MrExcel
LIBRARY

Excel® 2016 Pivot Table Data Crunching

Bill Jelen

Michael Alexander

que®

800 East 96th Street,
Indianapolis, Indiana 46240 USA

Contents at a Glance

Excel 2016 Pivot Table Data Crunching

ISBN-13: 978-0-7897-5629-9
ISBN-10: 0-7897-5629-3

Library of Congress Control Number: 2015949493

Printed in the United States of America

First Printing: November 2015

Trademarks

All terms mentioned in this book that are known to be trademarks or service marks have been appropriately capitalized. Que Publishing cannot attest to the accuracy of this information. Use of a term in this book should not be regarded as affecting the validity of any trademark or service mark.

Warning and Disclaimer

Special Sales

For information about buying this title in bulk quantities, or for special sales opportunities (which may include electronic versions; custom cover designs; and content particular to your business, training goals, marketing focus, or branding interests), please contact our corporate sales department at corpsales@pearsoned.com or (800) 382-3419.

For government sales inquiries, please contact governmentsales@pearsoned.com.

For questions about sales outside the U.S., please contact international@pearsoned.com.

Editor-in-Chief
Greg Wiegand

Acquisitions Editor
Joan Murray

Development Editor
Charlotte Kughen

Managing Editor
Sandra Schroeder

Project Editor
Seth Kerney

Copy Editor
Kitty Wilson

Indexer
Larry Sweazy

Proofreader
Megan Wade-Taxter

Technical Editor
Bob Umlas

Publishing Coordinator
Cindy Teeters

Book Designer
Anne Jones

Compositor
codeMantra

Contents

About the Authors

Bill Jelen, Excel MVP and the host of MrExcel.com, has been using spreadsheets since 1985, and he launched the MrExcel.com website in 1998. Bill was a regular guest on *Call for Help* with Leo Laporte and has produced more than 1,900 episodes of his daily video podcast, Learn Excel from MrExcel. He is the author of 49 books about Microsoft Excel and writes the monthly Excel column for *Strategic Finance* magazine. Before founding MrExcel.com, Bill Jelen spent 12 years in the trenches, working as a financial analyst for the finance, marketing, accounting, and operations departments of a $500 million public company. He lives in Merritt Island, Florida, with his wife, Mary Ellen.

Mike Alexander is a Microsoft Certified Application Developer (MCAD) and author of several books on advanced business analysis with Microsoft Access and Excel. He has more than 15 years of experience consulting and developing Office solutions. Mike has been named a Microsoft MVP for his ongoing contributions to the Excel community. In his spare time, he runs a free tutorial site, www.datapigtechnologies.com, where he shares basic Access and Excel tips to the Office community.

Dedication

To my friend, the recently departed Professor Simon Benninga
—Bill Jelen

To my 12 fans at datapigtechnologies.com
—Mike Alexander

Acknowledgments

Mike Alexander is the funniest guy doing live Excel seminars. I appreciate him as a coauthor on all five editions of this book, which has earned the #1 spot on the Amazon Computer Book bestseller list (for 54 minutes one day in January). Rob Collie of PowerPivotPro.com keeps me up to speed on PowerPivot. At Microsoft, thanks to Aviv Ezrachi and Ben Rampson for always being willing to answer quick questions. At MrExcel. com, thanks to an entire community of people who are passionate about Excel. Finally, thanks to my wife, Mary Ellen, for her support during the writing process.

—Bill Jelen

Thanks to Bill Jelen for deciding to coauthor this book with me many editions ago. His knowledge of Excel still blows me away to this day. My deepest thanks to the professionals at Pearson Education for all the hours of work put into bringing this book to life. Thanks also to Bob Umlas, whose technical editing has helped us make numerous improvements to the examples and text in this book. Finally, a special thank you goes to the wife and kids for putting up with all the time I spent locked away on this project.

—Mike Alexander

We Want to Hear from You!

As the reader of this book, *you* are our most important critic and commentator. We value your opinion and want to know what we're doing right, what we could do better, what areas you'd like to see us publish in, and any other words of wisdom you're willing to pass our way.

We welcome your comments. You can email or write to let us know what you did or didn't like about this book—as well as what we can do to make our books better.

Please note that we cannot help you with technical problems related to the topic of this book.

When you write, please be sure to include this book's title and author as well as your name and email address. We will carefully review your comments and share them with the author and editors who worked on the book.

E-mail: feedback@quepublishing.com

Mail: Que Publishing
        ATTN: Reader Feedback
        800 East 96th Street
        Indianapolis, IN 46240 USA

Reader Services

Visit our website and register this book at quepublishing.com/register for convenient access to any updates, downloads, or errata that might be available for this book.

INTRODUCTION

The pivot table is the single most powerful command in all of Excel. Pivot tables came along during the 1990s, when Microsoft and Lotus were locked in a bitter battle for dominance of the spreadsheet market. The race to continually add enhanced features to their respective products during the mid-1990s led to many incredible features, but none as powerful as the pivot table.

With a pivot table, you can transform one million rows of transactional data into a summary report in seconds. If you can drag a mouse, you can create a pivot table. In addition to quickly summarizing and calculating data, pivot tables enable you to change your analysis on the fly by simply moving fields from one area of a report to another.

No other tool in Excel gives you the flexibility and analytical power of a pivot table.

What You Will Learn from This Book

It is widely agreed that close to 60% of Excel users leave 80% of Excel untouched. That is, most users do not tap into the full potential of Excel's built-in utilities. Of these utilities, the most prolific by far is the pivot table. Despite the fact that pivot tables have been a cornerstone of Excel for almost 20 years, they remain one of the most underutilized tools in the entire Microsoft Office suite.

Having picked up this book, you are savvy enough to have heard of pivot tables—and you have perhaps even used them on occasion. You have a sense that pivot tables provide a power that you are not using, and you want to learn how to leverage that power to increase your productivity quickly.

Within the first two chapters, you will be able to create basic pivot tables, increase your productivity, and produce reports in minutes instead of hours. Within the first seven chapters, you will be able to output complex pivot reports with drill-down capabilities and accompanying charts. By the end of the book, you will be able to build a dynamic pivot table reporting system.

What Is New in Excel 2016's Pivot Tables

Luckily, Microsoft continues to invest heavily in business intelligence (BI), and pivot tables are the front end that let you access the new features. Some of the features added to Excel 2016 pivot tables include the following:

- Pivot tables now provide auto grouping for date or time columns. If you add a date column to the Rows or Columns area, Excel will automatically group the data up to Months and collapse to Months. If the data spans more than one year, Excel will add Quarters and Years as well. If you add a time column, Excel will automatically group to Seconds, Minutes, and Hours and collapse to show only the top level.

- Pivot charts offer expand and collapse buttons. If you add two or more fields to the Axis or Legend area of a pivot table, you can use the + and − icons on the pivot chart to zoom in and out on the hierarchy.

- Slicers now offer a Multi-Select icon to allow you to choose multiple items without using the Ctrl key. This feature was added for touchscreens.

- If your data has a geographic field such as for addresses or postal codes, you can build a pivot table on a map by using the 3D Maps icon on the Insert tab.

- If you need to import data for a pivot table, the Power Query tools found under Data, Get & Transform will assist you in cleaning and shaping that data.

- Power Pivot has an automatic feature for creating a calendar table.

- If you select Insert PivotTable from a blank cell, and if there is a Data Model in the workbook, Excel will offer to build the pivot table from the model.

- Power Pivot's Auto-Detect Relationships dialog offers a Manage Relationships button that allows you to review or correct any relationship that was detected.

If you skipped right over Excel 2013, you may not know about some of the new features it introduced. Here are some of the best ones:

- Beginning with 2013, Excel offers thumbnails for 10 recommended pivot tables when you choose Insert, Recommended Pivot Tables. If you are not sure how best to summarize your data, you'll find plenty of inspiration in this dialog.

- A timeline slicer enables you to easily filter a pivot table by month, quarter, or year.

- Excel 2013 introduced the Data Model as a way to build a pivot table from two tables. This is for the versions of Excel that do not offer Power Pivot.

- People using Office Professional Plus, Office 365 Pro Plus, or other high-end editions can enable the Power Pivot add-in. Power Pivot provides drag-and-drop functionality to link tables, worksheets, SQL Server, and more. Power Pivot adds better calculated fields.

- Power View enables you to animate pivot tables in an ad hoc query tool.

Skills Required to Use This Book

This book is a comprehensive enough reference for hard-core analysts yet relevant to casual users of Excel. The bulk of the book covers how to use pivot tables in the Excel user interface. Chapter 10, "Mashing Up Data with Power Pivot," delves into the Power Pivot window. Chapter 14, "Advanced Pivot Table Tips and Techniques," describes how to create pivot tables in Excel's powerful VBA macro language. Any user who has a firm grasp of basics such as preparing data, copying, pasting, and entering simple formulas should not have a problem understanding the concepts in this book.

CASE STUDY: LIFE BEFORE PIVOT TABLES

Say that your manager asks you to create a one-page summary of a sales database. He would like to see total revenue by region and product. Suppose you do not know how to use pivot tables. You will have to use dozens of keystrokes or mouse clicks to complete this task.

First, you have to build the outline of the report:

1. Copy the Product column to a blank section of the worksheet.
2. Select Data, Remove Duplicates to eliminate the duplicates.
3. Delete the Product heading.
4. Copy the unique list of products and then use Paste Special Transpose to turn the list sideways.
5. Delete the vertical list of products.
6. Copy the Region column to a blank section of the worksheet.
7. Select Data, Remove Duplicates to remove the duplicates.
8. Delete the Region heading.
9. Cut and paste the products so they appear left of and below the regions.

At this point, with 27 mouse clicks or keystrokes, you've built the shell of the final report, but there are no numbers inside yet (see Figure I.1).

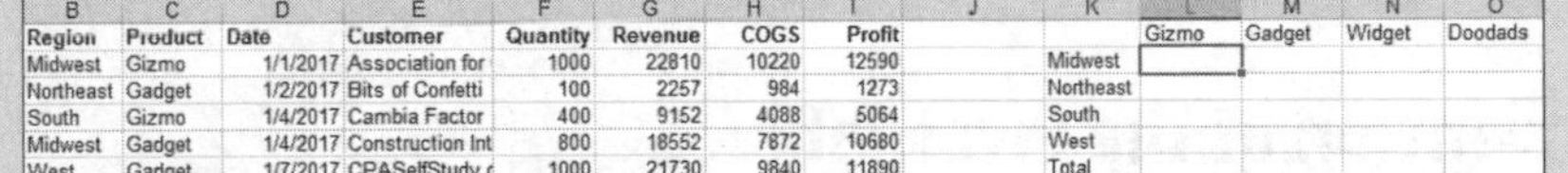

Figure I.1
It took 27 clicks to get to this point.

	B	C	D	E	F	G	H	I	J	K	L	M	N	O
	Region	Product	Date	Customer	Quantity	Revenue	COGS	Profit			Gizmo	Gadget	Widget	Doodads
	Midwest	Gizmo	1/1/2017	Association for	1000	22810	10220	12590		Midwest				
	Northeast	Gadget	1/2/2017	Bits of Confetti	100	2257	984	1273		Northeast				
	South	Gizmo	1/4/2017	Cambia Factor	400	9152	4088	5064		South				
	Midwest	Gadget	1/4/2017	Construction Int	800	18552	7872	10680		West				
	West	Gadget	1/7/2017	CPASelfStudy.c	1000	21730	9840	11890		Total				
	Midwest	Widget	1/7/2017	Data2Impact	400	8456	3388	5068						

Next, you need to build the relatively new SUMIFS function to total the revenue for the intersection of a region and product. As shown in Figure I.2, the formula =SUMIFS($G$2:$G$564,$C$2:$C$564,L$1,$B$2:$B$564,$K2) does the trick. It takes 52 characters plus the Enter key to finish the formula, but I managed to enter the formula in 36 clicks or keystrokes by using some clever navigation tricks I've learned over the years.

	K	L	M	N	O	P	Q
		Gizmo	Gadget	Widget	Doodads	Total	
	Midwest	=SUMIFS($G$2:$G$564,$C$2:$C$564,L$1,$B$2:$B$564,$K2)					
	Northeast						

If you are adept at using the fill handle, you need just two more mouse drags to copy the formula to the rest of the table.

Enter the heading Total for the total row and for the total column. You can do this in nine keystrokes if you type the first heading, press Ctrl+Enter to stay in the same cell and then use Copy, select the cell for the second heading, and use Paste.

If you select K1:P6 and press Alt+Equals, you can add the total formulas in three keystrokes.

With this method, which takes 77 clicks or keystrokes, you end up with a nice summary report, as shown in Figure I.3. If you could pull this off in 5 or 10 minutes, you would probably be fairly proud of your Excel prowess; there are some good tricks among those 77 operations.

K	Gizmo	Gadget	Widget	Doodads	Total
Midwest	652651	544772	537965	6036	1741424
Northeast	751724	714009	620019	38860	2124612
South	918588	839551	844186	0	2602325
West	70057	65382	75349	28663	239451
Total	2393020	2163714	2077519	73559	6707812

You hand the report to your manager. Within a few minutes, he comes back with one of the following requests, which will certainly cause a lot of rework:

- Could you put products down the side and regions across the top?
- Could you show me the same report for only the manufacturing customers?
- Could you show profit instead of revenue?
- Could you copy this report for each of the customers?

Invention of the Pivot Table

When the actual pivot table was invented is in dispute. The Excel team coined the term *pivot table*, which appeared in Excel in 1993. However, the concept was not new. Pito Salas and his team at Lotus were working on the pivot table concept in 1986 and released Lotus Improv in 1991. Before then, Javelin offered functionality similar to that of pivot tables.

The core concept behind a pivot table is that the data, formulas, and data views are stored separately. Each column has a name, and you can group and rearrange the data by dragging field names to various positions on the report.

CASE STUDY: LIFE AFTER PIVOT TABLES

Say that you're tired of working so hard to remake reports every time your manager wants a change. You're in luck: You can produce the same report as in the last case study but using a pivot table. Excel 2016 offers you 10 thumbnails of recommended pivot tables to get you close to the goal. Follow these steps:

1. Click the Insert tab of the ribbon.
2. Click Recommended PivotTables. The first recommended item is Revenue by Region (see Figure I.4).

Figure I.4
The first recommended pivot table is as close as you will get to the required report.

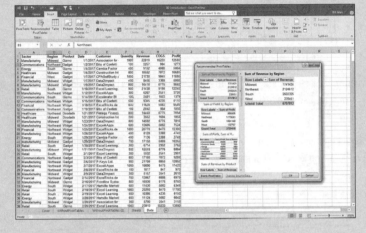

3. Click OK to accept the first pivot table.
4. Drag the Product field from the PivotTable Fields list to the Columns area (see Figure I.5).

Figure I.5
To finish the report, drag the Product heading to the Columns area.

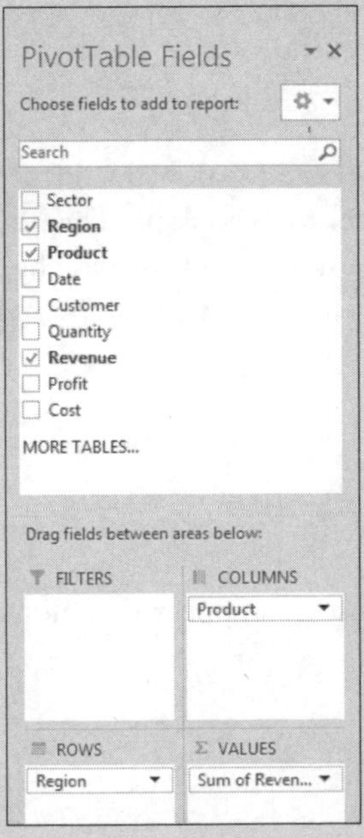

5. Unselect Field Headers on the right side of the ribbon.

With just five clicks of the mouse, you have the report shown in Figure I.6.

Figure I.6
It took five clicks to create this report.

◢	A	B	C	D	E	F
1						
2						
3	Sum of Revenue					
4		Doodads	Gadget	Gizmo	Widget	Grand Total
5	Midwest	6036	544772	652651	537965	1741424
6	Northeast	38860	714009	751724	620019	2124612
7	South		839551	918588	844186	2602325
8	West	28663	65382	70057	75349	239451
9	Grand Total	73559	2163714	2393020	2077519	6707812
10						
11						

In addition, when your manager comes back with a request like the ones near the end of the prior case study, you can easily use the pivot table makes to make the changes. Here's a quick overview of the changes you'll learn to make in the chapters that follow:

- Could you put products down the side and regions across the top? (This change will take you 10 seconds: Drag Product to Rows and Region to Columns.)
- Could you show me the same report for only the manufacturing customers? (15 seconds: Select Insert Slicer, Sector; click OK; click Manufacturing.)
- Could you show profit instead of revenue? (10 seconds: Uncheck Revenue, check Profit.)
- Could you copy this report for each of the customers? (30 seconds: Move Customer to Report Filter, open the tiny drop-down next to the Options button, choose Show Report Filter Pages, click OK.)

Sample Files Used in This Book

All data files used throughout this book are available for download from www.mrexcel.com/ pivotbookdata2016.html. You will find one Excel workbook per chapter and should be able to achieve exactly the same results shown in the figures in this book by starting with the raw data on the Data worksheet. If you simply want to work with the final pivot table, you can find it in the workbook as well.

Conventions Used in This Book

This book follows certain conventions:

- Monospace—Code and messages you see onscreen appear in a monospace font.
- **Bold**—Text you type appears in a bold font.

- *Italic*—New and important terms appear in italics.
- Initial Caps—Tab names, dialog names, and dialog elements are presented with initial capital letters so you can identify them easily.

Referring to Ribbon Commands

When the active cell is inside a pivot table, two new tabs appear on the ribbon. In the help files, Microsoft calls these tabs "PivotTable Tools | Analyze" and "PivotTable Tools | Design." For convenience, this book refers to these elements as the Analyze tab and the Design tab, respectively. The Slicer feature has a ribbon tab that Microsoft calls "Slicer Tools | Options." This book refers to this as the Slicer tab. Excel 2013 introduced the "Timeline Tools | Options" tab. This book calls this the Timeline tab.

In some cases, the ribbon icon leads to a drop-down with additional choices. In these cases, the book lists the hierarchy of ribbon, icon, menu choice, and submenu choice. For example, Figure I.7 shows what you would select if the book said "select Design, Report Layout, Repeat All Item Labels."

Figure I.7
For shorthand, instructions might say to select Design, Report Layout, Repeat All Item Labels.

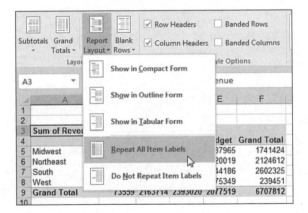

Special Elements

This book contains the following special elements:

CASE STUDY

Case studies provide real-world examples involving topics previously introduced in the chapter.

NOTE
Notes provide additional information outside the main thread of the chapter discussion that might be useful for you to know.

TIP
Tips provide quick workarounds and time-saving techniques to help you do your work more efficiently.

CAUTION
Cautions warn you about potential pitfalls you might encounter. Pay attention to cautions because they alert you to problems that could cause you hours of frustration.

Pivot Table Fundamentals

Defining a Pivot Table

Imagine that Excel is a large toolbox that contains different tools at your disposal. The pivot table is essentially one tool in your Excel toolbox. If a pivot table were indeed a physical tool that you could hold in your hand, a kaleidoscope would most accurately represent it.

When you look through a kaleidoscope at an object, you see that object in a different way. You can turn the kaleidoscope to move around the details of the object. The object itself doesn't change, and it's not connected to the kaleidoscope. The kaleidoscope is simply a tool you use to create a unique perspective on an ordinary object.

Think of a pivot table as a kaleidoscope that is pointed at a data set. When you look at a data set through a pivot table, you have the opportunity to see details in the data that you might not have noticed before. Furthermore, you can turn your pivot table to see your data from different perspectives. The data set itself doesn't change, and it's not connected to the pivot table. The pivot table is simply a tool you use to create a unique perspective on your data.

A pivot table enables you to create an interactive view of your data set, called a *pivot table report*. With a pivot table report, you can quickly and easily categorize your data into groups, summarize large amounts of data into meaningful information, and perform a variety of calculations in a fraction of the time it takes by hand. But the real power of a pivot table report is that you can use it to interactively drag and drop fields within your report, dynamically change your perspective, and recalculate totals to fit your current view.

Why You Should Use a Pivot Table

As a rule, what you do in Excel can be split into two categories:

- Calculating data
- Shaping (formatting) data

Although many built-in tools and formulas facilitate both of these tasks, using a pivot table is often the fastest and most efficient way to calculate and shape data. Let's look at one simple scenario that illustrates this point.

You have just given your manager some revenue information by month, and he has predictably asked for more information. He adds a note to the worksheet and emails it back to you. As you can see in Figure 1.1, he would like you to add a line that shows credits by month.

Figure 1.1
Your manager predictably changes his request after you provide the first pass of a report.

▲	A	B	C	D	E	F	G	H
1		Jan	Feb	Mar	Apr	May	Jun	Jul
2	Revenues	66,427,076	68,619,453	69,444,496	67,669,316	69,572,075	67,196,220	66,884,7
3		Please add a "credits" line and show the amount of credits for each month						

To meet this new requirement, you run a query from your legacy system that provides the needed data. As usual, the data is formatted specifically to make you suffer. Instead of data by month, the legacy system provides detailed transactional data by day, as shown in Figure 1.2.

Figure 1.2
The data from the legacy system is by day instead of by month.

▲	A	B	C
1	Document Number	In Balance Date	Credit Amount
2	D29210	01/03/12	(34.54)
3	D15775	01/03/12	(313.64)
4	D46035	01/03/12	(389.04)
5	D45826	01/03/12	(111.56)
6	D69172	01/03/12	(1,630.25)
7	D25388	01/03/12	(3,146.22)
8	D49302	01/03/12	(1,217.37)
9	D91669	01/03/12	(197.44)
10	D14289	01/03/12	(33.75)
11	D38471	01/03/12	(6,759.20)
12	D18645	01/03/12	(214.54)
13	D63807	01/03/12	(19.58)
14	D77943	01/03/12	(136.17)
15	D37446	01/03/12	(128.36)

Your challenge is to calculate the total dollar amount of credits by month and shape the results into an extract that fits the format of the original report. The final extract should look like the data shown in Figure 1.3.

Figure 1.3
Your goal is to produce a summary by month and transpose the data to a horizontal format.

Jan	Feb	Mar	Apr	May	Jun	Jul
-3,695,319	-3,698,537	-3,833,977	-3,624,967	-3,800,526	-3,603,367	-3,746,754

Creating the extract manually would take 18 mouse clicks and 3 keystrokes:

- Format dates to month: 3 clicks
- Create subtotals: 4 clicks
- Extract subtotals: 6 clicks, 3 keystrokes
- Transpose vertical to horizontal: 5 clicks

In contrast, creating the extract with a pivot table would take 9 mouse clicks:

- Create the pivot table report: 5 clicks
- Group dates into months: 3 clicks
- Transpose vertical to horizontal: 1 click

Both methods give you the same extract, which you can paste into the final report, as shown in Figure 1.4.

Figure 1.4
After adding credits to the report, you can calculate net revenue.

	A	B	C	D	E	F	G	H
1		Jan	Feb	Mar	Apr	May	Jun	Jul
2	Revenues	66,427,076	68,619,453	69,444,496	67,669,316	69,572,075	67,196,220	66,884,77
3	Credits	-3,695,319	-3,698,537	-3,833,977	-3,624,967	-3,800,526	-3,603,367	-3,746,754
4	Adjusted Revenues	62,731,757	64,920,916	65,610,519	64,044,349	65,771,549	63,592,853	63,138,01

Advantages of Using a Pivot Table

Using a pivot table to accomplish the task just described not only cuts down the number of actions by more than half but also reduces the possibility of human error. In addition, using a pivot table allows for the quick-and-easy shaping and formatting of the data.

This example shows that using a pivot table is not just about calculating and summarizing your data. Pivot tables can often help you do a number of tasks faster and better than conventional functions and formulas. For example, you can use pivot tables to instantly transpose large groups of data vertically or horizontally. You can use pivot tables to quickly find and count the unique values in your data. You can also use pivot tables to prepare your data to be used in charts.

The bottom line is that pivot tables can help you dramatically increase your efficiency and decrease your errors on a number of tasks you might have to accomplish with Excel. Pivot tables can't do everything for you, but knowing how to use just the basics of pivot table functionality can take your data analysis and productivity to a new level.

When to Use a Pivot Table

Large data sets, ever-changing impromptu data requests, and multilayered reporting are absolute productivity killers if you have to tackle them by hand. Going into hand-to-hand combat with one of these not only is time-consuming, but also opens up the possibility of an untold number of errors in your analysis. So how do you recognize when to use a pivot table before it's too late?

Generally, a pivot table would serve you well in any of the following situations:

■ You have a large amount of transactional data that has become increasingly difficult to analyze and summarize in a meaningful way.

■ You need to find relationships and groupings within your data.

■ You need to find a list of unique values for one field in your data.

■ You need to find data trends using various time periods.

■ You anticipate frequent requests for changes to your data analysis.

■ You need to create subtotals that frequently include new additions.

■ You need to organize your data into a format that's easy to chart.

Anatomy of a Pivot Table

Because the anatomy of a pivot table is what gives it its flexibility and, indeed, its ultimate functionality, truly understanding pivot tables would be difficult without understanding their basic structure.

A pivot table is composed of four areas:

■ Values area

■ Rows area

■ Columns area

■ Filters area

The data you place in these areas defines both the utility and appearance of the pivot table.

You will go through the process of creating a pivot table in the next chapter, and the following sections prepare you for that by taking a closer look at the four pivot table areas and the functionality around them.

Values Area

The *values area* is shown in Figure 1.5. It is a large rectangular area below and to the right of the headings. In this example, the values area contains a sum of the revenue field.

Figure 1.5
The heart of the pivot table is the values area. This area typically includes a total of one or more numeric fields.

	A	B	C	D	E	F
1	REGION	(All) ▾				
2						
3	Sum of REVENUE	MONTH ▾				
4	MODEL ▾	January	February	March	April	May
5	2500P	$33,073	$29,104	$25,612	$22,538	$19,834
6	3002C	$35,880	$31,574	$27,785	$24,451	$21,517
7	3002P	$90,258	$79,427	$69,896	$61,508	$54,127
8	4055T	$13,250	$11,660	$10,261	$9,030	$7,946
9	4500C	$100,197	$88,173	$77,593	$68,281	$60,088

The values area is the area that calculates. This area is required to include at least one field and one calculation on that field. The data fields you drop here are those you want to measure or calculate. The values area might include Sum of Revenue, Count of Units, and Average of Price.

It is also possible to have the same field dropped in the values area twice but with different calculations. For example, a marketing manager might want to see Minimum of Price, Average Price, and Maximum of Price.

Rows Area

The *rows area*, as shown in Figure 1.6, is composed of the headings that go down the left side of the pivot table.

Figure 1.6
The headings down the left side of the pivot table make up the rows area of the pivot table.

	A	B	C	D	E	F
1	REGION	(All) ▾				
2						
3	REVENUE	MONTH ▾				
4	MODEL ▾	January	February	March	April	May
5	2500P	$33,073	$29,104	$25,612	$22,538	$19,834
6	3002C	$35,880	$31,574	$27,785	$24,451	$21,517
7	3002P	$90,258	$79,427	$69,896	$61,508	$54,127
8	4055T	$13,250	$11,660	$10,261	$9,030	$7,946
9	4500C	$100,197	$88,173	$77,593	$68,281	$60,088

Dropping a field into the rows area displays the unique values from that field down the rows of the left side of the pivot table. The rows area typically has at least one field, although it is possible to have no fields. The example earlier in the chapter where you needed to produce a one-line report of credits is an example where there are no row fields.

The types of data fields you would drop here include those you want to group and categorize—for example, Products, Names, and Locations.

Columns Area

The *columns area* is composed of headings that stretch across the top of columns in the pivot table. In the pivot table in Figure 1.7, the Month field is in the columns area.

Figure 1.7
The columns area stretches across the top of the columns. In this example, it contains the unique list of months in your data set.

	A	B	C	D	E	F
1	REGION	(All)				
2						
3	Sum of REVENUE	MONTH				
4	MODEL	January	February	March	April	May
5	2500P	$33,073	$29,104	$25,612	$22,538	$19,834
6	3002C	$35,880	$31,574	$27,785	$24,451	$21,517
7	3002P	$90,258	$79,427	$69,896	$61,508	$54,127
8	4055T	$13,250	$11,660	$10,261	$9,030	$7,946
9	4500C	$100,197	$88,173	$77,593	$68,281	$60,088

Dropping fields into the columns area would display your items in column-oriented perspective. The columns area is ideal for showing trending over time. The types of data fields you would drop here include those you want to trend or show side by side—for example, Months, Periods, and Years.

Filters Area

The *filters area* is an optional set of one or more drop-downs at the top of the pivot table. In Figure 1.8, the filters area contains the Region field and the pivot table is set to show all regions.

Figure 1.8
Filter fields are great for quickly filtering a report. The Region drop-down in cell B1 enables you to print this report for one particular region manager.

	A	B	C	D	E	F
1	REGION	(All)				
2						
3	Sum of REVENUE	MONTH				
4	MODEL	January	February	March	April	May
5	2500P	$33,073	$29,104	$25,612	$22,538	$19,834
6	3002C	$35,880	$31,574	$27,785	$24,451	$21,517
7	3002P	$90,258	$79,427	$69,896	$61,508	$54,127
8	4055T	$13,250	$11,660	$10,261	$9,030	$7,946
9	4500C	$100,197	$88,173	$77,593	$68,281	$60,088

Dropping fields into the filters area would enable you to filter the data items in your fields. The filters area is optional and comes in handy when you need to filter your results dynamically. The types of data fields you would drop here include those you want to isolate and focus on—for example, Regions, Line of Business, and Employees.

Pivot Tables Behind the Scenes

It's important to know that pivot tables come with a few file space and memory implications for your system. To get an idea of what this means, let's look at what happens behind the scenes when you create a pivot table.

When you initiate the creation of a pivot table report, Excel takes a snapshot of your data set and stores it in a *pivot cache*, which is a special memory subsystem where your data source is duplicated for quick access. Although the pivot cache is not a physical object you can see, you can think of it as a container that stores a snapshot of the data source.

> ┌ **CAUTION** ────────────────────────────────
> Any changes you make to your data source are not picked up by your pivot table report until you take another snapshot of the data source or "refresh" the pivot cache. Refreshing is easy: Simply right-click the pivot table and click Refresh Data. You can also click the large Refresh button on the Options tab.

The benefit of working against the pivot cache and not your original data source is optimization. Any changes you make to the pivot table report, such as rearranging fields, adding new fields, or hiding items, are made rapidly and with minimal overhead.

Pivot Table Backward Compatibility

With Excel 2007, Microsoft introduced a dramatic increase in the number of rows and columns allowed in one worksheet. This increase in limits led to the creation of a new Excel file type: .xlsx. The.xlsx file type not only allows for more rows and columns than the legacy .xls files (used by Excel 2003 and prior versions), but also comes with limitation increases in many areas, including pivot tables.

Table 1.1 highlights the pivot table limits in both .xls and .xlsx file types. Whereas some of these limitations remain constant, others are highly dependent on available system memory.

Table 1.1   Pivot Table Limitations

Category	.xls Files	.xlsx Files
Number of row fields	Limited by available memory	1,048,576 (could be limited by available memory)
Number of column fields	256	16,384
Number of page fields	256	16,384
Number of data fields	256	16,384
Number of unique items in a single pivot field	32,500	1,048,576 (could be limited by available memory)
Number of calculated items	Limited by available memory	Limited by available memory
Number of pivot table reports on one worksheet	Limited by available memory	Limited by available memory

A Word About Compatibility

As you can imagine, the extraordinary increases in pivot table limitations lead to some serious compatibility questions. For instance, what if you create a pivot table that contains more than 256 column fields and more than 32,500 unique data items? How are users with previous versions of Excel affected by this? Luckily, Excel allows for some precautionary measures that can help you avoid compatibility issues.

The first precautionary measure is Compatibility mode. Compatibility mode is a state that Excel automatically enters when opening an .xls file. When Excel is in Compatibility mode, it artificially takes on the limitations of Excel 2003. This means that while you are working with an .xls file, you cannot exceed any of the .xls file pivot table limitations shown in Table 1.1. This effectively prevents you from unwittingly creating a pivot table that is not compatible with previous versions of Excel. If you want to get out of Compatibility mode, you have to save the .xls file as one of Excel's newer .xlsx or .xslm file formats (.xlsm files are macro-enabled Excel files).

> **CAUTION**
>
> Beware of the Convert option found under the Info section of the File menu. Although this command is designed to convert a previous file from Excel 2003 to Excel 2013, it actually deletes the Excel 2003 copy of the file.

The second precautionary measure is Excel's Compatibility Checker. The Compatibility Checker is a built-in tool that checks for any compatibility issues when you try to save an Excel workbook as an .xls file. If your pivot table exceeds the bounds of .xls file limitations, the Compatibility Checker alerts you with a dialog similar to the one shown in Figure 1.9.

Figure 1.9
The Compatibility Checker alerts you about any compatibility issues before you save to a previous version of Excel.

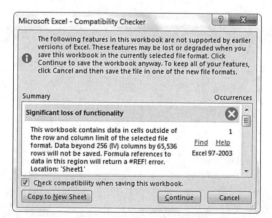

With this dialog, Excel gives you the option of saving your pivot data as hard values in the new .xls file. If you choose to do so, the data from your pivot table is saved as hard values, but the pivot table object and the pivot cache are lost.

NOTE

For information on Excel's compatibility tools, pick up Que Publishing's *Special Edition Using Microsoft Excel 2016*, by Bill Jelen.

Next Steps

In the next chapter, you'll learn how to prepare your data to be used by a pivot table. Chapter 2, "Creating a Basic Pivot Table," also walks through creating your first pivot table report using the Pivot Table Wizard.

Creating a Basic Pivot Table

2

Preparing Data for Pivot Table Reporting

When you have a family portrait taken, the photographer takes time to make sure that the lighting is right, the poses are natural, and everyone smiles his or her best smile. This preparation ensures that the resulting photo is effective in its purpose.

When you create a pivot table report, you're the photographer, taking a snapshot of your data. By taking time to make sure your data looks its best, you can ensure that your pivot table report is effective in accomplishing the task at hand.

One of the benefits of working in a spreadsheet is that you have the flexibility of laying out your data to suit your needs. Indeed, the layout you choose depends heavily on the task at hand. However, many of the data layouts used for presentations are not appropriate when used as the source data for a pivot table report.

> **TIP**
>
> As you read the following pages, which discuss preparing your data, keep in mind that pivot tables have only one hard rule pertaining to the data source: The data source must have column headings, which are labels in the first row of the data that describe the information in each column. Without column headings, you cannot create a pivot table report.

However, just because a pivot table report is created successfully does not mean that it's effective. A host of things can go wrong as a result of bad data preparation—from inaccurate reporting to problems with grouping and sorting.

Let's look at a few of the steps you can take to ensure that you end up with a viable pivot table report.

Ensuring That Data Is in a Tabular Layout

A perfect layout for the source data in a pivot table is a tabular layout. In tabular layout, there are no blank rows or columns. Every column has a heading. Every field has a value in every row. Columns do not contain repeating groups of data.

Figure 2.1 shows an example of data structured properly for a pivot table. There are headings for each column. Even though the values in D2:D6 are all the same model, the model number appears in each cell. Month data is organized down the page instead of across the columns.

Figure 2.1
This data is structured properly for use as a pivot table source.

	A	B	C	D	E	F
1	REGION	MARKET	STORE	MODEL	MONTH	REVENUE
2	North	Great Lakes	65061011	4055T	April	$2,354
3	North	Great Lakes	65061011	4055T	February	$3,040
4	North	Great Lakes	65061011	4055T	January	$3,454
5	North	Great Lakes	65061011	4055T	March	$2,675
6	North	Great Lakes	65061011	4055T	May	$2,071
7	North	New England	2105015	2500P	April	$11,851
8	North	New England	2105015	2500P	February	$15,304
9	North	New England	2105015	2500P	January	$17,391
10	North	New England	2105015	2500P	March	$13,468
11	North	New England	2105015	2500P	May	$10,429
12	North	New England	22022012	3002C	April	$256
13	North	New England	22022012	3002C	February	$330
14	North	New England	22022012	3002C	January	$375
16	North	New England	22022012	3002C	March	$200

Tabular layouts are *database centric*, meaning you would most commonly find these types of layouts in databases. These layouts are designed to store and maintain large amounts of data in a well-structured, scalable format.

> **TIP**
>
> You might work for a manager who demands that the column labels be split into two rows. For example, he might want the heading Gross Margin to be split, with Gross in row 1 and Margin in row 2. Because pivot tables require a unique heading one row high, your manager's preference can be problematic. To overcome this problem, start typing your heading; for example, type **Gross**. Before leaving the cell, press Alt+Enter and then type **Margin**. The result is a single cell that contains two lines of data.

Avoiding Storing Data in Section Headings

Examine the data in Figure 2.2. This spreadsheet shows a report of sales by month and model for the North region of a company. Because the data in rows 2 through 24 pertains to the North region, the author of the worksheet entered the title North as a single cell in C1. This approach is effective for display of the data, but it's not effective for a pivot table data source.

Figure 2.2
Region and model data are not formatted properly in this data set.

	A	B	C
1			North
2		January	33,073
3	Model 2500P	February	35,880
4		March	90,258
5		April	13,250
6		May	100,197
8		January	29,104
9	Model 3002P	February	31,574
10		March	79,427
11		April	11,660
12		May	88,173
14		January	35,880
15	Model 4055T	February	25,612
16		March	27,785
17		April	69,896
18		May	10,261
20		January	33,073
21	Model 4500T	February	25,612
22		March	27,785
23		April	69,896
24		May	10,261

Also in Figure 2.2, the author was very creative with the model information. The data in rows 2 through 6 applies to Model 2500P, so the author entered this value once in A2 and then applied a fancy vertical format combined with Merge Cells to create an interesting look for the report. Again, although this is a cool format, it is not useful for pivot table reporting.

Also, the worksheet in Figure 2.2 is missing column headings. You can guess that column A is Model, column B is Month, and column C is Sales, but for Excel to create a pivot table, this information must be included in the first row of the data.

Avoiding Repeating Groups as Columns

The format shown in Figure 2.3 is common. A time dimension is presented across several columns. Although it is possible to create a pivot table from this data, this format is not ideal.

Figure 2.3
This matrix format is common but not effective for pivot tables. The Month field is spread across several columns of the report.

	A	B	C	D	E	F	G	H
1								
2	North	MODEL	JANUARY	FEBRUARY	MARCH	APRIL	MAY	JUNE
3		4054T	$2,789	$2,454	$2,160	$1,901	$1,673	$1,472
4		4500C	$32,605	$28,692	$25,249	$22,219	$19,553	$17,207
5		3002P	$52,437	$46,145	$40,607	$35,734	$31,446	$27,673
6		2500P	$17,391	$15,304	$13,468	$11,851	$10,429	$9,178
7		4055T	$2,468	$2,172	$1,911	$1,682	$1,480	$1,302
8		3002C	$375	$330	$290	$256	$225	$198

The problem is that the headings spread across the top of the table pull double duty as column labels and actual data values. In a pivot table, this format would force you to manage and maintain six fields, each representing a different month.

Eliminating Gaps and Blank Cells in the Data Source

Delete all empty columns within your data source. An empty column in the middle of your data source causes your pivot table to fail on creation because the blank column, in most cases, does not have a column name.

Delete all empty rows within your data source. Empty rows may cause you to inadvertently leave out a large portion of your data range, making your pivot table report incomplete.

Fill in as many blank cells in your data source as possible. Although filling in cells is not required to create a workable pivot table, blank cells are generally errors waiting to happen. So a good practice is to represent missing values with some logical missing value code wherever possible.

> **NOTE** Although eliminating gaps and blank cells might seem like a step backward for those of you who are trying to create a nicely formatted report, it pays off in the end. When you are able to create a pivot table, there will be plenty of opportunities to apply some pleasant formatting.

> **NOTE** In Chapter 3, "Customizing a Pivot Table," you'll discover how to apply styles formatting to your pivot tables.

Applying Appropriate Type Formatting to Fields

Formatting fields appropriately helps you avoid a whole host of possible issues, from inaccurate reporting to problems with grouping and sorting.

Make certain that any fields to be used in calculations are explicitly formatted as a number, currency, or any other format appropriate for use in mathematical functions. Fields containing dates should also be formatted as any one of the available date formats.

Summary of Good Data Source Design

The attributes of an effective tabular design are as follows:

- The first row of your data source is made up of field labels or headings that describe the information in each column.
- Each column in your data source represents a unique category of data.
- Each row in your data source represents individual items in each column.
- None of the column names in your data source double as data items that will be used as filters or query criteria (that is, names of months, dates, years, names of locations, or names of employees).

CASE STUDY: CLEANING UP DATA FOR PIVOT TABLE ANALYSIS

The worksheet shown in Figure 2.4 is a great-looking report. However, it cannot be effectively used as a data source for a pivot table. Can you identify the problems with this data set?

Figure 2.4
Someone spent a lot of time formatting this report to look good, but what problems prevent it from being used as a data source for a pivot table?

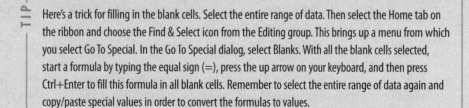

	A	B	C	D	E	F	G
1	Region	Market		Jan	Feb	Mar	Apr
2	Bar Equipment						
3	Midwest	Chicago		132	106	110	90
4		Kansas City		413	504	2,571	505
5		Omaha		332	543	372	424
6	North	Dakotas		130	136	106	90
7		Great Lakes		488	445	4,140	517
8							
9	Commercial Appliances						
10	Midwest	Chicago		780	76	851	76
11		Kansas City		3,352	76	8,442	2,831
12		Omaha		228	17,628	76	304
13	North	Dakotas		0	0	2,608	0
14		Great Lakes		990	76	11,435	76
15							
16	Concession Equipment						
17	Midwest	Chicago		808	0	3,912	0
18		Kansas City		824	1,761	11,181	1,616
19		Omaha		0	8,147	2,968	3,118
20	North	Dakotas		0	0	5,463	2,370
21		Great Lakes		751	808	13,814	1,632

These are the four problems with the data set and the fixes needed to get the data set pivot table ready:

■ The model information does not have its own column. Product category information appears in the Region column. To correct this problem, insert a new column titled Product Category and include the category name on every row.

■ There are blank columns and rows in the data. Column C should be deleted. The blank rows between models (such as rows 8 and 15) also should be deleted.

■ Blank cells present the data in an outline format. The person reading this worksheet would probably assume that cells A4:A5 fall into the Midwest region. These blank cells need to be filled in with the values from above.

> **TIP**
>
> Here's a trick for filling in the blank cells. Select the entire range of data. Then select the Home tab on the ribbon and choose the Find & Select icon from the Editing group. This brings up a menu from which you select Go To Special. In the Go To Special dialog, select Blanks. With all the blank cells selected, start a formula by typing the equal sign (=), press the up arrow on your keyboard, and then press Ctrl+Enter to fill this formula in all blank cells. Remember to select the entire range of data again and copy/paste special values in order to convert the formulas to values.

■ The worksheet presents the data for each month in several columns (one column per month). Columns D through G need to be reformatted as two columns. Place the month name in one column and the units for that month in the next column. This step either requires a fair amount of copying and pasting or a few lines of VBA macro code.

2

After you make the four changes described here, the data is ready for use as a pivot table data source. As you can see in Figure 2.5, each column has a heading. There are no blank cells, rows, or columns in the data. The monthly data is now presented down column E instead of across several columns.

Figure 2.5
Although this data will take up six times as many rows, it is perfectly formatted for pivot table analysis.

	A	B	C	D	E
1	Product Category	Region	Market	Month	Units
2	Bar Equipment	Midwest	Chicago	Jan	132
3	Bar Equipment	Midwest	Kansas City	Jan	413
4	Bar Equipment	Midwest	Omaha	Jan	332
5	Bar Equipment	North	Dakotas	Jan	130
6	Bar Equipment	North	Great Lakes	Jan	488
7	Commercial Appliances	Midwest	Chicago	Jan	780
8	Commercial Appliances	Midwest	Kansas City	Jan	3,352
9	Commercial Appliances	Midwest	Omaha	Jan	228
10	Commercial Appliances	North	Dakotas	Jan	0
11	Commercial Appliances	North	Great Lakes	Jan	990
12	Concession Equipment	Midwest	Chicago	Jan	808
13	Concession Equipment	Midwest	Kansas City	Jan	824
14	Concession Equipment	Midwest	Omaha	Jan	0
15	Concession Equipment	North	Dakotas	Jan	0
16	Concession Equipment	North	Great Lakes	Jan	751
17	Bar Equipment	Midwest	Chicago	Feb	106
18	Bar Equipment	Midwest	Kansas City	Feb	504
19	Bar Equipment	Midwest	Omaha	Feb	543

How to Create a Basic Pivot Table

Now that you have a good understanding of the importance of a well-structured data source, let's walk through creating a basic pivot table.

To ensure that the pivot table captures the range of your data source by default, click any single cell in your data source. Next, select the Insert tab and find the Tables group. In the Tables group, select PivotTable and then choose PivotTable from the drop-down list. Figure 2.6 demonstrates how to start a pivot table.

Figure 2.6
Start a pivot table by selecting PivotTable from the Insert tab.

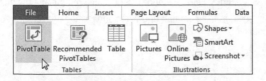

Choosing these options activates the Create PivotTable dialog, shown in Figure 2.7.

Figure 2.7
The Create PivotTable dialog.

TIP

You can also press the shortcut Alt+N+V to start a pivot table.

As you can see in Figure 2.7, the Create PivotTable dialog asks you only two fundamental questions: Where's the data that you want to analyze? and Where do you want to put the pivot table? Here's how you handle these two sections of the dialog:

- **Choose the Data That You Want to Analyze**—In this section, you tell Excel where your data set is. You can specify a data set that is located within your workbook, or you can tell Excel to look for an external data set. As you can see in Figure 2.7, Excel is smart enough to read your data set and fill in the range for you. However, you always should take note of the range Excel selects to ensure that you are capturing all your data.

- **Choose Where You Want the PivotTable Report to Be Placed**—In this section, you tell Excel where you want your pivot table to be placed. This is set to New Worksheet by default, meaning that your pivot table will be placed in a new worksheet within the current workbook. You will rarely change this setting because there are relatively few times you'll need your pivot table to be placed in a specific location.

NOTE

Note the presence of another option in the Create PivotTable dialog shown in Figure 2.7: the Add This Data to the Data Model option. You would select this option if you were trying to consolidate multiple data sources into one single pivot table.

The Add This Data to the Data Model option is covered this option in detail in Chapter 7, "Analyzing Disparate Data Sources with Pivot Tables," and in Chapter 10, "Mashing Up Data with Power Pivot."

In this chapter, we'll keep it basic by covering the steps to create a pivot table from using a single source, which means you can ignore this particular option.

After you have answered the two questions in the Create PivotTable dialog, simply click the OK button. At this point, Excel adds a new worksheet that contains an empty pivot table report. Next to that is the PivotTable Fields list, shown in Figure 2.8. This pane helps you build your pivot table.

Figure 2.8
You use the PivotTable Fields list to build a pivot table.

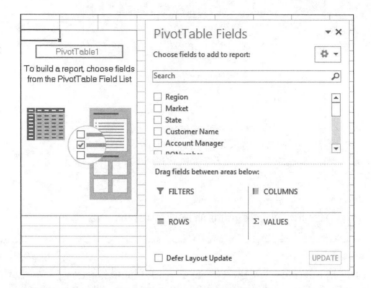

FINDING THE PIVOTTABLE FIELDS LIST

The PivotTable Fields list is your main work area in Excel 2016. This is the place where you add fields and make changes to a pivot table report. By default, this pane pops up when you place your cursor anywhere inside a pivot table. However, if you explicitly close this pane, you override the default and essentially tell the pane not to activate when you are in the pivot table.

If clicking on the pivot table does not activate the PivotTable Fields list, you can manually activate it by right-clicking anywhere inside the pivot table and selecting Show Fields list. You can also click anywhere inside the pivot table and then choose the large Fields List icon on the Analyze tab under PivotTable Tools in the ribbon.

Adding Fields to a Report

You can add the fields you need to a pivot table by using the four "areas" found in the PivotTable Fields list: Filters, Columns, Rows, and Values. These areas, which correspond to the four areas of the pivot table, are used to populate your pivot table with data:

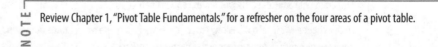

NOTE   Review Chapter 1, "Pivot Table Fundamentals," for a refresher on the four areas of a pivot table.

- **Filters**—Adding a field to the Filters area enables you to filter on its unique data items. In previous versions of Excel, this area was known as the Report Filters area.
- **Columns**—Adding a field into the Columns area displays the unique values from that field across the top of the pivot table.
- **Rows**—Adding a field into the Rows area displays the unique values from that field down the left side of the pivot table.
- **Values**—Adding a field into the Values area includes that field in the values area of your pivot table, allowing you to perform a specified calculation using the values in the field.

Fundamentals of Laying Out a Pivot Table Report

Now let's pause a moment and go over some fundamentals of laying out a pivot table report. This is generally the point where most new users get stuck. How do you know which field goes where?

Before you start dropping fields into the various areas, answer two questions: "What am I measuring?" and "How do I want to see it?" The answer to the first question tells you which fields in your data source you need to work with, and the answer to the second question tells you where to place the fields.

Say that in this case, you want to measure the dollar sales by region. This automatically tells you that you need to work with the Sale Amount field and the Region field. How do you want to see it? You want regions to go down the left side of the report and the sales amount to be calculated next to each region.

To achieve this effect, you need to add the Region field to the Rows area and add the Sale Amount field to the Values area.

Find the Region field in the PivotTable Fields list, and place a check in the check box next to it. As you can see in Figure 2.9, not only is the field automatically added to the Rows area, but your pivot table is updated to show the unique region names.

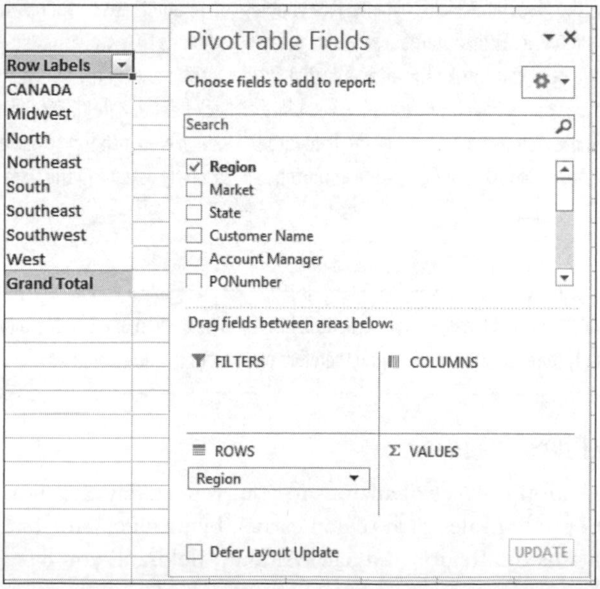

Figure 2.9
Place a check next to the Region field to automatically add that field to your pivot table.

Now that you have regions in your pivot table, it's time to add in the dollar sales. To do that, simply find the Sale Amount field and place a check next to it. As Figure 2.10 illustrates, the Sale Amount field is automatically added to the Values area, and your pivot table report now shows the total dollar sales for each region.

Figure 2.10
Place a check next to the Sale Amount field to add data to your pivot table report.

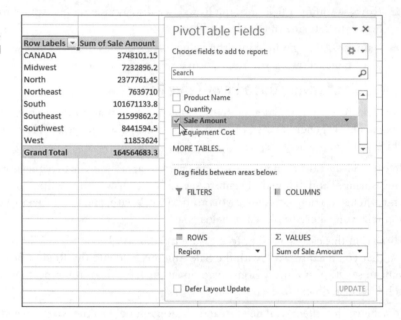

At this point, you have already created your first pivot table report!

HOW DOES EXCEL KNOW WHERE YOUR FIELDS GO?

As you've just experienced, the PivotTable Fields list interface enables you to add fields to your pivot table by simply placing a check next to each field name. Excel automatically adds the checked fields to the pivot table. But how does Excel know which area to use for a field you check? The answer is that Excel doesn't really know which area to use, but it makes a decision based on data type. Here's how it works: When you place a check next to a field, Excel evaluates the data type for that field. If the data type is numeric, Excel places the field into the Values area; otherwise, Excel places the field into the Rows area. This placement obviously underlines the importance of correctly assigning the data types for your fields.

┌ **CAUTION** ───
│ Watch out for blanks in your numeric fields. If you have even one blank cell in a numeric field, Excel
│ reads that cell as a Text field and therefore places it in the Rows area!
└──

Adding Layers to a Pivot Table

Now you can add another layer of analysis to your report. Say that now you want to measure the amount of dollar sales each region earned by product category. Because your pivot table already contains the Region and Sales Amount fields, all you have to do is place a check next to the Product Category field. As you can see in Figure 2.11, your pivot table automatically added a layer for Product Category and refreshed the calculations to include subtotals for each region. Because the data is stored efficiently in the pivot cache, this change took less than a second.

Figure 2.11
Without pivot tables, adding layers to analyses requires hours of work and complex formulas.

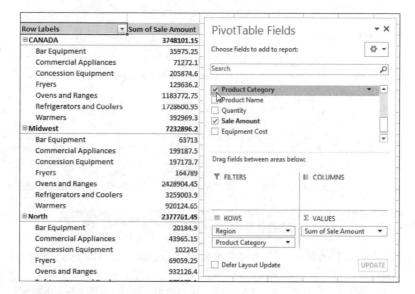

Rearranging a Pivot Table

Suppose that the view you've created doesn't work for your manager. He wants to see Product Categories across the top of the pivot table report. To make this change, simply drag the Product Category field from the Rows area to the Columns area, as illustrated in Figure 2.12.

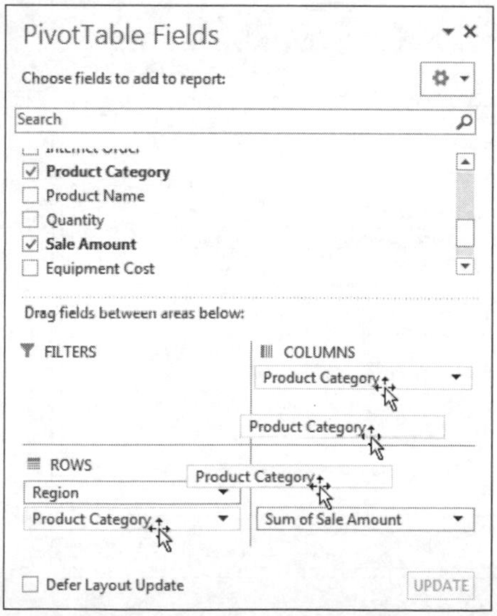

Figure 2.12
Rearranging a pivot table is as simple as dragging fields from one area to another.

2

> **N O T E**
>
> You don't have to move your fields into an area to be able to drag them around. You can actually drag fields directly from the list of fields in the PivotTable Fields list to the desired area. You can also move a field into an area by using that field's context menu: Click the black triangle next to the field name and then select the desired area.

The report is instantly restructured, as shown in Figure 2.13.

Figure 2.13
Your product categories are now column oriented.

Sum of Sale Amount	Column Labels			
Row Labels	Bar Equipment	Commercial Appliances	Concession Equipment	Fryers
CANADA	35975.25	71272.1	205874.6	129636.2
Midwest	63713	199187.5	197173.7	164789
North	20184.9	43965.15	102245	69059.25
Northeast	68407.1	285103.35	258557.4	190152.4
South	1191742.35	5923096.6	6971902.45	2420745
Southeast	283902.15	1525894.3	1569948.6	452579.35
Southwest	73528.5	289526.5	355845.45	268554.85
West	68684.65	296291.55	422201.2	276443.05
Grand Total	1806137.9	8634337.05	10083748.4	3971959.1

LONGING FOR DRAG-AND-DROP FUNCTIONALITY?

In Excel 2003 and previous versions, you had the ability to drag and drop fields directly onto the pivot table layout. This functionality is allowed only within the PivotTable Fields list (dragging into areas). However, Microsoft has provided the option of working with a classic pivot table layout, which enables the drag-and-drop functionality.

To activate the classic pivot table layout, right-click anywhere inside the pivot table and select Table Options. In the Table Options dialog, select the Display tab and place a check next to Classic PivotTable Layout, as demonstrated in Figure 2.14. Click the OK button to apply the change.

Figure 2.14
Place a check next to Classic PivotTable Layout.

At this point, you can drag and drop fields directly onto your pivot table layout.

Unfortunately, this setting is not global. That is, you have to go through the same steps to apply the classic layout to each new pivot table you create. However, this setting persists when a pivot table is copied.

Creating a Report Filter

You might be asked to produce different reports for particular regions, markets, or products. Instead of building separate pivot table reports for every possible analysis scenario, you can use the Filter field to create a report filter. For example, you can create a region-filtered report by simply dragging the Region field to the Filters area and the Product Category field to the Rows area. This way, you can analyze one particular region at a time. Figure 2.15 shows the totals for just the North region.

Figure 2.15
With this setup, you not only can see revenues by product clearly, but also can click the Region drop-down to focus on one region.

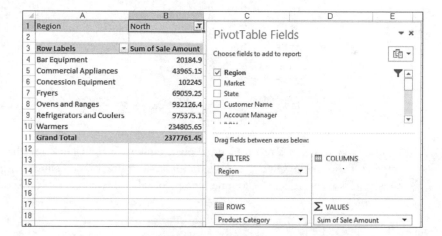

Understanding the Recommended Pivot Table Feature

With Excel 2013, Microsoft introduced a feature called Recommended PivotTables. You can find this feature next to the PivotTable icon on the Insert tab (see Figure 2.16).

Figure 2.16
The Recommended PivotTables icon helps you start a pivot table faster.

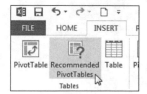

This feature is Microsoft's way of getting you up and running with pivot tables by simply creating one for you. The idea is simple: Place your cursor in a tabular range of data and then click the Recommended PivotTables icon. Excel shows you a menu of pivot tables it thinks it can create for you, based on the data in your range (see Figure 2.17). When you find one that looks good to you, click it and then click OK to have Excel create it.

Figure 2.17
Choose from the menu of recommended pivot tables to have Excel automatically create a pivot table for you.

Another way to get to a recommended pivot table is to right-click anywhere in your data range and choose the Quick Analysis option. The context menu shown in Figure 2.18 activates, and you can select a recommended pivot table under the Tables section.

Figure 2.18
You can also choose a recommended pivot table from the Quick Analysis context menu.

The reviews on this feature are mixed. On one hand, it does provide a quick and easy way to start a pivot table, especially for those of us who are not that experienced. On the other hand, Excel's recommendations are rudimentary at best. You will often find that you need to rearrange, add, or manipulate fields in the created pivot table to suit your needs. Although Excel *might* get it right the first time, it's unlikely that you will be able to leave the pivot table as is.

There is also a chance that Excel will simply not like the data range you pointed to. For example, the data in Figure 2.19 is a valid range, but Excel doesn't like the repeating dates. So it pops up a message to indicate that there are too many duplicates to recommend a pivot table; however, it will gladly create a blank one.

Figure 2.19
When Excel can't recommend a pivot table based on your data, it throws an error and gives you the option of starting with a blank pivot.

ument mber	In Balance Date	Credit Amount
9210	01/03/03	(34.54)
5775	01/03/03	(313.64)
6035	01/03/03	(389.04)
5826	01/03/03	(111.56)
9172	01/03/03	(1,630.25)
5388	01/03/03	(3,146.22)
9302	01/03/03	(1,217.37)
1669	01/03/03	(197.44)
4289	01/03/03	(33.75)
8471	01/03/03	(6,759.20)
8645	01/03/03	(214.54)
3807	01/03/03	(19.58)

Recommended PivotTables

We can't recommend any PivotTables for the selected data because there are too many blank cells or duplicate values, or not enough numerical columns.

Click OK to get a blank PivotTable.

All in all, the Recommended PivotTables feature can be a nice shortcut for getting a rudimentary pivot table started, but it's not a replacement for knowing how to create and manipulate pivot tables on your own.

Using Slicers

With Excel 2010, Microsoft introduced a feature called *slicers*. Slicers enable you to filter your pivot table in much the same way that the way Filter fields filter a pivot table. The difference is that slicers offer a user-friendly interface that enables you to easily see the current filter state.

Creating a Standard Slicer

To understand the concept behind slicers, place your cursor anywhere inside your pivot table and then select the Insert tab on the ribbon. Click the Slicer icon (see Figure 2.20).

Figure 2.20
Inserting a slicer.

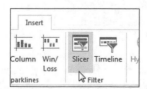

The Insert Slicers dialog, shown in Figure 2.21, opens. The idea is to select the dimensions you want to filter. In this example, the Region and Market slicers are selected.

Figure 2.21
Select the dimensions for which you want to create slicers.

After the slicers are created, you can simply click the filter values to filter your pivot table. As you can see in Figure 2.22, clicking Midwest in the Region slicer filters your pivot table, and also the Market slicer responds by highlighting the markets that belong to the Midwest region.

Figure 2.22
Select the dimensions you want to filter using slicers.

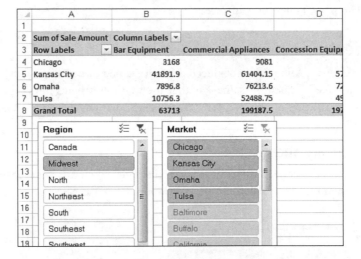

TIP

You can select multiple values by holding down the Ctrl key on your keyboard while selecting the needed filters. Alternatively, you can enable the Multi-Select toggle next to the filter icon at the top of the slicer.

In Figure 2.23, the Multi-Select toggle was enabled and then Baltimore, California, Charlotte, and Chicago were selected. Note that Excel highlights the selected markets in the Market slicer and also highlights their associated regions in the Region slicer.

Figure 2.23
The fact that they enable you to visually see the current filter state gives slicers a unique advantage over the Filter field.

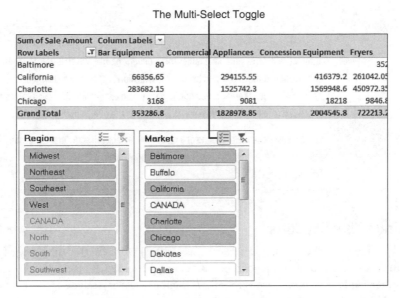

The Multi-Select Toggle

Another advantage you gain with slicers is that you can tie each slicer to more than one pivot table. In other words, any filter you apply to your slicer can be applied to multiple pivot tables.

To connect a slicer to more than one pivot table, simply right-click the slicer and select Report Connections. The Report Connections dialog, shown in Figure 2.24, opens. Place a check next to any pivot table that you want to filter using the current slicer.

Figure 2.24
Choose the pivot tables you want to filter using this slicer.

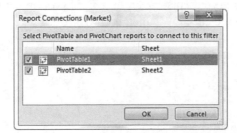

At this point, any filter applied via the slicer is applied to all the connected pivot tables. Again, slicers have a unique advantage over Filter fields in that they can control the filter state of multiple pivot tables. Filter fields can control only the pivot table in which they live.

> **NOTE**
>
> It's important to note that slicers are not part of a pivot table object. They are separate objects that you can use in a variety of ways. For a more detailed look at slicers, their functionality, and how to format them, pick up Que Publishing's *Special Edition Using Microsoft Excel 2016*, by Bill Jelen.

> **TIP**
>
> Notice that in Figure 2.24, the list of pivot tables is a bit ambiguous (PivotTable1, PivotTable2). Excel automatically gives your pivot tables these generic names, which it uses to identify them. You can imagine how difficult it would be to know which pivot table is which when working with more than a handful of pivots. Therefore, you might want to consider giving your pivot tables user-friendly names so you can recognize them in dialog boxes such as the one you see in Figure 2.24.
>
> You can easily change the name of a pivot table by placing your cursor anywhere inside the pivot table, selecting the Analyze tab, and entering a friendly name in the PivotTable Name input box found on the far left.

Creating a Timeline Slicer

The Timeline slicer (introduced with Excel 2013) works in the same way as a standard slicer in that it lets you filter a pivot table using a visual selection mechanism instead of the old Filter fields. The difference is that the Timeline slicer is designed to work exclusively with date fields, and it provides an excellent visual method to filter and group the dates in a pivot table.

> **NOTE**
>
> In order to create a Timeline slicer, your pivot table must contain a field where *all* the data is formatted as dates. This means that your source data table must contain at least one column where all the values are formatted as valid dates. If even only one value in the source date column is blank or not a valid date, Excel does not create a Timeline slicer.

To create a Timeline slicer, place your cursor anywhere inside your pivot table, select the Insert tab on the ribbon, and then click the Timeline icon (see Figure 2.25).

Figure 2.25
Inserting a Timeline slicer.

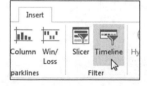

The Insert Timelines dialog shown in Figure 2.26 opens, showing you all the available date fields in the chosen pivot table. Here, you select the date fields for which you want to create slicers.

Figure 2.26
Select the date fields for which you want slicers created.

After your Timeline slicer is created, you can filter the data in your pivot table by using this dynamic data-selection mechanism. As you can see in Figure 2.27, clicking the April slicer filters the data in the pivot table to show only April data.

Figure 2.27
Click a date selection to filter your pivot table.

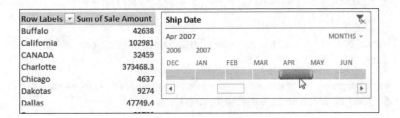

Figure 2.28 demonstrates how you can expand the slicer range with the mouse to include a wider range of dates in your filtered numbers.

Figure 2.28
You can expand the range on the Timeline slicer to include more data in the filtered numbers.

Row Labels ▼	Sum of Sale Amount
Buffalo	335113
California	543023
CANADA	147187.7
Charlotte	1178225.2
Chicago	6878
Dakotas	27353.8
Dallas	469309.15
Denver	291211

Want to quickly filter your pivot table by quarters? Well, you can easily do it with a Timeline slicer. Click the time period drop-down and select Quarters. As you can see in Figure 2.29, you also have the option of selecting Years or Days, if needed.

Figure 2.29
Quickly switch between filtering by years, quarters, months, and days.

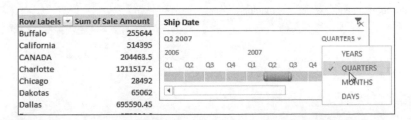

Be aware that Timeline slicers are not backward compatible, meaning that they are usable only in Excel 2013 and Excel 2016. If you open a workbook with Timeline slicers in Excel 2010 or earlier versions, the Timeline slicers are disabled.

CASE STUDY: ANALYZING ACTIVITY BY MARKET

Your organization has 18 markets that sell 7 types of products. You have been asked to build a report that breaks out each market and highlights the dollar sales for each product. You are starting with an intimidating transaction table that contains more than 91,000 rows of data. To start your report, do the following:

1. Place your cursor inside the data set, select the Insert tab, and click PivotTable.

2. When the Create PivotTable dialog appears, click the OK button. At this point, you should see an empty pivot table with the PivotTable Fields list.

3. Find the Market field in the PivotTable Fields list, and check the box next to it.

4. Find the Sale Amount field in the PivotTable Fields list, and check the box next to it.

5. To get the product breakouts, find the Product Category field in the PivotTable Fields list and drag it into the Columns area.

In five easy steps, you have calculated and designed a report that satisfies the requirements. After a little formatting, your pivot table report should look similar to the one shown in Figure 2.30.

Figure 2.30
This summary can be created in less than a minute.

Sum of Sale Amount	Column Labels			
Row Labels	Bar Equipment	Commercial Appliances	Concession Equipment	Frye
Baltimore	80			
Buffalo	37397.9	237297.85	187711	127
California	66356.65	294155.55	416379.2	261(
CANADA	35975.25	71272.1	205874.6	129
Charlotte	283682.15	1525742.3	1569948.6	4509
Chicago	3168	9081	18218	9
Dakotas	3386.5	7287.05	30619.2	180
Dallas	59580.3	255146	306037	151
Denver	34558.85	70068.8	75712.8	1200
Florida	1132162.05	5667950.6	6665865.45	2269
Great Lakes	16798.4	36678.1	71625.8	51
Kansas City	41891.9	61404.15	57300.7	5(
Knoxville	220	152		

Lest you lose sight of the analytical power you just harnessed, keep in mind that your data source has more than 91,000 rows and 14 columns, which is a hefty set of data by Excel standards. Despite the amount of data, you produced a relatively robust analysis in a matter of minutes.

Keeping Up with Changes in the Data Source

Let's go back to the family portrait analogy. As years go by, your family will change in appearance and might even grow to include some new members. The family portrait that was taken years ago remains static and no longer represents the family today. So another portrait needs to be taken.

As time goes by, your data might change and grow with newly added rows and columns. However, the pivot cache that feeds your pivot table report is disconnected from your data source, so it cannot represent any of the changes you make to your date source until you take another snapshot.

The action of updating your pivot cache by taking another snapshot of your data source is called *refreshing* your data. There are two reasons you might have to refresh your pivot table report:

- Changes have been made to your existing data source.
- Your data source's range has been expanded with the addition of rows or columns.

The following sections explain how to keep your pivot table synchronized with the changes in your data source.

Dealing with Changes Made to the Existing Data Source

If a few cells in your pivot table's source data have changed due to edits or updates, you can refresh your pivot table report with a few clicks. Simply right-click inside your pivot table report and select Refresh. This selection takes another snapshot of your data set, overwriting your previous pivot cache with the latest data.

> **NOTE**
> You can also refresh the data in a pivot table by selecting Analyze from the PivotTable Tools tab in the ribbon and then choosing Refresh.

> **TIP**
> Clicking anywhere inside a pivot table activates the PivotTable Tools tab just above the main ribbon.

Dealing with an Expanded Data Source Range Due to the Addition of Rows or Columns

When changes have been made to your data source that affect its range (for example, if you've added rows or columns), you have to update the range being captured by the pivot cache.

To do this, click anywhere inside the pivot table and then select Analyze from the PivotTable Tools tab in the ribbon. From here, select Change Data Source. This selection triggers the dialog shown in Figure 2.31.

Figure 2.31
The Change PivotTable Data Source dialog enables you to redefine the source data for your pivot table.

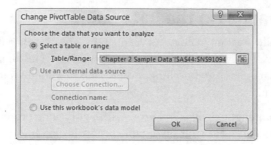

All you have to do here is update the range to include new rows and columns. After you have specified the appropriate range, click the OK button.

Sharing the Pivot Cache

You quite often need to analyze the same data set in multiple ways. In most cases, this process requires you to create separate pivot tables from the same data source. Keep in mind that every time you create a pivot table, you are storing a snapshot of the entire data set in a pivot cache. Every pivot cache that is created increases your memory usage and file size. For this reason, you should consider sharing your pivot cache.

> **NOTE** In situations where you need to create multiple pivot tables from the same data source, you can use the same pivot cache to feed multiple pivot tables. By using the same pivot cache for multiple pivot tables, you gain a certain level of efficiency when it comes to memory usage and file size.

In legacy versions of Excel, when you created a pivot table using a data set that was already being used in another pivot table, Excel actually gave you the option of using the same pivot cache. However, Excel 2016 does not give you such an option.

Instead, each time you create a new pivot table in Excel 2016, Excel automatically shares the pivot cache. Most of the time, this is beneficial: You can link as many pivot tables as you want to the same pivot cache with a negligible increase in memory and file size.

On the flip side, when you group one pivot table by month and year, all of the pivot tables are grouped in a similar fashion. If you want one pivot table by month and another pivot table by week, you have to force a separate pivot cache. You can force Excel to create a separate pivot cache by taking the following steps:

1. Press Alt+D+P on your keyboard to launch the Pivot Table Wizard.
2. Click the Next button to get past the first screen of the wizard.
3. On the second screen, select the range for your pivot table and click the Next button.
4. Excel displays a wordy message saying that you can use less memory if you click Yes. Instead, click No.
5. On the next screen, click the Finish button.

At this point, you have a blank pivot table that pulls from its own pivot cache.

> TIP
>
> If you already have an existing pivot table, you can use an alternative method for creating a separate pivot cache: Copy and paste the existing table to a new workbook and then copy and paste the pivot table back to a new sheet in the original workbook.

SIDE EFFECTS OF SHARING A PIVOT CACHE

It's important to note that there are a few side effects to sharing a pivot cache. For example, suppose you have two pivot tables using the same pivot cache. Certain actions affect both pivot tables:

- **Refreshing your data**—You cannot refresh one pivot table and not the other. Refreshing affects both tables.

- **Adding a calculated field**—If you create a calculated field in one pivot table, your newly created calculated field shows up in the PivotTable Fields list of the other pivot table.

- **Adding a calculated item**—If you create a calculated item in one pivot table, it shows in the other as well.

- **Grouping or ungrouping fields**—Any grouping or ungrouping you perform affects both pivot tables. For instance, suppose you group a date field in one pivot table to show months. The same date field in the other pivot table is also grouped to show months.

Although none of these side effects are critical flaws in the concept of sharing a pivot cache, it is important to keep them in mind when determining whether using a pivot table as your data source is the best option for your situation.

Saving Time with New Pivot Table Tools

Microsoft has invested a lot of time and effort in the overall pivot table experience. The results of these efforts are tools that make pivot table functionality more accessible and easier to use. The following sections look at a few of the tools that help you save time when managing pivot tables.

Deferring Layout Updates

The frustrating part of building a pivot table from a large data source is that each time you add a field to a pivot area, you are left waiting while Excel crunches through all that data. This can become a maddeningly time-consuming process if you have to add several fields to your pivot table.

Excel 2016 offers some relief for this problem by providing a way to defer layout changes until you are ready to apply them. You can activate this option by clicking the relatively inconspicuous Defer Layout Update check box in the PivotTable Fields list, as shown in Figure 2.32.

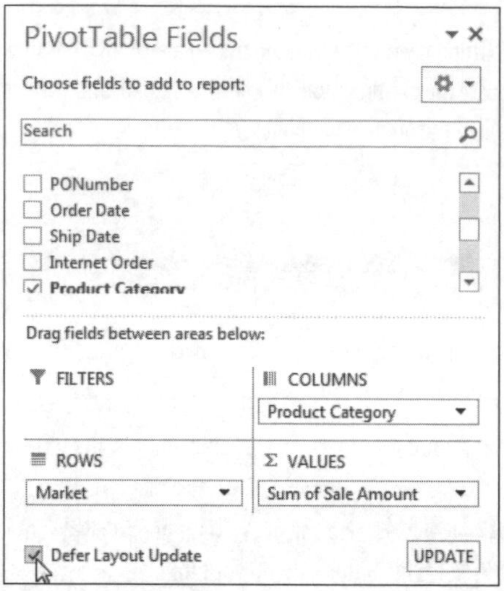

Figure 2.32
Click the Defer Layout Update check box to prevent your pivot table from updating while you add fields.

Here's how this feature works: With the Defer Layout Update check box selected, you prevent your pivot table from making real-time updates as you move your fields around without your pivot table. In Figure 2.32, notice that fields in the areas are not in the pivot table yet. The reason is that the Defer Layout Update check box is active. When you are ready to apply your changes, click the Update button on the lower-right corner of the PivotTable Fields list.

> **NOTE**
> Remember to remove the check from the Defer Layout Update check box when you are done building your pivot table. Leaving it checked results in your pivot table remaining in a state of manual updates, preventing you from using other features of the pivot table, such as sorting, filtering, and grouping.

> **TIP**
> Incidentally, the Defer Layout Update option is available through VBA. It can help improve the performance of any macro that automates the creation of pivot tables.

> **NOTE**
> For detailed information on how to use VBA to create pivot tables, refer to Chapter 13, "Using VBA to Create Pivot Tables."

Starting Over with One Click

Often you might want to start from scratch when working with your pivot table layouts. Excel 2016 provides a simple way to essentially start over without deleting your pivot cache. Select Analyze under the PivotTable Tools tab and select the Clear drop-down. As you can see in Figure 2.33, this command enables you to either clear your entire pivot table layout or remove any existing filters you might have applied in your pivot table.

Figure 2.33
The Clear command enables you to clear your pivot table fields or remove the applied filters from your pivot table.

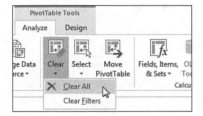

Relocating a Pivot Table

You might find that, after you have created a pivot table, you need to move it to another location. It might be in the way of other analyses on the worksheet, or you might simply need to move it to another worksheet. Although there are several ways to move a pivot table, the easiest is Excel 2016's no-frills way: Select Analyze under the PivotTable Tools tab and select Move PivotTable. This icon activates the Move PivotTable dialog, shown in Figure 2.34. All you have to do here is specify where you want your pivot table moved.

Figure 2.34
The Move PivotTable dialog enables you to quickly move your pivot table to another location.

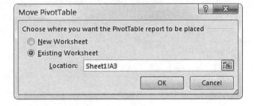

Next Steps

In Chapter 3, you'll learn how to enhance your pivot table reports by customizing your fields, changing field names, changing summary calculations, applying formats to data fields, adding and removing subtotals, and using the Show As setting.

Customizing a Pivot Table

3

Although pivot tables provide an extremely fast way to summarize data, sometimes the pivot table defaults are not exactly what you need. In such cases, you can use many powerful settings to tweak pivot tables. These tweaks range from making cosmetic changes to changing the underlying calculation used in the pivot table.

In Excel 2016, you find controls to customize a pivot table in myriad places: the Analyze tab, Design tab, Field Settings dialog, Data Field Settings dialog, PivotTable Options dialog, and context menus.

Rather than cover each set of controls sequentially, this chapter covers the following functional areas in making pivot table customization:

- **Minor cosmetic changes**—Change blanks to zeros, adjust the number format, and rename a field. The fact that you must correct these defaults in every pivot table that you create is annoying.

- **Layout changes**—Compare three possible layouts, show/hide subtotals and totals, and repeat row labels.

- **Major cosmetic changes**—Use pivot table styles to format a pivot table quickly.

- **Summary calculations**—Change from Sum to Count, Min, Max, and more. In a pivot table that defaults to Count of Revenue, change it to default to Sum of Revenue instead.

- **Advanced calculations**—Use settings to show data as a running total, percent of total, rank, percent of parent item, and more.

- **Other options**—Review some of the obscure options found throughout the Excel interface.

Making Common Cosmetic Changes

You need to make a few changes to almost every pivot table to make it easier to understand and interpret. Figure 3.1 shows a typical pivot table. To create this pivot table, open the Chapter 3 data file. Select Insert, Pivot Table, OK. Check the Sector, Customer, and Revenue fields, and drag the Region field to the Columns area.

Figure 3.1
A typical pivot table before customization.

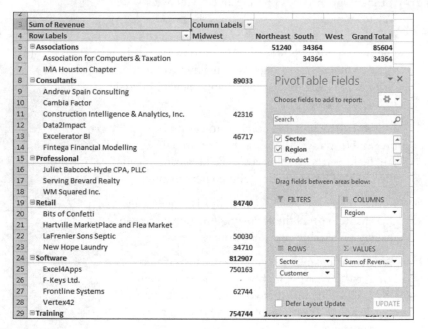

This default pivot table contains several annoying items that you might want to change quickly:

- The default table style uses no gridlines, which makes it difficult to follow the rows and columns across and down.

- Numbers in the Values area are in a general number format. There are no commas, currency symbols, and so on.

- For sparse data sets, many blanks appear in the Values area. The blank cell in B5 indicates that there were no Associations sales in the Midwest. Most people prefer to see zeros instead of blanks.

- Excel renames fields in the Values area with the unimaginative name Sum of Revenue. You can change this name.

You can correct each of these annoyances with just a few mouse clicks. The following sections address each issue.

Excel MVP Debra Dalgleish sells a Pivot Power Premium add-in that fixes most of the issues listed here. This add-in is great if you will be creating pivot tables frequently. For more information, visit `http://mrx.cl/pivpow16`.

Applying a Table Style to Restore Gridlines

The default pivot table layout contains no gridlines and is rather plain. Fortunately, you can apply a table style. Any table style that you choose is better than the default.

Follow these steps to apply a table style:

1. Make sure that the active cell is in the pivot table.
2. From the ribbon, select the Design tab. Three arrows appear at the right side of the PivotTable Style gallery.
3. Click the bottom arrow to open the complete gallery, which is shown in Figure 3.2.

Figure 3.2
The gallery contains 85 styles to choose from.

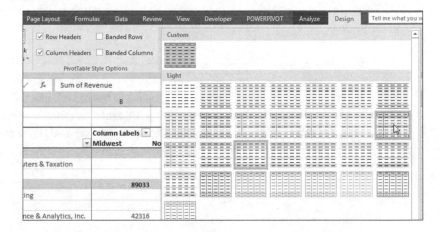

4. Choose any style other than the first style from the drop-down. Styles toward the bottom of the gallery tend to have more formatting.
5. Select the check box for Banded Rows to the left of the PivotTable Styles gallery. This draws gridlines in light styles and adds row stripes in dark styles.

It does not matter which style you choose from the gallery; any of the 84 other styles are better than the default style.

NOTE For more details about customizing styles, **see** "Customizing a Pivot Table's Appearance with Styles and Themes," **p. 60**.

Changing the Number Format to Add Thousands Separators

If you have gone to the trouble of formatting your underlying data, you might expect that the pivot table will capture some of this formatting. Unfortunately, it does not. Even if your underlying data fields were formatted with a certain numeric format, the default pivot table presents values formatted with a general format. As a sign of some progress, when you create pivot tables from PowerPivot, you can specify the number format for a field before creating the pivot table. This functionality has not come to regular pivot tables yet.

> **NOTE**   For more about PowerPivot, read Chapter 10, "Mashing Up Data with Power Pivot."

3

For example, in the figures in this chapter, the numbers are in the thousands or tens of thousands. At this level of sales, you would normally have a thousands separator and probably no decimal places. Although the original data had a numeric format applied, the pivot table routinely formats your numbers in an ugly general style.

> **CAUTION**
>
> You will be tempted to format the numbers using the right-click menu and choosing Number Format. This is not the best way to go. You will be tempted to format the cells using the tools on the Home tab. This is not the way to go. Either of these methods temporarily fixes the problem, but you lose the formatting as soon as you move a field in the pivot table. The right way to solve the problem is to use the Number Format button in the Value Field Settings dialog.

You have three ways to get to this dialog:

- Right-click a number in the Values area of the pivot table and select Value Field Settings.

- Click the drop-down to the right of the Sum of Revenue field in the areas of the PivotTable Fields list and then select Value Field Settings from the context menu.

- Select any cell in the Values area of the pivot table. From the Analyze tab, select Field Settings from the Active Field group.

As shown in Figure 3.3, the Value Field Settings dialog is displayed. To change the numeric format, click the Number Format button in the lower-left corner.

Figure 3.3
Display the Value Field
Settings dialog, and then
click Number Format.

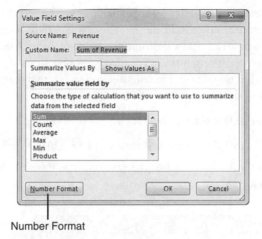

Number Format

In the Format Cells dialog that appears, you can choose any built-in number format or choose a custom format. For example, you can choose Currency, as shown in Figure 3.4.

3

Figure 3.4
Choose an easier-to-read
number format from the
Format Cells dialog.

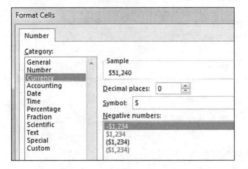

NOTE Although Excel 2016 offers a Live Preview feature for many formatting settings, the Format Cells dialog does not offer one. To see the changes, you must assign the number format, close the Format dialog, and then close the Value Field Settings dialog.

Replacing Blanks with Zeros

One of the elements of good spreadsheet design is that you should never leave blank cells in a numeric section of a worksheet. Even Microsoft believes in this rule; if your source data for a pivot table contains one million numeric cells and one blank cell, Excel 2016 treats the entire column as if it is text and chooses to count the column instead of sum it. This is why it is incredibly annoying that the default setting for a pivot table leaves many blanks in the Values area of some pivot tables.

A blank tells you that there were no sales for a particular combination of labels. In the default view, an actual zero is used to indicate that there was activity, but the total sales were zero. This value might mean that a customer bought something and then returned it, resulting in net sales of zero. Although there are limited applications in which you need to differentiate between having no sales and having net zero sales, this seems rare. In 99% of the cases, you should fill in the blank cells with zeros.

Follow these steps to change this setting for the current pivot table:

1. Right-click any cell in the pivot table and choose PivotTable Options.

2. On the Layout & Format tab in the Format section, type **0** next to the field labeled For Empty Cells Show (see Figure 3.5).

Figure 3.5
Enter a zero in the For Empty Cells Show box to replace the blank cells with zero.

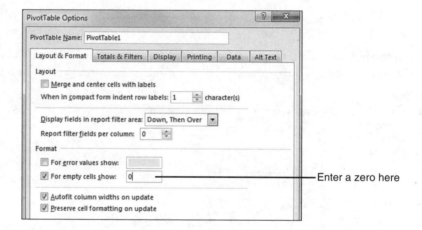

3. Click OK to accept the change.

The result is that the pivot table is filled with zeros instead of blanks, as shown in Figure 3.6.

Figure 3.6
Your report is now a solid contiguous block of non-blank cells.

	A	B	C	D	E	F
1						
2						
3	Sum of Revenue	Column Labels ▾				
4	Row Labels ▾	Midwest	Northeast	South	West	Grand Total
5	⊟ Associations	$0	$51,240	$34,364	$0	$85,604
6	Association for Computers & Taxation	$0	$0	$34,364	$0	$34,364
7	IMA Houston Chapter	$0	$51,240	$0	$0	$51,240
8	⊟ Consultants	$89,033	$0	$926,970	$115,132	$1,131,135
9	Andrew Spain Consulting	$0	$0	$869,454	$0	$869,454
10	Cambia Factor	$0	$0	$57,516	$0	$57,516
11	Construction Intelligence & Analytics, Inc.	$42,316	$0	$0	$0	$42,316
12	Data2Impact	$0	$0	$0	$59,881	$59,881
13	Excelerator BI	$46,717	$0	$0	$0	$46,717
14	Fintega Financial Modelling	$0	$0	$0	$55,251	$55,251
15	⊟ Professional	$0	$0	$437,695	$39,250	$476,945
16	Juliet Babcock-Hyde CPA, PLLC	$0	$0	$31,369	$0	$31,369
17	Serving Brevard Realty	$0	$0	$406,326	$0	$406,326
18	WM Squared Inc.	$0	$0	$0	$39,250	$39,250
19	⊟ Retail	$84,740	$0	$704,359	$31,021	$820,120

Changing a Field Name

Every field in a final pivot table has a name. Fields in the row, column, and filter areas inherit their names from the heading in the source data. Fields in the data section are given names such as Sum of Revenue. In some instances, you might prefer to print a different name in the pivot table. You might prefer Total Revenue instead of the default name. In these situations, the capability to change your field names comes in quite handy.

> **TIP**
> Although many of the names are inherited from headings in the original data set, when your data is from an external data source, you might not have control over field names. In these cases, you might want to change the names of the fields as well.

To change a field name in the Values area, follow these steps:

1. Select a cell in the pivot table that contains the appropriate type of value. You might have a pivot table with both Sum of Quantity and Sum of Revenue in the Values area. Choose a cell that contains a Sum of Revenue value.

2. Go to the Analyze tab in the ribbon. A Pivot Field Name text box appears below the heading Active Field. The box currently contains Sum of Revenue.

3. Type a new name in the box, as shown in Figure 3.7. Click a cell in your pivot table to complete the entry, and have the heading in A3 change. The name of the field title in the Values area also changes to reflect the new name.

Figure 3.7
The name typed in the Custom Name box appears in the pivot table. Although names should be unique, you can trick Excel into accepting a name that's similar to an existing name by adding a space to the end of it.

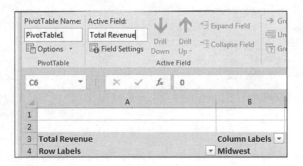

> **NOTE**
> One common frustration occurs when you would like to rename Sum of Revenue to Revenue. The problem is that this name is not allowed because it is not unique; you already have a Revenue field in the source data. To work around this limitation, you can name the field and add a space to the end of the name. Excel considers "Revenue" (with a space) to be different from "Revenue" (with no space). Because this change is only cosmetic, the readers of your spreadsheet do not notice the space after the name.

Making Report Layout Changes

Excel 2016 offers three report layout styles. The Excel team continues to offer the newer Compact layout as the default report layout, even though I continually hound them about the fact that people who work in the real world would rather use the Tabular report layout, or at least would like to have a choice about which one to use as a default.

If you consider three report layouts, and the ability to show subtotals at the top or bottom, plus choices for blank rows and Repeat All Item Labels, you have 16 different layout possibilities available.

Layout changes are controlled in the Layout group of the Design tab, as shown in Figure 3.8. This group offers four icons:

- **Subtotals**—Moves subtotals to the top or bottom of each group or turns them off.
- **Grand Totals**—Turns the grand totals on or off for rows and columns.
- **Report Layout**—Uses the Compact, Outline, or Tabular forms. Offers an option to repeat item labels.
- **Blank Rows**—Inserts or removes blank lines after each group.

Figure 3.8
The Layout group on the Design tab offers different layouts and options for totals.

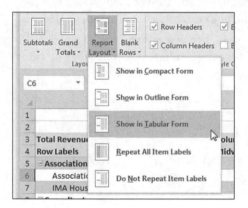

> NOTE
>
> You statisticians in the audience might think that 3 layouts × 2 repeat options × 2 subtotal location options × 2 blank row options would be 24 layouts. However, choosing Repeat All Item Labels does not work with the Compact layout, thus eliminating 4 of the combinations. In addition, Subtotals at the Top of Each Group does not work with the Tabular layout, eliminating another 4 combinations.

Using the Compact Layout

By default, all new pivot tables use the Compact layout that you saw in Figure 3.6. In this layout, multiple fields in the row area are stacked in column A. Note in the figure that the Consultants sector and the Andrew Spain Consulting customer are both in column A.

The Compact form is suited for using the Expand and Collapse icons. If you select one of the Sector value cells such as Associations in A5 and then click the Collapse Field icon on the Analyze tab, Excel hides all the customer details and shows only the sectors, as shown in Figure 3.9.

Figure 3.9
Click the Collapse Field icon to hide levels of detail.

	A	B	C	D	E	F
1						
2						
3	Total Revenue	Column Labels ▼				
4	Row Labels ▼	Midwest	Northeast	South	West	Grand Total
5	⊞ Associations	$0	$51,240	$34,364	$0	$85,604
6	⊞ Consultants	$89,033	$0	$926,970	$115,132	$1,131,135
7	⊞ Professional	$0	$0	$437,695	$39,250	$476,945
8	⊞ Retail	$84,740	$0	$704,359	$31,021	$820,120
9	⊞ Software	$812,907	$463,658	$0	$0	$1,276,565
10	⊞ Training	$754,744	$1,609,714	$498,937	$54,048	$2,917,443
11	Grand Total	$1,741,424	$2,124,612	$2,602,325	$239,451	$6,707,812

After a field is collapsed, you can show detail for individual items by using the plus icons in column A, or you can click Expand Field on the Analyze tab to see the detail again.

> **TIP** If you select a cell in the innermost row field and click Expand Field on the Options tab, Excel displays the Show Detail dialog, as shown in Figure 3.10, to enable you to add a new innermost row field.

Figure 3.10
When you attempt to expand the innermost field, Excel offers to add a new innermost field.

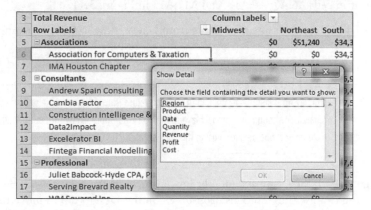

Using the Outline Layout

When you select Design, Layout, Report Layout, Show in Outline Form, Excel puts each row field in a separate column. The pivot table shown in Figure 3.11 is one column wider, with revenue values starting in C instead of B. This is a small price to pay for allowing each field to occupy its own column. Soon, you will find out how to convert a pivot table to values so you can further sort or filter. When you do this, you will want each field in its own column.

Figure 3.11
The Outline layout puts each row field in a separate column.

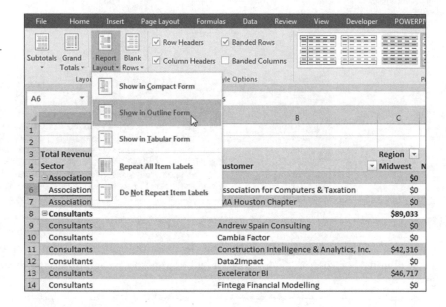

The Excel team added the Repeat All Item Labels option to the Report Layout tab starting in Excel 2010. This alleviated a lot of busy work because it takes just two clicks to fill in all the blank cells along the outer row fields. Choosing to repeat the item labels causes values to appear in cells A6:A7, A9:A10, and A12:A15 in Figure 3.11.

Figure 3.11 shows the same pivot table from before, now in Outline form and with labels repeated.

> **CAUTION**
> This layout is suitable if you plan to copy the values from the pivot table to a new location for further analysis. Although the Compact layout offers a clever approach by squeezing multiple fields into one column, it is not ideal for reusing the data later.

By default, both the Compact and Outline layouts put the subtotals at the top of each group. You can use the Subtotals drop-down on the Design tab to move the totals to the bottom of each group, as shown in Figure 3.12. In Outline view, this causes a not-really useful heading row to appear at the top of each group. Cell A5 contains "Associations" without any additional data in the columns to the right. Consequently, the pivot table occupies 44 rows instead of 37 rows because each of the 7 sector categories has an extra header.

Figure 3.12
With subtotals at the bottom of each group, the pivot table occupies several more rows.

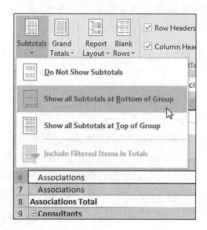

Using the Traditional Tabular Layout

Figure 3.13 shows the Tabular layout. This layout is similar to the one that has been used in pivot tables since their invention through Excel 2003. In this layout, the subtotals can never appear at the top of the group. The new Repeat All Item Labels works with this layout, as shown in Figure 3.13.

Figure 3.13
The Tabular layout is similar to pivot tables in legacy versions of Excel.

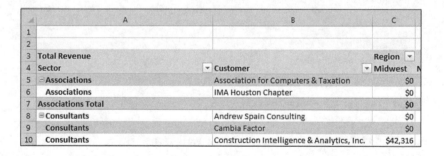

The Tabular layout is the best layout if you expect to use the resulting summary data in a subsequent analysis. If you wanted to reuse the table in Figure 3.13, you would do additional "flattening" of the pivot table by choosing Subtotals, Do Not Show Subtotals and Grand Totals, Off for Rows and Columns.

CASE STUDY: CONVERTING A PIVOT TABLE TO VALUES

Say that you want to convert the pivot table shown in Figure 3.13 to be a regular data set that you can sort, filter, chart, or export to another system. You don't need the Sectors totals in rows 7, 14, 18, and so on. You don't need the Grand Total at the bottom. And, depending on your future needs, you might want to move the Region field from the Columns area to the Rows area. This would allow you to add Cost and Profit as new columns in the final report.

Finally, you want to convert from a live pivot table to static values. To make these changes, follow these steps:

1. Select any cell in the pivot table.

2. From the Design tab, select Grand Totals, Off for Rows and Columns.

3. Select Design, Subtotals, Do Not Show Subtotals.

4. Drag the Region tile from the Columns area in the PivotTable Fields list. Drop this field between Sector and Customer in the Rows area.

5. Check Profit and Cost in the top of the PivotTable Fields list. Because both fields are numeric, they move to the Values area and appear in the pivot table as new columns. Rename both fields using the Current Field box on the Analyze tab. The report is now a contiguous solid block of data, as shown in Figure 3.14.

Figure 3.14
The pivot table now contains a solid block of data.

	A	B	C	D	E	F
1						
2						
3	Sector ▾	Region ▾	Customer ▾	Total Revenue	Total Profit	Total Cost
4	⊟Associations	⊟Northeast	IMA Houston Chapter	$51,240	22824	28416
5	Associations	⊟South	Association for Computers & Taxation	$34,364	15576	18788
6	⊟Consultants	⊟Midwest	Construction Intelligence & Analytics, Inc.	$42,316	18764	23552
7	Consultants	Midwest	Excelerator BI	$46,717	19961	26756
8	Consultants	⊟South	Andrew Spain Consulting	$869,454	382170	487284
9	Consultants	South	Cambia Factor	$57,516	26765	30751
10	Consultants	⊟West	Data2Impact	$59,881	25913	33968
11	Consultants	West	Fintega Financial Modelling	$55,251	24632	30619
12	⊟Professional	⊟South	Juliet Babcock-Hyde CPA, PLLC	$31,369	13730	17639
13	Professional	South	Serving Brevard Realty	$406,326	178585	227741

6. Select one cell in the pivot table. Press Ctrl+* to select all the data in the pivot table.

7. Press Ctrl+C to copy the data from the pivot table.

8. Select a blank section of a worksheet.

9. Right-click and choose Paste Values to open the fly-out menu. Select Paste Values and Number Formatting, as shown in Figure 3.15. Excel pastes a static copy of the report to the worksheet.

Figure 3.15
Use Paste Values to create a static version of the data.

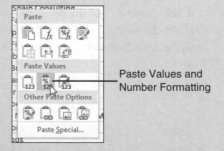

Paste Values and Number Formatting

10. If you no longer need the original pivot table, select the entire pivot table and press the Delete key to clear the cells from the pivot table and free up the area of memory that was holding the pivot table cache.

The result is a solid block of summary data. These 27 rows are a summary of the 500+ rows in the original data set, but they also are suitable for exporting to other systems.

Controlling Blank Lines, Grand Totals, and Other Settings

Additional settings on the Design tab enable you to toggle various elements.

The Blank Rows drop-down offers the choice Insert Blank Row After Each Item. This setting applies only to pivot tables with two or more row fields. Blank rows are not added after each item in the inner row field. You see a blank row after each group of items in the outer row fields. As shown in Figure 3.16, the blank row after each region makes the report easier to read. However, if you remove Sector from the report, you have only Region in the row fields, and no blank rows appear (see Figure 3.17).

3

	A	B	C	D	E	F
1						
2						
3	Total Revenue		Product			
4	Sector	Customer	Doodads	Gadget	Gizmo	Widget
5	Associations	Association for Computers & Taxation	$0	$4,270	$22,958	$7,136
6	Associations	IMA Houston Chapter	$0	$18,064	$18,072	$15,104
7	Associations Total		$0	$22,334	$41,030	$22,240
8						
9	Consultants	Andrew Spain Consulting	$0	$304,198	$288,409	$276,847
10	Consultants	Cambia Factor	$0	$16,784	$35,200	$5,532

Figure 3.16
The Blank Rows setting makes the report easier to read.

	A	B	C	D	E
1					
2					
3	Total Revenue	Product			
4	Customer	Doodads	Gadget	Gizmo	Widget
5	599CD.com	$0	$185,675	$245,491	$191,628
6	Andrew Spain Consulting	$0	$304,198	$288,409	$276,847
7	Association for Computers & Taxation	$0	$4,270	$22,958	$7,136
8	Bits of Confetti	$28,663	$2,358	$0	$0
9	Cambia Factor	$0	$16,784	$35,200	$5,532
10	Construction Intelligence & Analytics, Inc.	$6,036	$18,552	$17,728	$0
11	CPASelfStudy.com	$0	$190,533	$200,936	$177,382
12	Data2Impact	$0	$26,484	$19,544	$13,853
13	Excel4Apps	$0	$233,435	$235,761	$280,967

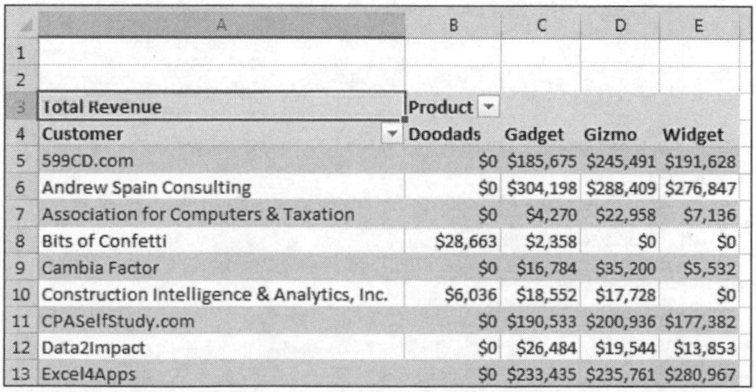

Figure 3.17
Blank rows will not appear when there is only one item in the row field.

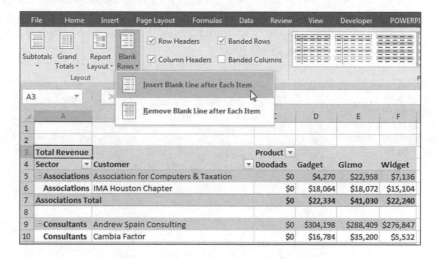

> **NOTE**
>
> For those of you following along with the sample files, you may have noticed quite a leap from the pivot table in Figure 3.14 to the one in Figure 3.16, but it is still the same pivot table. Here is how to make the changes:
>
> 1. Uncheck Sector, Customer, Profit, and Cost in the Pivot Table Fields list.
> 2. Drag the Product field to the Columns area.
> 3. Recheck the Sector field to move it to the second Row field.
> 4. Make sure the active cell is in column A.
> 5. On the Design tab of the ribbon, open Subtotals and choose Show All Subtotals at the Bottom of the Group.
> 6. As shown in Figure 3.16, open the Blank Rows drop-down and choose Insert Blank Row After Each Item.
> 7. To get to the pivot table shown in Figure 3.17, uncheck the Sector field.

Grand totals can appear at the bottom of each column and/or at the end of each row, or they can be turned off altogether. Settings for grand totals appear in the Grand Totals drop-down of the Layout group on the Design tab. The wording in this drop-down is a bit confusing, so Figure 3.18 shows what each option provides. The default is to show grand totals for rows and columns, as in Figure 3.17.

Figure 3.18
The wording is confusing, but you can toggle off the grand total column, row, or both.

Grand Totals On For Rows Only

Region	Doodads	Gadget	Gizmo	Widget	Grand Total
Keeps the Grand Total column					
Total Revenue Product					
Midwest	$6,036	$544,772	$652,651	$537,965	$1,741,424
Northeast	$38,860	$714,009	$751,724	$620,019	$2,124,612
South	$0	$839,551	$918,588	$844,186	$2,602,325
West	$28,663	$65,382	$70,057	$75,349	$239,451

Grand Totals On For Columns Only

Region	Doodads	Gadget	Gizmo	Widget
Keeps the Grand Total row				
Total Revenue Product				
Midwest	$6,036	$544,772	$652,651	$537,965
Northeast	$38,860	$714,009	$751,724	$620,019
South	$0	$839,551	$918,588	$844,186
West	$28,663	$65,382	$70,057	$75,349
Grand Total	$73,559	$2,163,714	$2,393,020	$2,077,519

Grand Totals Off For Rows and Columns

Region	Doodads	Gadget	Gizmo	Widget
Total Revenue Product				
Midwest	$6,036	$544,772	$652,651	$537,965
Northeast	$38,860	$714,009	$751,724	$620,019
South	$0	$839,551	$918,588	$844,186
West	$28,663	$65,382	$70,057	$75,349

If you want a grand total column but no grand total at the bottom, choose On for Rows Only, as shown at the top of Figure 3.18. To me, this seems backward. To keep the grand total column, you have to choose to turn on grand totals for rows only. I guess the rationale is that each cell in F5:F8 is a grand total of the row to the left of the cell. Hence, you are showing the grand totals for all the rows but not for the columns. Perhaps someday Microsoft will ship a version of Excel in English-Midwest where this setting would be called "Keep the Grand Total Column." But for now, it remains confusing.

In a similar fashion, to show a grand total row but no grand total column, you open the Grand Totals menu and choose On for Columns Only. Again, in some twisted version of the English language, cell B18 is totaling the cells in the column above it.

The final choice, Off for Rows and Columns, is simple enough. Excel shows neither a grand total column nor a grand total row.

Back in Excel 2003, pivot tables were shown in Tabular layout and logical headings such as Region and Product would appear in the pivot table, as shown in the top pivot table in Figure 3.19. When the Excel team switched to Compact form, they replaced those headings with Row Labels and Column Labels. These add nothing to the report. To toggle off those headings, look on the far right side of the Analyze tab for an icon called Field Headers and click it to remove Row Labels and Column Labels from your pivot tables in Compact form.

Figure 3.19
The Compact form introduced in Excel 2007 replaced useful headings with Row Labels. You can turn these off.

	A	B	C	D	E	F
1						
2	Tabular Form					
3	Revenue	Product	▼			
4	Region ▼	Doodads	Gadget	Gizmo	Widget	Grand Total
5	Midwest	$6,036	$544,772	$652,651	$537,965	$1,741,424
6	Northeast	$38,860	$714,009	$751,724	$620,019	$2,124,612
7	South	$0	$839,551	$918,588	$844,186	$2,602,325
8	West	$28,663	$65,382	$70,057	$75,349	$239,451
9						
10	Compact Form - "Region" becomes "Row Labels"					
11	Revenue	Column Labels	▼			
12	Row Lab ▼	Doodads	Gadget	Gizmo	Widget	Grand Total
13	Midwest	$6,036	$544,772	$652,651	$537,965	$1,741,424
14	Northeast	$38,860	$714,009	$751,724	$620,019	$2,124,612
15	South	$0	$839,551	$918,588	$844,186	$2,602,325
16	West	$28,663	$65,382	$70,057	$75,349	$239,451
17						
18	Compact Form - Toggle Off Field Headers					
19	Revenue					
20		Doodads	Gadget	Gizmo	Widget	Grand Total
21	Midwest	$6,036	$544,772	$652,651	$537,965	$1,741,424
22	Northeast	$38,860	$714,009	$751,724	$620,019	$2,124,612
23	South	$0	$839,551	$918,588	$844,186	$2,602,325
24	West	$28,663	$65,382	$70,057	$75,349	$239,451

> **CAUTION**
>
> When you arrange several pivot tables vertically, as in Figure 3.19, you'll notice that changes in one pivot table change the column widths for the entire column, often causing #### to appear in the other pivot tables. By default, Excel changes the column width to AutoFit the pivot table but ignores anything else in the column. To turn off this default behavior, right-click each pivot table and choose PivotTable Options. In the first tab of the Options dialog, the second-to-last check box is AutoFit Column Widths on Update. Uncheck this box.

Customizing a Pivot Table's Appearance with Styles and Themes

You can quickly apply color and formatting to a pivot table report by using the 85 built-in styles in the PivotTable Styles gallery on the Design tab. These 85 styles are further modified by the four check boxes to the left of the gallery. Throw in the 48 themes on the Page Layout tab, and you have 65,280 easy ways to format a pivot table. If none of those provide what you need, you can define a new style.

Start with the four check boxes in the PivotTable Style Options group of the Design tab of the ribbon. You can choose to apply special formatting to the row headers, column headers, banded rows, or banded columns. My favorite choice here is banded rows because it makes it easier for the reader's eye to follow a row across a wide report. You should choose from these settings first because the choices here will modify the thumbnails shown in the Styles gallery.

As mentioned earlier, the PivotTable Styles gallery on the Design tab offers 85 built-in styles. Grouped into 28 styles each of Light, Medium, and Dark, the gallery offers variations on the accent colors used in the current theme. In Figure 3.20, you can see which styles in the gallery truly support banded rows and which just offer a bottom border between rows.

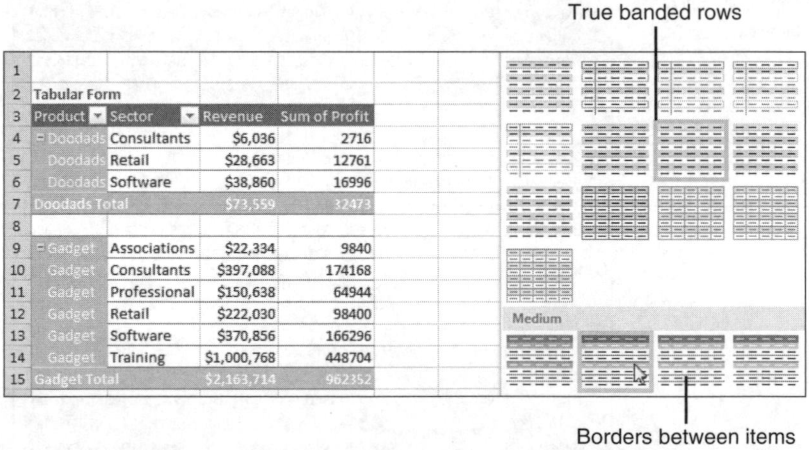

Figure 3.20

The styles are shown here with accents for row headers, column headers, and alternating colors in the columns.

True banded rows

Borders between items

> **TIP**
>
> Note that you can modify the thumbnails for the 85 styles shown in the gallery by using the four check boxes in the PivotTable Style Options group.

The Live Preview feature in Excel 2016 works in the Styles gallery. As you hover your mouse cursor over style thumbnails, the worksheet shows a preview of the style.

Customizing a Style

You can create your own pivot table styles, and the new styles are added to the gallery for the current workbook only. To use the custom style in another workbook, copy and temporarily paste the formatted pivot table to the other workbook. After the pivot table has been pasted, apply the custom style to an existing pivot table in your workbook and then delete the temporary pivot table.

Say that you want to create a pivot table style in which the banded colors are three rows high. Follow these steps to create the new style:

1. Find an existing style in the PivotTable Styles gallery that supports banded rows. Right-click the style in the gallery and select Duplicate. Excel displays the Modify PivotTable Quick Style dialog.

2. Choose a new name for the style. Excel initially appends a 2 to the existing style name, which means you have a name such as PivotStyleDark3 2. Type a better name, such as **Greenbar**.

3. In the Table Element list, click First Row Stripe. A new section called Stripe Size appears in the dialog.

4. Select 3 from the Stripe Size drop-down, as shown in Figure 3.21.

Figure 3.21
Customize the style in the Modify PivotTable Style dialog.

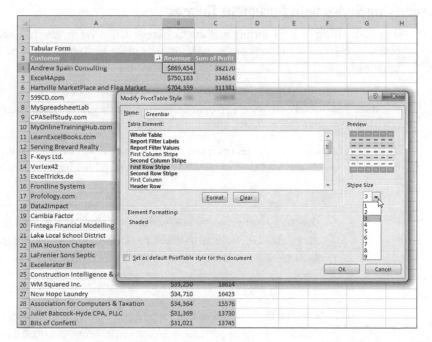

5. To change the stripe color, click the Format button. The Format Cells dialog appears. Click the Fill tab and then choose a fill color. If you want to be truly authentic, choose More Colors, Custom and use Red=200, Green=225, Blue=204 to simulate 1980s-era greenbar paper. Click OK to accept the color and return to the Modify PivotTable Quick Style dialog.

6. In the Table Element List, click Second Row Stripe. Select 3 from the Stripe Size drop-down. Modify the format to use a lighter color, such as white.

7. If you plan on creating more pivot tables in this workbook, choose the Set as Default PivotTable Style for This Document check box in the lower left.

8. Optionally edit the colors for Header Row and Grand Total Row.

9. Click OK to finish building the style. Strangely, Excel doesn't automatically apply this new style to the pivot table. After you put in a few minutes of work to tweak the style, the pivot table does not change.

10. Your new style should be the first thumbnail visible in the styles gallery. Click that style to apply it to the pivot table.

> **TIP** If you have not added more than seven custom styles, the thumbnail should be visible in the closed gallery, so you can choose it without reopening the gallery.

Modifying Styles with Document Themes

The formatting options for pivot tables in Excel 2016 are impressive. The 84 styles combined with 16 combinations of the Style options make for hundreds of possible format combinations.

In case you become tired of these combinations, you can visit the Themes drop-down on the Page Layout tab, where many built-in themes are available. Each theme has a new combination of accent colors, fonts, and shape effects.

To change a document theme, open the Themes drop-down on the Page Layout tab. Choose a new theme, and the colors used in the pivot table change to match the theme.

> **CAUTION** Changing the theme affects the entire workbook. It changes the colors and fonts and affects all charts, shapes, tables, and pivot tables on all worksheets of the active workbook. If you have several other pivot tables in the workbook, changing the theme will apply new colors to all of the pivot tables.

> **TIP** Some of the themes use unusual fonts. You can apply the colors from a theme without changing the fonts in your document by using the Colors drop-down next to the Themes menu, as shown in Figure 3.22.

Figure 3.22
Choose new colors from the Colors menu.

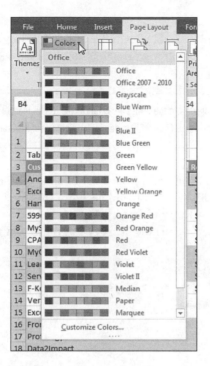

Changing Summary Calculations

When you create a pivot table report, by default Excel summarizes the data by either counting or summing the items. Instead of Sum or Count, you might want to choose functions such as Min, Max, and Count Numeric. In all, 11 options are available. However, the common reason to change a summary calculation is that Excel has incorrectly chosen to count instead of sum your data.

Understanding Why One Blank Cell Causes a Count

If all the cells in a column contain numeric data, Excel chooses to sum. If just one cell is either blank or contains text, Excel chooses to count.

In Figure 3.23, the worksheet contains mostly numeric entries but has a single blank cell in G2. The one blank cell is enough to cause Excel to count the data instead of summing.

Figure 3.23
The single blank cell in G2 causes problems in the default pivot table.

	A	B	C	D	E	F	G	H	I
1	Sector	Region	Product	Date	Customer	Quantity	Revenue	Profit	Cost
2	Training	Midwest	Gizmo	1/1/2017	599CD.com	1000		10220	12590
3	Software	Northeast	Gadget	1/2/2017	F-Keys Ltd.	100	2257	984	1273
4	Associations	South	Gizmo	1/4/2017	Association for Cor	400	9152	4088	5064
5	Consultants	Midwest	Gadget	1/4/2017	Construction Intell	800	18552	7872	10680
6	Consultants	West	Gadget	1/7/2017	Data2Impact	1000	21730	9840	11890
7	Software	Midwest	Widget	1/7/2017	Excel4Apps	400	8456	3388	5068
8	Software	Midwest	Widget	1/9/2017	Excel4Apps	800	16416	6776	9640

In Excel 2016, the first clue that you have a problem appears when you select the Revenue check box in the top section of the PivotTable Fields list. If Excel moves the Revenue field to the Rows area, you know that Excel considers the field to be text instead of numeric.

> **CAUTION**
>
> Be vigilant while dragging fields into the Values area. If a calculation appears to be dramatically low, check to see if the field name reads Count of Revenue instead of Sum of Revenue.

When you create the pivot table in Figure 3.24, you should notice that your company has only $562 in revenue instead of millions. This should be a hint that the heading in B3 reads Count of Revenue instead of Sum of Revenue. In fact, 562 is one less than the number of records in the data set; Excel doesn't include the blank cell in the Count function.

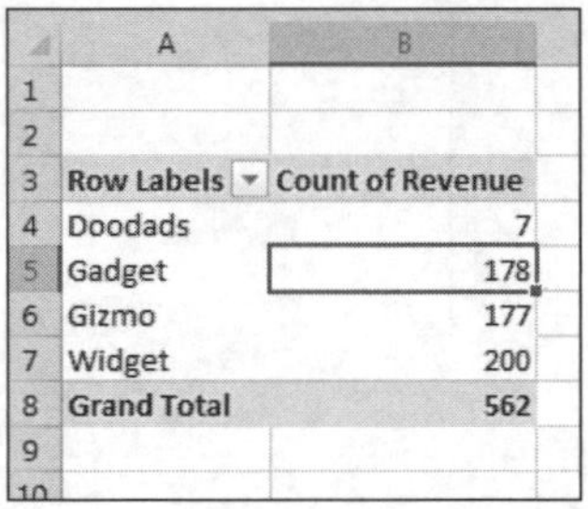

Figure 3.24
Your revenue numbers look anemic. Notice in cell B3 that Excel chose to count instead of sum the revenue. This often happens if you inadvertently have one blank cell in your Revenue column.

To override the incorrect Count calculation, right-click any pivot table cell in the Revenue column. Choose Summarize Values By and then choose Sum (see Figure 3.25).

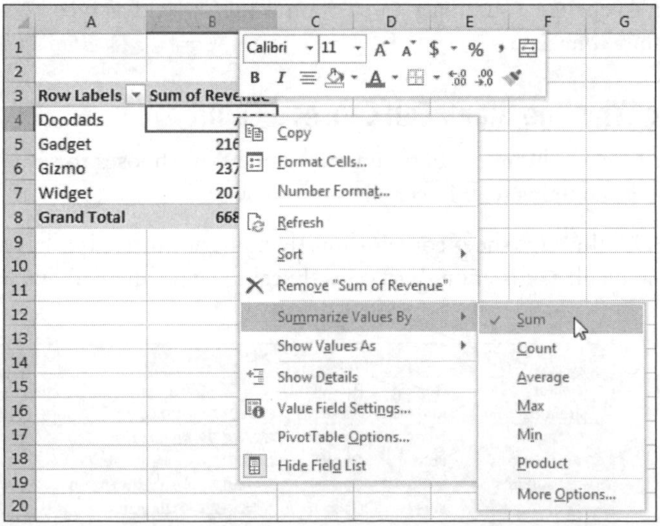

Figure 3.25
Change the function from Count to Sum in the Summarize Values By drop-down.

Using Functions Other Than Count or Sum

The settings for Summarize Values By and Show Values As were temporarily promoted to drop-downs in the Excel 2010 ribbon, but they are not in the ribbon in Excel 2016. All of the pivot table calculations icons for the Quick Access Toolbar were removed from Excel 2013 and are still gone in 2016. They were apparently removed to make space for Insert Timeline, Drill Down, Drill Up, and Recommended Pivot Tables. If you were a fan of Summarize Values By and Show Values As, you can continue to use them from the right-click menu or by selecting a cell and pressing Shift+F10. These options have always been available in the Value Field Settings dialog.

Excel offers six functions through the Summarize Values By command, plus five more options when you select More Options. The options available are as follows:

- **Sum**—Provides a total of all numeric data.
- **Count**—Counts all cells, including numeric, text, and error cells. This is equivalent to the Excel function =COUNTA().
- **Average**—Provides an average.
- **Max**—Shows the largest value.
- **Min**—Shows the smallest value.
- **Product**—Multiplies all the cells together. For example, if your data set has cells with values of 3, 4, and 5, the product is 60.
- **Count Nums**—Counts only the numeric cells. This is equivalent to the Excel function =COUNT().
- **StdDev and StdDevP**—Calculate the standard deviation. Use StdDevP if your data set contains the complete population. Use StdDev if your data set contains a sample of the population.
- **Var and VarP**—Calculate the statistical variance. Use VarP if your data contains a complete population. If your data contains only a sampling of the complete population, use Var to estimate the variance.

> **NOTE** Standard deviations explain how tightly results are grouped around the mean.

Adding and Removing Subtotals

Subtotals are an essential feature of pivot table reporting. Sometimes you might want to suppress the display of subtotals, and other times you might want to show more than one subtotal per field.

Suppressing Subtotals with Many Row Fields

When you have many row fields in a report, subtotals can obscure your view. For example, in Figure 3.26, there is no need to show subtotals for each market because there is only one sales rep for each market.

Figure 3.26
Sometimes you do not need subtotals at every level.

Region	Market	Rep	Sum of Revenue
Midwest	Chicago	Mike Mann	184425
	Chicago Total		184425
	Cincinnati	Richard Oldcorn	107016
	Cincinnati Total		107016
	Detroit	Anne Troy	1372957
	Detroit Total		1372957
	Louisville	John Cockerill	42316
	Louisville Total		42316
	Minneapolis	Sabine Hanschitz	34710
	Minneapolis Total		34710
Midwest Total			1741424
Northeast	New York	Jade Miller	2124612
	New York Total		2124612
Northeast Total			2124612
South	Arkla	Larry Vance	869454
	Arkla Total		869454

If you used the Subtotals drop-down on the Design tab, you would turn off all subtotals, including the Region subtotals and the Market subtotals. The Region subtotals are still providing good information, so you want to use the Subtotals setting in the Field Settings dialog. Choose one cell in the Market column. On the Analyze tab, choose Field Settings. Change the Subtotals setting from Automatic to None (see Figure 3.27).

Figure 3.27
Use the Subtotals setting in the field list to turn off subtotals for one field.

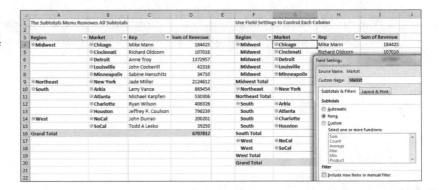

To remove subtotals for the Market field, click the Market field in the bottom section of the PivotTable Fields list. Select Field Settings. In the Field Settings dialog, select None under Subtotals, as shown in Figure 3.27.

Adding Multiple Subtotals for One Field

You can add customized subtotals to a row or column label field. Select the Region field in the bottom of the PivotTable Fields list, and select Field Settings.

In the Field Settings dialog for the Region field, select Custom and then select the types of subtotals you would like to see. The dialog in Figure 3.28 shows five custom subtotals selected for the Region field. It is rare to see pivot tables use this setting. It is not perfect. Note that the count of 211 records automatically gets a currency format like the rest of the column, even though this is not a dollar figure. Also, the average of $12,333 for South is an average of the detail records, not an average of the individual market totals.

Figure 3.28
By selecting the Custom option in the Subtotals section, you can specify multiple subtotals for one field.

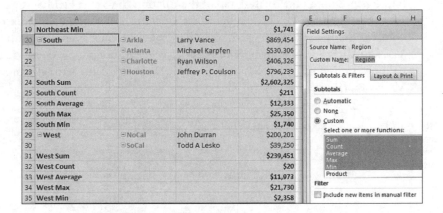

> **TIP** If you need to calculate the average of the four regions, you can do it with the DAX formula language and PowerPivot. See Chapter 10.

Changing the Calculation in a Value Field

The Value Field Settings dialog offers 11 options on the Summarize Values As tab and 15 main options on the Show Values As tab. The options on the first tab are the basic Sum, Average, Count, Max, and Min options that are ubiquitous throughout Excel; the 15 options under Show Values As are interesting ones such as % of Total, Running Total, and Ranks.

For Excel 2010 only, these options appeared as two drop-down menus in the ribbon. They are not on the Excel 2016 ribbon, but they still exist in the right-click menu. Because many of the calculations require one or two additional settings, you end up back in an extra dialog anyway. If you get in the habit of using the Value Field Settings dialog, you will have access to all the settings in one dialog.

Six of the Show Values As calculations were introduced in Excel 2010, including % of Parent Item, Rank, and % Running Total In.

The following examples show how to use the various calculation options. To contrast the settings, you can build a pivot table where you drag the Revenue field to the Values area nine separate times. Each one shows up as a new column in the pivot table. Over the course of the rest of the chapter, you will see the settings required for the calculations in each column.

To change the calculation for a field, select one value cell for the field and click the Field Settings button on the Analyze tab of the ribbon. The Value Field Settings dialog is similar to the Field Settings dialog, but it has two tabs. The first tab, Summarize Values By, contains Sum, Count, Average, Max, Min, Product, Count Numbers, StdDev, StdDevP, Var, and VarP. You can choose 1 of these 11 calculation options to change the data in the column. In Figure 3.29, columns B through D show various settings from the Summarize Values By tab.

Figure 3.29
Choose from the 11 summary calculations on this tab.

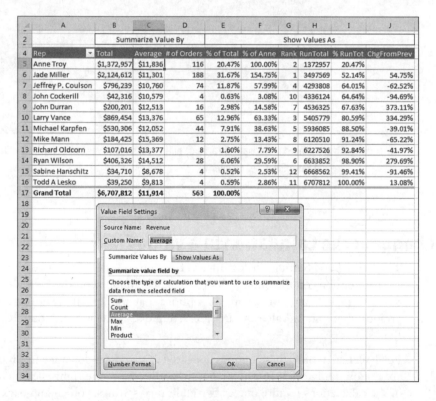

	A	B	C	D	E	F	G	H	I	J
2			Summarize Value By				Show Values As			
4	Rep	Total	Average	# of Orders	% of Total	% of Anne	Rank	RunTotal	% RunTot	ChgFromPrev
5	Anne Troy	$1,372,957	$11,836	116	20.47%	100.00%	2	1372957	20.47%	
6	Jade Miller	$2,124,612	$11,301	188	31.67%	154.75%	1	3497569	52.14%	54.75%
7	Jeffrey P. Coulson	$796,239	$10,760	74	11.87%	57.99%	4	4293808	64.01%	-62.52%
8	John Cockerill	$42,316	$10,579	4	0.63%	3.08%	10	4336124	64.64%	-94.69%
9	John Durran	$200,201	$12,513	16	2.98%	14.58%	7	4536325	67.63%	373.11%
10	Larry Vance	$869,454	$13,376	65	12.96%	63.33%	3	5405779	80.59%	334.29%
11	Michael Karpfen	$530,306	$12,052	44	7.91%	38.63%	5	5936085	88.50%	-39.01%
12	Mike Mann	$184,425	$15,369	12	2.75%	13.43%	8	6120510	91.24%	-65.22%
13	Richard Oldcorn	$107,016	$13,377	8	1.60%	7.79%	9	6227526	92.84%	-41.97%
14	Ryan Wilson	$406,326	$14,512	28	6.06%	29.59%	6	6633852	98.90%	279.69%
15	Sabine Hanschitz	$34,710	$8,678	4	0.52%	2.53%	12	6668562	99.41%	-91.46%
16	Todd A Lesko	$39,250	$9,813	4	0.59%	2.86%	11	6707812	100.00%	13.08%
17	Grand Total	$6,707,812	$11,914	563	100.00%					

Value Field Settings

Source Name: Revenue

Custom Name: Average

Summarize Values By | Show Values As

Summarize value field by

Choose the type of calculation that you want to use to summarize data from the selected field

Sum
Count
Average
Max
Min
Product

Number Format | OK | Cancel

Column B is the default Sum calculation. It shows the total of all records for a given market. Column C shows the average order for each item by market. Column D shows a count of the records. You can change the heading to say # of Orders or # of Records or whatever is appropriate. Note that the count is the actual count of records, not the count of distinct items.

> **NOTE**
> Counting distinct items has been difficult in pivot tables but is now easier using Power Pivot. See Chapter 10 for more details.

Far more interesting options appear on the Show Values As tab of the Value Field Settings dialog, as shown in Figure 3.30. Fifteen options appear in the drop-down. Depending on the option you choose, you might need to specify either a base field or a base field and a base item. Columns E through J in Figure 3.29 show some of the calculations possible using Show Values As.

Figure 3.30
Fifteen different ways to show that data is available on this tab.

Rename field as appropriate

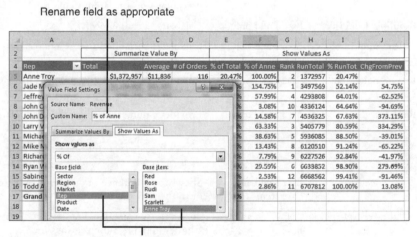

Base Field and Base Item are selectively enabled

Table 3.1 summarizes the Show Values As options.

Table 3.1   Calculations in Show Value As

Show Value As	Additional Required Information	Description
No Calculation	None	
% of Grand Total	None	Shows percentages so all the detail cells in the pivot table total 100%
% of Column Total	None	Shows percentages that total up and down the pivot table to 100%
% of Row Total	None	Shows percentages that total across the pivot table to 100%
% of Parent Row Total	None	With multiple row fields, shows a percentage of the parent item's total row
% of Parent Column Total	None	With multiple column fields, shows a percentage of the parent column's total
Index	None	Calculates the relative importance of items
% of Parent Total	Base Field only	With multiple row and/or column fields, calculates a cell's percentage of the parent item's total
Running Total In	Base Field only	Calculates a running total
% Running Total In	Base Field only	Calculates a running total as a percentage of the total
Rank Smallest to Largest	Base Field only	Provides a numeric rank, with 1 as the smallest item
Rank Largest to Smallest	Base Field only	Provides a numeric rank, with 1 as the largest item
% of	Base Field and Base Item	Expresses the values for one item as a percentage of another item
Difference From	Base Field and Base Item	Shows the difference of one item compared to another item or to the previous item
% Difference From	Base Field and Base Item	Shows the percentage difference of one item compared to another item or to the previous item

The capability to create custom calculations is another example of the unique flexibility of pivot table reports. With the Show Data As setting, you can change the calculation for a particular data field to be based on other cells in the Values area.

The following sections illustrate a number of Show Values As options.

Showing Percentage of Total

In Figure 3.29, column E shows % of Total. Jade Miller, with $2.1 million in revenue, represents 31.67% of the $6.7 million total revenue. Column E uses % of Column Total on the Show Values As tab. Two other similar options are % of Row Total and % of Grand Total.

Choose one of these based on whether your text fields are going down the report, across the report, or both down and across.

Using % Of to Compare One Line to Another Line

The % Of option enables you to compare one item to another item. For example, in the current data set, Anne was the top sales rep in the previous year. Column F shows everyone's sales as a percentage of Anne's. Cell E7 in Figure 3.31 shows that Jeff's sales were almost 58% of Anne's sales.

Figure 3.31
This report is created using the % Of option with Anne Troy as the Base Item.

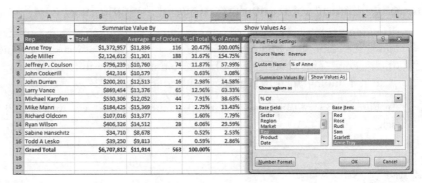

To set up this calculation, choose Show Values As, % Of. For Base Field, choose Rep because this is the only field in the Rows area. For Base Item, choose Anne Troy. The result is shown in Figure 3.31.

Showing Rank

Two ranking options are available. Column G in Figure 3.32 shows Rank Largest to Smallest. Jade Miller is ranked #1, and Sabine Hanschitz is #12. A similar option is Rank Smallest to Largest, which would be good for the pro golf tour.

Figure 3.32
The Rank options were added in Excel 2010.

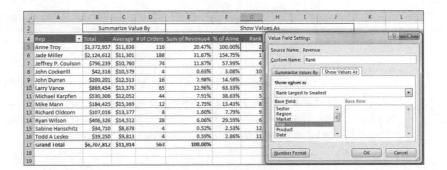

To set up a rank, choose Value Field Settings, Show Values As, Rank Largest to Smallest. You are required to choose base field. In this example, because Rep is the only row field, it is the selection under Base Field.

These rank options show that pivot tables have a strange way of dealing with ties. I say *strange* because they do not match any of the methods already established by the Excel functions =RANK(), =RANK.AVG(), and =RANK.EQ(). For example, if the top two markets have a tie, they are both assigned a rank of 1, and the third market is assigned a rank of 2.

Tracking Running Total and Percentage of Running Total

Running total calculations are common in reports where you have months running down the column or when you want to show that the top N customers make up $N\%$ of the revenue. The Running Total In calculation has been in Excel for many versions. The % Running Total In setting was added in Excel 2010.

In Figure 3.33, cell I8 shows that the top four sales reps account for 76.97% of the total sales.

Figure 3.33
Show running totals or a running percentage of total.

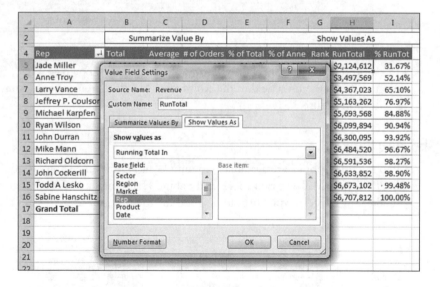

> **NOTE** To produce this figure, you have to use the Sort feature, which is discussed in depth in Chapter 4, "Grouping, Sorting, and Filtering Pivot Data." To create a similar analysis with the sample file, go to the drop-down in A4 and choose More Sort Options, Descending, by Total. Also note that the % Change From calculation shown in the next example is not compatible with sorting.

To specify Running Total In (as shown in Column H) or % Running Total In (Column J), select Field Settings, Show Values As, Running Total In. You have to specify a base field, which in this case is the row field: Rep.

Displaying a Change from a Previous Field

Figure 3.34 shows the % Difference From setting. This calculation requires a base field and base item. You could show how each market compares to Anne Troy by specifying Anne Troy as the base item. This would be similar to Figure 3.31, except each market would be shown as a percentage of Anne Troy.

Figure 3.34
The % Difference From options enable you to compare each row to the previous or next row.

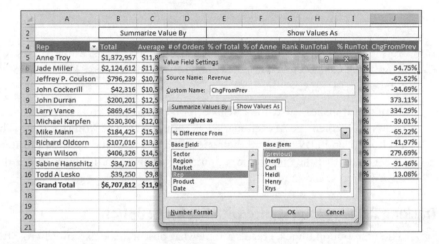

With date fields, it would make sense to use % Difference From and choose (previous) as the base item. Note that the first cell will not have a calculation because there is no previous data in the pivot table.

Tracking the Percentage of a Parent Item

The legacy % of Total settings always divides the current item by the grand total. In Figure 3.35, cell E4 says that Chicago is 2.75% of the total data set. A common question at the MrExcel.com message board is how to calculate Chicago's revenue as a percentage of the Midwest region total. This was possible but difficult in older versions of Excel. Starting in Excel 2010, though, Excel added the % of Parent Row, % of Parent Column, and % of Parent Total options.

Figure 3.35
An option in Excel enables you to calculate a percentage of the parent row.

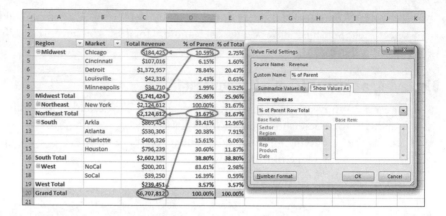

To set up this calculation in Excel 2016, use Field Settings, Show Values As, % of Parent Row Total. Cell D4 in Figure 3.35 shows that Chicago's $184,425 is 10.59% of the Midwest total of $1,741,424.

Although it makes sense, the calculation on the subtotal rows might seem confusing. D4:D8 shows the percentage of each market as compared to the Midwest total. The values in D9, D11, D16, and D19 compare the region total to the grand total. For example, the 31.67% in D11 says that the Northeast region's $2.1 million is a little less than a third of the $6.7 million grand total.

Tracking Relative Importance with the Index Option

The final option, Index, creates a somewhat obscure calculation. Microsoft claims that this calculation describes the relative importance of a cell within a column. In Figure 3.36, Georgia peaches have an index of 2.55, and California peaches have an index of 0.50. This shows that if the peach crop is wiped out next year, it will be more devastating to Georgia fruit production than to California fruit production.

Figure 3.36
Using the Index function, Excel shows that peach sales are more important in Georgia than in California.

	A	B	C	D	E	F G	H	I
1	Sum of Sales	State					GA Peach	180
2	Crop	California	Georgia	Ohio	Grand Total		/ GA Total	210
3	Apple	100	10	30	140		A = Worth of Peaches to GA	0.86
4	Banana	200	10	1	211			
5	Kiwi	200	10	1	211		Peach Total	285
6	Peach	100	180	5	285		/ Total	847
7	Grand Total	600	210	37	847		B = Worth of Peaches	0.34
8								
9							Index is A/B	2.55
10	Index	State						
11	Crop	California	Georgia	Ohio	Grand Total			
12	Apple	1.01	0.29	4.91	1.00		$= \dfrac{GeorgiaPeach + GeorgiaTotal}{PeachTotal \div Total}$	
13	Banana	1.34	0.19	0.11	1.00			
14	Kiwi	1.34	0.19	0.11	1.00			
15	Peach	0.50	2.55	0.40	1.00			
16	Grand Total	1.00	1.00	1.00	1.00			

Here is the exact calculation: First, divide Georgia peaches by the Georgia total. This is 180/210, or 0.857. Next, divide total peach production (285) by total fruit production (847). This shows that peaches have an importance ratio of 0.336. Now, divide the first ratio by the second ratio: 0.857/0.336.

In Ohio, apples have an index of 4.91, so an apple blight would be bad for the Ohio fruit industry.

I have to admit that, even after writing about this calculation for 10 years, there are parts that I don't quite comprehend. What if a state like Hawaii relied on productions of lychees, but lychees were nearly immaterial to U.S. fruit production? If lychees were half of Hawaii's fruit production but 0.001 of U.S. fruit production, the Index calculation would skyrocket to 500.

Next Steps

Note that the following pivot table customizations are covered in subsequent chapters:

- Sorting a pivot table is covered in Chapter 4.
- Filtering records in a pivot table is covered in Chapter 4.
- Grouping daily dates up to months or years is covered in Chapter 4.
- Adding new calculated fields is covered in Chapter 5, "Performing Calculations in Pivot Tables."
- Using data visualizations and conditional formatting in a pivot table is covered in Chapter 4.

Grouping, Sorting, and Filtering Pivot Data

With Excel 2016, Microsoft has added some interesting features for grouping, sorting, and filtering pivot tables. When you add a time or date field to a pivot table, Excel 2016 automatically groups the daily dates up to months and quarters—and possibly years. It was possible to do this manually in Excel 2013, but how to do it was difficult to discover.

A related feature is that pivot charts that include the date hierarchy offer a expand and collapse feature.

This chapter covers grouping, sorting, filtering, data visualizations, and pivot table options.

Automatically Grouping Dates

Say that you have a column in your data set with daily dates that span two years. When you add this Date field to the Columns area of your pivot table, you will see columns for each year instead of hundreds of daily dates (see Figure 4.1).

When you look in the Pivot Table Fields list, you see that the column area automatically includes three fields: Year, Quarter, and Date. All three of these are virtual fields created by grouping the daily dates up to months, quarters, and years.

The three fields are added to either the Rows area or the Columns area. However, only the highest level of the hierarchy will be showing. To see the quarters and years, click one cell that contains a year and then click the Expand button in the Analyze tab of the ribbon. To see months, select a cell containing a quarter and click the Expand button again.

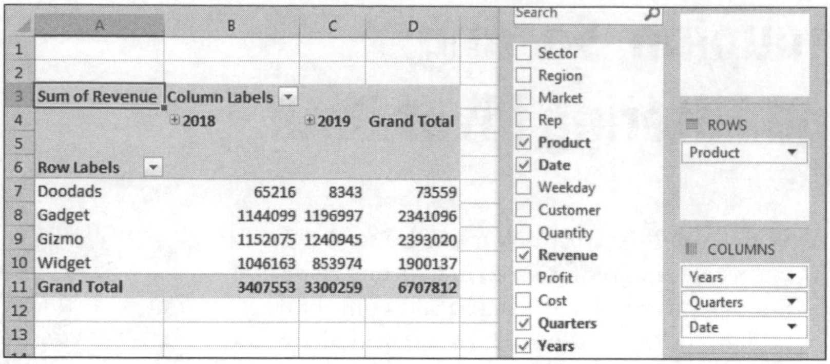

Figure 4.1
Excel 2016 automatically groups two years' worth of daily dates up to months, quarters, and years.

Undoing Automatic Grouping

For the most part, automatic grouping is a welcome addition to Excel 2016. However, if you don't like the feature, you should click Ctrl+Z to undo immediately after adding the Date field to the pivot table. To disable the Auto Group functionality on both native and data model pivot tables and pivot charts, you can add a new DWORD (32-bit) Value registry key: HKEY_CURRENT_USER\Software\Microsoft\Office\16.0\Excel\Options\ DateAutoGroupingDisabled. After adding the key, edit it to set its value data to "1".

If you have missed the opportunity to undo by taking some other action, you can ungroup by following these steps:

1. Choose a cell that contains one of the rolled-up dates.
2. On the Analyze tab in the ribbon, choose Ungroup.

Understanding How Excel 2016 Decides What to Group

If you have daily dates that include an entire year or that fall in two or more years, Excel 2016 groups the daily dates to include years, quarters, and months. If you need to report by daily dates, you will have to select any date cell, choose Group Field, and add Days.

If you have daily dates that fall within one calendar year, Excel groups the daily dates to month and includes daily dates.

> ┌ C A U T I O N ─────────────────
> If your company is closed on New Year's Day and you have no sales on January 1, a data set that stretches from January 2 to December 31 will fit the "less than a full year" case and will include months and daily dates.

If your data contains times that do not cross over midnight, you get hours, minutes, and seconds. If the times span more than one day, you get days, hours, minutes, and seconds.

Grouping Date Fields Manually

Sometimes you might prefer to group your dates manually instead of using the automatic grouping that Excel 2016 offers. Excel provides a straightforward way to group date fields. Select any date cell in your pivot table. On the Analyze tab, click Group Field in the Group option.

When your field contains date information, the Grouping dialog appears. By default, the Months option is selected. You have choices to group by Seconds, Minutes, Hours, Days, Months, Quarters, and Years. It is possible—and usually advisable—o select more than one field in the Grouping dialog. In this case, select Months and Years, as shown in Figure 4.2.

Figure 4.2
Business users of Excel usually group by months (or quarters) and years.

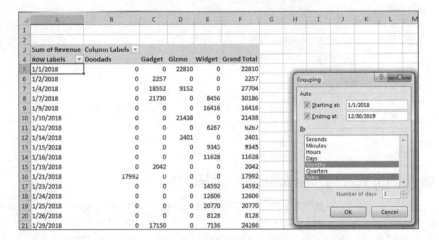

There are several interesting points to note about the resulting pivot table. First, notice that the Years field has been added to the PivotTable Fields list. Don't let this fool you. Your source data is not changed to include the new field. Instead, this field is now part of your pivot cache in memory.

Another interesting point is that, by default, the Years field is automatically added to the same area as the original date field in the pivot table layout, as shown in Figure 4.3. Although this happens automatically, you are free to pivot months and years onto the opposite axis of the report. This is a quick way to create a year-over-year sales report.

Also, the Years field will be set up to not display subtotals. To add subtotals, select cell A5 in Figure 4.3. Choose Field Settings and change the Subtotals setting from None to Automatic, as shown in Figure 4.4.

Figure 4.3
By default, Excel adds the new grouped date field to your pivot table layout.

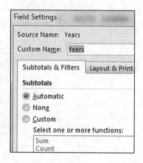

Sum of Revenue	Column Labels	
Row Labels	Doodads	Gadget
⊟ 2018		
Jan	17992	68445
Feb	0	95259
Mar	0	98570
Apr	4948	64754
May	0	147716
Jun	0	89088
Jul	0	117410
Aug	17856	67859
Sep	0	111585
Oct	0	102644
Nov	24420	99953
Dec	0	80816
⊟ 2019		
Jan	0	36413

Figure 4.4
Add subtotals to the outer row fields.

Field Settings

Source Name: Years

Custom Name: Years

Subtotals & Filters   Layout & Print

Subtotals
- ◉ Automatic
- ○ None
- ○ Custom
  Select one or more functions:
  Sum
  Count

Including Years When Grouping by Months

Although this point is not immediately obvious, it is important to understand that if you group a date field by month, you also need to include the year in the grouping. If your data set includes January 2018 and January 2019, selecting only months in the Grouping dialog will result in both January 2018 and January 2019 being combined into a single row called January (see Figure 4.5).

Figure 4.5
If you fail to include the Year field in the grouping, the report mixes sales from January 2018 and January 2019 in the same number.

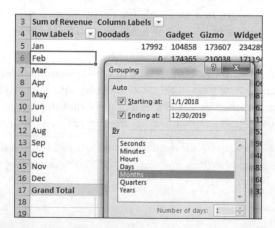

	Sum of Revenue	Column Labels			
3					
4	Row Labels	Doodads	Gadget	Gizmo	Widget
5	Jan	17992	104858	173607	234289
6	Feb	0	174365	210038	171194
7	Mar				
8	Apr				
9	May				
10	Jun				
11	Jul				
12	Aug				
13	Sep				
14	Oct				
15	Nov				
16	Dec				
17	Grand Total				
18					
19					

Grouping

Auto
☑ Starting at: 1/1/2018
☑ Ending at: 12/30/2019

By
Seconds
Minutes
Hours
Days
Months
Quarters
Years

Number of days: 1

Grouping Date Fields by Week

The Grouping dialog offers choices to group by second, minute, hour, day, month, quarter, and year. It is also possible to group on a weekly or biweekly basis.

The first step is to find either a paper calendar or an electronic calendar, such as the Calendar feature in Outlook, for the year in question. If your data starts on January 1, 2018, it is helpful to know that January 1 is a Monday that year. You need to decide if weeks should start on Sunday or Monday or any other day. For example, you can check the paper or electronic calendar to learn that the nearest starting Sunday is December 31, 2017.

Select any date heading in your pivot table. Then select Group Field from the Analyze tab. In the Grouping dialog, clear all the By options and select only the Days field. This enables the spin button for Number of Days. To produce a report by week, increase the number of days from 1 to 7.

Next, you need to set up the Starting At date. If you were to accept the default of starting at January 1, 2018, all your weekly periods would run from Monday through Sunday. By checking a calendar before you begin, you know that you want the first group to start on December 31, 2017, to have weeks that run Sunday through Monday. Figure 4.6 shows the settings in the Grouping dialog and the resulting report.

Figure 4.6
Group dates up to weekly periods.

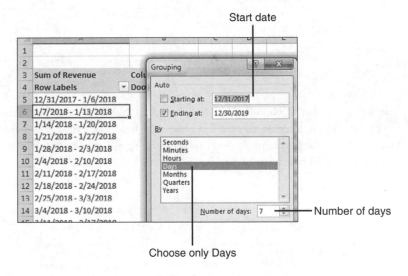

Start date

Number of days

Choose only Days

Grouping Numeric Fields

The Grouping dialog for numeric fields enables you to group items into equal ranges. This can be useful for creating frequency distributions. The pivot table in Figure 4.7 is quite the opposite of anything you've seen so far in this book. The numeric field—Revenue—is in the Rows area. A text field—Customer—is in the Values area. When you put a text field in the Values area, you get a count of how many records match the criteria. In its present state, this pivot table is not that fascinating; it is telling you that exactly one record in the database has a total revenue of $23,990.

Figure 4.7
Nothing interesting here—just lots of order totals that appear exactly one time in the database.

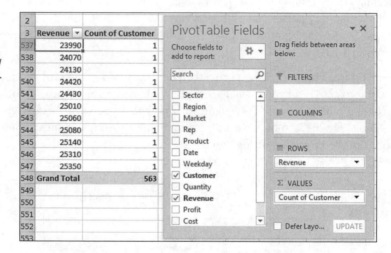

Select one number in column A of the pivot table. Select Group Field from the Analyze tab of the ribbon. Because this field is not a date field, the Grouping dialog offers fields for Starting At, Ending At, and By. As shown in Figure 4.8, you can choose to show amounts from 0 to 30,000 in groups of 5,000.

Figure 4.8
Create a frequency distribution by grouping the order size into $5,000 buckets.

Revenue	# of Invoices	Total $	% of $
0-4999	104	326674	4.9%
5000-9999	125	937212	14.0%
10000-14999	142	1769165	26.4%
15000-19999	123	2149079	32.0%
20000-24999	63	1374732	20.5%
25000-30000	6	150950	2.3%
Grand Total	563	6707812	100.0%

Grouping
Auto
☐ Starting at: 0
☐ Ending at: 30000
By: 5000
OK   Cancel

After grouping the order size into buckets, you might want to add additional fields, such as Revenue and % of Revenue shown as a percentage of the total.

CASE STUDY: GROUPING TEXT FIELDS FOR REDISTRICTING

Say that you get a call from the VP of Sales. The Sales Department is secretly considering a massive reorganization of the sales regions. The VP would like to see a report showing revenue after redistricting. You have been around long enough to know that the proposed regions will change several times before the reorganization happens, so you are not willing to change the Region field in your source data quite yet.

First, build a report showing revenue by market. The VP of Sales is proposing eliminating two regional managers and redistricting the country into three super-regions. While holding down the Ctrl key, highlight the five regions that will make up the new West region. Figure 4.9 shows the pivot table before the first group is created.

Figure 4.9
Use the Ctrl key to select the noncontiguous cells that make up the new region.

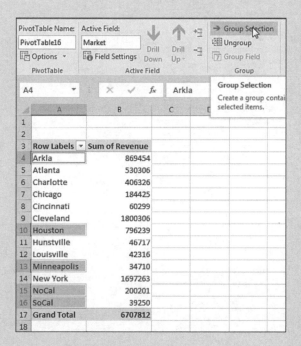

From the Analyze tab, click Group Selection. Excel adds a new field called Market2. The five selected regions are arbitrarily rolled up to a new territory called Group1. While holding down the Ctrl key, select the markets for the South region (see Figure 4.10).

Click Group Selection to group the markets in the proposed Southeast region. Repeat to group the remaining regions into the proposed Northeast region. Figure 4.11 shows what it looks like when you have grouped the markets into new regions. Five things need further adjustment: the names of Group1, Group2, Group3, and Market2 and the lack of subtotals for the outer row field.

Figure 4.10
The first super-region is arbitrarily called Group1.

3	Row Labels ▾	Sum of Revenue
4	⊟Group1	
5	Arkla	869454
6	Houston	796239
7	Minneapolis	34710
8	NoCal	200201
9	SoCal	39250
10	⊟Atlanta	
11	Atlanta	530306
12	⊟Charlotte	
13	Charlotte	406326
14	⊟Chicago	
15	Chicago	184425
16	⊟Cincinnati	
17	Cincinnati	60299
18	⊟Cleveland	
19	Cleveland	1800306
20	⊟Hunstville	
21	Hunstville	46717
22	⊟Louisville	
23	Louisville	42316
24	⊟New York	
25	New York	1697263
26	Grand Total	6707812

Figure 4.11
The markets are grouped, but you have to do some cleanup.

3	Row Labels ▾	Sum of Revenue
4	⊟Group1	
5	Arkla	869454
6	Houston	796239
7	Minneapolis	34710
8	NoCal	200201
9	SoCal	39250
10	⊟Group2	
11	Atlanta	530306
12	Charlotte	406326
13	Hunstville	46717
14	Louisville	42316
15	⊟Group3	
16	Chicago	184425
17	Cincinnati	60299
18	Cleveland	1800306
19	New York	1697263
20	Grand Total	6707812

Cleaning up the report takes only a few moments:

1. Select cell A4. Type **West** to replace the arbitrary name Group1.

2. Select cell A10. Type **Southeast** to replace the arbitrary name Group2.

3. Select A15. Type **Northeast** to replace Group3.

4. Select any outer heading in A4, A10, or A15. Click Field Settings on the Analyze tab.

5. In the Field Settings dialog, replace the Custom Name of Market2 with Proposed Region. Also in the Field Settings dialog, change the Subtotals setting from None to Automatic.

Figure 4.12 shows the pivot table that results, which is ready for the VP of Sales.

Figure 4.12
It is now easy to
see that these
regions are heavily
unbalanced.

	Row Labels	Sum of Revenue
3	Row Labels ▼	Sum of Revenue
4	⊟West	1939854
5	Arkla	869454
6	Houston	796239
7	Minneapolis	34710
8	NoCal	200201
9	SoCal	39250
10	⊟Southeast	1025665
11	Atlanta	530306
12	Charlotte	406326
13	Hunstville	46717
14	Louisville	42316
15	⊟Northeast	3742293
16	Chicago	184425
17	Cincinnati	60299
18	Cleveland	1800306
19	New York	1697263
20	**Grand Total**	**6707812**

You can probably predict that the Sales Department needs to shuffle markets to balance the regions. To go back to the original regions, select any Proposed Region cell in A4, A10, or A15 and choose Ungroup. You can then start over, grouping regions in new combinations.

4

Using the PivotTable Fields List

The entry points for sorting and filtering are spread throughout the Excel interface. It is worth taking a closer look at the row header drop-downs and the PivotTable Fields list before diving in to sorting and filtering.

As you've seen in these pages, I rarely use the Compact form for a pivot table. My first step with most pivot tables is to ditch the Compact form and select Tabular layout instead. Although there are many good reasons for this, one is illustrated in Figures 4.13 and 4.14.

Figure 4.13
The drop-down in B3 for Customer is separate from the drop-down for Region.

Figure 4.14
In Compact form, one single drop-down tries to control sorting and filtering for all the row fields.

In Figure 4.13, a Region drop-down appears in A3. A Customer drop-down appears in B3. Each of these separate drop-downs offers great settings for sorting and filtering.

When you leave the pivot table in the Compact form, there are not separate headings for Region and Customer. Both fields are crammed into column A, with the silly heading Row Labels. This means the drop-down always offers sorting and filtering options for Region. Every time you go back to the A3 drop-down with hopes of filtering or sorting the Customer field, you have to reselect Customer from a drop-down at the top of the menu. This is an extra click. If you are making five changes to the Customer field, you are reselecting Customer over and over and over and over and over. This should be enough to convince you to abandon the Compact layout.

If you decide to keep the Compact layout and get frustrated with the consolidated Row Labels drop-down, you can directly access the invisible drop-down for the correct field by using the PivotTable Fields list, which contains a visible drop-down for every field in the areas at the bottom. Those visible drop-downs do not contain the sorting and filtering options.

The good drop-downs are actually in the top of the fields list, but you have to hover over the field to see the drop-down appear. After you hover as shown in Figure 4.15, you can directly access the same customer drop-down shown in Figure 4.13.

Figure 4.15
Hover over the field in the top of the fields list to directly access the sorting and filtering settings for that field.

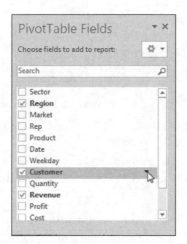

Docking and Undocking the PivotTable Fields List

The PivotTable Fields list starts out docked on the right side of the Excel window. Hover over the green PivotTable Fields heading in the pane, and the mouse pointer changes to a four-headed arrow. Drag to the left to enable the pane to float anywhere in your Excel window.

After you have undocked the PivotTable Fields list, you might find that it is difficult to redock it on either side of the screen. To redock the fields list, you must grab the title bar and drag until at least 85% of the fields list is off the edge of the window. Pretend that you are trying to remove the floating fields list completely from the screen. Eventually, Excel gets the hint and redocks it. Note that you can dock the PivotTable Fields list on either the right side or the left side of the screen.

Rearranging the PivotTable Fields List

As shown in Figure 4.16, a small gear-wheel icon appears near the top of the PivotTable Fields list. Select this drop-down to see its five possible arrangements. Although the default is to have the Fields section at the top of the list and the Areas section at the bottom of the list, four other arrangements are possible. Other options let you control whether the fields in the list appear alphabetically or in the same sequence that they appeared in the original data set.

Figure 4.16
Use this drop-down to
rearrange the PivotTable
Fields list.

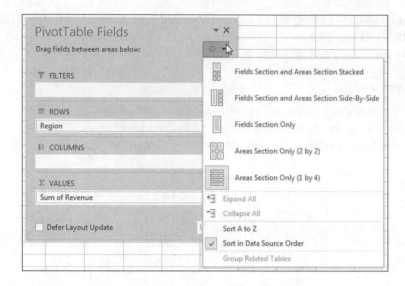

4

The final three arrangements offered in the drop-down are rather confusing. If someone changes the PivotTable Fields list to show only the Areas section, you cannot see new fields to add to the pivot table.

If you ever encounter a version of the PivotTable Fields list with only the Areas section (see Figure 4.16) or only the Fields section, remember that you can return to a less confusing view of the data by using the arrangement drop-down.

Using the Areas Section Drop-Downs

As shown in Figure 4.17, every field in the Areas section has a visible drop-down arrow. When you select this drop-down arrow, you see four categories of choices:

- The first four choices enable you to rearrange the field within the list of fields in that area of the pivot table. You can accomplish this by dragging the field up or down in area.

- The next four choices enable you to move the field to a new area. You could also accomplish this by dragging the field to a new area.

- The next choice enables you to remove the field from the pivot table. You can also accomplish this by dragging the field outside the fields list.

- The final choice displays the Field Settings dialog for the field.

Figure 4.17
Use this drop-down to rearrange the PivotTable Fields list.

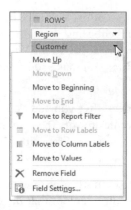

Sorting in a Pivot Table

Items in the row area and column area of a pivot table are sorted in ascending order by any custom list first. This allows weekday and month names to sort into Monday, Tuesday, Wednesday,...instead of the alphabetical order Friday, Monday, Saturday,..., Wednesday.

If the items do not appear in a custom list, they will be sorted in ascending order. This is fine, but in many situations, you want the customer with the largest revenue to appear at the top of the list. When you sort in descending order using a pivot table, you are setting up a rule that controls how that field is sorted, even after new fields are added to the pivot table.

> **TIP** Excel 2016 includes four custom lists by default, but you can add your own custom list to control the sort order of future pivot tables. See the section "Using a Custom List for Sorting," later in this chapter.

Sorting Customers into High-to-Low Sequence Based on Revenue

Three pivot tables appear in Figure 4.18. The first pivot table shows the default sort for a pivot table: Customers are arranged alphabetically, starting with Adaept, Callelia, and so on.

Figure 4.18
When you override the default sort, Excel remembers the sort as additional fields are added.

	A	B	C	D	E	F	G	H
1	Customers AZ is default			Sort descending by revenue			After adding fields, sort rule remains	
2								
3	Customer	Total $		Customer	Total $			Total $
4	Adaept Information Mana	498937		MySpreadsheetLab	869454		⊟Consulting	2555333
5	Calleia Company	406326		Surten Excel	750163		Surten Excel	750163
6	Excel Design Solutions Ltd	71651		SkyWire, Inc.	704359		NetCom Computer	613514
7	Excel Learning Zone	72680		SpringBoard	622794		Adaept Information N	498937
8	Excel4Apps	91320		NetCom Computer	613514		Calleia Company	406326
9	Excel-Translator.de	42316		St. Peter's Prep	568851		Excel Design Solution	71651
10	F-Keys Ltd.	34710		Adaept Information Mana	498937		Yesenita	62744
11	JEVS Human Services	50030		The Salem Ohio Historical	427349		Symons	55251
12	LearnExcelBooks.com	34364		Calleia Company	406326		JEVS Human Services	50030
13	MyExcelOnline.com	54048		MyOnlineTrainingHub.cor	390978		Spain Enterprises	46717
14	MyOnlineTrainingHub.cor	390978		Excel4Apps	91320		⊟Museums	427349
15	MySpreadsheetLab	869454		Excel Learning Zone	72680		The Salem Ohio Histo	427349

In the second pivot table, the report is sorted in descending sequence by Total Revenue. This pivot table was sorted by selecting cell E3 and choosing the ZA icon in the Data tab of the ribbon. Although that sounds like a regular sort, it is better. When you sort inside a pivot table, Excel sets up a rule that will be used after you make additional changes to the pivot table.

The pivot table in columns G:H shows what happens after you add Sector as a new outer row field. Within each sector, the pivot table continues to sort the data in descending order by revenue. Within Consulting, Surten Excel appears first, with $750K, followed by NetCom, with $614K.

You could remove Customer from the pivot table, do more adjustments, and then add Customer back to the column area, and Excel would remember that the customers should be presented from high to low.

If you could see the entire pivot table in G3:H35 in Figure 4.18, you would notice that the sectors are sorted alphabetically. It might make more sense, though, to put the largest sectors at the top. The following tricks can be used for sorting an outer row field by revenue:

- You can select cell G4 and then use Collapse Field on the Analyze tab to hide the customer detail. When you have only the sectors showing, select H4 and click ZA to sort descending. Excel understands that you want to set up a sort rule for the Sector field.
- You can temporarily remove Customer from the pivot table, sort descending by revenue, and then add Customer back.
- You can use More Sort Options, as described in the following paragraphs.

To sort the Sector field, you should open the drop-down menu for the Sector field. Hover over Sector in the top of the PivotTable Fields list, and click the drop-down arrow that appears (see Figure 4.19). Or, if your pivot table is shown in Tabular layout or Outline layout, you can simply open the drop-down arrow in cell G3.

Figure 4.19
For explicit control over sort order, open this drop-down menu.

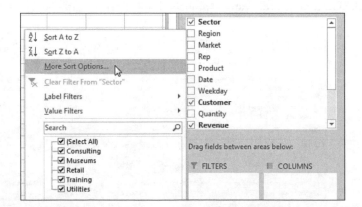

Inside the drop-down menu, choose More Sort Options to open the Sort (Sector) dialog. In this dialog, you can choose to sort the Sector field in Descending order by Total $ (see Figure 4.20).

Figure 4.20
Choose to sort Sector based on the Total $ field.

The Sort (Sector) dialog shown in Figure 4.20 includes a More Options button in the lower left. If you click this button, you arrive at the More Sort Options dialog, in which you can specify a custom list to be used for the first key sort order. You can also specify that the sorting should be based on a column other than Grand Total.

In Figure 4.21, the pivot table includes Product in the column area. If you wanted to sort the customers based on total gadget revenue instead of total revenue, for example, you could do so with the More Sort Options dialog. Here are the steps:

1. Open the Customer heading drop-down in B4.
2. Choose More Sort Options.
3. In the Sort (Customer) dialog, choose More Options.
4. In the More Sort Options (Customer) dialog, choose the Sort By Values in Selected Column option (see Figure 4.21).
5. Click in the reference box and then click cell D5. Note that you cannot click the Gadget heading in D4; you have to choose one of the Gadget value cells.
6. Click OK twice to return to the pivot table.

Figure 4.21
Using More Sort Options, you can sort by a specific pivot field item.

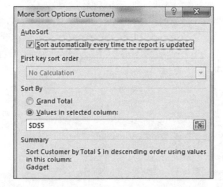

If your pivot table has only one field in the Rows area, you can set up the "Sort by Doodads" rule by doing a simple sort using the Data tab. Select any cell in B5:B30 and choose Data, ZA. The pivot table will be sorted with the largest Doodads customers at the top (see Figure 4.22).

Figure 4.22
Sort by column E to sort by Doodads.

3	Total $	Product ▾				
4	Customer	↴ Doodads	Gadget	Gizmo	Widget	Grand Total
5	Excel Learning Zone	38860	22140	11680		72680
6	Excel4Apps	28663	20115	30068	12474	91320
7	Excel-Translator.de	6036	18552	17728		42316
8	Tennessee Moon		13249	13962	4158	31369
9	SpringBoard		185675	245491	191628	622794
10	Calleia Company		133009	159354	113963	406326

Using a Manual Sort Sequence

The Sort dialog offers something called a *manual sort*. Rather than using the dialog, you can invoke a manual sort in a surprising way.

Note that the products in Figure 4.23 are in the following order: Doodads, Gadget, Gizmo, and Widget. It appears that the Doodads product line is a minor product line and probably would not fall first in the product list.

Figure 4.23
Initially, the products across the top of the report are sorted alphabetically.

3	Total $	Product ▾				
4	Years ▾	Doodads	Gadget	Gizmo	Widget	Grand Total
5	2018	65216	1144099	1152075	1046163	3407553
6	2019	8343	1196997	1240945	853974	3300259
7	Grand Total	73559	2341096	2393020	1900137	6707812

Place the cell pointer in cell E4 and type the word **Doodads**. When you press Enter, Excel figures out that you want to move the Doodads column to be last. All the values for this product line move from column B to column E. The values for the remaining products shift to the left.

This behavior is completely unintuitive. You should never try this behavior with a regular (non–pivot table) data set in Excel. You would never expect Excel to change the data sequence just by moving the labels. Figure 4.24 shows the pivot table after a new column heading has been typed in cell E4.

Figure 4.24
Simply type a heading in E4 to rearrange the columns.

3	Total $	Product ▾				
4	Years ▾	Gadget	Gizmo	Widget	Doodads	Grand Total
5	2018	1144099	1152075	1046163	65216	3407553
6	2019	1196997	1240945	853974	8343	3300259
7	Grand Total	2341096	2393020	1900137	73559	6707812

If you prefer to use the mouse, you can drag and drop the column heading to a new location. Select a column heading. Hover over the edge of the active cell border until the mouse changes to a four-headed arrow. Drag the cell to a new location, as shown in Figure 4.25. When you release the mouse, all of the value settings move to the new column.

Figure 4.25
Use drag and drop to move a column to a new position.

3	Total $	Product ▼				
4	Years ▼	Gadget	Gizmo	Widget	Doodads	Grand Total
5	2018	1144099	1152075	1046163	65216	3407553
6	2019	1196997	1240945	853974	8343	3300259
7	Grand Total	2341096	2393020	1900137	73559	6707812

─ CAUTION ───

After you use a manual sort, any new products you add to the data source are automatically added to the end of the list rather than appearing alphabetically.

Using a Custom List for Sorting

Another way to permanently change the order of items along a dimension is to set up a custom list. All future pivot tables created on your computer will automatically respect the order of the items in a custom list.

The pivot table at the top of Figure 4.26 includes weekday names. The weekday names were added to the original data set by using =TEXT(F2,"DDD") and copying down. Excel automatically puts Sunday first and Saturday last, even though this is not the alphabetical sequence of these words. This happens because Excel ships with four custom lists to control the days of the week, months of the year, and the three-letter abbreviations for both.

Figure 4.26
The weekday names in B2:H2 follow the order specified in the Custom Lists dialog.

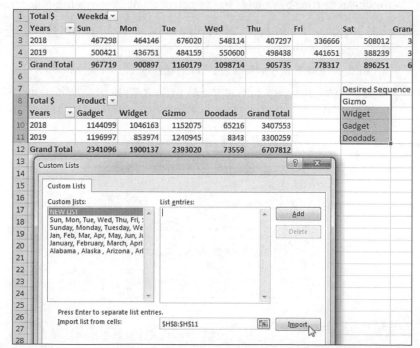

You can define your own custom list to control the sort order of pivot tables. Follow these steps to set up a custom list:

1. In an out-of-the-way section of the worksheet, type the products in their proper sequence. Type one product per cell, going down a column.

2. Select the cells containing the list of regions in the proper sequence.

3. Click the File tab and select Options.

4. Select the Advanced category in the left navigation bar. Scroll down to the General group and click the Edit Custom Lists button. In the Custom Lists dialog, your selection address is entered in the Import text box, as shown in Figure 4.26.

5. Click Import to bring the products in as a new list.

6. Click OK to close the Custom Lists dialog, and then click OK to close the Excel Options dialog.

The custom list is now stored on your computer and is available for all future Excel sessions. All future pivot tables will automatically show the product field in the order specified in the custom list. Figure 4.27 shows a new pivot table created after the custom list was set up.

Figure 4.27
After you define a custom list, all future pivot tables will follow the order in the list.

3	Sum of Revenue					
4		Gizmo	Widget	Gadget	Doodads	Grand Total
5	⊞ 2018	1152075	1046163	1144099	65216	3407553
6	⊞ 2019	1240945	853974	1196997	8343	3300259
7	Grand Total	2393020	1900137	2341096	73559	6707812

To sort an existing pivot table by the newly defined custom list, follow these steps:

1. Open the Product header drop-down and choose More Sort Options.

2. In the Sort (Product) dialog, choose More Options.

3. In the More Sort Options (Product) dialog, clear the AutoSort check box.

4. As shown in Figure 4.28, in the More Sort Options (Product) dialog, open the First Key Sort Order drop-down and select the custom list with your product names.

Figure 4.28
Choose to sort by the custom list.

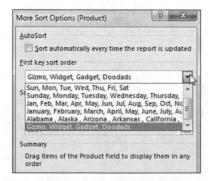

5. Click OK twice.

Filtering a Pivot Table: An Overview

Excel 2016 provides dozens of ways to filter a pivot table. Figure 4.29 shows some of the filters available. These methods, and the best way to use each one, are discussed in the following sections.

Figure 4.29
This figure shows a fraction of the available filtering choices.

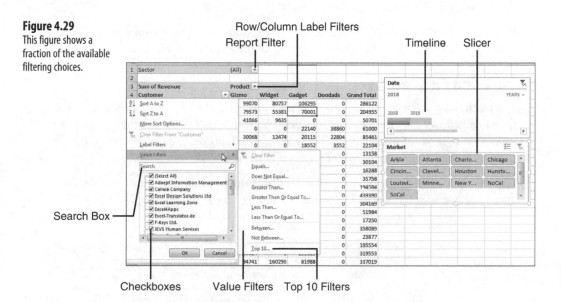

There are four ways to filter a pivot table, as shown in Figure 4.29:

- The Date timeline filter in G2:K9 was introduced in Excel 2013.
- The Market filter in G10:K17 is an example of the slicer introduced in Excel 2010.
- A drop-downs in B1 offers what were known as page filters in Excel 2003, report filters in Excel 2010, and now simply filters.
- Cell G4 offers the top-secret AutoFilter location.

Drop-downs in A4 and B3 lead to even more filters:

- You see the traditional check box filters for each pivot item.
- A Search box filter was introduced in Excel 2010.
- A fly-out menu has Label Filters.
- Depending on the field type, you might see a Value Filters fly-out menu, including the powerful Top 10 filter, which can do Top 10, Bottom 5, Bottom 3%, Top $8 Million, and more.
- Depending on the field type, you might see a Date Filters fly-out menu, with 37 virtual filters such as Next Month, Last Year, and Year to Date.

4

Using Filters for Row and Column Fields

If you have a field (or fields) in the row or column area of a pivot table, a drop-down with filtering choices appears on the header cell for that field. In Figure 4.29, a Customer drop-down appears in A4, and a Product drop-down appears in B3. The pivot table in that figure is using Tabular layout. If your pivot tables use Compact layout, you see a drop-down on the cell with Row Labels or Column Labels.

If you have multiple row fields, it is just as easy to sort using the invisible drop-downs that appear when you hover over a field in the top of the PivotTable Fields list.

Filtering Using the Check Boxes

You might have a few annoying products appear in a pivot table. In the present example, the Doodads product line is a specialty product with very little sales. It might be an old legacy product that is out of line, but it still gets an occasional order from the scrap bin. Every company seems to have these orphan sales that no one really wants to see.

The check box filter provides an easy way to hide these items. Open the Product drop-down and uncheck Doodads. The product is hidden from view (see Figure 4.30).

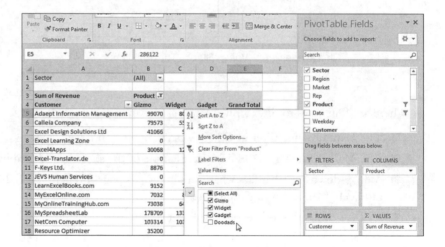

Figure 4.30
Open the Product filter and uncheck Doodads.

What if you need to uncheck hundreds of items in order to leave only a few items selected? You can toggle all items off or on by using the Select All check box at the top of the list. You can then select the few items that you want to show in the pivot table.

In Figure 4.31, Select All turned off all customers and then two clicks re-selected Excel4Apps and F-Keys Ltd.

Figure 4.31
Use Select All to toggle all items off or on.

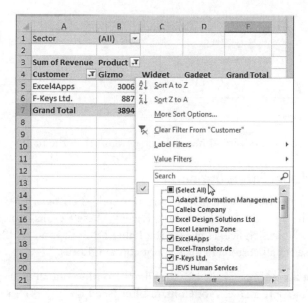

The check boxes work great in this tiny data set with 26 customers. In real life, with 500 customers in the list, it will not be this easy to filter your data set by using the check boxes.

Filtering Using the Search Box

When you have hundreds of customers, the search box can be a great timesaver. In Figure 4.32, the database includes consultants, trainers, and other companies. If you want to narrow the list to companies with *Excel* or *spreadsheet* in their name, you can follow these steps:

1. Open the Customer drop-down.
2. Type **Excel** in the search box (see Figure 4.32).

Figure 4.32
Select the results of the first search.

3. By default, Select All Search Results is selected. Click OK.
4. Open the Customer drop-down again.
5. Type **spreadsheet** in the search box.
6. Choose Add Current Selection to Filter, as shown in Figure 4.33. Click OK.

Figure 4.33
For the second search, add these results to the existing filter.

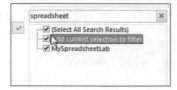

You now have all customers with either *Excel* or *spreadsheet* in the name.

Filtering Using the Label Filters Option

The search box isn't perfect. What if you want to find all the Lotus 1-2-3 consultants and turn those off? There is no Select Everything Except These Results choice. Nor is there a Toggle All Filter Choices choice. However, the Label Filters option enables you to handle queries such as "select all customers that do not contain 'Lotus.'"

Text fields offer a fly-out menu called Label Filters. To filter out all of the Insurance customers, you can apply a Does Not Contain filter (see Figure 4.34). In the next dialog, you can specify that you want customers that do not contain Excel, Exc, or Exc* (see Figure 4.35).

Figure 4.34
Choose Label Filters, Does Not Contain.

Figure 4.35
Specify to exclude customers containing Excel.

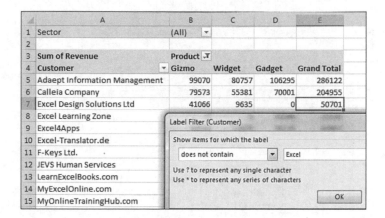

Note that label filters are not additive. You can only apply one label filter at a time. If you take the data in Figure 4.34 and apply a new label filter of between D and Fzz, some Excel customers that were filtered out in Figure 4.35 come back, as shown in Figure 4.36.

Figure 4.36
Note that a second label filter does not get added to the previous filter. Excel is back in.

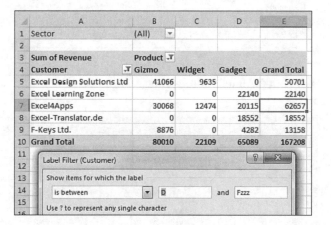

Filtering a Label Column Using Information in a Values Column

The Value Filters fly-out menu enables you to filter customers based on information in the Values columns. Perhaps you want to see customers who had between $20,000 and $30,000 of revenue. You can use the Customer heading drop-down to control this. Here's how:

1. Open the Customer drop-down.

2. Choose Label Filters.

3. Choose Between (see Figure 4.37).

Figure 4.37
Value Filters for the
Customer column will
look at values in the
Revenue field.

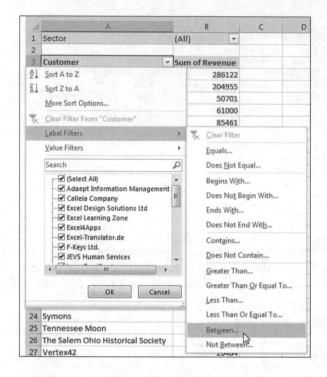

4

4. Type the values **20000** and **30000**, as shown in Figure 4.38.

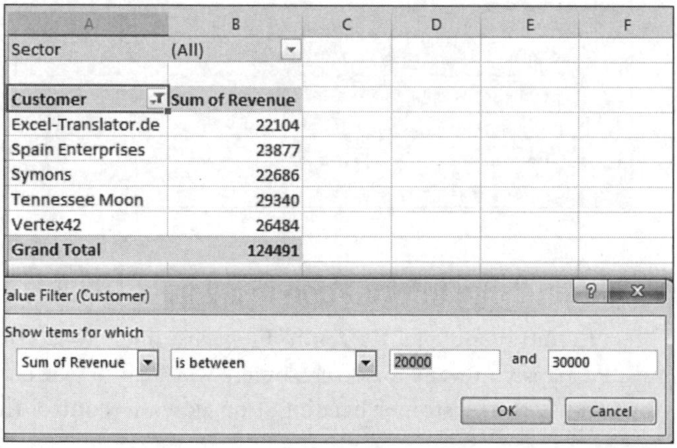

Figure 4.38
Choose customers
between $20,000 and
$30,000, inclusive.

5. Click OK.

The results are inclusive; if a customer had exactly $20,000 or exactly $30,000, they are
returned along with the customers between $20,000 and $30,000.

> **NOTE**
>
> Choosing a value filter clears out any previous label filters.

Creating a Top-Five Report Using the Top 10 Filter

One of the more interesting value filters is the Top 10 filter. If you are sending a report to the VP of Sales, she is not going to want to see hundreds of pages of customers. One short summary with the top customers is almost more than her attention span can handle. Here's how to create it:

1. Go to the Customer drop-down and choose Value Filters, Top 10.

2. In the Top 10 Filter dialog, which enables you to choose Top or Bottom, leave the setting at the default of Top.

3. In the second field, enter any number of customers: 10, 5, 7, 12, or something else.

4. In the third drop-down on the dialog, select from Items, Percent, and Sum. You could ask for the top 10 items. You could ask for the top 80% of revenue (which the theory says should be 20% of the customers). Or you could ask for enough customers to reach a sum of $5 million (see Figure 4.39).

Figure 4.39
Create a report of the top five customers.

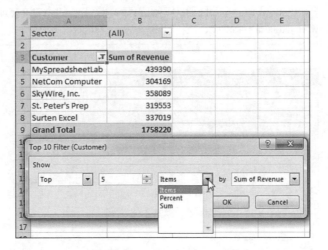

The $1,758,220 total shown in cell B9 in Figure 4.39 is the revenue of only the visible customers. It does not include the revenue for the remaining customers. You might want to show the grand total of all customers at the bottom of the list. You have a few options:

- A setting on the Design tab, under the Subtotals drop-down, enables you to include values from filtered items in the totals. This option is available only for OLAP data sets. However, you can make a regular data set into an OLAP data set by running it through Power Pivot.

NOTE See Chapter 10, "Mashing Up Data with Power Pivot," for more information on working with Power Pivot.

■ You can remove the grand total from the pivot table in Figure 4.39 and build another one-row pivot table just below this data set. Hide the heading row from the second pivot table, and you will appear to have the true grand total at the bottom of the pivot table.

■ If you select the blank cell to the right of the last heading (C3 in Figure 4.39), you can turn on the filter on the Data tab. This filter is not designed for pivot tables and is usually grayed out. After you've added the regular filters, open the drop-down in B3. Choose Top 10 Filter and ask for the top six items, as shown in Figure 4.40. This returns the top five customers and the grand total from the data set.

CAUTION

Be aware that this method is taking advantage of a bug in Excel. Normally, the Filter found on the Data tab is not allowed in a pivot table. If you use this method and later refresh the pivot table, the Excel team will not update the filter for you. As far as they know, the option to filter is greyed out when you are in a pivot table.

Figure 4.40
You are taking advantage of a hole in the fabric of Excel to apply a regular AutoFilter to a pivot table.

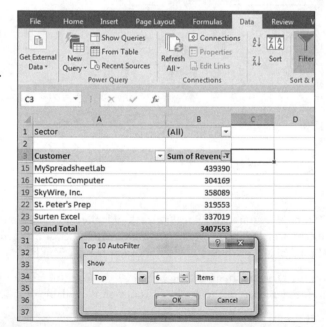

Filtering Using the Date Filters in the Label Drop-down

If your label field contains all dates, Excel replaces the Label Filter fly-out with a Date Filters fly-out. These filters offer many virtual filters, such as Next Week, This Month, Last Quarter, and so on (see Figure 4.41).

Figure 4.41
The Date Filters menu offers various virtual date periods.

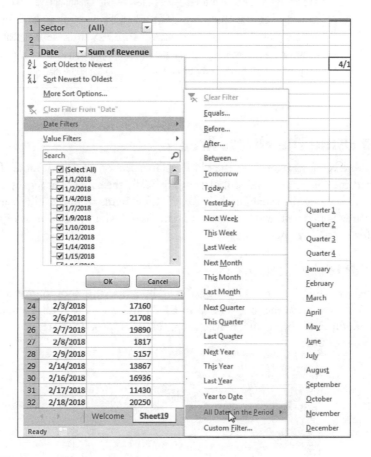

If you choose Equals, Before, After, or Between, you can specify a date or a range of dates.

Options for the current, past, or next day, week, month, quarter, or year occupy 15 options. Combined with Year to Date, these options change day after day. You can pivot a list of projects by due date and always see the projects that are due in the next week by using this option. When you open the workbook on another day, the report recalculates.

> **TIP**
> A week runs from Sunday through Saturday. If you select Next Week, the report always shows a period from the next Sunday through the following Saturday.

When you select All Dates in the Period, a new fly-out menu offers options such as Each Month and Each Quarter.

┌─ CAUTION ──┐

If your date field contains dates and times, the Date Filters might not work as expected. You might ask for dates equal to 4/15/2018, and Excel will say that no records are found. The problem is that 6:00 p.m. on 4/15/2018 is stored internally as 43205.75, with the ".75" representing the 18 hours elapsed in the day between midnight and 6:00 p.m. If you want to return all records that happened at any point on April 15, check the Whole Days box in the Date Filter dialog.

└──┘

Filtering Using the Filters Area

Pivot table veterans remember the old Page area section of a pivot table. This area has been renamed the Filters area and still operates basically the same as in legacy versions of Excel. Microsoft did add the capability to select multiple items from the Filters area. Although the Filters area is not as showy as slicers, it is still useful when you need to replicate your pivot table for every customer.

Adding Fields to the Filters Area

The pivot table in Figure 4.42 is a perfect ad hoc reporting tool to give to a high-level executive. He can use the drop-downs in B1:B4 and E1:E4 to find revenue quickly for any combination of sector, region, market, rep, customer, product, date, or weekday. This is a typical use of filters.

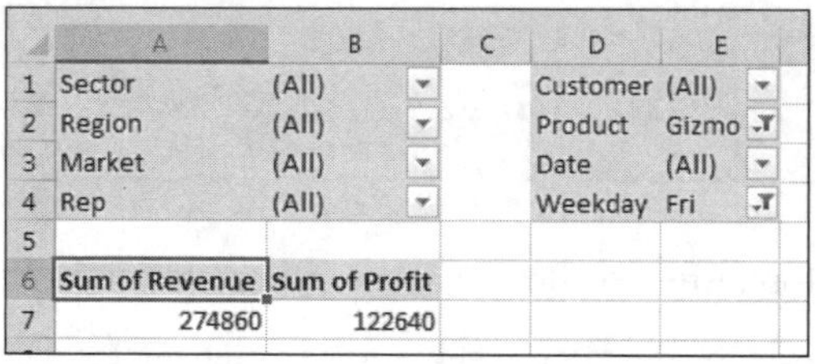

Figure 4.42
With multiple fields in the Filters area, this pivot table can answer many ad hoc queries.

	A	B	C	D	E
1	Sector	(All) ▼		Customer	(All) ▼
2	Region	(All) ▼		Product	Gizmo .T
3	Market	(All) ▼		Date	(All) ▼
4	Rep	(All) ▼		Weekday	Fri .T
5					
6	Sum of Revenue	Sum of Profit			
7	274860	122640			

To set up the report, drag Revenue and Cost to the Values area and then drag as many fields as desired to the Filters area.

If you add many fields to the Filters area, you might want to use one of the obscure pivot table options settings. Click Options on the Analyze tab. On the Layout & Format tab of the PivotTable Options dialog, change Report Filter Fields per Column from 0 to a positive number. Excel rearranges the filter fields into multiple columns. Figure 4.42 shows the filters with four fields per column. You can also change Down, Then Over to Over, Then Down to rearrange the sequence of the filter fields.

Choosing One Item from a Filter

To filter the pivot table, click any drop-down in the Filters area of the pivot table. The drop-down always starts with (All) but then lists the complete unique set of items available in that field.

Choosing Multiple Items from a Filter

At the bottom of the Filters drop-down is a check box labeled Select Multiple Items. If you select this box, Excel adds a check box next to each item in the drop-down. This enables you to check multiple items from the list.

In Figure 4.43, the pivot table is filtered to show revenue from multiple sectors, but it is impossible to tell which sectors are included.

Figure 4.43
You can select multiple items, but after the filter drop-down closes, you cannot tell which items were selected.

⊿	A	B	C	D	E
1					
2					
3					
4					
5	Sector	(All) ▼		Customer	(All) ▼
6	Region	(All) ▼		Product	Gizmo ⊤
7	Market	(All) ▼		Date	(All) ▼
8	Rep	(All) ▼		Weekday	Fri ⊤
9					
10	Sum of Revenue	Sum of Profit			
11	274860	122640			
12					
13					

4

> **TIP** Selecting multiple items from the Filter leads to a situation where the person reading the report will not know which items are included. Slicers solve this problem.

Replicating a Pivot Table Report for Each Item in a Filter

Although slicers are now the darlings of the pivot table report, the good old-fashioned report filter can still do one trick that slicers cannot do. Say you have created a report that you would like to share with the industry managers. You have a report showing customers with revenue and profit. You would like each industry manager to see only the customers in their area of responsibility.

Follow these steps to quickly replicate the pivot table:

1. Make sure the formatting in the pivot table looks good before you start. You are about to make several copies of the pivot table, and you don't want to format each worksheet in the workbook, so double-check the number formatting and headings now.

2. Add the Sector field to the Filters area. Leave the Sector filter set to (All).

3. Select one cell in the pivot table so that you can see the Analyze tab in the ribbon.

4. Find the Options button in the left side of the Analyze tab. Next to the options tab is a drop-down. Don't click the big Options button. Instead, open the drop-down (see Figure 4.44).

Figure 4.44
Click the tiny drop-down arrow next to the Options button.

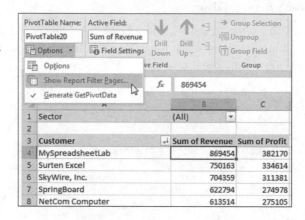

4

5. Choose Show Report Filter Pages. In the Show Report Filter Pages dialog, you see a list of all the fields in the report area. Because this pivot table has only the Sector field, this is the only choice (see Figure 4.45).

Figure 4.45
Select the field by which to replicate the report.

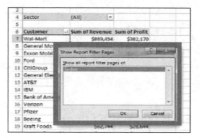

6. Click OK and stand back.

Excel inserts a new worksheet for every item in the Sector field. On the first new worksheet, Excel chooses the first sector as the filter value for that sheet. Excel renames the worksheet to match the sector. Figure 4.46 shows the new Consulting worksheet, with neighboring tabs that contain Museums, Retail, Training, and Utilities.

Figure 4.46
Excel quickly adds one
page per sector.

	A	B	C
1	Sector	Consulting ⏷	
2			
3	**Customer** ⏷	**Sum of Revenue**	**Sum of Profit**
4	Surten Excel	750163	334614
5	NetCom Computer	613514	275105
6	Adaept Information Management	498937	219978
7	Calleia Company	406326	178585
8	Excel Design Solutions Ltd	71651	32471
9	Yesenita	62744	28644
10	Symons	55251	24632
11	JEVS Human Services	50030	21612
12	Spain Enterprises	46717	19961
13	**Grand Total**	**2555333**	**1135602**
14			

◀ ▶ ... **Consulting** Museums Retail Training Utilitie

> **TIP**
> If the underlying data changes, you can refresh all of the Sector worksheets by using Refresh on one
> Sector pivot table. After you refresh the Consulting worksheet, all of the pivot tables refresh.

Filtering Using Slicers and Timelines

Slicers are graphical versions of the Report Filter fields. Rather than hiding the items
selected in the filter drop-down behind a heading such as (Multiple Items), the slicer provides a large array of buttons that show at a glance which items are included or excluded.

To add slicers, click the Insert Slicer icon on the Analyze tab. Excel displays the Insert
Slicers dialog. Choose all the fields for which you want to create graphical filters, as shown
in Figure 4.47.

Figure 4.47
Choose fields for slicers.

Initially, Excel chooses one-column slicers of similar color in a tiled arrangement (see Figure 4.48). However, you can change these settings by selecting a slicer and using the Slicer Tools Options tab in the ribbon.

Figure 4.48
The slicers appear with one column each.

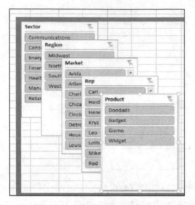

You can add more columns to a slicer. If you have to show 50 two-letter state abbreviations, that will look much better as 5 rows of 10 columns than as 50 rows of 1 column. Click the slicer to get access to the Slicer Tools Analyze tab. Use the Columns spin button to increase the number of columns in the slicer. Use the resize handles in the slicer to make the slicer wider or shorter. To add visual interest, choose a different color from the Slicer Styles gallery for each field.

After formatting the slicers, arrange them in a blank section of the worksheet, as shown in Figure 4.49.

Figure 4.49
After formatting, your slicers might fit on a single screen.

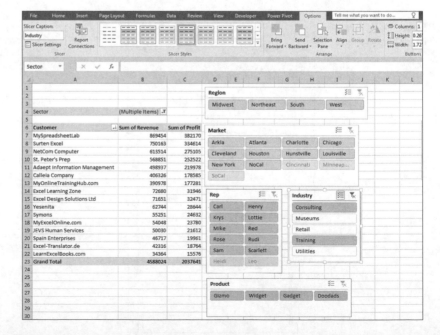

Three colors might appear in a slicer. The dark color indicates items that are selected. White boxes often mean the item has no records because of other slicers. Gray boxes indicate items that are not selected.

Note that you can control the heading for the slicer and the order of items in the slicer by using the Slicer Settings icon on the Slicer Tools Options tab of the ribbon. Just as you can define a new pivot table style, you can also right-click an existing slicer style and choose Duplicate. You can change the font, colors, and so on.

A new icon appears in Excel 2016, in the top bar of the slicer. The icon appears as three check marks. When you select this icon, you can select multiple items from the slicer without having to hold down the Ctrl key.

Using Timelines to Filter by Date

After slicers were introduced in Excel 2010, there was some feedback that using slicers was not an ideal way to deal with date fields. You might end up adding some fields to your original data set to show (perhaps) a decade and then use the group feature for year, quarter, and month. You would end up with a whole bunch of slicers all trying to select a time period, as shown in Figure 4.50.

Figure 4.50
Four different slicers are necessary to filter by date.

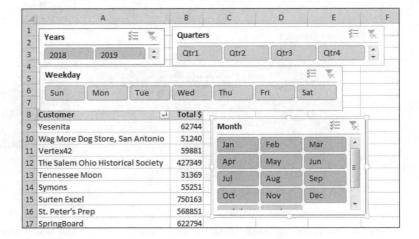

For Excel 2013, Microsoft introduced a new kind of filter called a *Timeline slicer*. To use one, select one cell in your pivot table and choose Insert Timeline from the Analyze tab. Timeline slicers can only apply to fields that contain dates. Excel gives you a list of date fields to choose from, although in most cases there is only one date field from which to choose.

Figure 4.51 shows a Timeline slicer. Perhaps the best part of a Timeline slicer is the dropdown that lets you repurpose the timeline for days, months, quarters, or years. This works even if you have not grouped your daily dates up to months, quarters, or years.

Figure 4.51
A single Timeline slicer can filter your pivot table by month, quarter, year, or day.

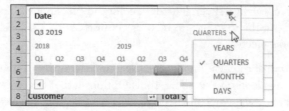

Driving Multiple Pivot Tables from One Set of Slicers

Chapter 12, "Enhancing Pivot Tables with Macros," includes a tiny macro that lets you drive two pivot tables with one set of filters. This has historically been difficult to do unless you used a macro.

Now, one set of slicers or timelines can be used to drive multiple pivot tables or pivot charts. In Figure 4.52, the Market slicer is driving three elements. It drives the pivot table in the top left with year-over-year sales by quarter. It drives a pivot table behind the top-right chart with sales by product line. It drives the bottom-right chart with sales by sector.

Figure 4.52
Three pivot elements controlled by the same slicer.

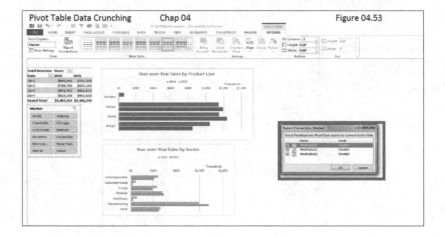

→ For more information about how to create pivot charts, refer to Chapter 6, "Using Pivot Charts and Other Visualizations."

The following steps show you how to create three pivot tables that are tied to a single slicer:

1. Create your first pivot table.
2. Select the entire pivot table.
3. Copy with Ctrl+C or the Copy command.
4. Select a new blank area of the worksheet.

5. Paste. Excel creates a second pivot table that shares the pivot cache with the first pivot table. In order for one slicer to run multiple pivot tables, they must share the same pivot cache.

6. Change the fields in the second pivot table to show some other interesting analysis.

7. Repeat steps 2–6 to create a third copy of the pivot table.

8. Select a cell in the first pivot table. Choose Insert Slicer. Choose one or more fields to be used as a slicer. Alternatively, insert a Timeline slicer for a date field.

9. Format the slicer with columns and colors. At this point, the slicer is only driving the first pivot table.

10. Click the slicer to select it. When the slicer is selected, the Slicer Tools Design tab of the ribbon appears.

11. Select the Slicer Tools Design tab and choose Report Connections. Excel displays the Report Connections (Market) dialog. Initially, only the first pivot table is selected.

12. As shown in Figure 4.53, choose the other pivot tables in the dialog and click OK.

Figure 4.53
Choose to hook this slicer up to the other pivot tables.

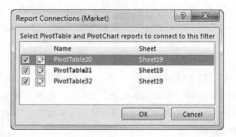

13. If you created multiple slicers and/or timelines in step 8, repeat steps 11 and 12 for the other slicers.

The result is a dashboard in which all of the pivot tables and pivot charts update in response to selections made in the slicer (see Figure 4.54).

4

Figure 4.54
All of the pivot charts
and pivot tables update
when you choose from
the slicer.

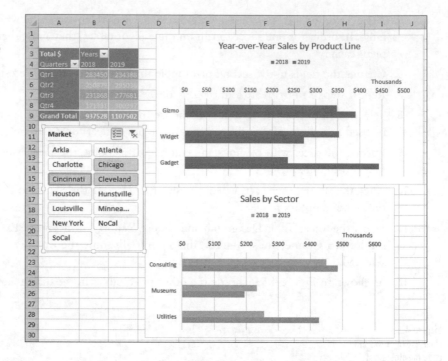

T I P   The worksheet in Figure 4.54 would be a perfect worksheet to publish to SharePoint or to your
OneDrive. You can share the workbook with co-workers and allow them to interact with the slicers.
They won't need to worry about the underlying data or enter any numbers; they can just click on the
slicer to see the reports update.

Next Steps

In Chapter 5, "Performing Calculations in Pivot Tables," you'll learn how to use pivot table
formulas to add new virtual fields to a pivot table.

Performing Calculations in Pivot Tables

5

Introducing Calculated Fields and Calculated Items

When analyzing data with pivot tables, you will often need to expand your analysis to include data based on calculations that are not in your original data set. Excel provides a way to perform calculations within a pivot table through calculated fields and calculated items.

A *calculated field* is a data field you create by executing a calculation against existing fields in the pivot table. Think of a calculated field as a virtual column added to your data set. This column takes up no space in your source data, contains the data you define with a formula, and interacts with your pivot data as a field—just like all the other fields in your pivot table.

A *calculated item* is a data item you create by executing a calculation against existing items within a data field. Think of a calculated item as a virtual row of data added to your data set. This virtual row takes up no space in your source data and contains summarized values based on calculations performed on other rows in the same field. Calculated items interact with your pivot data as data items—just like all the other items in your pivot table.

With calculated fields and calculated items, you can insert a formula into a pivot table to create your own custom field or data item. Your newly created data becomes a part of your pivot table, interacting with other pivot data, recalculating when you refresh and supplying you with a calculated metric that does not exist in your source data.

The example in Figure 5.1 demonstrates how a basic calculated field can add another perspective on your data. Your pivot table shows total sales amount and contracted hours for each market. A calculated field that shows you average dollar per hour enhances this analysis and adds another dimension to your data.

Figure 5.1
Avg Dollar per Hour is a calculated field that adds another perspective to your data analysis.

	A	B	C	D
1				
2	Row Labels ▼	Sales_Amount	Contracted Hours	Avg Dollar Per Hour
3	BUFFALO	$450,478	6,864	$65.63
4	CALIFORNIA	$2,254,735	33,014	$68.30
5	CANADA	$776,245	12,103	$64.14
6	CHARLOTTE	$890,522	14,525	$61.31
7	DALLAS	$467,089	6,393	$73.06
8	DENVER	$645,583	8,641	$74.71
9	FLORIDA	$1,450,392	22,640	$64.06
10	KANSASCITY	$574,899	8,547	$67.26
11	MICHIGAN	$678,705	10,744	$63.17
12	NEWORLEANS	$333,454	5,057	$65.94
13	NEWYORK	$873,581	14,213	$61.46
14	PHOENIX	$570,255	10,167	$56.09
15	SEATTLE	$179,827	2,889	$62.25
16	TULSA	$628,405	9,583	$65.57
17	Grand Total	$10,774,172	165,380	$65.15

Now, you might look at Figure 5.1 and ask, "Why go through all the trouble of creating calculated fields or calculated items? Why not just use formulas in surrounding cells or even add the calculation directly into the source table to get the information needed?"

To answer these questions, in the next sections, we will look at the three different methods you can use to create the calculated field in Figure 5.1:

- Manually add the calculated field to your data source
- Use a formula outside your pivot table to create the calculated field
- Insert a calculated field directly into your pivot table

Method 1: Manually Add a Calculated Field to the Data Source

If you manually add a calculated field to your data source, the pivot table can pick up the field as a regular data field (see Figure 5.2). On the surface, this option looks simple, but this method of precalculating metrics and incorporating them into your data source is impractical on several levels.

Figure 5.2
Precalculating calculated fields in your data source is both cumbersome and impractical.

	N	O	P	Q	R
1	Sales_Amount	Contracted Hours	Sales_Period	Sales_Rep	Avg Dollar Per Hour
2	$197.95	2	P08	5060	$98.98
3	$197.95	2	P08	5060	$98.98
4	$191.28	3	P08	5060	$63.76
5	$240.07	4	P11	44651	$60.02
6	$147.22	2	P08	160410	$73.61
7	$163.51	2	P02	243	$81.76
8	$134.01	3	P02	243	$44.67
9	$134.01	3	P02	243	$44.67
10	$134.01	3	P02	243	$44.67
11	$239.00	3	P01	4244	$79.67
12	$215.87	4	P02	5030	$53.97
13	$180.57	4	P02	64610	$45.14
14	$240.07	4	P02	213	$60.02

If the definitions of your calculated fields change, you have to go back to the data source, recalculate the metric for each row, and refresh your pivot table. If you have to add a metric, you have go back to the data source, add a new calculated field, and then change the range of your pivot table to capture the new field.

Method 2: Use a Formula Outside a Pivot Table to Create a Calculated Field

You can add a calculated field by performing the calculation in an external cell with a formula. In the example shown in Figure 5.3, the Avg Dollar per Hour column was created with formulas referencing the pivot table.

Figure 5.3
Typing a formula next to your pivot table essentially gives you a calculated field that refreshes when your pivot table is refreshed.

	A	B	C	D
	Row Labels	Sales_Amount	Contracted Hours	Avg Dollar Per Hour
3	BUFFALO	$450,478	6,864	$65.63
4	CALIFORNIA	$2,254,735	33,014	$68.30
5	CANADA	$776,245	12,103	$64.14
6	CHARLOTTE	$890,522	14,525	$61.31
7	DALLAS	$467,089	6,393	$73.06
8	DENVER	$645,583	8,641	$74.71
9	FLORIDA	$1,450,392	22,640	$64.06
10	KANSASCITY	$574,899	8,547	$67.26
11	MICHIGAN	$678,705	10,744	$63.17
12	NEWORLEANS	$333,454	5,057	$65.94
13	NEWYORK	$873,581	14,213	$61.46
14	PHOENIX	$570,255	10,167	$56.09
15	SEATTLE	$179,827	2,889	$62.25
16	TULSA	$628,405	9,583	$65.57
17	Grand Total	$10,774,172	165,380	$65.15

(D3 = B3/C3)

Although this method gives you a calculated field that updates when your pivot table is refreshed, any changes in the structure of your pivot table have the potential of rendering your formula useless.

As you can see in Figure 5.4, moving the Market field to the Filters area changes the structure of your pivot table—and exposes the weakness of makeshift calculated fields that use external formulas.

Figure 5.4
External formulas can cause errors when the pivot table structure is changed.

	A	B	C	D
1	Market	(All)		
2				Avg Dollar Per Hour
3	Sales_Amount	Contracted Hours		#VALUE!
4	$10,774,172	165,380		#DIV/0!
5				#DIV/0!
6				#DIV/0!
7				#DIV/0!
8				#DIV/0!
9				#DIV/0!
10				#DIV/0!
11				#DIV/0!
12				#DIV/0!
13				#DIV/0!
14				#DIV/0!
15				#DIV/0!
16				#DIV/0!
17				#DIV/0!

5

Method 3: Insert a Calculated Field Directly into a Pivot Table

Inserting a calculated field directly into a pivot table is the best option. Going this route eliminates the need to manage formulas, provides for scalability when your data source grows or changes, and allows for flexibility in the event that your metric definitions change.

Another huge advantage of this method is that you can alter your pivot table's structure and even measure different data fields against your calculated field without worrying about errors in your formulas or losing cell references.

The pivot table report shown in Figure 5.5 is the same one you see in Figure 5.1, except it has been restructured to show the average dollar per hour by market and product.

Figure 5.5
Your calculated field remains viable even when your pivot table's structure changes to accommodate new dimensions.

	A	B	C	D	E
1					
2	**Market**	**Product_Description**	**Sales_Amount**	**Contracted Hours**	**Avg Dollar Per Hour**
3	⊟BUFFALO	Cleaning & Housekeeping Services	$66,845	982	$68.07
4		Facility Maintenance and Repair	$69,570	821	$84.74
5		Fleet Maintenance	$86,460	1,439	$60.08
6		Green Plants and Foliage Care	$34,831	490	$71.08
7		Landscaping/Grounds Care	$65,465	1,172	$55.86
8		Predictive Maintenance/Preventative Maintenance	$127,307	1,960	$64.95
9	**BUFFALO Total**		**$450,478**	**6,864**	**$65.63**
10	⊟CALIFORNIA	Cleaning & Housekeeping Services	$37,401	531	$70.44
11		Facility Maintenance and Repair	$281,198	3,103	$90.62
12		Fleet Maintenance	$337,225	5,737	$58.78
13		Green Plants and Foliage Care	$830,413	11,900	$69.78
14		Landscaping/Grounds Care	$248,343	3,421	$72.59
15		Predictive Maintenance/Preventative Maintenance	$520,156	8,322	$62.50
16	**CALIFORNIA Total**		**$2,254,735**	**33,014**	**$68.30**

The bottom line is that there are significant benefits to integrating your custom calculations into a pivot table, including the following:

- Elimination of potential formula and cell reference errors
- Ability to add or remove data from your pivot table without affecting your calculations
- Ability to auto-recalculate when your pivot table is changed or refreshed
- Flexibility to change calculations easily when your metric definitions change
- Ability to manage and maintain your calculations effectively

> **NOTE**
> If you move your data to PowerPivot, you can use the DAX formula language to create more powerful calculations. **See** Chapter 10, "Mashing Up Data with Power Pivot," to get a concise look at the DAX formula language.

Creating a Calculated Field

Before you create a calculated field, you must first have a pivot table, so build the pivot table shown in Figure 5.6.

Once you have a pivot table, it's time to create your first calculated field. To do this, you must activate the Insert Calculated Field dialog. Select Analyze under the PivotTable Tools tab and then select Fields, Items, & Sets from the Calculations group. Selecting this option activates a drop-down menu from which you can select Calculated Field, as demonstrated in Figure 5.7.

Figure 5.6
Create the pivot table shown here.

	A	B	C
1			
2	**Market** ▼	Sales_Amount	Contracted Hours
3	BUFFALO	$450,478	6,864
4	CALIFORNIA	$2,254,735	33,014
5	CANADA	$776,245	12,103
6	CHARLOTTE	$890,522	14,525
7	DALLAS	$467,089	6,393
8	DENVER	$645,583	8,641
9	FLORIDA	$1,450,392	22,640
10	KANSASCITY	$574,899	8,547
11	MICHIGAN	$678,705	10,744
12	NEWORLEANS	$333,454	5,057
13	NEWYORK	$873,581	14,213
14	PHOENIX	$570,255	10,167
15	SEATTLE	$179,827	2,889
16	TULSA	$628,405	9,583
17	**Grand Total**	$10,774,172	165,380

Figure 5.7
Start the creation of your calculated field by selecting Calculated Field.

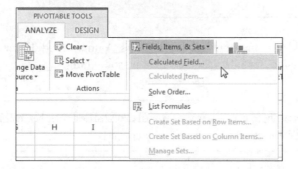

After you select Calculated Field, Excel activates the Insert Calculated Field dialog, as shown in Figure 5.8.

Figure 5.8
The Insert Calculated Field dialog assists you in creating a calculated field in a pivot table.

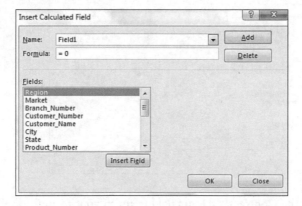

Notice the two input boxes, Name and Formula, at the top of the dialog box. The objective here is to give your calculated field a name and then build the formula by selecting the combination of data fields and mathematical operators that provide the metric you are looking for.

As you can see in Figure 5.9, you first give your calculated field a descriptive name—that is, a name that describes the utility of the mathematical operation. In this case, enter **Avg Dollar per Hour** in the Name input box.

Figure 5.9
Give your calculated field a descriptive name.

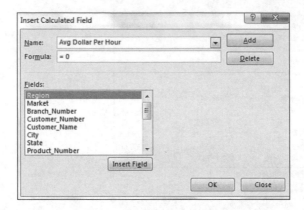

Next, go to the Fields list and double-click the Sales_Amount field. Enter **/** to let Excel know you plan to divide the Sales_Amount field by something.

> ┌─ C A U T I O N ───
> By default, the Formula input box in the Insert Calculated Field dialog box contains = 0. Ensure that you delete the zero before continuing with your formula.

At this point, your dialog should look similar to the one shown in Figure 5.10.

Figure 5.10
Start your formula with
= Sales_Amount /.

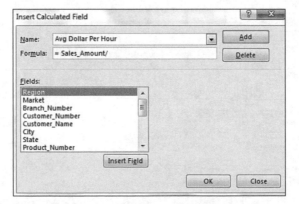

Next, double-click the Contracted Hours field to finish your formula, as illustrated in Figure 5.11.

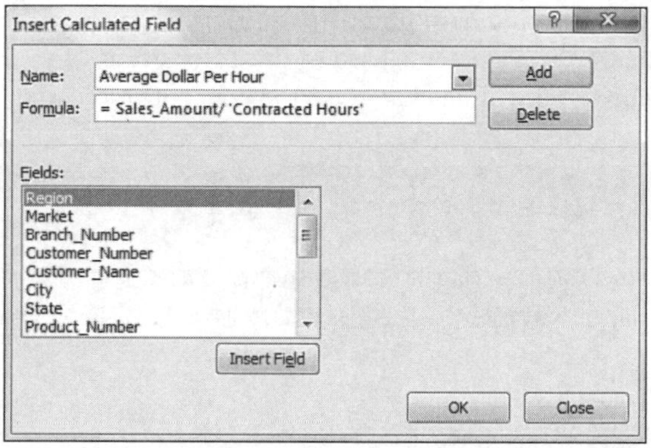

Figure 5.11
The full formula, =
`Sales_Amount/`
`'Contracted`
`Hours'`, gives you the
calculated field you need.

Finally, select Add and then click OK to create the new calculated field.

As you can see in Figure 5.12, the pivot table creates a new field called Sum of Avg Dollar per Hour. Note that in addition to adding your calculated field to the pivot table, Excel also adds your new field to the PivotTable Fields list.

Figure 5.12
You can change the
settings on your new
calculated field—for
example, field name,
number format, color—
just as you would on any
other field.

	A	B	C	D
1				
2	Market	Sales_Amount	Contracted Hours	Sum of Avg Dollar Per Hour
3	BUFFALO	$450,478	6,864	65.62911859
4	CALIFORNIA	$2,254,735	33,014	68.29634034
5	CANADA	$776,245	12,103	64.13660002
6	CHARLOTTE	$890,522	14,525	61.30963787
7	DALLAS	$467,089	6,393	73.06264195
8	DENVER	$645,583	8,641	74.71164101
9	FLORIDA	$1,450,392	22,640	64.06325088
10	KANSASCITY	$574,899	8,547	67.26324675
11	MICHIGAN	$678,705	10,744	63.1706022
12	NEWORLEANS	$333,454	5,057	65.93902511
13	NEWYORK	$873,581	14,213	61.46351298
14	PHOENIX	$570,255	10,167	56.08882561
15	SEATTLE	$179,827	2,889	62.24548633
16	TULSA	$628,405	9,583	65.57495878
17	Grand Total	$10,774,172	165,380	65.14797303

5

> **NOTE** The resulting values from a calculated field are not formatted. You can easily apply any desired formatting by using some of the techniques from Chapter 3, "Customizing a Pivot Table."

Does this mean you have just added a column to your data source? The answer is no.

Calculated fields are similar to the pivot table's default subtotal and grand total calculations in that they are all mathematical functions that recalculate when the pivot table changes or is refreshed. Calculated fields merely mimic the hard fields in your data source; you can drag them, change field settings, and use them with other calculated fields.

Take a moment and take another close look at Figure 5.11. Notice that the formula entered there is in a format similar to the one used in the standard Excel formula bar. The obvious difference is that instead of using hard numbers or cell references, you are referencing pivot data fields to define the arguments used in this calculation. If you have worked with formulas in Excel before, you will quickly grasp the concept of creating calculated fields.

CASE STUDY: SUMMARIZING NEXT YEAR'S FORECAST

All the branch managers in your company have submitted their initial revenue forecasts for next year. Your task is to take the first-pass numbers they submitted and create a summary report that shows the following:

- Total revenue forecast by market
- Total percentage growth over last year
- Total contribution margin by market

Because these numbers are first-pass submissions and you know they will change over the course of the next two weeks, you decide to use a pivot table to create the requested forecast summary.

Start by building the initial pivot table, shown in Figure 5.13, to include Revenue Last Year and Forecast Next Year for each market. After creating the pivot table, you will see that by virtue of adding the Forecast Next Year field in the data area, you have met your first requirement: to show total revenue forecast by market.

Figure 5.13
The initial pivot table is basic, but it provides the data for your first requirement: show total revenue forecast by market.

MARKET	Revenue Last Year	Forecast Next Year
BUFFALO	$450,478	$411,246
CALIFORNIA	$2,254,735	$2,423,007
CANADA	$776,245	$746,384
CHARLOTTE	$890,522	$965,361
DALLAS	$467,089	$510,635
DENVER	$645,583	$722,695
FLORIDA	$1,450,392	$1,421,507
KANSASCITY	$574,899	$607,226
MICHIGAN	$678,705	$870,447
NEWORLEANS	$333,454	$366,174
NEWYORK	$873,581	$953,010
PHOENIX	$570,255	$746,721
SEATTLE	$179,827	$214,621
TULSA	$628,405	$661,726
Grand Total	$10,774,172	$11,620,760

The next metric you need is percentage growth over last year. To get this data, you need to add a calculated field that calculates the following formula:

```
(Forecast Next Year / Revenue Last Year) - 1
```

To achieve this, do the following:

1. Activate the Insert Calculated Field dialog, and name your new field **Percent Growth** (see Figure 5.14).
2. Delete the 0 in the Formula input box.
3. Enter ((an opening parenthesis).

Figure 5.14
Name your new field
Percent Growth.

4. Double-click the Forecast Next Year field.

5. Enter / (a division sign).

6. Double-click the Revenue Last Year field.

7. Enter) (a closing parenthesis).

8. Enter - (a minus sign).

9. Enter the number **1**.

> **TIP**
>
> You can use any constant in your pivot table calculations. Constants are static values that do not change. In this example, the number 1 is a constant. While the value of Revenue Last Year or Forecast Next Year will almost certainly change based on the available data, the number 1 will always have the same value.

After you have entered the full formula, your dialog should look like the one shown in Figure 5.15.

With your formula typed in, you can now click OK to add your new field. After changing the format of the resulting values to percentages, you have a nicely formatted Percent Growth calculation in your pivot table. At this point, your pivot table should look like the one shown in Figure 5.16.

Figure 5.15
With just a few clicks, you have created a variance formula!

5

Figure 5.16
You have added a Percent Growth calculation to your pivot table.

	A	B	C	D
1				
2				
3	MARKET ▾	Revenue Last Year	Forecast Next Year	Sum of Percent Growth
4	BUFFALO	$450,478	$411,246	-8.7%
5	CALIFORNIA	$2,254,735	$2,423,007	7.5%
6	CANADA	$776,245	$746,384	-3.8%
7	CHARLOTTE	$890,522	$965,361	8.4%
8	DALLAS	$467,089	$510,635	9.3%
9	DENVER	$645,583	$722,695	11.9%
10	FLORIDA	$1,450,392	$1,421,507	-2.0%
11	KANSASCITY	$574,899	$607,226	5.6%
12	MICHIGAN	$678,705	$870,447	28.3%
13	NEWORLEANS	$333,454	$366,174	9.8%
14	NEWYORK	$873,581	$953,010	9.1%
15	PHOENIX	$570,255	$746,721	30.9%
16	SEATTLE	$179,827	$214,621	19.3%
17	TULSA	$628,405	$661,726	5.3%
18	Grand Total	$10,774,172	$11,620,760	7.9%

With this newly created view into your data, you can easily see that three markets need to resubmit their forecasts to reflect positive growth over last year (see Figure 5.17).

Figure 5.17
You can already discern some information from the calculated field, which identifies three problematic markets.

	A	B	C	D
1				
2				
3	MARKET ▾	Revenue Last Year	Forecast Next Year	Sum of Percent Growth
4	BUFFALO	$450,478	$411,246	-8.7%
5	CALIFORNIA	$2,254,735	$2,423,007	7.5%
6	CANADA	$776,245	$746,384	-3.8%
7	CHARLOTTE	$890,522	$965,361	8.4%
8	DALLAS	$467,089	$510,635	9.3%
9	DENVER	$645,583	$722,695	11.9%
10	FLORIDA	$1,450,392	$1,421,507	-2.0%
11	KANSASCITY	$574,899	$607,226	5.6%
12	MICHIGAN	$678,705	$870,447	28.3%
13	NEWORLEANS	$333,454	$366,174	9.8%
14	NEWYORK	$873,581	$953,010	9.1%
15	PHOENIX	$570,255	$746,721	30.9%
16	SEATTLE	$179,827	$214,621	19.3%
17	TULSA	$628,405	$661,726	5.3%
18	Grand Total	$10,774,172	$11,620,760	7.9%

Now it's time to focus on your last requirement, which is to find total contribution margin by market. To get this data, you need to add a calculated field that calculates the following formula:

```
Forecast Next Year + Variable Cost Next Year
```

> **NOTE** A quick look at Figure 5.17 confirms that the Variable Cost Next Year field is not displayed in the pivot table report. Can you build pivot table formulas with fields that are currently *not even in* the pivot table? The answer is yes; you can use any field that is available to you in the PivotTable Fields list, even if the field is not shown in the pivot table.

To create this field, do the following:

1. Activate the Insert Calculated Field dialog box and name your new field **Contribution Margin**.

2. Delete the 0 in the Formula input box.

3. Double-click the Forecast Next Year field.

4. Enter + (a plus sign).

5. Double-click the Variable Cost Next Year field.

After you have entered the full formula, your dialog should look like the one shown in Figure 5.18.

Figure 5.18
With just a few clicks, you have created a formula that calculates contribution margin.

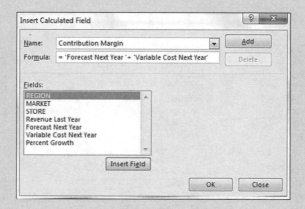

Now that you have created the Contribution Margin calculation, this report is ready to be formatted and delivered (see Figure 5.19).

With this pivot table report, you can easily analyze any new forecast submissions by refreshing your report with the new updates.

Figure 5.19
Contribution Margin is now a data field in your pivot table report, thanks to your calculated field.

	A	B	C	D	E
1					
2					
3	**MARKET**	**Revenue Last Year**	**Forecast Next Year**	**Sum of Percent Growth**	**Sum of Contribution Margin**
4	BUFFALO	$450,478	$411,246	-8.7%	($169,546)
5	CALIFORNIA	$2,254,735	$2,423,007	7.5%	$1,152,641
6	CANADA	$776,245	$746,384	-3.8%	$118,415
7	CHARLOTTE	$890,522	$965,361	8.4%	$360,343
8	DALLAS	$467,089	$510,635	9.3%	($908,021)
9	DENVER	$645,583	$722,695	11.9%	($697,393)
10	FLORIDA	$1,450,392	$1,421,507	-2.0%	$865,700
11	KANSASCITY	$574,899	$607,226	5.6%	($328,773)
12	MICHIGAN	$678,705	$870,447	28.3%	($92,813)
13	NEWORLEANS	$333,454	$366,174	9.8%	($586,405)
14	NEWYORK	$873,581	$953,010	9.1%	$506,335
15	PHOENIX	$570,255	$746,721	30.9%	$318,496
16	SEATTLE	$179,827	$214,621	19.3%	($163,738)
17	TULSA	$628,405	$661,726	5.3%	($1,193,984)
18	**Grand Total**	$10,774,172	$11,620,760	7.9%	($818,743)

Creating a Calculated Item

As you learned at the beginning of this chapter, a calculated item is a virtual data item you create by executing a calculation against existing items within a data field. Calculated items come in especially handy when you need to group and aggregate a set of data items.

For example, the pivot table in Figure 5.20 gives you sales amount by sales period. Imagine that you need to compare the average performance of the most recent six sales periods to the average of the prior seven periods. That is, you want to take the average of P01–P07 and compare it to the average of P08–P13.

Figure 5.20
You want to compare the most recent six sales periods to the average of the prior seven periods.

	A	B
1		
2		
3	Row Labels ▼	Sum of Sales_Amount
4	P01	$681,865
5	P02	$1,116,916
6	P03	$657,611
7	P04	$865,498
8	P05	$925,802
9	P06	$868,930
10	P07	$640,587
11	P08	$1,170,262
12	P09	$604,552
13	P10	$891,253
14	P11	$949,605
15	P12	$887,665
16	P13	$513,625
17	**Grand Total**	**$10,774,172**

Place your cursor on any data item in the Sales_Period field, and then select Fields, Items, & Sets from the Calculations group. Next, select Calculated Item, as shown in Figure 5.21.

Figure 5.21
Start the creation of your calculated item by selecting Calculated Item.

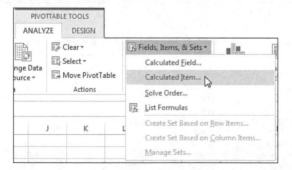

Selecting this option opens the Insert Calculated Item dialog. A quick glance at Figure 5.22 shows you that the top of the dialog identifies which field you are working with. In this case, it is the Sales_Period field. In addition, notice that the Items list box is automatically filled with all the items in the Sales_Period field.

Figure 5.22
The Insert Calculated Item dialog is automatically populated to reflect the field with which you are working.

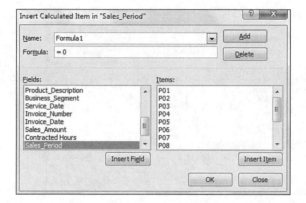

You need to give your calculated item a name and then build its formula by selecting the combination of data items and operators that provide the metric you are looking for.

In this example, name your first calculated item **Avg P1-P7 Sales**, as shown in Figure 5.23.

Next, you can build your formula in the Formula input box by selecting the appropriate data items from the Items list. In this scenario, you want to create the following formula:

```
=Average(P01, P02, P03, P04, P05, P06, P07)
```

Enter the formula shown in Figure 5.24 into the Formula input box.

Click OK to activate your new calculated item. As you can see in Figure 5.25, you now have a data item called Avg P1-P7 Sales.

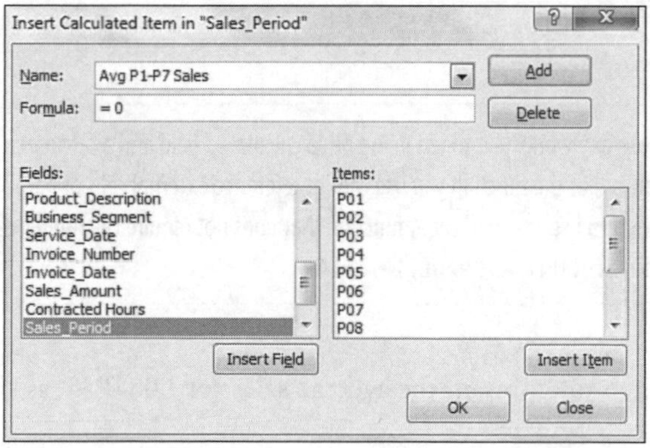

Figure 5.23
Give your calculated item a descriptive name.

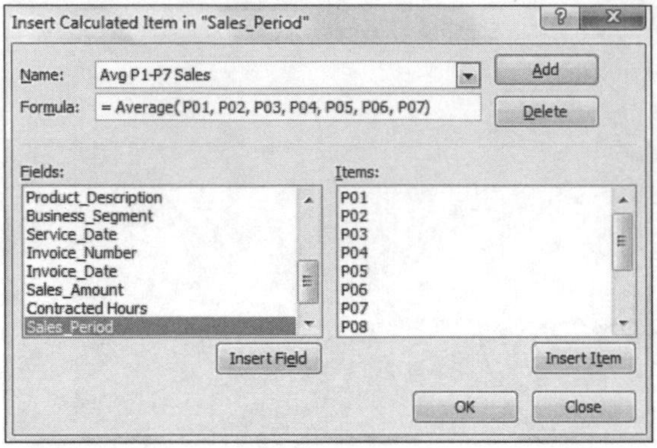

Figure 5.24
Enter a formula that gives you the average of P01–P07.

Figure 5.25
You have successfully added a calculated item to your pivot table.

	A	B
1		
2		
3	**Row Labels** ▾	**Sum of Sales_Amount**
4	P01	$681,865
5	P02	$1,116,916
6	P03	$657,611
7	P04	$865,498
8	P05	$925,802
9	P06	$868,930
10	P07	$640,587
11	P08	$1,170,262
12	P09	$604,552
13	P10	$891,253
14	P11	$949,605
15	P12	$887,665
16	P13	$513,625
17	Avg P1-P7 Sales	$822,458
18	**Grand Total**	**$11,596,630**

> **TIP**
> You can use any worksheet function in both a calculated field and a calculated item. The only restriction is that the function you use cannot reference external cells or named ranges. In effect, this means you can use any worksheet function that does not require cell references or defined names to work (such as COUNT, AVERAGE, IF, and OR).

Create a calculated item to represent the average sales for P08–P13, as shown in Figure 5.26.

Figure 5.26
Create a second calculated item.

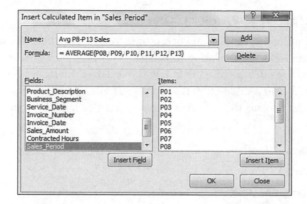

Now you can hide the individual sales periods so that the report shows only the two calculated items. As shown in Figure 5.27, after a little formatting, your calculated items allow you to compare the average performance of the six most recent sales periods to the average of the prior seven periods.

Figure 5.27
You can now compare the most recent six sales periods to the average of the prior seven periods.

	A	B
1		
2		
3	**Row Labels**	**Sum of Sales_Amount**
4	Avg P1-P7 Sales	$822,458
5	Avg P8-P13 Sales	$836,160
6	**Grand Total**	**$1,658,619**

> **CAUTION**
>
> It is often prudent to hide the data items you used to create your calculated item. In Figure 5.27, notice that all periods have been hidden. This prevents any grand totals and subtotals from showing incorrect aggregations.

5

Understanding the Rules and Shortcomings of Pivot Table Calculations

There is no better way to integrate your calculations into a pivot table than by using calculated fields and calculated items. However, calculated fields and calculated items do come with their own set of drawbacks. It's important you understand what goes on behind the scenes when you use pivot table calculations, and it's even more important to be aware of the boundaries and limitations of calculated fields and calculated items to avoid potential errors in your data analysis.

The following sections highlight the rules related to calculated fields and calculated items that you will most likely encounter when working with pivot table calculations.

Remembering the Order of Operator Precedence

Just as in a spreadsheet, you can use any operator in your calculation formulas—meaning any symbol that represents a calculation to perform (+, –, *, /, %, ^). Moreover, just as in a spreadsheet, calculations in a pivot table follow the order of operator precedence. In other words, when you perform a calculation that combines several operators, as in (2+3) * 4/50%, Excel evaluates and performs the calculation in a specific order. The order of operations for Excel is as follows:

- Evaluate items in parentheses.
- Evaluate ranges (:).
- Evaluate intersections (spaces).
- Evaluate unions (,).
- Perform negation (–).
- Convert percentages (%).
- Perform exponentiation (^).
- Perform multiplication (*) and division (/), which are of equal precedence.
- Perform addition (+) and subtraction (–), which are of equal precedence.
- Evaluate text operators (&).
- Perform comparisons (=, <>, <=, >=).

> **NOTE** Operations that are equal in precedence are performed left to right.

Consider this basic example. The correct answer to (2+3)*4 is 20. However, if you leave off the parentheses, so that you have 2+3*4, Excel performs the calculation like this: 3*4 = 12 + 2 = 14. The order of operator precedence mandates that Excel perform multiplication before addition. Entering 2+3*4 gives you the wrong answer. Because Excel evaluates and performs all calculations in parentheses first, placing 2+3 inside parentheses ensures the correct answer.

Here is another widely demonstrated example. If you enter 10^2, which represents the exponent 10 to the second power as a formula, Excel returns 100 as the answer. If you enter –10^2, you expect –100 to be the result, but instead Excel returns 100 yet again. The reason is that Excel performs negation before exponentiation, which means Excel converts 10 to –10 before doing the exponentiation, effectively calculating –10*–10, which indeed equals 100. When you use parentheses in the formula, –(10^2), Excel calculates the exponent before negating the answer, giving you –100.

Understanding the order of operations helps you avoid miscalculating your data.

Using Cell References and Named Ranges

When you create calculations in a pivot table, you are essentially working in a vacuum. The only data available to you is the data that exists in the pivot cache. Therefore, you cannot reach outside the confines of the pivot cache to reference cells or named ranges in your formula.

Using Worksheet Functions

When you build calculated fields or calculated items, Excel enables you to use any worksheet function that accepts numeric values as arguments and returns numeric values as the result. Some of the many functions that fall into this category are COUNT, AVERAGE, IF, AND, NOT, and OR.

Some examples of functions you cannot use are VLOOKUP, INDEX, SUMIF, COUNTIF, LEFT, and RIGHT. Again, these are all impossible to use because they either require cell array references or return textual values as the result.

Using Constants

You can use any constant in your pivot table calculations. Constants are static values that do not change. For example, in the formula [Units Sold]*5, 5 is a constant. Though the value of Units Sold might change based on the available data, 5 always has the same value.

Referencing Totals

Your calculation formulas cannot reference a pivot table's subtotals or grand total. This means that you cannot use the result of a subtotal or grand total as a variable or an argument in a calculated field.

Rules Specific to Calculated Fields

Calculated field calculations are always performed against the sum of the data. In basic terms, Excel always calculates data fields, subtotals, and grand totals before evaluating a calculated field. This means that your calculated field is always applied to the sum of the underlying data. The example shown in Figure 5.28 demonstrates how this can adversely affect your data analysis.

Figure 5.28
Although the calculated field is correct for the individual data items in your pivot table, the subtotal is mathematically incorrect.

⊿	A	B	C	D	E	F	G	H
1			Data					
2	Qtr	Product	Number of Units	Price	CalcField Unit*Price			
3	⊟Q1	A	10	22	$220			
4		B	5	30	$150			
5		C	5	·44	$220			
6		D	11	54	$594			
7	Q1 Total		31	150	$4,650		$1,184 <--Real Q1 Subtotal	

In each quarter, you need to get the total revenue for every product by multiplying the number of units sold by the price. If you look at Q1 first, you can immediately see the problem. Instead of returning the sum of 220+150+220+594, which would be $1,184, the subtotal is calculating the sum of number of units times the sum of price, which is the wrong answer.

As you can see in Figure 5.29, including the whole year in your analysis compounds the problem.

Figure 5.29
The grand total for the year as a whole is completely wrong.

	A	B	C	D	E	F	G	H
1			Data					
2	Qtr	Product	Number of Units	Price	CalcField Unit*Price			
3	Q1	A	10	22	$220			
4		B	5	30	$150			
5		C	5	44	$220			
6		D	11	54	$594			
7	Q1 Total		31	150	$4,650		$1,184 <--Real Q1 Subtotal	
8	Q2	A	7	19	$133			
9		B	12	25	$300			
10		C	9	39	$351			
11		D	5	52	$260			
12	Q2 Total		33	135	$4,455		$1,044 <--Real Q2 Subtotal	
13	Q3	A	6	17	$102			
14		B	8	21	$168			
15		C	6	40	$240			
16		D	7	55	$385			
17	Q3 Total		27	133	$3,591		$895 <--Real Q3 Subtotal	
18	Q4	A	8	22	$176			
19		B	7	31	$217			
20		C	6	35	$210			
21		D	10	49	$490			
22	Q4 Total		31	137	$4,247		$1,093 <--Real Q4 Subtotal	
23	Grand Total		122	555	$67,710		$4,216 <--Real Grand Total	

Unfortunately, there is no solution to this problem, but there is a workaround. In worst-case scenarios, you can configure your settings to eliminate subtotals and grand totals and then calculate your own totals. Figure 5.30 demonstrates this workaround.

Figure 5.30
Calculating your own totals can prevent reporting incorrect data.

	A	B	C	D	E
1			Data		
2	Qtr	Product	Number of Units	Price	CalcField Unit*Price
3	Q1	A	10	22	$220
4		B	5	30	$150
5		C	5	44	$220
6		D	11	54	$594
7	Q2	A	7	19	$133
8		B	12	25	$300
9		C	9	39	$351
10		D	5	52	$260
11	Q3	A	6	17	$102
12		B	8	21	$168
13		C	6	40	$240
14		D	7	55	$385
15	Q4	A	8	22	$176
16		B	7	31	$217
17		C	6	35	$210
18		D	10	49	$490
19					
20					$4,216

Rules Specific to Calculated Items

To use calculated items effectively, it is important that you understand a few ground rules:

- You cannot use calculated items in a pivot table that uses averages, standard deviations, or variances. Conversely, you cannot use averages, standard deviations, or variances in a pivot table that contains a calculated item.

- You cannot use a page field to create a calculated item, nor can you move any calculated item to the report filter area.

- You cannot add a calculated item to a report that has a grouped field, nor can you group any field in a pivot table that contains a calculated item.

- When building your calculated item formula, you cannot reference items from a field other than the one you are working with.

As you think about the pages you have just read, don't be put off by these shortcomings of pivot tables. Despite the clear limitations highlighted, the capability to create custom calculations directly into your pivot table remains a powerful and practical feature that can enhance your data analysis.

Now that you are aware of the inner workings of pivot table calculations and understand the limitations of calculated fields and items, you can avoid the pitfalls and use these features with confidence.

Managing and Maintaining Pivot Table Calculations

In your dealings with pivot tables, you will find that sometimes you don't keep a pivot table for more than the time it takes to say, "Copy, Paste Values." Other times, however, it will be more cost-effective to keep a pivot table and all its functionality intact.

When you find yourself maintaining and managing pivot tables through changing requirements and growing data, you might find the need to maintain and manage your calculated fields and calculated items as well.

Editing and Deleting Pivot Table Calculations

When a calculation's parameters change or you no longer need a calculated field or calculated item, you can activate the appropriate dialog to edit or remove the calculation.

Simply activate the Insert Calculated Field or Insert Calculated Item dialog, and select the Name drop-down, as demonstrated in Figure 5.31.

Figure 5.31
Opening the drop-down list under Name reveals all the calculated fields or items in the pivot table.

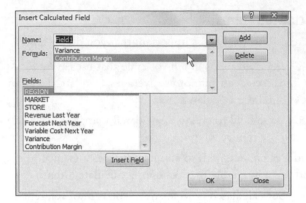

As you can see in Figure 5.32, after you select a calculated field or item, you have the option of deleting the calculation or modifying the formula.

Figure 5.32
After you select the appropriate calculated field or item, you can either delete or modify the calculation.

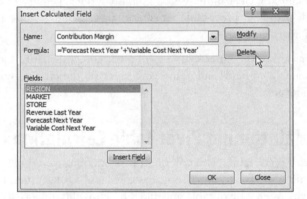

Changing the Solve Order of Calculated Items

If the value of a cell in your pivot table is dependent on the results of two or more calculated items, you have the option of changing the solve order of the calculated items. That is, you can specify the order in which the individual calculations are performed.

To specify the order of calculations, you need the Solve Order dialog. To get there, place your cursor anywhere in the pivot table, select Fields, Items, & Sets from the Calculations group, and then select Solve Order, as shown in Figure 5.33.

Figure 5.33
Activate the Solve Order dialog.

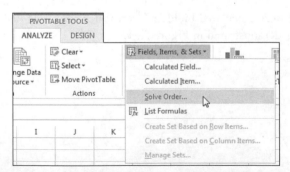

The Solve Order dialog, shown in Figure 5.34, lists all the calculated items that currently exist in the pivot table. The order in which the formulas are listed here is the order in which the pivot table will perform the operations. To make changes to this order, select any of the calculated items you see and then click Move Up, Move Down, or Delete, as appropriate.

Figure 5.34
After you identify the calculated item you are working with, simply move the item up or down to change the solve order. You also have the option of deleting items in this dialog.

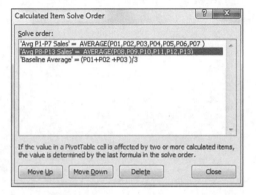

Documenting Formulas

Excel provides a nice little function that lists the calculated fields and calculated items used in a pivot table, along with details on the solve order and formulas. This feature comes in especially handy if you need to quickly determine what calculations are being applied in a pivot table and which fields or items those calculations affect.

To list your pivot table calculations, simply place your cursor anywhere in the pivot table and select Fields, Items, & Sets and then select List Formulas. Excel creates a new tab in your workbook that lists the calculated fields and calculated items in the current pivot table. Figure 5.35 shows an example of a tab created by the List Formulas command.

Figure 5.35
The List Formulas command documents the details of your pivot table calculations quickly and easily.

Calculated Field			
Solve Order	Field	Formula	
Calculated Item			
Solve Order	Item	Formula	
1	'Avg P1-P7 Sales'	= AVERAGE(P01,P02,P03,P04,P05,P06,P07)	
2	'Avg P8-P13 Sales'	= AVERAGE(P08,P09,P10,P11,P12,P13)	
3	'Baseline Average'	=(P01+P02 +P03)/3	
Note:	When a cell is updated by more than one formula,		
	the value is set by the formula with the last solve order.		
	To change formula solve orders,		
	use the Solve Order command on the Pivot Formulas drop down menu.		

5

Next Steps

In Chapter 6, "Using Pivot Charts and Other Visualizations," you will discover the fundamentals of pivot charts and the basics of representing your pivot data graphically. You'll also get a firm understanding of the limitations of pivot charts and alternatives to using pivot charts.

5

Using Pivot Charts and Other Visualizations

What Is a Pivot Chart...Really?

When sharing your analyses with others, you will quickly find that there is no getting around the fact that people want charts. Pivot tables are nice, but they show a lot of pesky numbers that take time to absorb. Charts, on the other hand, enable users to make split-second determinations about what the data is actually revealing. Charts offer instant gratification, allowing users to immediately see relationships, point out differences, and observe trends. The bottom line is that managers today want to absorb data as fast as possible, and nothing delivers that capability faster than a chart. This is where pivot charts come into play. Whereas pivot tables offer the analytical, pivot charts offer the visual.

A common definition of a pivot chart is a graphical representation of the data in a pivot table. Although this definition is technically correct, it somehow misses the mark on what a pivot chart truly does.

When you create a standard chart from data that is not in a pivot table, you feed the chart a range made up of individual cells holding individual pieces of data. Each cell is an individual object with its own piece of data, so your chart treats each cell as an individual data point and thus charts each one separately.

However, the data in a pivot table is part of a larger object. The pieces of data you see inside a pivot table are not individual pieces of data that occupy individual cells. Rather, they are items inside a larger pivot table object that is occupying space on your worksheet.

When you create a chart from a pivot table, you are not feeding it individual pieces of data inside individual cells; you are feeding it the entire pivot table layout. Indeed, a *pivot chart* is a chart that uses a PivotLayout object to view and control the data in a pivot table.

Using the PivotLayout object allows you to interactively add, remove, filter, and refresh data fields inside a pivot chart just like in a pivot table. The result of all this action is a graphical representation of the data you see in a pivot table.

Creating a Pivot Chart

Based on the rather complicated definition just provided, you might get the impression that creating a pivot chart is difficult. The reality is that it's quite a simple task, as you'll see in this section.

The pivot table in Figure 6.1 provides for a simple view of revenue by market. The Business_Segment field in the report filter area lets you parse out revenue by line of business.

Figure 6.1
This basic pivot table shows revenue by market and allows for filtering by line of business.

	A	B
1	Business_Segment (All)	
2		
3	**Row Labels**	**Sum of Sales_Amount**
4	BUFFALO	$450,478
5	CALIFORNIA	$2,254,735
6	CANADA	$776,245
7	CHARLOTTE	$890,522
8	DALLAS	$467,089
9	DENVER	$645,583
10	FLORIDA	$1,450,392
11	KANSASCITY	$574,899
12	MICHIGAN	$678,705
13	NEWORLEANS	$333,454
14	NEWYORK	$873,581
15	PHOENIX	$570,255
16	SEATTLE	$179,827
17	TULSA	$628,405
18	**Grand Total**	**$10,774,172**

Creating a pivot chart from this data would not only allow for an instant view of the performance of each market, but would also permit you to retain the ability to filter by line of business.

To start the process, place your cursor anywhere inside the pivot table and click the Insert tab on the ribbon. On the Insert tab, you can see the Charts group displaying the various types of charts you can create. Here, you can choose the chart type you would like to use for your pivot chart. For this example, click the Column chart icon and select the first 2-D column chart, as shown in Figure 6.2.

Figure 6.2
Select the chart type you want to use.

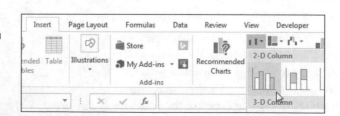

Figure 6.3 shows the chart Excel creates after you choose a chart type.

Figure 6.3
Excel creates your pivot chart on the same sheet as your pivot table.

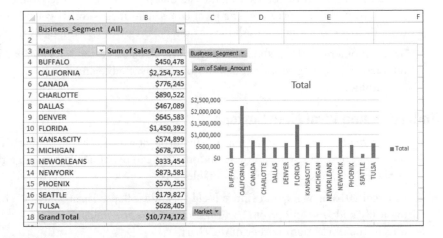

TIP

Notice that pivot charts are now, by default, placed on the same sheet as the source pivot table. If you long for the days when pivot charts were located on their own chart sheets, you are in luck. All you have to do is place your cursor inside a pivot table and then press F11 to create a pivot chart on its own sheet.

You can easily change the location of a pivot chart by right-clicking the chart (outside the plot area) and selecting Move Chart. This activates the Move Chart dialog, in which you can specify the new location.

You now have a chart that is a visual representation of your pivot table. More than that, because the pivot chart is tied to the underlying pivot table, changing the pivot table in any way changes the chart. For example, as Figure 6.4 illustrates, adding the Region field to the pivot table adds a region dimension to your chart.

Figure 6.4
The pivot chart displays the same fields that the underlying pivot table displays.

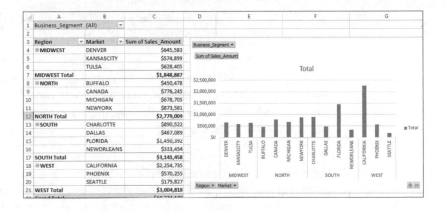

6

NOTE

The pivot chart in Figure 6.4 does not display the subtotals shown in the pivot table. When creating a pivot chart, Excel ignores subtotals and grand totals.

In addition, filtering a business segment not only filters the pivot table, but also the pivot chart. All this behavior comes from the fact that pivot charts use the same pivot cache and pivot layout as their corresponding pivot tables. This means that if you add or remove data from the data source and refresh the pivot table, the pivot chart updates to reflect the changes.

Take a moment to think about the possibilities. You can essentially create a fairly robust interactive reporting tool on the power of one pivot table and one pivot chart—no programming necessary.

Understanding Pivot Field Buttons

In Figure 6.4, notice the gray buttons and drop-downs on the pivot chart. These are called pivot field buttons. By using these buttons, you can dynamically rearrange the chart and apply filters to the underlying pivot table.

In Excel 2016, new Expand Entire Field (+) and Collapse Entire Field (–) buttons are automatically added to any pivot chart that contains nested fields. Figure 6.4 shows these buttons in the lower-right corner of the chart.

Clicking Collapse Entire Field (–) on the chart collapses the data series and aggregates the data points. For example, Figure 6.5 shows the same chart collapsed to the Region level. You can click Expand Entire Field (+) to drill back down to the Market level. These new buttons enable customers to interactively drill down or roll up the data shown in pivot charts.

Figure 6.5
The new Expand Entire Field (+) and Collapse Entire Field (–) buttons allow for dynamic drill-down and grouping of chart series.

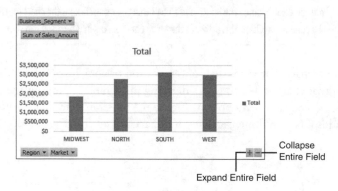

TIP

Keep in mind that pivot field buttons are visible when you print a pivot table. If you aren't too keen on showing the pivot field buttons directly on your pivot charts, you can remove them by clicking your chart and then selecting the Analyze tab. On the Analyze tab, you can use the Field Buttons drop-down to hide some or all of the pivot field buttons.

TIP

Did you know you can also use slicers with pivot charts? Simply click a pivot chart, select the Analyze tab, and then click the Insert Slicer icon to take advantage of all the benefits of slicers with your pivot chart!

NOTE

See "Using Slicers" in Chapter 2, "Creating a Basic Pivot Table," to get a quick refresher on slicers.

CREATING A PIVOT CHART FROM SCRATCH

You don't have to build a pivot table before creating a pivot chart. You can go straight from raw data to a pivot chart. Simply click any single cell in your data source and select the Insert tab. From there, select the PivotChart drop-down and then choose PivotChart. This activates the Create PivotChart dialog. At this point, you go through the same steps you would take if you were building a pivot table.

→   In Chapter 9, "Working with and Analyzing OLAP Data," you will find out how to create pivot charts that are completely decoupled from any pivot table.

Keeping Pivot Chart Rules in Mind

As with other aspects of pivot table technology, pivot charts come with their own set of rules and limitations. The following sections give you a better understanding of the boundaries and restrictions of pivot charts.

Changes in the Underlying Pivot Table Affect a Pivot Chart

The primary rule you should always be cognizant of is that a pivot chart that is based on a pivot table is merely an extension of the pivot table. If you refresh, move a field, add a field, remove a field, hide a data item, show a data item, or apply a filter, the pivot chart reflects your changes.

Placement of Data Fields in a Pivot Table Might Not Be Best Suited for a Pivot Chart

One common mistake people make when using pivot charts is assuming that Excel places the values in the column area of the pivot table in the x-axis of the pivot chart.

For instance, the pivot table in Figure 6.6 is in a format that is easy to read and comprehend. The structure chosen shows Sales_Period in the column area and Region in the row area. This structure works fine in the pivot table view.

Figure 6.6
The placement of the data fields works for a pivot table view.

⬜	A	B	C	D	E	F	G
1	Business_Segment	(All)					
2							
3	Sum of Sales_Amount	Column Labels					
4	Row Labels	P01	P02	P03	P04	P05	P06	P0
5	MIDWEST	$109,498	$207,329	$101,861	$155,431	$159,298	$149,426	$1
6	NORTH	$180,772	$260,507	$183,151	$214,665	$235,369	$221,791	$1
7	SOUTH	$198,415	$334,189	$189,493	$255,558	$283,012	$249,258	$1
8	WEST	$193,180	$314,891	$183,106	$239,843	$248,124	$248,456	$1
9	Grand Total	$681,865	$1,116,916	$657,611	$865,498	$925,802	$868,930	$6

Suppose you decide to create a pivot chart from this pivot table. You would instinctively expect to see fiscal periods across the x-axis and lines of business along the y-axis. However, as you can see in Figure 6.7, the pivot chart comes out with Region on the x-axis and Sales_Period on the y-axis.

Figure 6.7
Creating a pivot chart from your nicely structured pivot table does not yield the results you were expecting.

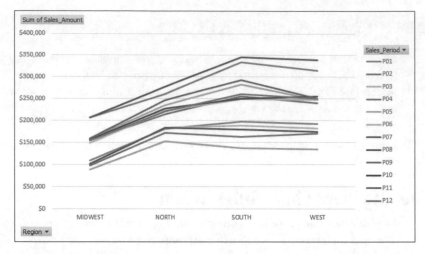

So why does the structure in the pivot table not translate to a clean pivot chart? The answer has to do with the way pivot charts handle the different areas of a pivot table.

In a pivot chart, both the x-axis and y-axis correspond to specific areas in your pivot table:

- **y-axis**—Corresponds to the column area in a pivot table and makes up the y-axis of a pivot chart
- **x-axis**—Corresponds to the row area in a pivot table and makes up the x-axis of a pivot chart

Given this information, look again at the pivot table in Figure 6.6. This structure says that the Sales_Period field will be treated as the y-axis because it is in the column area. Meanwhile, the Region field will be treated as the x-axis because it is in the row area.

Now suppose you were to rearrange the pivot table to show fiscal periods in the row area and lines of business in the column area, as shown in Figure 6.8.

Figure 6.8
This format makes for slightly more difficult reading in a pivot table view but allows a pivot chart to give you the effect you are looking for.

	A	B	C	D	E	F
1	Business_Segment	(All)				
2						
3	Sum of Sales_Amount	Column Labels				
4	Row Labels	MIDWEST	NORTH	SOUTH	WEST	Grand Total
5	P01	$109,498	$180,772	$198,415	$193,180	$681,865
6	P02	$207,329	$260,507	$334,189	$314,891	$1,116,916
7	P03	$101,861	$183,151	$189,493	$183,106	$657,611
8	P04	$155,431	$214,665	$255,558	$239,843	$865,498
9	P05	$159,298	$235,369	$283,012	$248,124	$925,802
10	P06	$149,426	$221,791	$249,258	$248,456	$868,930
11	P07	$101,809	$184,350	$180,146	$174,282	$640,587
12	P08	$207,278	$277,905	$345,842	$339,236	$1,170,262
13	P09	$98,129	$172,271	$163,153	$171,000	$604,552
14	P10	$156,974	$227,469	$251,042	$255,769	$891,253
15	P11	$159,130	$246,435	$293,184	$250,855	$949,605
16	P12	$154,276	$221,242	$261,113	$251,034	$887,665
17	P13	$88,448	$153,083	$137,053	$135,041	$513,625
18	Grand Total	$1,848,887	$2,779,009	$3,141,458	$3,004,818	$10,774,172

6

This arrangement generates the pivot chart shown in Figure 6.9.

Figure 6.9
With the new arrange-
ment in your pivot table,
you get a pivot chart that
makes sense.

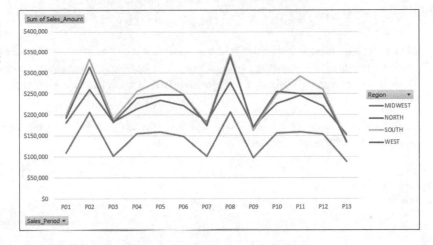

A Few Formatting Limitations Still Exist in Excel 2016

With versions of Excel prior to Excel 2007, many users avoided using pivot charts because of their many formatting limitations. These limitations included the inability to resize or move key components of the pivot chart, the loss of formatting when underlying pivot tables were changed, and the inability to use certain chart types. Because of these limitations, most users viewed pivot charts as being too clunky and impractical to use.

Over the last few versions of Excel, Microsoft introduced substantial improvements to the pivot chart functionality. Today, the pivot charts in Excel 2016 look and behave very much like standard charts. However, a few limitations persist in this version of Excel that you should keep in mind:

■ You still cannot use XY (scatter) charts, bubble charts, and stock charts when creating a pivot chart. This includes the new sunburst and waterfall chart types introduced in Excel 2016.

■ Applied trend lines can be lost when you add or remove fields in the underlying pivot table.

■ The chart titles in the pivot chart cannot be resized.

TIP   Although you cannot resize the chart titles in a pivot chart, you can make the font bigger or smaller to indirectly resize a chart title. Alternatively, you can opt to create your own chart title by simply adding a text box that will serve as the title for your chart. To add a text box, select the Text Box command on the Insert tab and then click on your pivot chart. The resulting text box will be fully customizable to suit your needs.

CASE STUDY: CREATING AN INTERACTIVE REPORT SHOWING REVENUE BY PRODUCT AND TIME PERIOD

You have been asked to provide both region and market managers with an interactive reporting tool that will allow them to easily see revenues across products for a variety of time periods. Your solution needs to give managers the flexibility to filter out a region or market if needed, as well as give managers the ability to dynamically filter the chart for specific periods.

Given the amount of data in your source table and the possibility that this will be a recurring exercise, you decide to use a pivot chart. Start by building the pivot table shown in Figure 6.10.

Figure 6.10
The initial pivot table meets all the data requirements.

	A	B
1		
2	Region	(All)
3	Market	(All)
4		
5	**Product_Description**	**Sum of Sales_Amount**
6	Cleaning & Housekeeping Services	$1,138,593
7	Facility Maintenance and Repair	$2,361,158
8	Fleet Maintenance	$2,627,798
9	Green Plants and Foliage Care	$1,276,783
10	Landscaping/Grounds Care	$1,190,915
11	Predictive Maintenance/Preventative Maintenance	$2,178,925
12	**Grand Total**	**$10,774,172**

Next, place your cursor anywhere inside the pivot table and click Insert. On the Insert tab, you can see the Charts menu displaying the various types of charts you can create. Choose the Column chart icon and select the first 2-D column chart. You immediately see a chart like the one in Figure 6.11.

Figure 6.11
Your raw pivot chart needs some formatting to meet requirements.

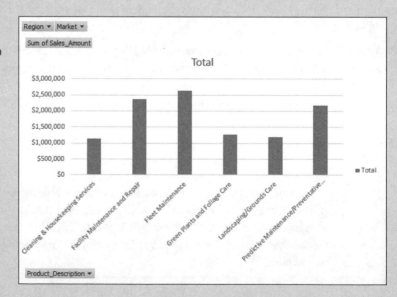

Next, click the newly created chart and select Insert Timeline from the Analyze tab under PivotChart Tools (see Figure 6.12).

Figure 6.12
Insert a Timeline slicer.

Excel opens the Insert Timelines dialog, shown in Figure 6.13, which lists the available date fields in the pivot table. From the list of, select Invoice_Date.

Figure 6.13
Insert a Timeline slicer for Invoice_Date.

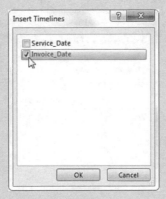

You have created a slicer that aggregates and filters the pivot chart by time-specific periods (see Figure 6.14).

Figure 6.14
A pivot chart and slicer combination makes for a powerful reporting mechanism.

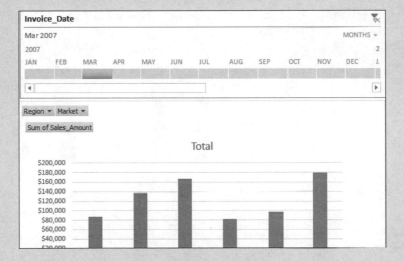

See "Using Slicers" in Chapter 2 to get a quick refresher on Timeline slicers.

At this point, you can remove any superfluous pivot field buttons from the chart. In this case, the only buttons you need are the Region and Market drop-downs, which give your users an interactive way to filter the pivot chart. The other gray buttons you see on the chart are not necessary.

You can remove superfluous pivot field buttons by clicking the chart and selecting the Analyze tab in the ribbon. You can then use the Field Buttons drop-down to choose the field buttons you want to be visible in the chart. In this case, you want only the Report filter field buttons to be visible, so select only that option (see Figure 6.15).

Figure 6.15
Use the Field Buttons drop-down to hide any unwanted pivot field buttons on the chart.

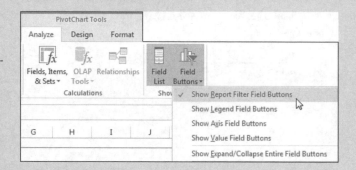

Your final pivot chart should look like the one in Figure 6.16.

Figure 6.16
Your final report meets all the requirements of content and interactivity.

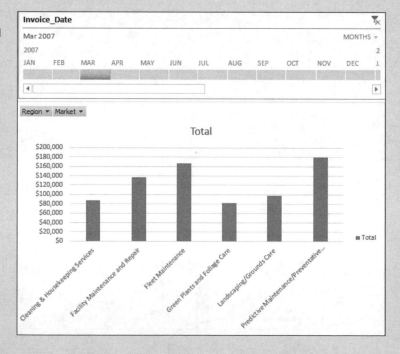

You now have a pivot chart that enables a manager to interactively review revenue by product and time period. This pivot chart also gives anyone using this report the ability to filter by region and market.

Examining Alternatives to Using Pivot Charts

There are generally two reasons you would need an alternative to using pivot charts:

- You do not want the overhead that comes with a pivot chart.
- You want to avoid some of the formatting limitations of pivot charts.

In fact, sometimes you might create a pivot table simply to summarize and shape data in preparation for charting. In these situations, you don't plan on keeping the source data, and you definitely don't want a pivot cache taking up memory and file space.

The example in Figure 6.17 shows a pivot table that summarizes revenue by quarter for each product.

Figure 6.17
This pivot table was created to summarize and chart revenue by quarter for each product.

	A	B	C	D	E	F
1						
2	Sum of Sales_Amount	Invoice_Date				
3	Product_Description	Qtr1	Qtr2	Qtr3	Qtr4	Grand Total
4	Cleaning & Housekeeping Services	$257,218	$290,074	$297,251	$294,049	$1,138,593
5	Facility Maintenance and Repair	$563,799	$621,715	$600,810	$574,834	$2,361,158
6	Fleet Maintenance	$612,496	$691,440	$674,592	$649,269	$2,627,798
7	Green Plants and Foliage Care	$293,194	$325,276	$329,787	$328,527	$1,276,783
8	Landscaping/Grounds Care	$288,797	$310,670	$303,086	$288,363	$1,190,915
9	Predictive Maintenance/Preventative Maintenance	$533,127	$567,391	$552,380	$526,027	$2,178,925
10	Grand Total	$2,548,631	$2,806,566	$2,757,906	$2,661,069	$10,774,172

Keep in mind that you need this pivot table only to summarize and shape data for charting. You don't want to keep the source data, nor do you want to keep the pivot table, with all its overhead.

> **CAUTION**
>
> If you try to create a chart using the data in the pivot table, you'll inevitably create a pivot chart. This effectively means you have all the overhead of the pivot table looming in the background. Of course, this could be problematic if you do not want to share your source data with end users or if you don't want to inundate them with unnecessarily large files.

The good news is, you can use a few simple techniques to create a chart from a pivot table but not end up with a pivot chart. Any one of the following four methods does the trick:

- Turn the pivot table into hard values.
- Delete the underlying pivot table.
- Distribute a picture of the pivot table.
- Use cells linked back to the pivot table as the source data for the chart.

Details about how to use each of these methods are discussed in the next sections.

Method 1: Turn the Pivot Table into Hard Values

After you have created and structured a pivot table appropriately, select the entire pivot table and copy it. Then select Paste Values from the Insert tab, as demonstrated in Figure 6.18. This action essentially deletes your pivot table, leaving you with the last values that were displayed in the pivot table. You can subsequently use these values to create a standard chart.

6

> **NOTE**
>
> This technique effectively disables the dynamic functionality of your pivot chart. That is, the pivot chart becomes a standard chart that cannot be interactively filtered or refreshed. This is also true with · method 2 and method 3, which are outlined in the following sections.

Figure 6.18
The Paste Values functionality is useful when you want to create hard-coded values from pivot tables.

Method 2: Delete the Underlying Pivot Table

If you have already created a pivot chart, you can turn it into a standard chart by simply deleting the underlying pivot table. To do this, select the entire pivot table and press the Delete key on the keyboard. Keep in mind that with this method, unlike with method 1, you are left with none of the values that made up the source data for the chart. In other words, if anyone asks for the data that feeds the chart, you will not have it.

> **TIP**
>
> Here is a handy tip to keep in the back of your mind: If you ever find yourself in a situation where you have a chart but the data source is not available, activate the chart's data table. The data table lets you see the data values that feed each series in the chart.

Method 3: Distribute a Picture of the Pivot Chart

Now, it might seem strange to distribute pictures of a pivot chart, but this is an entirely viable method of distributing your analysis without a lot of overhead. In addition to very small file sizes, you also get the added benefit of controlling what your clients can see.

To use this method, simply copy a pivot chart by right-clicking the chart itself (outside the plot area) and selecting Copy. Then open a new workbook. Right-click anywhere in the new workbook, select Paste Special, and then select the picture format you prefer. A picture of your pivot chart is placed in the new workbook.

> **CAUTION**
>
> If you have pivot field buttons on your chart, they will also show up in the copied picture. This will not only be unsightly but might leave your audience confused because the buttons don't work. Be sure to hide all pivot field buttons before copying a pivot chart as a picture. You can remove them by clicking on your chart and then selecting the Analyze tab. On the Analyze tab, you can use the Field Buttons drop-down to hide all the pivot field buttons.

Method 4: Use Cells Linked Back to the Pivot Table as the Source Data for the Chart

Many Excel users shy away from using pivot charts solely based on the formatting restrictions and issues they encounter when working with them. Often these users give up the functionality of a pivot table to avoid the limitations of pivot charts.

However, if you want to retain key functionality in your pivot table, such as report filters and top 10 ranking, you can link a standard chart to your pivot table without creating a pivot chart.

In the example in Figure 6.19, a pivot table shows the top 10 markets by contracted hours, along with their total revenue. Notice that the report filter area allows you to filter by business segment so you can see the top 10 markets segment.

Figure 6.19
This pivot table allows you to filter by business segment to see the top 10 markets by total contracted hours and revenue.

	A	B	C
1	Business_Segment (All)		
2			
3	**Market**	**Contracted Hours**	**Sales_Amount**
4	CALIFORNIA	33,014	$2,254,735
5	FLORIDA	22,640	$1,450,392
6	CHARLOTTE	14,525	$890,522
7	NEWYORK	14,213	$873,581
8	CANADA	12,103	$776,245
9	MICHIGAN	10,744	$678,705
10	PHOENIX	10,167	$570,255
11	TULSA	9,583	$628,405
12	DENVER	8,641	$645,583
13	KANSASCITY	8,547	$574,899
14	**Grand Total**	**144,177**	**$9,343,323**

Suppose you want to turn this view into an XY scatter chart to be able to point out the relationship between the contracted hours and revenues.

Well, a pivot chart is definitely out because you can't build pivot charts with XY scatter charts. The techniques outlined in methods 1, 2, and 3 are also out because those methods disable the interactivity you need.

So what's the solution? Use the cells around the pivot table to link back to the data you need, and then chart those cells. In other words, you can build a mini data set that feeds your standard chart. This data set links back to the data items in your pivot table, so when your pivot table changes, so does your data set.

Click your cursor in a cell next to your pivot table, as demonstrated in Figure 6.20, and reference the first data item that you need to create the range you will feed to your standard chart.

Now copy the formula you just entered, and paste that formula down and across to create your complete data set. At this point, you should have a data set that looks like the one shown in Figure 6.21.

6

Figure 6.20
Start your linked data set by referencing the first data item you need to capture.

	A	B	C	D	E
1	Business_Segment (All)	▾			
2					
3	**Market**	⊤ Contracted Hours	Sales_Amount		
4	CALIFORNIA	33,014	$2,254,735		=B4
5	FLORIDA	22,640	$1,450,392		
6	CHARLOTTE	14,525	$890,522		
7	NEWYORK	14,213	$873,581		
8	CANADA	12,103	$776,245		
9	MICHIGAN	10,744	$678,705		
10	PHOENIX	10,167	$570,255		
11	TULSA	9,583	$628,405		
12	DENVER	8,641	$645,583		
13	KANSASCITY	8,547	$574,899		
14	**Grand Total**	144,177	$9,343,323		

Figure 6.21
Copy the formula and paste it down and across to create your complete data set.

	A	B	C	D	E	F
1	Business_Segment (All)	▾				
2						
3	**Market**	⊤ Contracted Hours	Sales_Amount		Contracted Hours	Sales_Amount
4	CALIFORNIA	33,014	$2,254,735		33,014	2,254,735
5	FLORIDA	22,640	$1,450,392		22,640	1,450,392
6	CHARLOTTE	14,525	$890,522		14,525	890,522
7	NEWYORK	14,213	$873,581		14,213	873,581
8	CANADA	12,103	$776,245		12,103	776,245
9	MICHIGAN	10,744	$678,705		10,744	678,705
10	PHOENIX	10,167	$570,255		10,167	570,255
11	TULSA	9,583	$628,405		9,583	628,405
12	DENVER	8,641	$645,583		8,641	645,583
13	KANSASCITY	8,547	$574,899		8,547	574,899
14	**Grand Total**	144,177	$9,343,323			

When your linked data set is complete, you can use it to create a standard chart. In this example, you are creating an XY scatter chart with this data. You could never do this with a pivot chart.

Figure 6.22 demonstrates how this solution offers the best of both worlds. You have the ability to filter out a particular business segment using the page field, and you also have all the formatting freedom of a standard chart without any of the issues related to using a pivot chart.

Figure 6.22
This solution allows you to continue using the functionality of your pivot table without any of the formatting limitations you would have with a pivot chart.

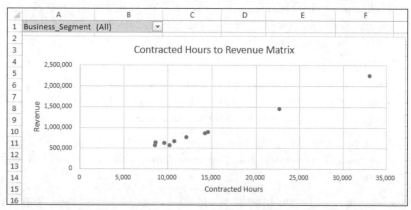

NOTE Another alternative to using pivot charts is to create a Power View dashboard. See Chapter 11, "Dashboarding with Power View and Power Map."

Using Conditional Formatting with Pivot Tables

In the next sections, you'll learn how to leverage the magic combination of pivot tables and conditional formatting to create interactive visualizations that serve as an alternative to pivot charts.

An Example of Using Conditional Formatting

To start the first example, create the pivot table shown in Figure 6.23.

Figure 6.23
Create this pivot table.

	A	B	C
1			
2	Market ▼	Sum of Sales_Amount	Sum of Sales_Amount2
3	BUFFALO	$450,478	450,478
4	CALIFORNIA	$2,254,735	2,254,735
5	CANADA	$776,245	776,245
6	CHARLOTTE	$890,522	890,522
7	DALLAS	$467,089	467,089
8	DENVER	$645,583	645,583
9	FLORIDA	$1,450,392	1,450,392
10	KANSASCITY	$574,899	574,899
11	MICHIGAN	$678,705	678,705
12	NEWORLEANS	$333,454	333,454
13	NEWYORK	$873,581	873,581
14	PHOENIX	$570,255	570,255
15	SEATTLE	$179,827	179,827
16	TULSA	$628,405	628,405
17	Grand Total	$10,774,172	10,774,172

Suppose you want to create a report that enables your managers to see the performance of each sales period graphically. You could build a pivot chart, but you decide to use conditional formatting. In this example, you'll go the easy route and quickly apply some data bars.

Select all the Sum of Sales_Amount2 values in the values area. After you have highlighted the revenue for each Sales_Period, click the Home tab and select Conditional Formatting in the Styles group. Then select Data Bars and select one of the Solid Fill options, as shown in Figure 6.24.

You immediately see data bars in your pivot table, along with the values in the Sum of Sales_Amount2 field. You want to hide the actual value and show only the data bar. To do this, follow these steps:

1. Click the Conditional Formatting drop-down on the Home tab, and select Manage Rules.

2. In the Rules Manager dialog, select the data bar rule you just created and select Edit Rule.

3. Place a check next to Show Bar Only (see Figure 6.25).

6

Figure 6.24
Apply data bars to the values in your pivot table.

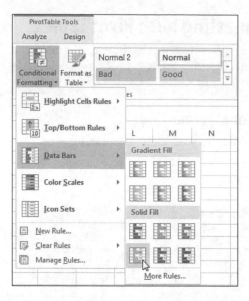

Figure 6.25
Check the Show Bar Only option to get a clean view of just the data bars.

As you can see in Figure 6.26, you now have a set of bars that correspond to the values in your pivot table. This visualization looks like a sideways chart, doesn't it? What's more impressive is that as you filter the markets in the report filter area, the data bars dynamically update to correspond with the data for the selected market.

Figure 6.26
You have applied conditional data bars with just three easy clicks!

	A	B	C
1			
2	**Market**	**Sum of Sales_Amount**	**Sum of Sales_Amount2**
3	BUFFALO	$450,478	
4	CALIFORNIA	$2,254,735	
5	CANADA	$776,245	
6	CHARLOTTE	$890,522	
7	DALLAS	$467,089	
8	DENVER	$645,583	
9	FLORIDA	$1,450,392	
10	KANSASCITY	$574,899	
11	MICHIGAN	$678,705	
12	NEWORLEANS	$333,454	
13	NEWYORK	$873,581	
14	PHOENIX	$570,255	
15	SEATTLE	$179,827	
16	TULSA	$628,405	
17	**Grand Total**	**$10,774,172**	**10,774,172**

Preprogrammed Scenarios for Condition Levels

In the previous example, you did not have to trudge through a dialog to define the condition levels. How can that be? Excel 2016 has a handful of preprogrammed scenarios that you can leverage when you want to spend less time configuring your conditional formatting and more time analyzing your data.

For example, to create the data bars you've just employed, Excel uses a predefined algorithm that takes the largest and smallest values in the selected range and calculates the condition level for each bar.

Other examples of preprogrammed scenarios include the following:

- Top Nth Items
- Top Nth %
- Bottom Nth Items
- Bottom Nth %
- Above Average
- Below Average

As you can see, Excel 2016 makes an effort to offer the conditions that are most commonly used in data analysis.

> **NOTE** To remove the applied conditional formatting, place your cursor inside the pivot table, click the Home tab, and select Conditional Formatting in the Styles group. From there, select Clear Rules and then select Clear Rules from This PivotTable.

Creating Custom Conditional Formatting Rules

It's important to note that you are by no means limited to the preprogrammed scenarios mentioned in the previous section. You can still create your own custom conditions.

To see how this works, you need to begin by creating the pivot table shown in Figure 6.27.

Figure 6.27
This pivot shows Sales_Amount, Contracted_Hours, and a calculated field that calculates Dollars per Hour.

	A	B	C	D
1	Product_Description (All)			
2				
3	Market	Sales_Amount	Contracted Hours	Dollars Per Hour
4	BUFFALO	$450,478	6,864	$65.63
5	CALIFORNIA	$2,254,735	33,014	$68.30
6	CANADA	$776,245	12,103	$64.14
7	CHARLOTTE	$890,522	14,525	$61.31
8	DALLAS	$467,089	6,393	$73.06
9	DENVER	$645,583	8,641	$74.71
10	FLORIDA	$1,450,392	22,640	$64.06
11	KANSASCITY	$574,899	8,547	$67.26
12	MICHIGAN	$678,705	10,744	$63.17
13	NEWORLEANS	$333,454	5,057	$65.94
14	NEWYORK	$873,581	14,213	$61.46
15	PHOENIX	$570,255	10,167	$56.09
16	SEATTLE	$179,827	2,889	$62.25
17	TULSA	$628,405	9,583	$65.57
18	Grand Total	$10,774,172	165,380	$65.15

In this scenario, you want to evaluate the relationship between total revenue and dollars per hour. The idea is that some strategically applied conditional formatting helps identify opportunities for improvement.

Place your cursor in the Sales_Amount column. Click the Home tab and select Conditional Formatting. Then select New Rule. This activates the New Formatting Rule dialog, shown in Figure 6.28. In this dialog, you need to identify the cells where the conditional formatting will be applied, specify the rule type to use, and define the details of the conditional formatting.

First, you must identify the cells where your conditional formatting will be applied. You have three choices:

- **Selected Cells**—This selection applies conditional formatting to only the selected cells.
- **All Cells Showing "Sales_Amount" Values**—This selection applies conditional formatting to all values in the Sales_Amount column, including all subtotals and grand totals. This selection is ideal for use in analyses using averages, percentages, or other calculations where a single conditional formatting rule makes sense for all levels of analysis.
- **All Cells Showing "Sales_Amount" Values for "Market"**—This selection applies conditional formatting to all values in the Sales_Amount column at the Market level only. (It excludes subtotals and grand totals.) This selection is ideal for use in analyses using calculations that make sense only within the context of the level being measured.

Figure 6.28
The New Formatting Rule
dialog.

The words *Sales_Amount* and *Market* are not permanent fixtures of the New Formatting Rule dialog. These words change to reflect the fields in your pivot table. Sales_Amount is used here because the cursor is in that column. Market is used because the active data items in the pivot table are in the Market field.

In this example, the third selection (All Cells Showing "Sales_Amount" Values for "Market") makes the most sense, so click that radio button, as shown in Figure 6.29.

Next, in the Select a Rule Type section, you must specify the rule type you want to use for the conditional format. You can select one of five rule types:

- **Format All Cells Based on Their Values**—This selection enables you to apply conditional formatting based on some comparison of the actual values of the selected range. That is, the values in the selected range are measured against each other. This selection is ideal when you want to identify general anomalies in your data set.

- **Format Only Cells That Contain**—This selection enables you to apply conditional formatting to cells that meet specific criteria you define. Keep in mind that the values in your range are not measured against each other when you use this rule type. This selection is useful when you are comparing your values against a predefined benchmark.

- **Format Only Top or Bottom Ranked Values**—This selection enables you to apply conditional formatting to cells that are ranked in the top or bottom Nth number or percentage of all the values in the range.

6

Figure 6.29
Click the radio button next to All Cells Showing "Sales_Amount" Values for "Market".

- **Format Only Values That Are Above or Below Average**—This selection enables you to apply conditional formatting to values that are mathematically above or below the average of all values in the selected range.

- **Use a Formula to Determine Which Cells to Format**—This selection enables you to specify your own formula and evaluate each value in the selected range against that formula. If the values evaluate to true, the conditional formatting is applied. This selection comes in handy when you are applying conditions based on the results of an advanced formula or mathematical operation.

> **NOTE**
> You can use data bars, color scales, and icon sets only when the selected cells are formatted based on their values. This means that if you want to use data bars, color scales, and icon sets, you must select the Format All Cells Based on Their Values rule type.

In this scenario, you want to identify problem areas using icon sets; therefore, you want to format the cells based on their values, so select Format All Cells Based on Their Values.

Finally, you need to define the details of the conditional formatting in the Edit the Rule Description section. Again, you want to identify problem areas using the slick icon sets that are offered by Excel 2016. Therefore, select Icon Sets from the Format Style drop-down box.

After selecting Icon Sets, select a style appropriate to your analysis. The style selected in Figure 6.30 is ideal in situations in which your pivot tables cannot always be viewed in color.

Figure 6.30
Select Icon Sets from the
Format Style drop-down
box.

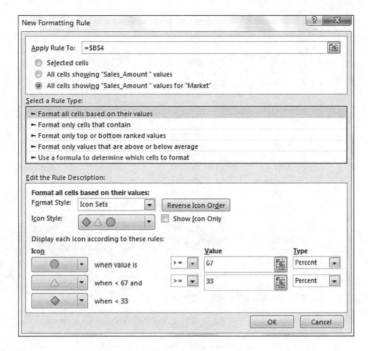

With this configuration, Excel applies the sign icons based on the percentile bands >=67, >=33, and <33. Keep in mind that you can change the actual percentile bands based on your needs. In this scenario, the default percentile bands are sufficient.

Click the OK button to apply the conditional formatting. As you can see in Figure 6.31, you now have icons that enable you to quickly determine where each market falls in relation to other markets in terms of revenue.

Now apply the same conditional formatting to the Dollars per Hour field. When you are done, your pivot table should look like the one shown in Figure 6.32.

Take a moment to analyze what you have here. With this view, a manager can analyze the relationship between total revenue and dollars per hour. For example, the Dallas market manager can see that he is in the bottom percentile for revenue but in the top percentile for dollars per hour. With this information, he immediately sees that his dollars per hour rates might be too high for his market. Conversely, the New York market manager can see that she is in the top percentile for revenue but in the bottom percentile for dollars per hour. This tells her that her dollars per hour rates might be too low for her market.

Remember that this in an interactive report. Each manager can view the same analysis by product by simply filtering the report filter area!

6

Figure 6.31
You have applied your first custom conditional formatting!

	A	B	C	D
1	Product_Description (All) ▼			
2				
3	**Market** ▼	Sales_Amount	Contracted Hours	Dollars Per Hour
4	BUFFALO	◆ $450,478	6,864	$65.63
5	CALIFORNIA	⬤ $2,254,735	33,014	$68.30
6	CANADA	◆ $776,245	12,103	$64.14
7	CHARLOTTE	△ $890,522	14,525	$61.31
8	DALLAS	◆ $467,089	6,393	$73.06
9	DENVER	◆ $645,583	8,641	$74.71
10	FLORIDA	△ $1,450,392	22,640	$64.06
11	KANSASCITY	◆ $574,899	8,547	$67.26
12	MICHIGAN	◆ $678,705	10,744	$63.17
13	NEWORLEANS	◆ $333,454	5,057	$65.94
14	NEWYORK	△ $873,581	14,213	$61.46
15	PHOENIX	◆ $570,255	10,167	$56.09
16	SEATTLE	◆ $179,827	2,889	$62.25
17	TULSA	◆ $628,405	9,583	$65.57
18	**Grand Total**	$10,774,172	165,380	$65.15

Figure 6.32
You have successfully created an interactive visualization.

	A	B	C	D
1	Product_Description (All) ▼			
2				
3	**Market** ▼	Sales_Amount	Contracted Hours	Dollars Per Hour
4	BUFFALO	◆ $450,478	6,864 △	$65.63
5	CALIFORNIA	⬤ $2,254,735	33,014 △	$68.30
6	CANADA	◆ $776,245	12,103 △	$64.14
7	CHARLOTTE	△ $890,522	14,525 ◆	$61.31
8	DALLAS	◆ $467,089	6,393 ⬤	$73.06
9	DENVER	◆ $645,583	8,641 ⬤	$74.71
10	FLORIDA	△ $1,450,392	22,640 △	$64.06
11	KANSASCITY	◆ $574,899	8,547 △	$67.26
12	MICHIGAN	◆ $678,705	10,744 △	$63.17
13	NEWORLEANS	◆ $333,454	5,057 △	$65.94
14	NEWYORK	△ $873,581	14,213 ◆	$61.46
15	PHOENIX	◆ $570,255	10,167 ◆	$56.09
16	SEATTLE	◆ $179,827	2,889 △	$62.25
17	TULSA	◆ $628,405	9,583 △	$65.57
18	**Grand Total**	$10,774,172	165,380	$65.15

Next Steps

In Chapter 7, "Analyzing Disparate Data Sources with Pivot Tables," you will find out how to bring together disparate data sources into one pivot table. You will create a pivot table from multiple data sets and learn the basics of creating pivot tables from other pivot tables.

Analyzing Disparate Data Sources with Pivot Tables

7

Up to this point, you have been working with one local table located in the worksheet within which you are operating. Indeed, it would be wonderful if every data set you came across were neatly packed in one easy-to-use Excel table. Unfortunately, the business of data analysis does not always work out that way.

The reality is that some of the data you encounter will come from disparate data sources—sets of data that are from separate systems, stored in different locations, or saved in a variety of formats. In an Excel environment, disparate data sources generally fall into one of two categories:

- **External data**—External data is exactly what it sounds like—data that is not located in the Excel workbook in which you are operating. Some examples of external data sources are text files, Access tables, SQL Server tables, and other Excel workbooks.

- **Multiple ranges**—Multiple ranges are separate data sets located in the same workbook but separated either by blank cells or by different worksheets. For example, if your workbook has three tables on three different worksheets, each of your data sets covers a range of cells. You are therefore working with multiple ranges.

A pivot table can be an effective tool when you need to summarize data that is not neatly packed into one table. With a pivot table, you can quickly bring together either data found in an external source or data found in multiple tables within your workbook. In this chapter, you'll discover various techniques for working with external data sources and data sets located in multiple ranges within a workbook.

Using the Internal Data Model

Excel 2013 introduced a new in-memory analytics engine called the Data Model. Every workbook has one internal Data Model that enables you to work with and analyze disparate data sources like never before.

The idea behind the Data Model is simple. Let's say you have two tables: a Customers table and an Orders table. The Orders table contains basic information about invoices (customer number, invoice date, and revenue). The Customers table contains information such as customer number, customer name, and state. If you want to analyze revenue by state, you have to join the two tables and aggregate the Revenue field in the Orders table by the State field in the Customers table.

In the past, in order to do this, you would have had to go through a series of gyrations involving using VLOOKUP, SUMIF, or other functions. With the new Data Model, however, you can simply tell Excel how the two tables are related (they both have customer number) and then pull them into the internal Data Model. The Excel Data Model then builds an analytical cube based on that customer number relationship and exposes the data through a pivot table. With the pivot table, you can create the aggregation by state with a few mouse clicks.

➔ The internal Data Model is secretly using the Power Pivot data engine. If you have Excel Pro Plus or higher, you can take the Data Model further. See Chapter 10, "Mashing Up Data with PowerPivot."

Building Out Your First Data Model

Imagine that you have the Transactions table shown in Figure 7.1. On another worksheet, you have the Employees table shown in Figure 7.2.

Figure 7.1
This table shows transactions by employee number.

	A	B	C	D
1	Sales_Rep	Invoice_Date	Sales_Amount	Contracted Hours
2	4416	1/5/2007	111.79	2
3	4416	1/5/2007	111.79	2
4	160006	1/5/2007	112.13	2
5	6444	1/5/2007	112.13	2
6	160006	1/5/2007	145.02	3
7	52661	1/5/2007	196.58	4
8	6444	1/5/2007	204.20	4
9	51552	1/5/2007	225.24	3
10	55662	1/6/2007	86.31	2
11	1336	1/6/2007	86.31	2
12	60224	1/6/2007	86.31	2
13	54564	1/6/2007	86.31	2
14	56146	1/6/2007	89.26	2
15	5412	1/6/2007	90.24	1

7

Figure 7.2
This table provides information on employees: first name, last name, and job title.

⊿	A	B	C	D
1	Employee_Number	Last_Name	First_Name	Job_Title
2	21	SIOCAT	ROBERT	SERVICE REPRESENTATIVE 3
3	42	BREWN	DONNA	SERVICE REPRESENTATIVE 3
4	45	VAN HUILE	KENNETH	SERVICE REPRESENTATIVE 2
5	104	WIBB	MAURICE	SERVICE REPRESENTATIVE 2
6	106	CESTENGIAY	LUC	SERVICE REPRESENTATIVE 2
7	113	TRIDIL	ROCH	SERVICE REPRESENTATIVE 2
8	142	CETE	GUY	SERVICE REPRESENTATIVE 3
9	145	ERSINEILT	MIKE	SERVICE REPRESENTATIVE 2
10	162	GEBLE	MICHAEL	SERVICE REPRESENTATIVE 2
11	165	CERDANAL	ALAIN	SERVICE REPRESENTATIVE 3
12	201	GEIDRIOU	DOMINIC	TEAMLEAD 1

You need to create an analysis that shows sales by job title. This would normally be difficult, given the fact that sales and job title are in two separate tables. But with the new Data Model, you can follow these simple steps:

1. Click inside the Transactions data table and start a new pivot table (by using Insert, Pivot Table on the ribbon).

2. In the Create PivotTable dialog, be sure to place a check next to the Add This Data to the Data Model option (see Figure 7.3).

Figure 7.3
Create a new pivot table from the Transactions table. Make sure you select Add This Data to the Data Model.

3. Click inside the Employees data table and start a new pivot table. Again, be sure to place a check next to the Add This Data to the Data Model option, as demonstrated in Figure 7.4.

7

Figure 7.4
Create a new pivot
table from the Employees
table. Make sure to select
Add This Data to the Data
Model.

> **NOTE**
>
> Notice that in Figures 7.3 and 7.4, the Create PivotTable dialogs are referencing named ranges. That
> is to say, each table was given a specific name. When you're adding data to the Data Model, it's a best
> practice to name your data tables. This way, you can easily recognize your tables in the Data Model. If
> you don't name your tables, the Data Model shows them as Range1, Range2, and so on.
>
> To give a data table a name, simply highlight all the data in the table, select the Formulas tab on the
> ribbon, and then click the Define Name command. In the dialog, enter a name for the table. Repeat for
> all other tables.

4. Once both tables have been added to the Data Model, activate the PivotTable Fields
   list and choose ALL, as shown in Figure 7.5, to see both ranges in the fields list.

Figure 7.5
Select ALL in the
PivotTable Fields list to
see both tables in your
Data Model.

PivotTable Fields   ▾ ✕

ACTIVE   ALL

Choose fields to add to report: ⚙ ▾

Search   🔎

▷ 🎫 Employees

▷ 🎫 Transactions

Drag fields between areas below:

▼ FILTERS   ▥ COLUMNS

≡ ROWS   Σ VALUES

☐ Defer Layout Update   UPDATE

5. Build out your pivot table as normal. In this case, Job_Title goes to the Rows area and Sales_Amount goes to the Values area. As you can see in Figure 7.6, Excel immediately recognizes that you are using two tables from your Data Model and prompts you to create a relationship between them. You can let Excel auto-detect the relationships between your tables, or you can click the Create button. It's best to create relationships yourself to avoid any possibility of Excel getting it wrong, so click the Create button.

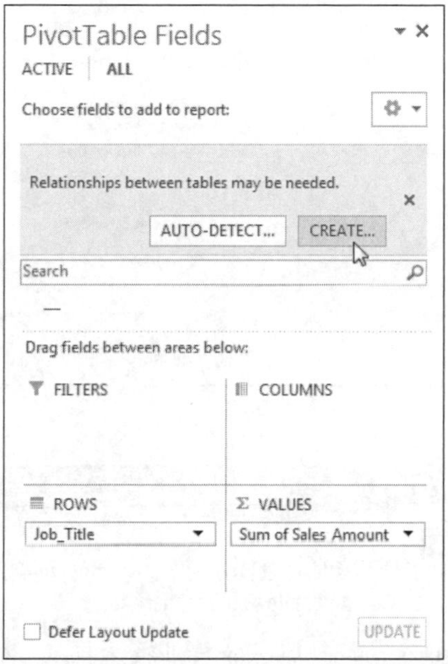

Figure 7.6
When Excel prompts you, choose to create the relationship between the two tables.

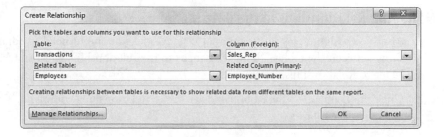

6. Excel activates the Create Relationship dialog shown in Figure 7.7. Here, you select the tables and fields that define the relationship. In Figure 7.7, you can see that the Transactions table has a Sales_Rep field. It is related to the Employees table via the Employee_Number field.

Figure 7.7
Build the appropriate relationship by using the Table and Column drop-downs.

7

After you create the relationship, you have a single pivot table that effectively uses data from both tables to create the analysis you need. Figure 7.8 illustrates that using the Excel Data Model, you have achieved the goal of showing sales by job title.

Figure 7.8
You have achieved your goal of showing sales by job title.

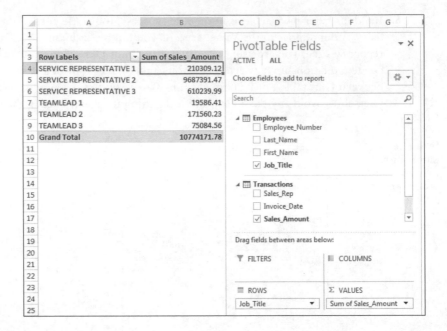

THE IMPORTANCE OF PRIMARY KEYS

In Figure 7.7, the lower-right drop-down is called Related Column (Primary). The term *Primary* in this case means that the internal Data Model uses this field from the associated table as the primary key.

A *primary key* is a field that contains only unique non-null values (no duplicates or blanks). Primary key fields are necessary in the Data Model to prevent aggregation errors and duplications. Every relationship you create must have a field designated as the primary key.

In the scenario in Figure 7.7, the Employees table must have all unique values in the Employee_Number field, with no blanks or null values. This is the only way Excel can ensure data integrity when joining multiple tables.

Managing Relationships in the Data Model

After you assign tables to the internal Data Model, you might need to adjust the relationships between the tables. To make changes to the relationships in a Data Model, activate the Manage Relationships dialog.

Click the Data tab in the ribbon and select the Relationships command. The dialog shown in Figure 7.9 appears.

7

Figure 7.9
The Manage Relationships dialog enables you to make changes to the relationships in the Data Model.

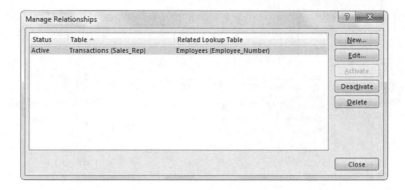

The Manage Relationships dialog offers the following buttons:

- **New**—Create a new relationship between two tables in the Data Model.
- **Edit**—Alter the selected relationship.
- **Activate**—Enforce the selected relationship; that is, tell Excel to consider the relationship when aggregating and analyzing the data in the Data Model.
- **Deactivate**—Turn off the selected relationship; that is, tell Excel to ignore the relationship when aggregating and analyzing the data in the Data Model.
- **Delete**—Remove the selected relationship.

Adding a New Table to the Data Model

You can add a new table to the Data Model in one of two ways. The easiest way is to simply create a pivot table from the new table and then choose the Add This Data to the Data Model option. Excel adds your table to the Data Model and produces a pivot table. After your table has been added, you can open the Manage Relationships dialog and create the needed relationship.

The second and more flexible method is to manually define a table and add it to the Data Model. Here's how:

1. Place your cursor inside a data table and select Insert Table. The Create Table dialog, shown in Figure 7.10, appears.
2. In the Create Table dialog, specify the range for your data. Excel turns that range into a defined table that the internal Data Model can recognize.

Figure 7.10
Convert your range into a defined table.

3. On the Table Tools Design tab, change the Table Name field (in the Properties group) to something appropriate that's easy to remember (see Figure 7.11).

Figure 7.11
Give your newly created table a friendly name.

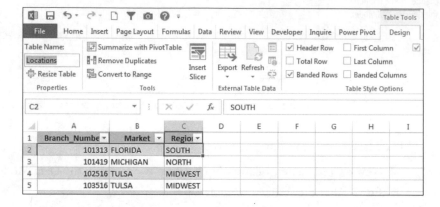

4. Go to the Data tab in the ribbon and select Connections to open the Workbook Connections dialog, shown in Figure 7.12. Click the drop-down next to Add and choose the Add to the Data Model option.

Figure 7.12
Open the Workbook Connections dialog and select Add to the Data Model.

5. In the Existing Connections dialog that appears (see Figure 7.13), select the Tables tab. Then find and select your newly created table. Click the Open button to add the table to the Data Model.

7

Figure 7.13
Select your newly created table and click the Open button.

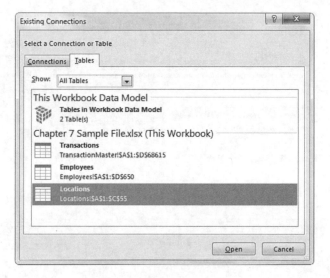

At this point, all pivot tables built on the Data Model are updated to reflect the new table. Be sure to open the Manage Relationships dialog and create the needed relationship.

CAUTION

Be aware that every table you add to the Data Model is essentially stored with the workbook, effectively increasing the size of your Excel file. Read more about the size limitations of the Excel Data Model later in the chapter.

Removing a Table from the Data Model

You might find that you want to remove a table or data source altogether from the Data Model. To do so, click the Data tab in the ribbon and then click Connections. The Workbook Connections dialog, shown in Figure 7.14, opens.

Click the table you want to remove from the Data Model (Employees, in this case), and then click the Remove button.

7

Figure 7.14
Use the Workbook Connections dialog to remove any table from the internal Data Model.

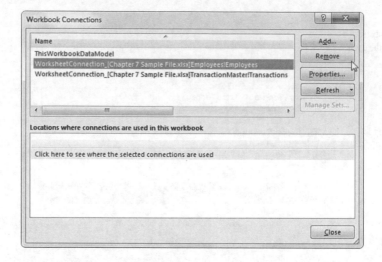

Creating a New Pivot Table Using the Data Model

There might be instances when you want to create a pivot table from scratch using the existing internal Data Model as the source data. Here are the steps to do so:

1. Activate the Create PivotTable dialog by clicking Insert, PivotTable. Click the Use an External Data Source option (see Figure 7.15). Then click the Choose Connection button.

Figure 7.15
Open the Create PivotTable dialog and choose the external data source option.

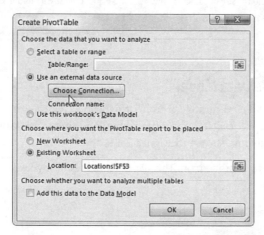

2. In the Existing Connections dialog that appears (see Figure 7.16), select the Tables tab. Then select Tables in Workbook Data Model and click the Open button.

Figure 7.16
Use the Existing
Connections dialog to
select the internal Data
Model as the data source
for the pivot table.

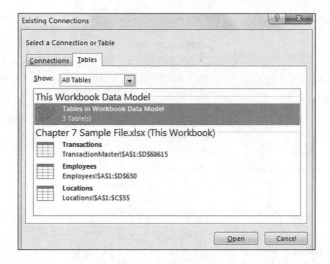

3. When Excel takes you back to the Create PivotTable dialog, click the OK button to create the pivot table. If all goes well, the PivotTable Fields list now shows all the tables that are included in the internal Data Model (see Figure 7.17).

Figure 7.17
Your newly created pivot
table shows all the tables
in the internal Data
Model.

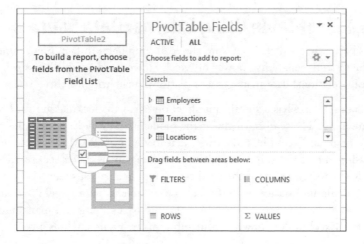

Limitations of the Internal Data Model

As with everything else in Excel, the internal Data Model does have limitations. Table 7.1 highlights the maximum and configurable limits for the Excel Data Model.

7

Table 7.1   Data Model Limitations

Object	Specification
Data Model size	In 32-bit environments, Excel workbooks are subject to a 2GB limit. This includes the in-memory space shared by Excel, the internal Data Model, and add-ins that run in the same process. In 64-bit environments, there are no hard limits on file size. Workbook size is limited only by available memory and system resources.
Number of tables in the Data Model	There are no hard limits on the count of tables. However, all tables in the Data Model cannot cumulatively exceed 2,147,483,647 bytes.
Number of rows in each table in the Data Model	The limit is 1,999,999,997 rows.
Number of columns and calculated columns in each table in the Data Model	The limit is 2,147,483,647 bytes.
Number of distinct values in a column	The limit is 1,999,999,997 values.
Characters in a column name	The limit is 100 characters.
String length in each field	The limit is 536,870,912 bytes (512MB), which is equivalent to 268,435,456 Unicode characters (256 mega-characters).

Building a Pivot Table Using External Data Sources

Excel is certainly good at processing and analyzing data. In fact, pivot tables themselves are a testament to the analytical power of Excel. However, despite all its strengths, Excel makes for a poor relational data management platform, primarily for three reasons:

■ A data set's size has a significant effect on performance, making for less efficient data crunching. The reason for this is the fundamental way Excel handles memory. When you open an Excel file, the entire file is loaded into RAM to ensure quick data processing and access. The drawback to this behavior is that Excel requires a great deal of RAM to process even the smallest change in a spreadsheet (and typically gives you a "Calculating" indicator in the status bar). So although Excel 2016 offers more than 1 million rows and more than 16,000 columns, creating and managing large data sets causes Excel to slow down considerably, making data analysis a painful endeavor.

■ The lack of a relational data structure forces the use of flat tables that promote redundant data. This also increases the chance for errors.

■ There is no way to index data fields in Excel to optimize performance when you're attempting to retrieve large amounts of data.

In smart organizations, the task of data management is not performed by Excel; rather, it is primarily performed by relational database systems such as Microsoft Access and SQL Server. These databases are used to store millions of records that can be rapidly searched and retrieved. The effect of this separation in tasks is that you have a data management layer (your database) and a presentation layer (Excel). The trick is to find the best way to get information from your data management layer to your presentation layer for use by your pivot table.

Managing your data is the general idea behind building a pivot table using an external data source. Building pivot tables from external systems enables you to leverage environments that are better suited to data management. This means you can let Excel do what it does best: analyze and create a presentation layer for your data. The following sections walk you through several techniques for building pivot tables using external data.

Building a Pivot Table with Microsoft Access Data

Often Access is used to manage a series of tables that interact with each other, such as a Customers table, an Orders table, and an Invoices table. Managing data in Access provides the benefit of a relational database where you can ensure data integrity, prevent redundancy, and easily generate data sets via queries.

Most Excel users use an Access query to create a subset of data and then import that data into Excel. From there, the data can be analyzed with pivot tables. The problem with this method is that it forces the Excel workbook to hold two copies of the imported data sets: one on the spreadsheet and one in the pivot cache. Holding two copies obviously causes the workbook to be twice as big as it needs to be, and it introduces the possibility of performance issues.

Excel 2016 offers a surprisingly easy way to use your Access data without creating two copies of it. To see how easy it is, open Excel and start a new workbook. Then click the Data tab and look for the group called Get External Data. Then click the From Access selection, as shown in Figure 7.18.

Figure 7.18
Click the From Access button to get data from a Access database.

Clicking the From Access button activates a dialog asking you to select the database you want to work with. Select your database.

> **TIP**
> The sample database used in this chapter is available for download from www.mrexcel.com/pivotbookdata2016.html.

After your database has been selected, the dialog shown in Figure 7.19 appears. This dialog lists all the tables and queries available. In this example, select the query called Sales_By_Employee and click the OK button.

Figure 7.19
Select the table or query you want to analyze.

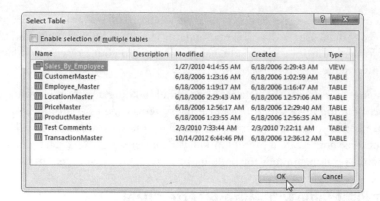

In Figure 7.19, notice that the Select Table dialog contains a column called Type. There are two types of Access objects you can work with: views and tables. View indicates that the data set listed is an Access query, and Table indicates that the data set is an Access table.

In this example, notice that Sales_By_Employee is actually an Access query. This means that you import the results of the query. This is true interaction at work: Access does all the back-end data management and aggregation, and Excel handles the analysis and presentation!

Next, you see the Import Data dialog, where you select the format in which you want to import the data. As you can see in Figure 7.20, you have the option of importing the data as a table, as a pivot table, or as a pivot table with an accompanying pivot chart. You also have the option to tell Excel where to place the data.

Select the radio button next to PivotTable Report, and click the OK button.

Figure 7.20
Select the radio button next to PivotTable Report.

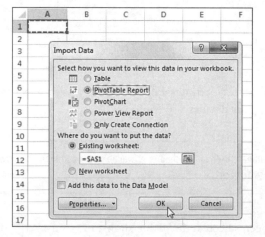

At this point, you should see the PivotTable Fields list shown in Figure 7.21. From here, you can use this pivot table just as you normally would.

The wonderful thing about this technique is that you can refresh the data simply by refreshing the pivot table. When you refresh, Excel takes a new snapshot of the data source and updates the pivot cache.

Figure 7.21
Your pivot table is ready to use.

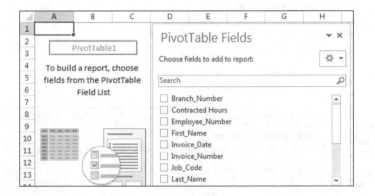

CAUTION

If you create a pivot table that uses an Access database as its source, you can refresh that pivot table only if the table or view is available. That is to say, deleting, moving, or renaming the database used to create the pivot table destroys the link to the external data set, thus destroying your ability to refresh the data. Deleting or renaming the source table or query has the same effect.

Following that reasoning, any clients using your linked pivot table cannot refresh the pivot table unless the source is available to them. If you need your clients to be able to refresh, you might want to make the data source available via a shared network directory.

Building a Pivot Table with SQL Server Data

In the spirit of collaboration, Excel 2016 vastly improves your ability to connect to transactional databases such as SQL Server. With the connection functionality found in Excel, creating a pivot table from SQL Server data is as easy as ever.

Start on the Data tab and select From Other Sources to see the drop-down menu shown in Figure 7.22. Then select From SQL Server.

Figure 7.22
From the drop-down menu, select From SQL Server.

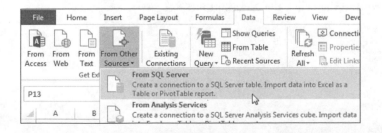

7

Selecting this option activates the Data Connection Wizard, as shown in Figure 7.23. The idea here is to configure your connection settings so Excel can establish a link to the server.

> **NOTE** There is no sample file for this example. The essence of this demonstration is the interaction between Excel and a SQL server data source. The actions you take to connect to your particular database are the same as demonstrated here.

You need to provide Excel with some authentication information. As you can see in Figure 7.23, you enter the name of your server as well as your username and password.

Figure 7.23
Enter your authentication information and click the Next button.

> **NOTE** If you are typically authenticated via Windows Authentication, you simply select the Use Windows Authentication option.

Next, you select the database with which you are working from a drop-down menu containing all available databases on the specified server. As you can see in Figure 7.24, a database called AdventureWorks2012 has been selected in the drop-down box. Selecting this database causes all the tables and views in it to be exposed in the list of objects below the drop-down menu. All that is left to do in this dialog is to choose the table or view you want to analyze and then click the Next button.

Figure 7.24
Specify your database and then choose the table or view you want to analyze.

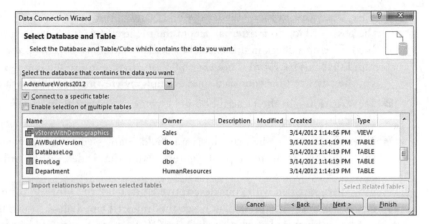

The next screen in the wizard, shown in Figure 7.25, enables you to enter some descriptive information about the connection you've just created.

Figure 7.25
Enter descriptive information for your connection.

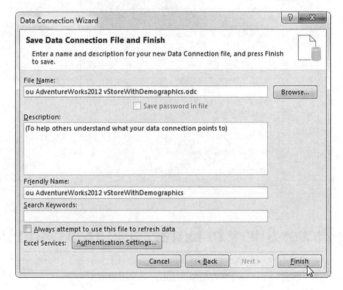

> **NOTE**
> All the fields in the dialog shown in Figure 7.25 are optional edits only. That is, if you bypass this screen without editing anything, your connection works fine.

Here are the fields you'll use most often:

- **File Name**—In the File Name input box, you can change the filename of the .odc (Office Data Connection) file generated to store the configuration information for the link you just created.

■ **Save Password in File**—Under the File Name input box, you have the option of saving the password for your external data in the file itself (via the Save Password in File check box). Placing a check in this check box actually enters your password in the file. Keep in mind that this password is not encrypted, so anyone interested enough could potentially get the password for your data source simply by viewing your file with a text editor.

■ **Description**—In the Description field, you can enter a plain description of what this particular data connection does.

■ **Friendly Name**—The Friendly Name field enables you to specify your own name for the external source. You typically enter a name that is descriptive and easy to read.

When you are satisfied with your descriptive edits, click the Finish button to finalize your connection settings. You immediately see the Import Data dialog, shown in Figure 7.26. In it you select a pivot table and then click the OK button to start building your pivot table.

Figure 7.26
When your connection is finalized, you can start building your pivot table.

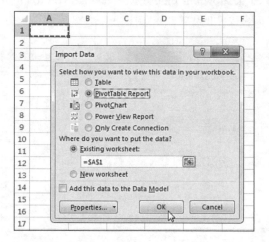

Leveraging Power Query to Extract and Transform Data

Every day, millions of Excel users manually pull data from some source location, manipulate that data, and integrate it into their pivot table reporting.

This process of extracting, manipulating, and integrating data is called ETL. ETL refers to the three separate functions typically required to integrate disparate data sources: extraction, transformation, and loading. The extraction function involves reading data from a specified source and extracting a desired subset of data. The transformation function involves cleaning, shaping, and aggregating data to convert it to the desired structure. The loading function involves actually importing or using the resulting data.

In an attempt to empower Excel analysts to develop robust and reusable ETL processes, Microsoft created Power Query. Power Query enhances the ETL experience by offering an intuitive mechanism to extract data from a wide variety of sources, perform complex transformations on that data, and then load the data into a workbook or the internal Data Model.

7

In the following sections, you'll see how Power Query works and discover some of the innovative ways you can use it to help save time and automate the steps for importing clean data into your pivot table reporting models.

POWER QUERY: NO LONGER AN ADD-IN

In Excel 2016, Power Query is not an add-in. It's a native feature of Excel, just like charts and pivot tables are native features.

You may have previously installed the Power Query add-in when you were working with Excel 2010 or Excel 2013. Indeed, Microsoft still offers the Power Query add-in for previous versions of Excel. Simply enter the search term "Excel Power Query Add-in" into your favorite search engine to find the free Excel 2010 and 2013 installation packages.

Again, don't expect to find an Excel 2016 version of the Power Query add-in, as it's already built into Excel.

Power Query Basics

Although Power Query is relatively intuitive, it's worth taking to the time to walk through a basic scenario to understand its high-level features. To start this basic look at Power Query, you need to import Microsoft Corporation stock prices from the past 30 days by using Yahoo Finance. For this scenario, you need to perform a web query to pull the data needed from Yahoo Finance. As shown in the following example, the Get & Transform group of the Data tab contains all the commands you need to start this query.

To start your query, follow these steps:

1. Select the New Query command on the Data tab and then select From Other Sources, From Web, as shown in Figure 7.27.

Figure 7.27
Starting a Power Query web query.

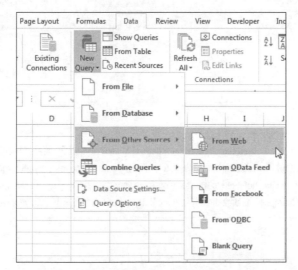

2. In the dialog box that appears (see Figure 7.28), enter in the URL for the data you need—in this case, http://finance.yahoo.com/q/hp?s=MSFT.

Figure 7.28
Enter the target URL containing the data you need.

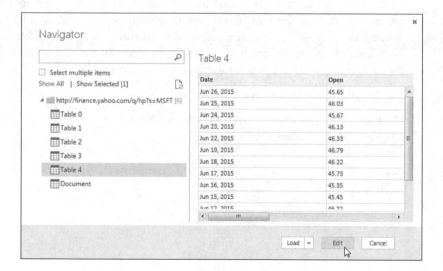

From Web

Enter a Web page URL.

URL

http://finance.yahoo.com/q/hp?s=MSFT+Historical+Prices

OK   Cancel

3. After a bit of gyrating, the Navigator pane shown in Figure 7.29 appears. Here, you select the data source you want extracted. You can click on each table to see a preview of the data. In this case, Table 4 holds the historical stock data you need, so click on Table 4 and then click the Edit button.

Figure 7.29
Select the correct data source and then click the Edit button.

Navigator

☐ Select multiple items
Show All | Show Selected [1]

▲ ▦ http://finance.yahoo.com/q/hp?s=MSFT [6]
  ▦ Table 0
  ▦ Table 1
  ▦ Table 2
  ▦ Table 3
  ▦ Table 4
  ▦ Document

Table 4

Date	Open
Jun 26, 2015	45.65
Jun 25, 2015	46.03
Jun 24, 2015	45.67
Jun 23, 2015	46.13
Jun 22, 2015	46.33
Jun 19, 2015	46.79
Jun 18, 2015	46.22
Jun 17, 2015	45.73
Jun 16, 2015	45.35
Jun 15, 2015	45.45
Jun 12, 2015	46.22

Load ▾   Edit   Cancel

NOTE You may have noticed that the Navigator pane shown in Figure 7.29 offers a Load button (next to the Edit button). The Load button allows you to skip any editing and import your targeted data as-is. If you are sure you will not need to transform or shape your data in any way, you can opt to click the Load button to import the data directly into the Data Model or a spreadsheet in your workbook.

> **CAUTION**
>
> Excel has another From Web command button on the Data tab under the Get External Data group. This unfortunate duplicate command is actually the legacy web scraping capability found in all Excel versions going back to Excel 2000.
>
> The Power Query version of the From Web command (found under New Query, From Other Sources, From Web) goes beyond simple web scraping. Power Query is able to pull data from advanced web pages and is able to manipulate the data. Make sure you are using the correct feature when pulling data from the Web.

When you click the Edit button, Power Query activates a new Query Editor window, which contains its own Ribbon and a preview pane that shows a preview of the data (see Figure 7.30). Here, you can apply certain actions to shape, clean, and transform the data before importing.

Figure 7.30
The Query Editor window allows you to shape, clean, and transform data.

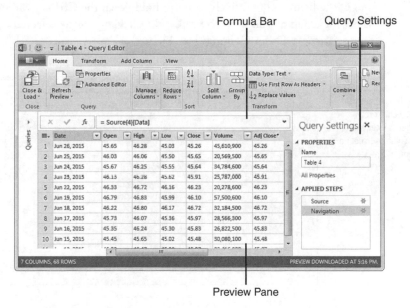

Formula Bar   Query Settings

Preview Pane

The idea is to work with each column shown in the Query Editor, applying the necessary actions that will give you the data and structure you need. You'll dive deeper into column actions later in this chapter. For now, you need to continue toward the goal of getting the last 30 days of stock prices for Microsoft Corporation.

4. Right-click the Date field to see the available column actions, as shown in Figure 7.31. Select Change Type and then Date to ensure that the Date field is formatted as a proper date.

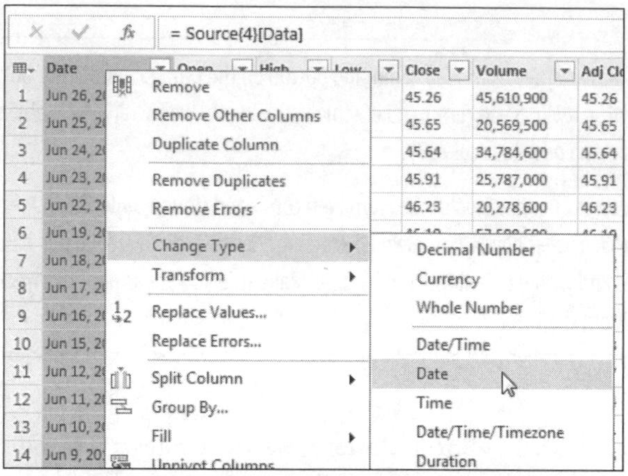

Figure 7.31
Right-click the Date column and choose to change the data type to a date format.

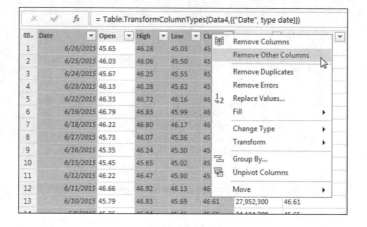

5. Remove all the columns you do not need by right-clicking each one and clicking Remove. (Besides the Date field, the only other columns you need are the High, Low, and Close fields.) Alternatively, you can hold down the Ctrl key on your keyboard, select the columns you want to keep, right-click any of the selected columns, and then choose Remove Other Columns (see Figure 7.32).

Figure 7.32
Select the columns you do not want to keep and then select Remove Other Columns to get rid of them.

6. Ensure that the High, Low, and Close fields are formatted as proper numbers. To do this, hold down the Ctrl key on your keyboard, select the three columns, right-click, and then select Change Type, Decimal Number. After you do this, you may notice that some of the rows show the word Error. These are rows that contained text values that could not be converted.

7. Remove the Error rows by selecting Remove Errors from the Table Actions list (next to the Date field), as shown in Figure 7.33.

Figure 7.33
You can click the Table Actions icon to select actions (such as Remove Errors) that you want applied to the entire data table.

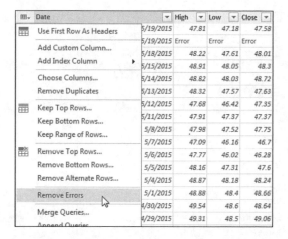

8. Once all the errors are removed, add a Week Of field that displays the week each date in the table belongs to. To do this, right-click the Date field and select the Duplicate Column option. A new column is added to the preview. Right-click the newly added column, select the Rename option, and then rename the column Week Of.

9. Select the Transform tab on the Power Query ribbon and then choose Date, Week, Start of the Week, as shown in Figure 7.34. Excel transforms the date to display the start of the week for a given date.

Figure 7.34
The Power Query ribbon can be used to apply transformation actions such as displaying the start of the week for a given date.

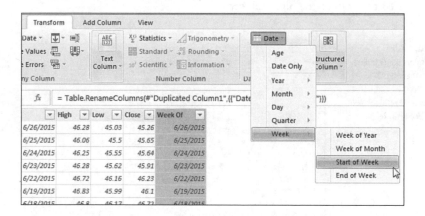

10. When you've finished configuring your Power Query feed, save and output the results. To do this, click the Close & Load drop-down found on the Home tab of the Power Query ribbon to reveal the two options shown in Figure 7.35. The Close & Load option saves your query and outputs the results to a new worksheet in your workbook as an Excel table. The Close & Load To option activates the Load To dialog box, where you can choose to output the results to a specific worksheet or to the internal Data Model. Alternatively, you can choose to save the query as a query connection only, which means you will be able to use the query in various in-memory processes without needing to actually output the results anywhere. Choose to output your results as a table on a new worksheet.

7

Figure 7.35
The Load To dialog box gives you more control over how the results of queries are used.

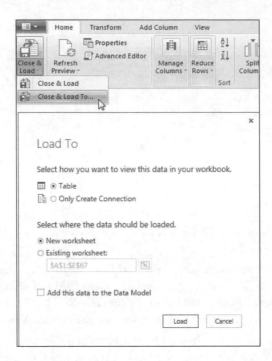

At this point, you will have a table similar to the one shown in Figure 7.36, which can be used to produce the pivot table you need.

Figure 7.36
Your final query pulled from the Internet—transformed, put into an Excel table, and ready to use in a pivot table.

	A	B	C	D	E
1	Date	High	Low	Close	Week Of
2	6/26/2015	46.28	45.03	45.26	6/21/2015
3	6/25/2015	46.06	45.5	45.65	6/21/2015
4	6/24/2015	46.25	45.55	45.64	6/21/2015
5	6/23/2015	46.28	45.62	45.91	6/21/2015
6	6/22/2015	46.72	46.16	46.23	6/21/2015
7	6/19/2015	46.83	45.99	46.1	6/14/2015
8	6/18/2015	46.8	46.17	46.72	6/14/2015
9	6/17/2015	46.07	45.36	45.97	6/14/2015
10	6/16/2015	46.24	45.3	45.83	6/14/2015
11	6/15/2015	45.65	45.02	45.48	6/14/2015
12	6/12/2015	46.47	45.9	45.97	6/7/2015
13	6/11/2015	46.92	46.13	46.44	6/7/2015
14	6/10/2015	46.83	45.69	46.61	6/7/2015
15	6/9/2015	45.94	45.46	45.65	6/7/2015

Take a moment to appreciate what Power Query allowed you to do just now. With a few clicks, you searched the Internet, found some base data, shaped the data to keep only the columns you needed, and even manipulated that data to add an extra Week Of dimension to the base data. This is what Power Query is about: enabling you to easily extract, filter, and reshape data without the need for any programmatic coding skills.

Understanding Query Steps

Power Query uses its own formula language (known as the "M" language) to codify your queries. As with macro recording, each action you take when working with Power Query results in a line of code being written into a query step. Query steps are embedded M code that allow your actions to be repeated each time you refresh your Power Query data.

You can see the query steps for your queries by activating the Query Settings pane. Simply click the Query Settings command on the View tab of the Query Editor ribbon. You can also place a check in the Formula Bar option to enhance your analysis of each step with a formula bar that displays the syntax for the given step.

The Query Settings pane appears to the right of the preview pane, as shown in Figure 7.37. The formula bar is located directly above the preview pane.

Figure 7.37
Query steps can be viewed and managed in the Applied Steps section of the Query Settings pane.

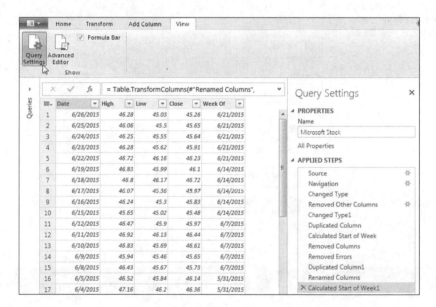

Each query step represents an action you took to get to a data table. You can click on any step to see the underlying M code in the Power Query formula bar. For example, clicking the step called Removed Errors reveals the code for that step in the formula bar.

> **NOTE**
> When you click on a query step, the data shown in the preview pane is a preview of what the data looked like up to and including the step you clicked. For example, in Figure 7.37, clicking the step before the Removed Other Columns step lets you see what the data looked like before you removed the non essential columns.

7

You can right-click on any step to see a menu of options for managing your query steps. Figure 7.38 illustrates the following options:

- **Edit Settings**—Edit the arguments or parameters that defines the selected step.
- **Rename**—Give the selected step a meaningful name.
- **Delete**—Remove the selected step. Be aware that removing a step can cause errors if subsequent steps depend on the deleted step.
- **Delete Until End**—Remove the selected step and all following steps.
- **Move Up**—Move the selected step up in the order of steps.
- **Move Down**—Move the selected step down in the order of steps.

Figure 7.38
Right-click on any query step to edit, rename, delete, or move the step.

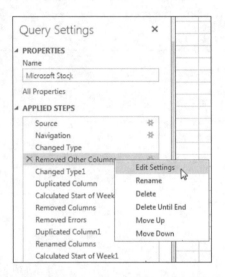

VIEWING THE ADVANCED QUERY EDITOR

Power Query gives you the option of viewing and editing a query's embedded M code directly. While in the Query Editor window, click the View tab of the ribbon and select Advanced Editor. The Advanced Editor dialog box is little more than a space for you to type your own M code. Advanced users can use the M language to extend the capabilities of Power Query by directly coding their own steps in the Advanced Editor. The M language is a fairly robust topic that falls outside the scope of this book.

If you're interested in learning more about M and coding your own steps, start with the M language specification guide by Microsoft. To get it, simply enter "Microsoft Power Query Formula Language Specification" into your favorite search engine.

Refreshing Power Query Data

It's important to note that Power Query data is not in any way connected to the source data used to extract it. A Power Query data table is merely a snapshot. In other words, as the source data changes, Power Query will not automatically keep up with the changes; you need to intentionally refresh your query.

If you chose to load your Power Query results to an Excel table in the existing workbook, you can manually refresh by right-clicking on the table and selecting the Refresh option.

If you chose to load your Power Query data to the internal Data Model, you need to open the Power Pivot window, select your Power Query data, and then click the Refresh command on the Home tab of the Power Query window.

To get a bit more automated with the refreshing of your queries, you can configure your data sources to automatically refresh your Power Query data. To do so, follow these steps:

1. Go to the Data tab in the Excel ribbon and select the Connections command. The Workbook Connections dialog box appears.

2. Select the Power Query data connection you want to refresh, and then click the Properties button.

3. With the Properties dialog box open, select the Usage tab.

4. Set the options to refresh the chosen data connection:

   ■ **Refresh Every X Minutes**—Placing a check next to this option tells Excel to automatically refresh the chosen data every a specified number of minutes. Excel will refresh all tables associated with that connection.

   ■ **Refresh Data When Opening the File**—Placing a check next to this option tells Excel to automatically refresh the chosen data connection upon opening the workbook. Excel will refresh all tables associated with that connection as soon as the workbook is opened.

These refresh options are useful when you want to ensure that your customers are working with the latest data. Of course, setting these options does not preclude the ability manually refresh the data using the Refresh command on the Home tab.

Managing Existing Queries

As you add various queries to a workbook, you will need a way to manage them. Excel accommodates this need by offering the Workbook Queries pane, which enables you to edit, duplicate, refresh, and generally manage all the existing queries in the workbook. Activate the Workbook Queries pane by selecting the Show Queries command on the Data tab of the Excel ribbon.

You need to find the query you want to work with and then right-click it to take any one of these actions (see Figure 7.39):

7

Figure 7.39
Right-click any query in the Workbook Queries pane to see the available management options.

- **Edit**—Open the Query Editor, where you can modify the query steps.
- **Delete**—Delete the selected query.
- **Refresh**—Refresh the data in the selected query.
- **Load To**—Activate the Load To dialog box, where you can redefine where the selected query's results are used.
- **Duplicate**—Create a copy of the query.
- **Reference**—Create a new query that references the output of the original query.
- **Merge**—Merge the selected query with another query in the workbook by matching specified columns.
- **Append**—Append the results of another query in the workbook to the selected query.
- **Send to Data Catalog**—Publish and share the selected query via a Power BI server that your IT department sets up and manages.
- **Move to Group**—Move the selected query into a logical group you create for better organization.
- **Move Up**—Move the selected query up in the Workbook Queries pane.

- **Move Down**—Move the selected query down in the Workbook Queries pane.
- **Show the Peek**—Show a preview of the query results for the selected query.
- **Properties**—Rename the query and add a friendly description.

The Workbook Queries pane is especially useful when your workbook contains several queries. Think of it as a kind of table of contents that allows you to easily find and interact with the queries in your workbook.

Understanding Column-Level Actions

Right-clicking a column in the Query Editor activates a context menu that shows a full list of the actions you can take. You can also apply certain actions to multiple columns at one time by selecting two or more columns before right-clicking. Figure 7.40 shows the available column-level actions, and Table 7.2 explains them, as well as a few other actions that are available only in the Query Editor ribbon.

Figure 7.40
Right-click any column to see the column-level actions you can use to transform the data.

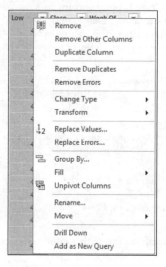

NOTE

Note that all of the column-level actions available in Power Query are also available in the Query Editor ribbon. So you can either opt for the convenience of right-clicking to quickly select an action or choose to utilize the more visual ribbon menu. There are a few useful column-level actions found only in the ribbon (see Table 7.2).

7

Table 7.2   Column-Level Actions

Action	Purpose	Available When Selecting Multiple Columns?
Remove	Remove the selected column from the Power Query data.	Yes
Remove Other Columns	Remove all non-selected columns from the Power Query data.	Yes
Duplicate Column	Create a duplicate of the selected column as a new column placed at the far right of the table. The name given to the new column is Copy of X, where X is the name of the original column.	No
Remove Duplicates	Remove all rows from the selected column where the values duplicate earlier values. The row with the first occurrence of a value is not removed.	Yes
Remove Errors	Remove rows containing errors in the selected column.	Yes
Change Type	Change the data type of the selected column to any of these types: Binary, Date, Date/Time, Date/Time/Timezone, Duration, Logical, Number, Text, Time, or Using Locale (which localizes data types to the country you specify).	Yes
Transform	Change the way values in the column are rendered. You can choose from the following options: Lowercase, Uppercase, Capitalize Each Word, Trim, Clean, Length, JSON, and XML. If the values in the column are date/time values, the options are Date, Time, Day, Month, Year, and Day Of Week. If the values in the column are number values, the options are Round, Absolute Value, Factorial, Base-10 Logarithm, Natural Logarithm, Power, and Square Root.	Yes
Replace Values	Replace one value in the selected column with another specified value.	Yes
Replace Errors	Replace unsightly error values with your own friendlier text.	Yes
Group By	Aggregate data by row values. For example, you can group by state and either count the number of cities in each state or sum the population of each state.	Yes
Fill	Fill empty cells in the column with the value of the first non-empty cell. You have the option of filling up or filling down.	Yes
Unpivot Columns	Transpose the selected columns from column oriented to row oriented or vice versa.	Yes
Rename	Rename the selected column to a name you specify.	No

(Continued)

7

Action	Purpose	Available When Selecting Multiple Columns?
Move	Move the selected column to a different location in the table. You have these choices for moving the column: Left, Right, To Beginning, and To End.	Yes
Drill Down	Navigate to the contents of the column. This is used with tables that contain meta-data representing embedded information.	No
Add as New Query	Create a new query with the contents of the column. This is done by referencing the original query in the new one. The name of the new query is the same as the column header of the selected column.	No
Split Column (ribbon only)	Split the value of a single column into two or more columns, based on a number of characters or a given delimiter, such as a comma, semicolon, or tab.	No
Merge Column (ribbon only)	Merge the values of two or more columns into a single column that contains a specified delimiter, such as a comma, semicolon, or tab.	Yes
Date & Time Transformation (ribbon only)	Allow for mathematical operations for a column formatted as Date or Time. You have the option of returning values such as Age or Duration. Or you can choose to return dates that represent time dimensions such as End of Month, Start of Week, End of Quarter, or Day of Year.	No

Understanding Table Actions

While you're in the Query Editor, Power Query allows you to apply certain actions to an entire data table. You can see the available table-level actions by clicking the Table Actions icon shown in Figure 7.41.

Figure 7.41
Click the Table Actions icon in the upper-left corner of the Query Editor Preview pane to see the table-level actions you can use to transform the data.

7

Table 7.3 lists the table-level actions and describes the primary purpose of each one.

Table 7.3   Table-Level Actions

Action	Purpose
Use First Row as Headers	Replace each table header name with the values in the first row of each column.
Add Custom Column	Insert a new column after the last column of the table. The values in the new column are determined by the value or formula you define.
Add Index Column	Insert a new column containing a sequential list of numbers starting from 1, 0, or another specified value you define.
Choose Columns	Choose the columns you want to keep in the query results.
Remove Duplicates	Remove all rows where the values in the selected columns duplicate earlier values. The row with the first occurrence of a value set is not removed.
Keep Top Rows	Remove all but the top N number of rows. You specify the number threshold.
Keep Bottom Rows	Remove all but the bottom N number of rows. You specify the number threshold.
Keep Range of Rows	Remove all rows except the ones that fall within a range you specify.
Remove Top Rows	Remove the top N rows from the table.
Remove Bottom Rows	Remove the bottom N rows from the table.
Remove Alternate Rows	Remove alternate rows from the table, starting at the first row to remove and specifying the number of rows to remove and the number of rows to keep.
Remove Errors	Remove rows containing errors in the currently selected columns.
Merge Queries	Create a new query that merges the current table with another query in the workbook by matching specified columns.
Append Queries	Create a new query that appends the results of another query in the workbook to the current table.

> **NOTE**
> Note that all of the table-level actions available in Power Query are also available in the Query Editor ribbon. So you can either opt for the convenience of right-clicking to quickly select an action or choose to utilize the more visual ribbon menu.

Power Query Connection Types

Microsoft has invested a great deal of time and resources in ensuring that Power Query has the ability to connect to a wide array of data sources. Whether you need to pull data from an external website, a text file, a database system, Facebook, or a web service, Power Query can accommodate most, if not all, your source data needs.

You can see all the available connection types by clicking on the New Query drop-down on the Data tab. As Figure 7.42 shows, Power Query offers the ability to pull from a wide array of data sources:

- **From File**—Pull data from a specified Excel file, text file, CSV file, XML file, or folder.

- **From Database**—Pull data from a relational Microsoft Access, SQL Server, or SQL Server Analysis Services database.

- **From Other Sources**—Pull data from a wide array of Internet, cloud, and other ODBC data sources.

- **From Table**—Query data from a defined Excel Table within the current workbook.

Figure 7.42
Power Query has the ability to connect to a wide array of text, database, and Internet data sources.

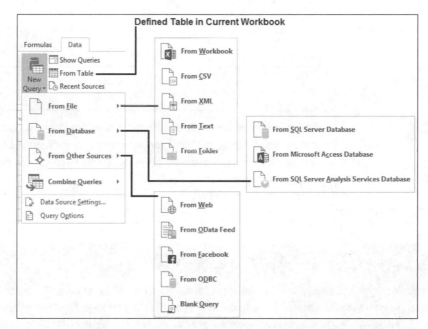

Clicking any of the connection types shown in Figure 7.42 activates a set of dialog boxes for the selected connection. These dialog boxes ask for the basic parameters Power Query needs to connect to the data source—parameters such as file path, URL, server name, and credentials.

Each connection type requires its own unique set of parameters, so each of their dialog boxes are different. Luckily, Power Query rarely needs more than a handful of parameters to connect to any one data source, so the dialog boxes are relatively intuitive and hassle free.

Power Query saves the data source parameters for each data source connection you have used. You can view, edit, or delete any of the data source connections by selecting Data Source Settings at the bottom of the New Query drop-down (see Figure 7.43). Click any of the connections in the Data Source Settings pane to edit or delete the selected connection.

7

Figure 7.43
The Data Source Settings pane allows you to edit and delete previously used data connections.

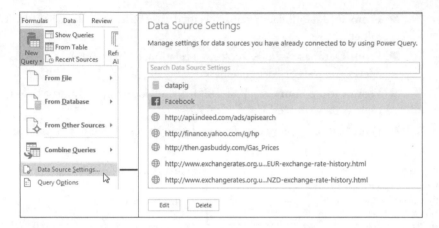

CAUTION

Deleting a connection does not delete any of its associated data that you may have already loaded in your workbook or internal Data Model. However, when you try to refresh the data, Power Query won't have any of the connection parameters (because you deleted them), so it will ask you for the connection parameters again.

CASE STUDY: TRANSPOSING A DATA SET WITH POWER QUERY

In Chapter 2, "Creating a Basic Pivot Table," you learned that the perfect layout for the source data in a pivot table is Tabular layout. Tabular layout is a particular table structure where there are no blank rows or columns, every column has a heading, every field has a value in every row, and columns do not contain repeating groups of data.

Unfortunately, you often encounter data sets like the one shown in Figure 7.44. The problem here is that the month headings are spread across the top of the table, doing double duty as column labels and actual data values. In a pivot table, this format would force you to manage and maintain 12 fields, each representing a different month.

Figure 7.44
You need to convert this matrix-style table to a Tabular data set so it can be used in a pivot table.

	A	B	C	D	E	F	
1	Market	Product_Description	Jan	Feb	Mar	Apr	May
2	BUFFALO	Cleaning & Housekeeping Services	$6,220	$4,264	$5,386	$6,444	$4
3	BUFFALO	Facility Maintenance and Repair	$3,256	$9,490	$4,409	$4,958	$8
4	BUFFALO	Fleet Maintenance	$5,350	$8,925	$6,394	$6,522	$9
5	BUFFALO	Green Plants and Foliage Care	$2,415	$2,580	$2,402	$2,981	$2
6	BUFFALO	Landscaping/Grounds Care	$5,474	$4,501	$5,324	$5,706	$5
7	BUFFALO	Predictive Maintenance/Preventative	$9,811	$10,180	$9,626	$11,701	$10
8	CALIFORNIA	Cleaning & Housekeeping Services	$2,841	$2,997	$2,097	$4,102	
9	CALIFORNIA	Facility Maintenance and Repair	$16,251	$35,879	$18,369	$21,844	$28
10	CALIFORNIA	Fleet Maintenance	$22,575	$36,895	$22,016	$27,871	$31
11	CALIFORNIA	Green Plants and Foliage Care	$48,251	$90,013	$51,130	$75,528	$69

7

You can leverage Power Query to easily transform this matrix-style data set to one that is appropriate for use with a pivot table. Follow these steps:

1. Place your cursor inside your data table and select Insert, Table. In the resulting Create Table dialog box, specify the range for your data. Excel turns that range into a defined table that Power Query can recognize.

2. On the Data tab, select From Table to use your newly created table as the source for the query. The Query Editor appears.

3. In the Query Editor, hold down the Ctrl key as you select the Market and Product_Description fields (which are the fields you do not want to transpose).

4. Go to the Transform tab on the Query Editor ribbon, select the Unpivot Columns drop-down, and then select Unpivot Other Columns (see Figure 7.45). All of the month names now fall under a column called Attributes.

Figure 7.45
Power Query's Unpivot transformation makes quick work of tricky transpose operations.

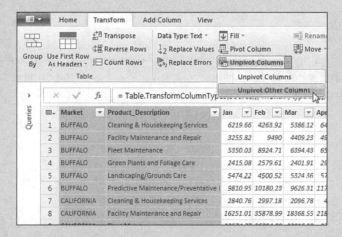

5. Rename the Attributes column Month.

6. Click the Home tab on the Query Editor ribbon and select the Close & Load command to send the results to a new worksheet in the current workbook.

Amazingly, that is it! If all went well, you should now have a table similar to the one shown in Figure 7.46.

Figure 7.46
Your data is now ready for use in a pivot table.

	A	B	C	D
1	Market	Product_Description	Month	Value
2	BUFFALO	Cleaning & Housekeeping Services	Jan	6219.66
3	BUFFALO	Cleaning & Housekeeping Services	Feb	4263.92
4	BUFFALO	Cleaning & Housekeeping Services	Mar	5386.12
5	BUFFALO	Cleaning & Housekeeping Services	Apr	6443.99
6	BUFFALO	Cleaning & Housekeeping Services	May	4360.14
7	BUFFALO	Cleaning & Housekeeping Services	Jun	5097.46
8	BUFFALO	Cleaning & Housekeeping Services	Jul	7566.19
9	BUFFALO	Cleaning & Housekeeping Services	Aug	4263.92
10	BUFFALO	Cleaning & Housekeeping Services	Sep	7245.64
11	BUFFALO	Cleaning & Housekeeping Services	Oct	3847.15
12	BUFFALO	Cleaning & Housekeeping Services	Nov	6540.21
13	BUFFALO	Cleaning & Housekeeping Services	Dec	5610.45
14	BUFFALO	Facility Maintenance and Repair	Jan	3255.82
15	BUFFALO	Facility Maintenance and Repair	Feb	9490
16	BUFFALO	Facility Maintenance and Repair	Mar	4409.23
17	BUFFALO	Facility Maintenance and Repair	Apr	4957.62
18	BUFFALO	Facility Maintenance and Repair	May	8851.72

7

In just a few clicks, you were able to transpose your data set in preparation for use in a pivot table. Even better, this query can be refreshed! So as new month columns or rows are added to the source table, Power Query will rerun your steps and automatically include any new data in the resulting table.

The new Power Query functionality is an exciting addition to Excel 2016. In the past, it was a chore to import and clean external data in preparation for pivot table reporting. Now with Power Query, you can create automated extraction and transformation procedures that traditionally would require personnel and skillsets found only in the IT department.

Next Steps

Chapter 8, "Sharing Pivot Tables with Others," covers the ins and outs of sharing pivot tables with the world. In that chapter, you will find out how you can distribute your pivot tables through the Web.

Sharing Pivot Tables with Others

8

Say that you've built an awesome pivot table with slicers. You would like people to be able to interact with the pivot table, but you don't want them to be able to rearrange the pivot table, nor do you want them to be able to access the underlying data. This is now possible via a couple avenues:

- Excel Online and OneDrive let you turn your Excel workbook into an interactive web app with ease. A OneDrive account is free, and this method will accommodate files up to 10MB in size.

- As of July 2015, you can publish a workbook to Power BI. Then you can use the Power BI Desktop to build pivot tables, pivot charts, and slicers. You can share these dashboards with anyone who shares the same business domain.

Designing a Workbook as an Interactive Web Page

You can use the Excel client to design a workbook for use as a web page. Imagine a set of slicers at the top, then a pivot table and a few pivot charts all on one screen of data. A person who visits your workbook in a browser can interact with the slicers and see the results. And here is the best part: You can protect your intellectual property. You can choose to publish Sheet1 in the browser and not show other worksheets. The pivot tables on Sheet1 reach back to use information on Sheet2, but no one is able to hack in and unhide Sheet2. They can't see your formulas.

Figure 8.1 shows a top customers report with several slicers. The source data and the source pivot table are located on back worksheets.

Figure 8.1
You can make and share a worksheet that does not look like Excel.

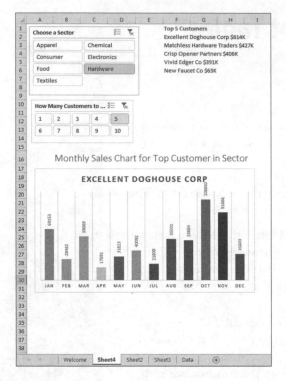

Adapting the workbook to create a web page might involve these tasks:

■ Isolate the visible parts of the report on a single worksheet. Cut anything that does not need to be seen from the first worksheet, and paste it to the hidden worksheet. In this example, you could cut the formula for first-year interest and put it on the hidden worksheet.

■ Consider whether any input cells can be changed to slicers. Slicers are excellent for selecting values in a web page. The How Many Customers to Show slicer in Figure 8.1 is tied to a simple 10-row data set and pivot table on the hidden worksheet. The formulas in F2:F11 pulls the top values from the pivot table. When someone chooses from the slicer, the proper number of top customers are shown.

■ Take a few steps to make your worksheet not look like Excel: On the View tab, uncheck Formula Bar, Gridlines, and Headings.

Figure 8.1 shows the workbook in the Excel client. The first worksheet is visible, but most of the data is on the hidden worksheet.

You need to control what is shown in the browser, so choose File, Info, Browser View Options. In the Show tab, open the drop-down and change Entire Workbook to Sheets. You can then uncheck the hidden worksheet (see Figure 8.2).

Figure 8.2
Choose which worksheet will be visible and which ones will be hidden.

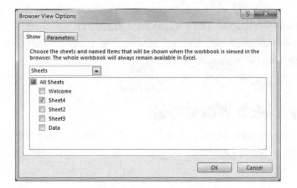

Save the workbook to your OneDrive account.

> **TIP**
> You should test the workbook before sharing it. Make sure that the parameters work and that everything looks correct. When you are signed in to OneDrive and open your own workbook, it might automatically open in Edit mode. Go to the View tab and choose Reading View.

Figure 8.3 shows the workbook in the browser. If you click a slicer, the filters change and the pivot tables and pivot charts update.

Figure 8.3
This is a cool interactive web page, all created using Excel skills.

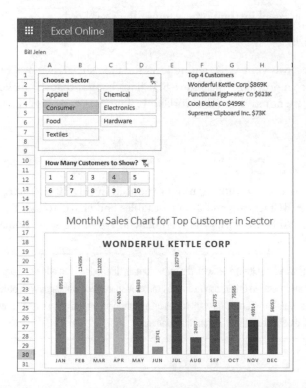

8

If you are reading this book, I bet that you know a lot about Microsoft Excel. You can probably knock out amazing formulas that do all sorts of calculations. Now, with just that knowledge, you can create amazing interactive web pages.

Sharing a Link to a Web Workbook

The easiest way to share a web workbook is to use the Share with People command in OneDrive. This enables other people to interact with your workbook, but it also lets them download the whole workbook to their computers.

While you are viewing the workbook, use Share, Share with People, as shown in Figure 8.4.

Figure 8.4
While viewing the workbook in OneDrive, click Share, Share with People.

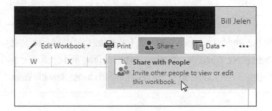

The Share dialog offers two categories:

■ You can send an email inviting others to use the workbook.

■ You can get a link that you can distribute.

When someone receives your URL and follows the link, she arrives at a read-only copy of the application shown previously in Figure 8.3. Any changes that she makes to the slicer or the parameters are not saved to the workbook. The next person gets a fresh copy of the workbook.

Sharing with Power BI

Power BI Desktop is a new authoring tool introduced in July 2015. You can upload your Excel files to Power BI Desktop and use pivot tables and charts to build a dashboard. You can then share the dashboard with other people who are in the same domain as you.

NOTE   For me, as a consultant, the "with the same domain" limitation is an odd one. I sign in to Power BI with the domain @Jelen.OnMicrosoft.com, so I can only share my dashboards with other people who use @Jelen.OnMicrosoft.com. If I want to design a dashboard for a client, I have to convince them to set up a new email account for me from their domain.

Power BI comes in free and paid versions. With the free version, data can be refreshed once per day, and you are limited to 1GB per person. For $10 per person per month, you get 10GB per person and an hourly refresh.

Preparing Data for Power BI

Before you can use Power BI, you need to prepare the data you want to use in it. To do this, build an Excel workbook and format each data set as a table. Then, using the Power Pivot tab, add each table to the workbook Data Model. Save this workbook to your Office 365 OneDrive or OneDrive for Business account with an .xlsx extension.

> **NOTE** When creating an Excel workbook, keep in mind that files with .xlsm extensions are not supported in Power BI.

Importing Data to Power BI

Once your data is properly prepared, you can import it into Power BI. Sign in to PowerBI.Microsoft.com. On the bottom left of the main screen, click the Get Data icon (see Figure 8.5).

Figure 8.5
Add data to Power BI.

On the Get Data screen, click Get in the third tile, Files, to import a file (see Figure 8.6).

Figure 8.6
Import your Excel file.

Get Data

Need more guidance? Try this tutorial

Content Pack Library

My Organization
Browse content packs that other people in your organization have published.

Get ↗

Services
Choose content packs from online services that you use.

Get ↗

Import or Connect to Data

Files
Bring in your reports, workbooks, or data from Excel, Power BI Desktop or CSV files.

Get ↗

Databases
Connect to live data in Azure SQL Database and more.

Get ↗

Samples

8

In the next screen, shown in Figure 8.7, choose to import from either OneDrive—Personal or OneDrive—Business, depending on where you saved your data.

Figure 8.7
Import your data from
OneDrive.

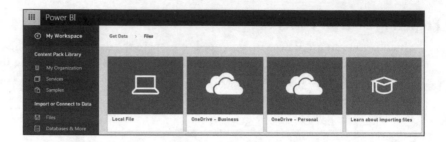

Choose the file to import and then click Connect in the top-right corner (see Figure 8.8).

Figure 8.8
Connect to one of your
OneDrive files.

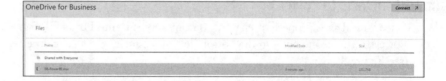

> **NOTE**
> The next screen, shown in Figure 8.9, offers two choices: Import and Connect. When you choose Import, any changes made in OneDrive are automatically refreshed. When you choose Connect, the data is only imported during the hourly or daily refresh. Choose Import. After this, if you save new data to OneDrive, it will be updated in Power BI.

Figure 8.9
Import your Excel data
into Power BI.

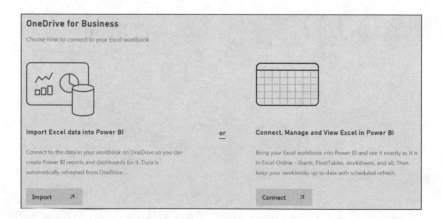

Building a Report in Power BI

In Figure 8.10, you can see a list of fields on the right and an array of icons representing many visualizations. Power BI makes it easy to start a good-looking report: Just select one of the visualizations.

8

Figure 8.10
Choose a visualization to begin building a report.

> **NOTE** Power BI allows open source visualizations, so you can add more chart types than you initially see onscreen. For details, see http://microsoft.github.io/PowerBI-visuals/docs/index.html.

When you choose a chart type, a PivotTable Fields list appears. Drag fields to the appropriate areas and the chart updates, as shown in Figure 8.11.

8

Figure 8.11
When you drag fields to
the PivotTable Fields list
areas, the chart updates.

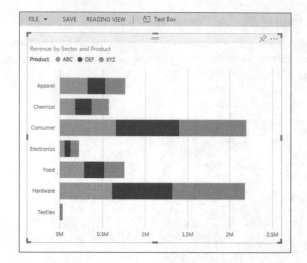

See the ellipsis icon at the top right of the chart? Open it to access additional options, such as sorting, as shown in Figure 8.12.

Figure 8.12
Where you find the tools
for sorting a chart is not
obvious: Click the ellipsis
icon.

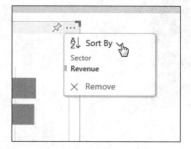

When you finish the first chart, click in the white space outside the chart and repeat the process to add another visualization.

Save the Report by clicking the Save button. You can combine multiple reports into a dashboard by using the + symbol next to the Dashboard section in the left navigation pane.

Using Q&A to Query Data

When you view a report, a box at the top allows you to ask questions. As you type, Power BI creates charts or tables on the fly to try to answer your question.

Make sure to include a value field in your question. For example, typing "Top five cities" will give you a list of cities. Typing "Top five cities by revenue" will give you a sorted bar chart of revenue by city, as shown in Figure 8.13.

Figure 8.14 and Figure 8.15 show the results from other queries. The algorithm is fairly impressive.

Figure 8.13
The Q&A portion of Power
BI allows natural language
queries of the data.

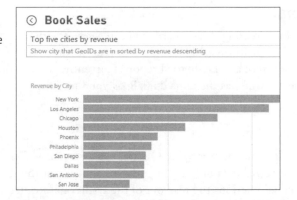

Figure 8.14
Ask about profit by year.

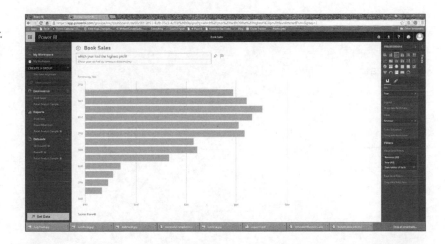

Figure 8.15
Ask about revenue by
channel.

8

Sharing Your Dashboard

When you have finished creating a dashboard, you can share it with others in your organization. They can use Power BI on a tablet such as an iPad to view reports. Find the Share Dashboard icon at the top of any Dashboard report. Currently, you can only share the workbook with someone who has the same domain as your account.

Next Steps

In Chapter 9, "Working with and Analyzing OLAP Data," returns to Excel and shows you how you can analyze external data in Excel pivot tables. Check out the section at the end of Chapter 9 on using cube functions to break out of the traditional format of pivot tables.

Working with and Analyzing OLAP Data

9

Introduction to OLAP

Online analytical processing (OLAP) is a category of data warehousing that enables you to mine and analyze vast amounts of data with ease and efficiency. Unlike other types of databases, OLAP databases are designed specifically for reporting and data mining. In fact, there are several key differences between standard transactional databases, such as Access and SQL Server, and OLAP databases.

Records within a transactional database are routinely added, deleted, and updated. OLAP databases, on the other hand, contain only snapshots of data. The data in an OLAP database is typically archived data, stored solely for reporting purposes. Although new data may be appended on a regular basis, existing data is rarely edited or deleted.

Another difference between transactional databases and OLAP databases is structure. Transactional databases typically contain many tables; each table usually contains multiple relationships with other tables. Indeed, some transactional databases contain so many tables that it can be difficult to determine how each table relates to another.

In an OLAP database, however, all the relationships between the various data points have been predefined and stored in *OLAP cubes*. These cubes already contain the relationships and hierarchies you need to easily navigate the data within. Consequently, you can build reports without needing to know how the data tables relate to one another.

The biggest difference between OLAP and transactional databases is the way the data is stored. The data in an OLAP cube is rarely stored in raw form. OLAP cubes typically store data in views that are already organized and aggregated. That is, grouping, sorting, and aggregations are pre-defined and ready to use. This makes querying and browsing for data far more efficient than in a transactional database, where you have to group, aggregate, and sort records on the fly.

> **NOTE** An OLAP database is typically set up and maintained by the database administrator in your IT depart-ment. If your organization does not utilize OLAP databases, you might want to speak with your data-base administrator about the possibility of using some OLAP reporting solutions.

Connecting to an OLAP Cube

Before you can browse OLAP data, you must establish a connection to an OLAP cube. Start on the Data tab and select From Other Sources to see the drop-down menu shown in Figure 9.1. Then select the From Analysis Services option.

Figure 9.1
Select the From Analysis Services option.

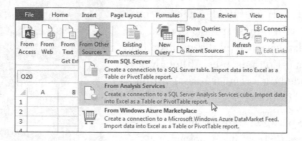

Selecting this option activates the Data Connection Wizard, shown in Figure 9.2. The idea here is that you configure your connection settings so Excel can establish a link to the server. Here are the steps to follow:

> **NOTE** The examples in this chapter have been created using the Analysis Services Tutorial cube that comes with SQL Server Analysis Services 2012. The actions you take to connect to and work with *your* OLAP database are the same as demonstrated here because the concepts are applicable to any OLAP cube you are using.

1. Provide Excel with authentication information. Enter the name of your server as well as your username and password, as demonstrated in Figure 9.2. Then click Next.

Figure 9.2
Enter your authentication information and click Next.

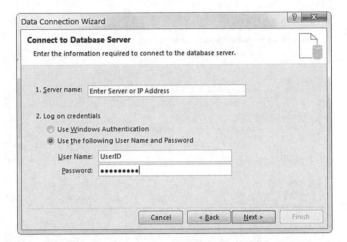

> **NOTE** If you are typically authenticated via Windows Authentication, you simply select the Use Windows Authentication option.

2. Select the database with which you are working from the drop-down box. As Figure 9.3 illustrates, the Analysis Services Tutorial database is selected for this scenario. Selecting this database causes all the available OLAP cubes to be exposed in the list of objects below the drop-down menu. Choose the cube you want to analyze and then click Next.

Figure 9.3
Specify your database and then choose the OLAP cube you want to analyze.

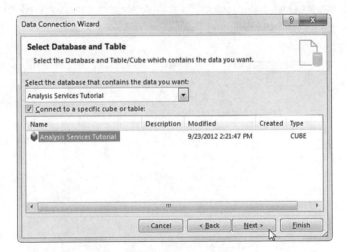

3. On the next screen, shown in Figure 9.4, enter some descriptive information about the connection you've just created.

Figure 9.4
Edit descriptive informa-
tion for your connection.

9

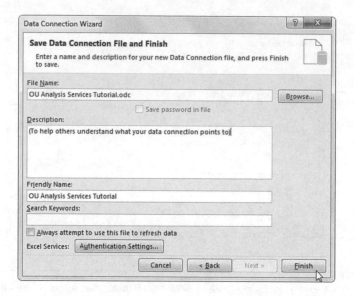

> **NOTE**
> All the fields in the screen shown in Figure 9.4 are optional. That is, you can bypass this screen without editing anything, and your connection will work fine.

4. Click the Finish button to finalize your connection settings. You immediately see the Import Data dialog, as shown in Figure 9.5.

5. In the Import Data dialog, select PivotTable Report and then click the OK button to start building your pivot table.

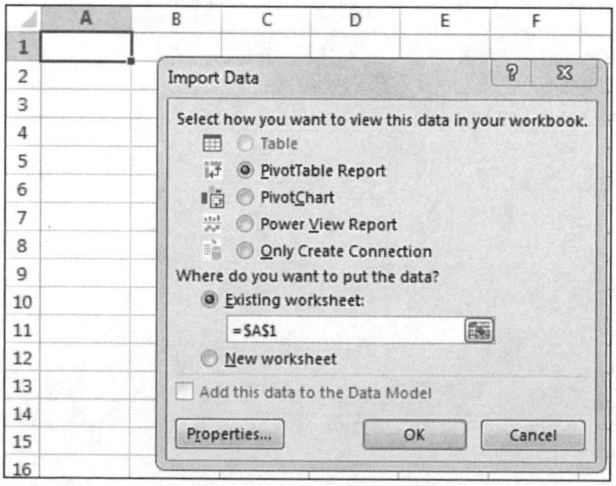

Figure 9.5
When your connection is
finalized, you can start
building your pivot table.

Understanding the Structure of an OLAP Cube

When a pivot table is created, you might notice that the PivotTable Fields list looks somewhat different from that of a standard pivot table. The reason is that the PivotTable Fields list for an OLAP pivot table is arranged to represent the structure of the OLAP cube you are connected to.

To effectively browse an OLAP cube, you need to understand the component parts of OLAP cubes and the way they interact with one another. Figure 9.6 illustrates the basic structure of a typical OLAP cube.

Figure 9.6
The basic structure of an OLAP cube.

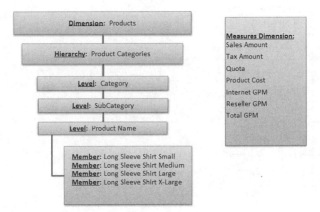

As you can see, the main components of an OLAP cube are dimensions, hierarchies, levels, members, and measures:

- **Dimensions**—Major classifications of data that contain the data items that are analyzed. Some common examples of dimensions are the Products dimension, Customer dimension, and Employee dimension. The structure shown in Figure 9.6 is the Products dimension.

- **Hierarchies**—Predefined aggregations of levels within a particular dimension. A hierarchy enables you to pivot and analyze multiple levels at one time without having any knowledge of the relationships between the levels. In the example in Figure 9.6, the Products dimension has three levels that are aggregated into one hierarchy called Product Categories.

- **Levels**—Categories of data that are aggregated within a hierarchy. You can think of levels as data fields that can be queried and analyzed individually. In Figure 9.6, note that there are three levels: Category, Subcategory, and Product Name.

- **Members**—The individual data items within a dimension. Members are typically accessed via the OLAP structure of dimension, hierarchy, level, and member. In the example shown in Figure 9.6, the members you see belong to the Product Name level. The other levels have their own members and are not shown here.

■ **Measures**—The data values within the OLAP cube. Measures are stored within their own dimension, appropriately called the *Measures dimension*. The idea is that you can use any combination of dimension, hierarchy, level, and member to query the measures. This is called *slicing the measures*.

Now that you understand how the data in an OLAP cube is structured, take a look at the PivotTable Fields list in Figure 9.7, and the arrangement of the available fields should begin to make sense.

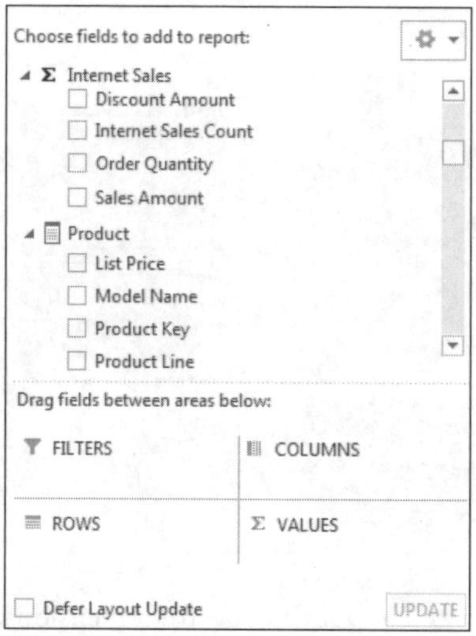

Figure 9.7
The PivotTable Fields list for an OLAP pivot table.

As you can see, the measures are listed first under the Sigma icon. These are the only items you can drop in the Values area of the pivot table. Next, you see dimensions represented next to the table icon. In this example, you see the Product dimension. Under the Product dimension, you see the Product Categories hierarchy that can be drilled into. Drilling into the Product Categories hierarchy enables you to see the individual levels.

The cool thing is that you are able to browse the entire cube structure by simply navigating through your PivotTable Fields list! From here, you can build your OLAP pivot table report just as you would build a standard pivot table.

Understanding the Limitations of OLAP Pivot Tables

When working with OLAP pivot tables, you must remember that the source data is maintained and controlled in the Analysis Services OLAP environment. This means that every aspect of the cube's behavior—from the dimensions and measures included in the cube to the ability to drill into the details of a dimension—is controlled via Analysis Services. This reality translates into some limitations on the actions you can take with your OLAP pivot tables.

When your pivot table report is based on an OLAP data source, keep in mind the following:

- You cannot place any field other than measures into the Values area of the pivot table.
- You cannot change the function used to summarize a data field.
- The Show Report Filter Pages command is disabled.
- The Show Items with No Data option is disabled.
- The Subtotal Hidden Page Items setting is disabled.
- The Background Query option is not available.
- Double-clicking in the Values field returns only the first 1,000 records of the pivot cache.
- The Optimize Memory check box in the PivotTable Options dialog is disabled.

Creating an Offline Cube

With a standard pivot table, the source data is typically stored on your local drive. This way, you can work with and analyze your data while you're disconnected from the network. However, this is not the case with OLAP pivot tables. With an OLAP pivot table, the pivot cache is never brought to your local drive. This means that while you are disconnected from the network, your pivot table is out of commission. You can't even move a field while disconnected.

If you need to analyze your OLAP data while disconnected from your network, you need to create an offline cube. An *offline cube* is essentially a file that acts as a pivot cache, locally storing OLAP data so that you can browse that data while disconnected from the network.

To create an offline cube, start with an OLAP-based pivot table. Place your cursor anywhere inside the pivot table and click the OLAP Tools drop-down menu button on the PivotTable Tools Analyze tab. Then select Offline OLAP, as shown in Figure 9.8.

Selecting this option activates the Offline OLAP Settings dialog (see Figure 9.9), where you click the Create Offline Data File button. The Create Cube File wizard, shown in Figure 9.10, appears. Click Next to start the process.

Figure 9.8
Select the Offline OLAP option to start the creation of an offline cube.

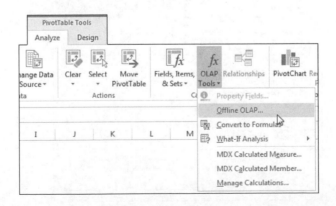

9

Figure 9.9
Start the Create Cube File wizard.

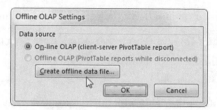

As you can see in Figure 9.10, you first select the dimensions and levels you want included in your offline cube. Your selections tell Excel which data you want to import from the OLAP database. The idea is to select only the dimensions that you need available to you while you're disconnected from the server. The more dimensions you select, the more disk space your offline cube file takes up.

Figure 9.10
Select the dimensions and level you want included in your offline cube.

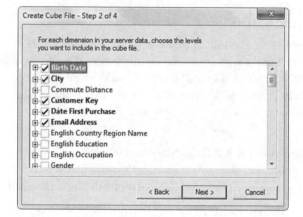

Clicking Next moves you to the next dialog, shown in Figure 9.11. Here, you are given the opportunity to filter out any members or data items you do not want included. For instance, the Extended Amount measure is not needed, so the check has been removed from its selection box. Deselecting this box ensures that this measure will not be imported and therefore will not take up unnecessary disk space.

Figure 9.11
Deselect any members you do not need to see offline.

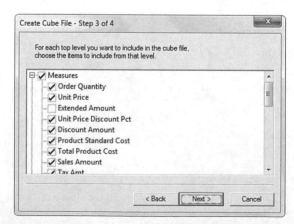

The final step is to specify a name and location for your cube file. In Figure 9.12, the cube file is named MyOfflineCube.cub, and it will be placed in a directory called Documents.

Figure 9.12
Specify a name and location for your cube file.

After a few moments of crunching, Excel outputs your offline cube file to your chosen directory. To test it, simply double-click the file to automatically generate an Excel workbook that is linked to the offline cube via a pivot table.

After your offline cube file has been created, you can distribute it to others and use it while disconnected from the network.

TIP When you're connected to the network, you can open your offline cube file and refresh the pivot table within. This automatically refreshes the data in the cube file. The idea is that you can use the data within the cube file while you are disconnected from the network and can refresh the cube file while a data connection is available. Any attempt to refresh an offline cube while disconnected causes an error.

Breaking Out of the Pivot Table Mold with Cube Functions

Cube functions are Excel functions that can be used to access OLAP data outside a pivot table object. In pre-2010 versions of Excel, you could find cube functions only if you installed the Analysis Services add-in. In Excel 2010, cube functions were brought into the native Excel environment. To fully understand the benefit of cube functions, take a moment to walk through an example.

Exploring Cube Functions

One of the easiest ways to start exploring cube functions is to allow Excel to convert your OLAP-based pivot table into cube formulas. Converting a pivot table to cube formulas is a delightfully easy way to create a few cube formulas without doing any of the work yourself. The idea is to tell Excel to replace all cells in the pivot table with a formula that connects to the OLAP database. Figure 9.13 shows a pivot table connected to an OLAP database.

Figure 9.13
A normal OLAP pivot table.

Customer Geography	United States		
Internet Sales-Sales An			
	CY 2003	CY 2004	Grand Total
⊟ **Accessories**			
⊞ Bike Racks	$7,680	$9,480	$17,160
⊞ Bike Stands	$6,996	$6,519	$13,515
⊞ Bottles and Cages	$8,292	$12,738	$21,030
⊞ Cleaners	$1,240	$1,590	$2,830
⊞ Fenders	$8,880	$12,946	$21,826
⊞ Helmets	$31,771	$45,522	$77,293
⊞ Hydration Packs	$6,049	$9,073	$15,122
⊞ Tires and Tubes	$38,001	$51,520	$89,521
Accessories Total	**$108,909**	**$149,388**	**$258,298**

With just a few clicks, you can convert any OLAP pivot table into a series of cube formulas. Place the cursor anywhere inside the pivot table and click the OLAP Tools drop-down menu button on the PivotTable Tools Analyze tab. Select Convert to Formulas, as shown in Figure 9.14.

Figure 9.14
Select the Convert to Formulas option to convert your pivot table to cube formulas.

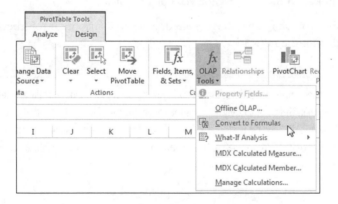

If your pivot table contains a report filter field, the dialog shown in Figure 9.15 appears. This dialog gives you the option of converting your filter drop-down selectors to cube formulas. If you select this option, the drop-down selectors are removed, leaving a static formula. If you need to have your filter drop-down selectors intact so that you can continue to interactively change the selections in the filter field, leave the Convert Report Filters option unchecked.

Figure 9.15
Excel gives you the option of converting your report filter fields.

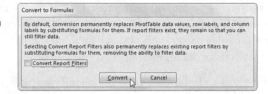

> **NOTE**
> If you are working with a pivot table in Compatibility mode, Excel automatically converts the filter fields to formulas.

After a second or two, the cells that used to house a pivot table are now homes for cube formulas. Note that, as shown in Figure 9.16, any styles you have applied are removed.

So why is this capability useful? Well, now that the values you see are no longer part of a pivot table object, you can insert rows and columns, you can add your own calculations, you can combine the data with other external data, and you can modify the report in all sorts of ways by simply moving the formulas around.

Figure 9.16
Note in the formula bar that these cells are now a series of cube formulas!

The spreadsheet shown:

Formula bar: `C6` `fx` `=CUBEVALUE("AdventureWorks OLAP Cube",$B$1,$A$3,$B6,C$4)`

	A	B	C	D	E
1	Customer Geography	United States			
2					
3	Internet Sales-Sales Amount				
4			CY 2003	CY 2004	Grand Total
5	Accessories				
6		Bike Racks	$7,680.00	$9,480.00	$17,160.00
7		Bike Stands	$6,996.00	$6,519.00	$13,515.00
8		Bottles and Cages	$8,292.26	$12,738.04	$21,030.30
9		Cleaners	$1,240.20	$1,590.00	$2,830.20
10		Fenders	$8,879.92	$12,946.22	$21,826.14
11		Helmets	$31,770.92	$45,521.99	$77,292.91
12		Hydration Packs	$6,048.90	$9,073.35	$15,122.25
13		Tires and Tubes	$38,001.19	$51,519.83	$89,521.02
14	Accessories Total		$108,909.39	$149,388.43	$258,297.82

Adding Calculations to OLAP Pivot Tables

In Excel 2010 and earlier, OLAP pivot tables were limited in that you could not build your own calculations within OLAP pivot tables. This means you could not add the extra layer of analysis provided by the calculated fields and calculated items functionality in standard pivot tables.

> **NOTE**
> Calculated fields and calculated items are covered in Chapter 5, "Performing Calculations in Pivot Tables." If you haven't read it already, you might find it helpful to read that chapter first in order to build the foundation for this section.

Excel 2013 changed that with the introduction of the new OLAP tools—calculated measures and calculated members. With these two tools, you are no longer limited to just using the measures and members provided through the OLAP cube by the database administrator. You can add your own analysis by building your own calculations.

In this section, you'll explore how to build your own calculated measures and calculated members.

A WORD ABOUT MDX

When you are using a pivot table with an OLAP cube, you are sending MDX (multidimensional expressions) queries to the OLAP database. MDX is an expression language that is used to return data from multidimensional data sources (that is, OLAP cubes).

As your OLAP pivot table is refreshed or changed, subsequent MDX queries are passed to the OLAP database. The results of the query are sent back to Excel and displayed through the pivot table. This is how you are able to work with OLAP data without having a local copy of a pivot cache.

When building calculated measures and calculated members, you need to utilize MDX syntax. This is the only way the pivot table can communicate your calculation to the back-end OLAP database.

The examples in this book use basic MDX constructs in order to demonstrate the calculated measures and calculated members functionality. If you need to create complex calculated measures and calculated members, you will want to invest some time learning more about MDX.

That being said, the topic of MDX is robust and beyond the scope of this book. If, after reading this section, you have a desire to learn more about MDX, consider picking up *MDX Solutions* (by George Spofford et al), an excellent guide to MDX that is both easy to understand and comprehensive.

Creating Calculated Measures

A *calculated measure* is essentially the OLAP version of a calculated field. When you create a calculated measure, you basically create a new data field based on some mathematical operation that uses the existing OLAP fields.

In the example shown in Figure 9.17, an OLAP pivot table contains products along with their respective quantities and revenues. Say that you want to add a new measure that calculates average sales price per unit.

Figure 9.17
You want to add a calcu-
lation to this OLAP pivot
table to show average
sales price per unit.

	A	B	C
1	**Row Labels** ▾	**Order Quantity**	**Sales Amount**
2	All-Purpose Bike Stand	249	$39,591
3	Bike Wash	908	$7,219
4	Classic Vest	562	$35,687
5	Cycling Cap	2,190	$19,688
6	Fender Set - Mountain	2,121	$46,620
7	Half-Finger Gloves	1,430	$35,021
8	Hitch Rack - 4-Bike	328	$39,360
9	HL Mountain Tire	1,396	$48,860
10	HL Road Tire	858	$27,971
11	Hydration Pack	733	$40,308
12	LL Mountain Tire	862	$21,541
13	LL Road Tire	1,044	$22,436
14	Long-Sleeve Logo Jersey	1,736	$86,783
15	ML Mountain Tire	1,161	$34,818

9

Place your cursor anywhere in the pivot table and select the PivotTable Tools Analyze tab.
Then select MDX Calculated Measure, as shown in Figure 9.18. This activates the New
Calculated Measure dialog, shown in Figure 9.19.

Figure 9.18
Choose the MDX
Calculated Measure
command.

Figure 9.19
Use the New Calculated
Measure dialog to build
your calculated measure.

Name your Measure   Assign a Measure Group   Enter your Calculation

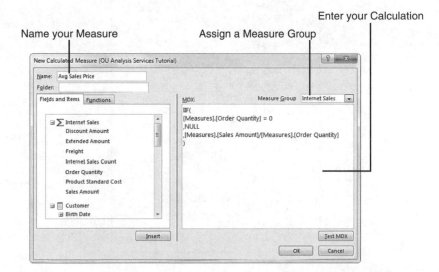

In the New Calculated Measure dialog, take the following actions:

1. Give your calculated measure a name by entering it in the Name input box.

2. Choose a measure group where Excel should place your calculated measure. If you don't choose one, Excel automatically places your measure in the first available measure group.

3. Enter the MDX syntax for your calculation in the MDX input box. To save a little time, you can use the list on the left to choose the existing measures you need for your calculation. Simply double-click the measures needed, and Excel pops them into the MDX input box. In this example, the calculation for the average sales price is `IIF([Measures].[Order Quantity] = 0,NULL,[Measures].[Sales Amount]/[Measures].[Order Quantity])`.

4. Click OK.

> **TIP**
>
> In the New Calculated Measure dialog, shown in Figure 9.19, notice the Test MDX button. You can click this to ensure that the MDX you entered is well formed. Excel lets you know via a message box if your syntax contains any errors.

After you have built your calculated measure, you can go to the PivotTable Fields list and select your newly created calculation (see Figure 9.20).

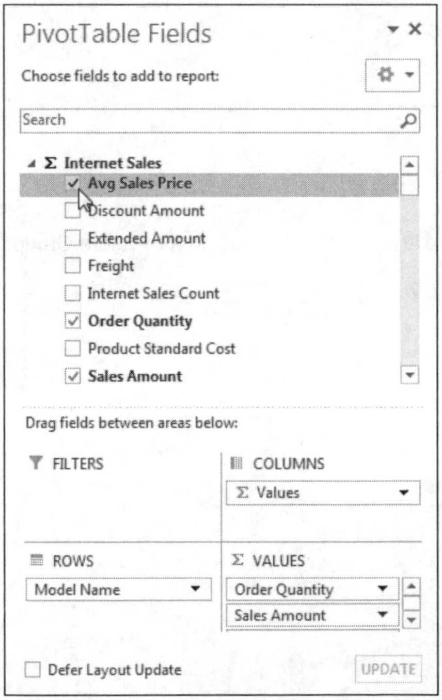

Figure 9.20
Add your newly created calculation to your pivot table via the PivotTable Fields list.

As you can see in Figure 9.21, your calculated measure adds a meaningful layer of analysis to the pivot table.

Figure 9.21
Your pivot table now contains your calculated measure!

Row Labels	Order Quantity	Sales Amount	Avg Sales Price
All-Purpose Bike Stand	249	$39,591	$159.00
Bike Wash	908	$7,219	$7.95
Classic Vest	562	$35,687	$63.50
Cycling Cap	2,190	$19,688	$8.99
Fender Set - Mountain	2,121	$46,620	$21.98
Half-Finger Gloves	1,430	$35,021	$24.49
Hitch Rack - 4-Bike	328	$39,360	$120.00
HL Mountain Tire	1,396	$48,860	$35.00
HL Road Tire	858	$27,971	$32.60
Hydration Pack	733	$40,308	$54.99
LL Mountain Tire	862	$21,541	$24.99
LL Road Tire	1,044	$22,436	$21.49
Long-Sleeve Logo Jersey	1,736	$86,783	$49.99
ML Mountain Tire	1,161	$34,818	$29.99

NOTE It's important to note that when you create a calculated measure, it exists in your workbook only. In other words, you are not building your calculation directly in the OLAP cube on the server. This means no one else connected to the OLAP cube will be able to see your calculations unless you share or distribute your workbook.

Creating Calculated Members

A *calculated member* is essentially the OLAP version of a calculated item. When you create a calculated member, you basically create a new data item based on some mathematical operation that uses the existing OLAP members.

In the example shown in Figure 9.22, an OLAP pivot table contains sales information for each quarter in the year. Let's say you want to aggregate quarters 1 and 2 into a new data item called First Half of Year. You also want to aggregate quarters 3 and 4 into a new data item called Second Half of Year.

Figure 9.22
You want to add new calculated members to aggregate the four quarters into First Half of Year and Second Half of Year.

Row Labels	Order Quantity	Sales Amount	Avg Sales Price
1	15,425	$7,586,624	$491.84
2	17,465	$8,893,345	$509.21
3	13,011	$6,009,120	$461.85
4	14,497	$6,869,588	$473.86
Grand Total	60,398	$29,358,677	$486.09

Place your cursor anywhere in the pivot table and select the PivotTable Tools Analyze tab. Then select MDX Calculated Member, as shown in Figure 9.23. The New Calculated Member dialog opens (see Figure 9.24).

Figure 9.23
Choose the MDX Calculated Member command.

Figure 9.24
Use the New Calculated Member dialog to build your calculated member.

Name your Measure   Choose a Parent Heirarchy   Enter your Calculation

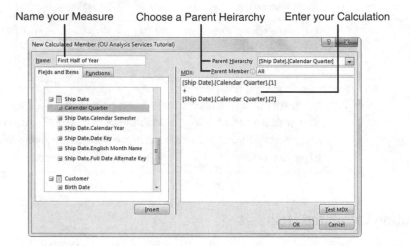

In the New Calculated Member dialog, take the following actions:

1. Give your calculated member a name by entering it in the Name input box.

2. Choose the parent hierarchy for which you are creating new members. Be sure to leave Parent Member set to All. This ensures that Excel takes into account all members in the parent hierarchy when evaluating your calculation.

3. Enter the MDX syntax for your calculation in the MDX input box. To save a little time, you can use the list on the left to choose the existing members you need for your calculation. Simply double-click the member needed, and Excel pops them into the MDX input box. In the example in Figure 9.24, you are adding quarter 1 and quarter 2:
   `[Ship Date]·[Calendar Quarter]·[1] + [Ship Date]·[Calendar Quarter]·[2].`

4. Click OK.

As soon as you click OK, Excel shows your newly created calculated member in the pivot table. As you can see in Figure 9.25, your calculated member is included with the other original members of the pivot field.

Figure 9.25
Excel immediately adds your calculated member to your pivot field.

	A	B	C	D
1	Row Labels ▾	Order Quantity	Sales Amount	Avg Sales Price
2	1	15,425	$7,586,624	$491.84
3	2	17,465	$8,893,345	$509.21
4	3	13,011	$6,009,120	$461.85
5	4	14,497	$6,869,588	$473.86
6	First Half of Year	32,890	$16,479,969	$501.06
7	Grand Total	60,398	$29,358,677	$486.09

Figure 9.26 shows how you repeat the process to calculate the Second Half of Year member.

Figure 9.26
Repeat the process for any additional calculated members.

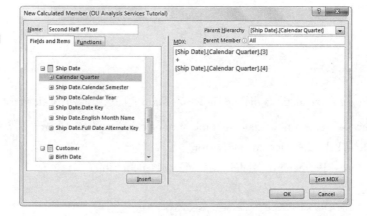

Notice in Figure 9.27 that Excel makes no attempt to remove any of the original members. In this case, you see that quarters 1 through 4 are still in the pivot table. This might be fine for your situation, but in most scenarios, you will likely hide these members to avoid confusion.

Figure 9.27
Excel shows your final calculated members along with the original members. It is a best practice to remove the original members to avoid confusion.

	A	B	C	D
1	Row Labels ▾	Order Quantity	Sales Amount	Avg Sales Price
2	1	15,425	$7,586,624	$491.84
3	2	17,465	$8,893,345	$509.21
4	3	13,011	$6,009,120	$461.85
5	4	14,497	$6,869,588	$473.86
6	First Half of Year	32,890	$16,479,969	$501.06
7	Second Half of Year	27,508	$12,878,709	$468.18
8	Grand Total	60,398	$29,358,677	$486.09

NOTE

Remember that your calculated member exists in your workbook only. No one else connected to the OLAP cube is able to see your calculations unless you share or distribute your workbook.

CAUTION

If the parent hierarchy or parent member is changed in the OLAP cube, your calculated member ceases to function. You must re-create the calculated member.

Managing OLAP Calculations

Excel provides an interface for managing the calculated measures and calculated members in an OLAP pivot table. Simply place your cursor anywhere in the pivot table and select the PivotTable Tools Analyze tab. Then select Manage Calculations, as shown in Figure 9.28.

Figure 9.28
Activate the Manage Calculations dialog.

The Manage Calculations dialog, shown in Figure 9.29, appears, offering three commands:

- **New**—Create a new calculated measure or calculated member.
- **Edit**—Edit the selected calculation.
- **Delete**—Permanently delete the selected calculation.

Figure 9.29
The Manage Calculations dialog enables you to create a new calculation, edit an existing calculation, or delete an existing calculation.

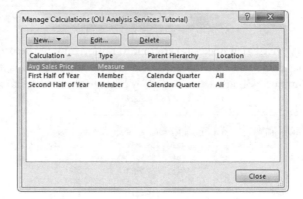

Performing What-If Analysis with OLAP Data

Another piece of functionality that Microsoft introduced in Excel 2013 is the ability to perform what-if analysis with the data in OLAP pivot tables. With this functionality, you have the ability to actually edit the values in a pivot table and recalculate your measures and members based on your changes. You even have the ability to publish your changes back to the OLAP cube.

To make use of the what-if analysis functionality, create an OLAP pivot table and then go to the PivotTable Tools Analyze tab. Once there, select What-If Analysis, Enable What-If Analysis, as shown in Figure 9.30.

Figure 9.30
Enabling what-if analysis allows you to change the values in a pivot table.

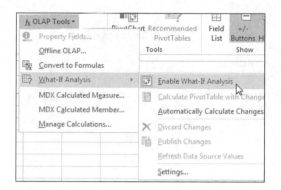

At this point, you can edit the values in your pivot table. After you have made changes, you can right-click any of the changed values and choose Calculate PivotTable with Change (see Figure 9.31). This forces Excel to reevaluate all the calculations in the pivot table based on your edits—including your calculated members and measures.

Figure 9.31
Choose Calculate PivotTable with Change to reevaluate all your calculations.

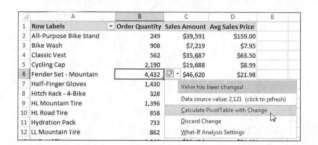

The edits you make to your pivot table while using what-if analysis are, by default, local edits only. If you are committed to your changes and would like to actually make the changes on the OLAP server, you can tell Excel to publish your changes. To do this, in the PivotTable Tools Analyze tab, select What-If Analysis, Publish Changes (see Figure 9.32). This triggers a "write-back" to the OLAP server, meaning the edited values are sent to the source OLAP cube.

> **NOTE**
> You need adequate server permissions to publish changes to the OLAP server. Your database administrator can guide you through the process of getting write access to your OLAP database.

Figure 9.32
Excel lets you publish your changes to the source OLAP cube!

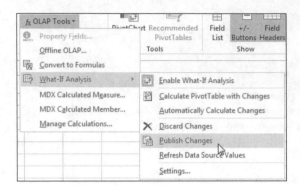

Next Steps

In Chapter 10, "Mashing Up Data with Power Pivot," you'll find out how to use PowerPivot to create powerful reporting models that are able to process and analyze millions of rows of data in a single pivot table.

Mashing Up Data with Power Pivot

10

Power Pivot debuted in Excel 2010 as a free add-in with six jaw-dropping features. It was an amazing product, created outside the Excel team. You've already seen the Data Model in Chapter 7, "Analyzing Disparate Data Sources with Pivot Tables." The Data Model is really the Power Pivot engine, and it was first built into Excel 2013.

The Data Model gives you some of the Power Pivot features, but many more features require the Power Pivot add-in, which ships with Office 365 Pro Plus or the E3 level of Office volume licensing.

> **NOTE**
> If you have Office 2016 Standard, you can still use the Power Pivot engine as the Data Model, but you are locked out of the Power Pivot window and some other features. You have to upgrade to a higher version of Office 2016 to unlock these features.

Understanding the Benefits and Drawbacks of Power Pivot and the Data Model

Let's start with the three most important benefits of Power Pivot and analyze what is in each version of Excel. These features are joining two related tables, analyzing more than 1 million records, and creating calculations using DAX.

Merging Data from Multiple Tables Without Using VLOOKUP

Everyone using Excel 2016 can merge data from multiple tables without using VLOOKUP. If you have the Standard edition, you won't see the Power Pivot branding; rather, you'll just be using the Data Model.

■ To learn how to build a multitable analysis, **see** "Joining Multiple Tables Using the Data Model in Regular Excel 2016," **p. 226**.

> **TIP**
> If you have the Power Pivot add-in, building relationships is easier using a graphic view.

Importing 100 Million Rows into a Workbook

The Power Pivot grid holds unlimited rows. I've personally seen 100 million rows. Your only limit is the 2GB maximum file size for a workbook and available memory. Thanks to the VertiPaq compression algorithm, a 50MB text file frequently fits into 4MB when it is in the Power Pivot grid. For a 10-column data set, that means you can get about 950 million rows of data in one workbook. Loading more than 1,048,576 records is available to all versions of Excel 2016.

With Office Standard, you can import huge numbers of records and produce pivot tables; however, you aren't allowed to browse the records. You need the Power Pivot add-in to browse. This is an intense psychological hurdle. I want to be able to see my data before reporting on it. It would be like putting a Maserati engine in a jalopy, but then welding the hood shut so I can't actually look at the engine. Yes, I can still drive the car really fast, but I simply have this intense need to be able to browse my data. It makes me feel better. Maybe you feel the same.

Creating Better Calculations Using the DAX Formula Language

The DAX language, discussed later in this chapter, is not available in Standard editions of Excel 2016. You need the Power Pivot add-in in order to add new calculations to the Power Pivot grid and to add new calculated columns to a pivot table.

As you'll learn shortly, the DAX language provides a lot of flexibility. Although it's the hardest feature of Power Pivot to learn, it offers the biggest paybacks.

Other Benefits of the Power Pivot Data Model in All Editions of Excel

You get a number of other side-effect benefits of running your data through the Data Model:

■ Count Distinct becomes a calculation option. This type of calculation was previously hard to do. Excel tricksters would add a column to the original data that divided 1 by the COUNTIF of a field. If a customer showed up five times, the calculation would evaluate to 1/5, or 0.2. They would then add up the five records with 0.2 and to get one unique customer. If you've ever gone through this painful process, you will be thrilled to know that, thanks to the Data Model, Count Distinct is two clicks away. Ditto for those of you who wanted a distinct count but could never get the workaround to work.

■ You can include filtered items in grand totals. Create a pivot table showing the top 10 customers. The grand total has always been just the 10 customers you see. Now you can make that total include all of the small customers who were filtered out of the report. This feature has always been in the Subtotals drop-down on the left side of the Design tab in the ribbon, but it was perpetually grayed out. Run your data through the Data Model, and it becomes available.

- Named sets were introduced in Excel 2010, but only for people with OLAP data. Named sets let you create pivot tables, for example, with last year's actuals and next year's budget. By taking your data through the Data Model, you cause named sets to become available.

- If you ever use the GETPIVOTDATA function to extract values from pivot tables, you can save a step and convert your pivot table to cube formulas. Cut and paste these into any format desired.

Benefits of the Full Power Pivot Add-in with Excel Pro Plus

If you have Excel Pro Plus and the full Power Pivot add-in, you also have access to these features:

- You can access the Power Pivot grid, where you can actually browse through the 100 million rows. You can sort, filter, and add calculations in the grid.

- In a graphical design view, you can build relationships by dragging between fields.

- You have the ability to change the properties of fields in the model. You can choose which fields should appear in the PivotTable Fields list and which should not.

- You can specify that FieldA (for example, month name) should be sorted by FieldB (for example, month number).

- You can define a default number format to use when the field appears in a pivot table. How many times have you wished for this in a regular pivot table?

- You can define a field as representing a product, a geographic area, or a link to an image.

- You get access to a weak implementation of key performance indicators. This would be simpler to use icon sets in your resultant pivot table.

- You get access to Power View dashboards. This is discussed in Chapter 11, "Dashboarding with Power View and 3D Map."

Understanding the Limitations of the Data Model

When you use the Data Model, you transform your regular Excel data into an OLAP model. There are annoying limitations and some benefits available to pivot tables built on OLAP models. The Excel team tried to mitigate some of the limitations for Excel 2016, but many are still present. Here are some of the limitations:

- **Fewer calculation options**—Although you now have access to Distinct Count, you lose access to other calculation options such as Product.

- **Less grouping**—While Excel 2016 introduced the Auto Group feature for dates, you cannot use the Group feature of pivot tables to create territories or to group numeric values into bins.

- **Strange drill-down**—Usually, you can double-click a cell in a pivot table and see the rows that make up that cell. This does work with the Data Model, but only for the first 1,000 rows.

- **No calculated fields or calculated items**—The Data Model does not support calculated fields or calculated items. If you have Power Pivot, the DAX measures run circles around those old calculations. However, if you don't have Power Pivot, you are going to be frustrated using the Data Model.

Joining Multiple Tables Using the Data Model in Regular Excel 2016

Microsoft faced a marketing dilemma. It had built the best features of Power Pivot right into Excel 2013, but it then tried to get customers to spend extra money for Office Pro Plus to get Power Pivot, Power View, and Inquire.

> **NOTE** Although the name Power Pivot sounds really awesome and powerful, Microsoft doesn't include the product in the Standard edition so they had to come up with another name to describe the Power Pivot engine in Standard Excel 2016. When you see the capitalized words *Data Model* in Excel 2016, that is Microsoft's way of saying you are using Power Pivot without calling it Power Pivot.

Figure 10.1
When Excel 2016 refers to the Data Model, you are using the Power Pivot engine.

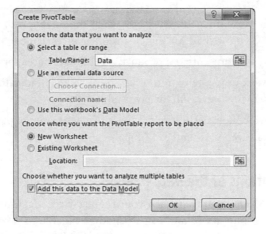

Figure 10.1 shows the Create PivotTable dialog. The Add This Data to the Data Model check box really means that you will be using the non-branded version of the Power Pivot engine.

Preparing Data for Use in the Data Model

When you are planning on using the Data Model to join multiple tables, you should always convert your Excel ranges to tables before you begin. You theoretically do not have to convert the ranges to tables, but joining the tables is far easier if you convert the ranges to tables and name the tables.

> **CAUTION**
>
> If you don't convert the ranges to tables first, Excel secretly does it in the background and gives your tables meaningless names such as Range.

Figure 10.2 shows two ranges in Excel. Columns A:H contain a transactional data set. Columns J:K contain a customer lookup table to add an industry sector for each customer. Say that you would like to create a pivot table showing revenue by sector.

Figure 10.2
You want to join these two tables together in a single pivot table.

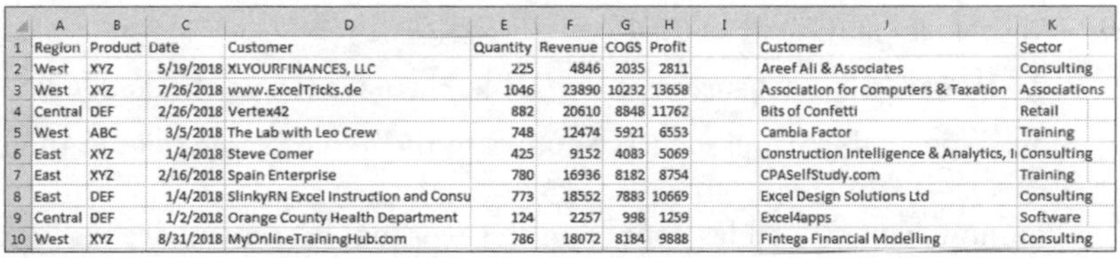

	A	B	C	D	E	F	G	H	I	J	K
1	Region	Product	Date	Customer	Quantity	Revenue	COGS	Profit		Customer	Sector
2	West	XYZ	5/19/2018	XLYOURFINANCES, LLC	225	4846	2035	2811		Areef Ali & Associates	Consulting
3	West	XYZ	7/26/2018	www.ExcelTricks.de	1046	23890	10232	13658		Association for Computers & Taxation	Associations
4	Central	DEF	2/26/2018	Vertex42	882	20610	8848	11762		Bits of Confetti	Retail
5	West	ABC	3/5/2018	The Lab with Leo Crew	748	12474	5921	6553		Cambia Factor	Training
6	East	XYZ	1/4/2018	Steve Comer	425	9152	4083	5069		Construction Intelligence & Analytics, I	Consulting
7	East	XYZ	2/16/2018	Spain Enterprise	780	16936	8182	8754		CPASelfStudy.com	Training
8	East	DEF	1/4/2018	SlinkyRN Excel Instruction and Consu	773	18552	7883	10669		Excel Design Solutions Ltd	Consulting
9	Central	DEF	1/2/2018	Orange County Health Department	124	2257	998	1259		Excel4apps	Software
10	West	XYZ	8/31/2018	MyOnlineTrainingHub.com	786	18072	8184	9888		Fintega Financial Modelling	Consulting

Excel gurus are thinking, "Why don't you do a VLOOKUP to join the tables?" In this case, the tables are small and a VLOOKUP would calculate quickly. However, imagine that you have a million records in the transactional table and 10 columns in the lookup table. The VLOOKUP solution quickly becomes unwieldy. The Power Pivot engine available in the Data Model can join the tables without the overhead of VLOOKUP.

Convert the first data set to a table by following these steps:

1. Select any one cell in the first data set.

2. Press Ctrl+T or select Home, Format as Table and then select a format.

3. The Create Table dialog appears. Provided that you have no blank rows, the address will be correct. And if you have a heading above each column and three or more columns, the dialog will preselect My Table Has Headers. Make sure to check this box if it is not already checked. Click OK to convert the range to a table. You will immediately notice the AutoFilter drop-downs in each heading and that a formatting style has been applied to the first range. The formatting is not the important part. The important part is that Excel is now treating this data set like a database table. A Table Name field in the left part of the ribbon shows a table name such as Table1 (see Figure 10.3).

Figure 10.3
Excel uses a default table name.

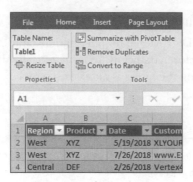

4. Click in the Table Name field and give the table a meaningful name. Database experts would call this the Fact table, but feel free to use Sales, Data, InvoiceRegister, or anything that describes the data. Sales is the table name for this example.

Now convert the second range to a table:

1. Select cell J1.

2. Press Ctrl+T. Ensure that My Table Has Headers is checked. Click OK.

3. Type a table name such as **Sectors** in the Table Name field in the ribbon.

You now have two tables defined in this workbook, and you are ready to begin building the pivot table.

Adding the First Table to the Data Model

Choose one cell in the first data set and select Insert, PivotTable from the ribbon. You can't use the Recommended Pivot Tables or Analysis Lens options to build a Data Model pivot table.

The table name appears in the Create PivotTable dialog. Choose the check box Add This Data to the Data Model, as shown previously in Figure 10.1.

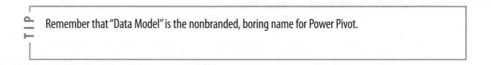

TIP

Remember that "Data Model" is the nonbranded, boring name for Power Pivot.

Click OK. Creating a Data Model pivot table takes several extra seconds as Excel converts and loads your data into the model.

Eventually, you get a new blank workbook with a pivot table icon in A3:C20, just like with a regular pivot table. The PivotTable Fields list appears, but it is a slightly different version. In Figure 10.4, note the addition of the choice of two tabs: Active and All.

Expand the Sales table and choose Revenue. You see a small pivot table with the total revenue amount.

Figure 10.4
The choices for Active or All indicate that you have a pivot table that's using the Power Pivot engine.

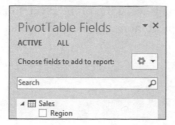

Adding the Second Table and Defining a Relationship

In the PivotTable Fields list, choose the All tab, and you see a list of all the defined tables in the workbook. At this moment, although the PivotTable Fields list is showing two tables, only the Sales field is actually loaded into the Data Model. Click the plus sign next to the Sector table.

Drag the Sector field from the top of the PivotTable Fields list to the Columns area in the bottom of the PivotTable Fields list. You should notice three things:

- The bottom of the PivotTable Fields list now shows fields from two different tables.
- The pivot table shows sectors, but the numbers are identical and clearly incorrect in the right column.
- A yellow warning appears at the top of the PivotTable Fields list, indicating that relationships between tables may be needed and offering a Create button (see Figure 10.5).

Figure 10.5
Excel warns that you need to define a relationship between the two tables.

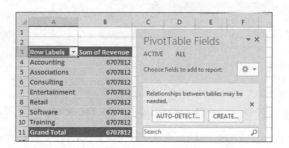

> **NOTE**
> In Excel 2016, you can use Relationships on the Data tab to explicitly define a relationship to avoid this awkward state of having wrong numbers in the pivot table.

Click the Auto-Detect button in the warning at the top of the Pivot Table Fields list, and Excel detects the relationship. Then the pivot table updates with correct numbers, as shown in Figure 10.6.

Figure 10.6
Without doing a VLOOKUP, you've successfully joined data from two tables in this report.

	A	B	C
1			
2			
3	Row Labels ▼	Sum of Revenue	
4	Accounting	750163	
5	Associations	479515	
6	Consulting	2225348	
7	Entertainment	91668	
8	Retail	652764	
9	Software	1223804	
10	Training	1284550	
11	Grand Total	6707812	
12			

If the Auto-Detect relationship fails, use Data, Relationships, Edit Relationship. Choose Sales as the first table and Customer as the column. Choose Sectors as the second table and Customer as the related column (see Figure 10.7).

Figure 10.7
It is easy to define a relationship.

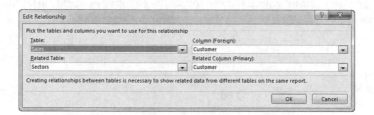

Tell Me Again—Why Is This Better Than Doing a VLOOKUP?

If you don't have the Power Pivot add-in, you may not be convinced that all of the hassle in the preceding section is worthwhile. You now have the ability to do some cool tricks that you could never do in a regular pivot-cache pivot table. The following case study provides some examples.

CASE STUDY: SHOWING TOP CUSTOMER BUT TOTAL REVENUE

The Top 10 filter in regular pivot tables lets you show the top *N* customers, but you cannot get a true total of all records. Now that your data is in the Data Model, you can do this easily.

Starting with the pivot table in Figure 10.8, which shows Sector and Revenue, perform these steps:

1. Choose Customer from the Sales table in the PivotTable Fields list. Customer becomes the inner row field.

Figure 10.8
With Show Top 1 Customer per Sector, the totals are not useful.

	A	B	C
1			
2			
3	Row Labels	Sum of Revenue	
4	Accounting	$750,163	
5	Juliet Babcock-Hyde CPA, PLLC	$750,163	
6	Associations	$390,978	
7	Orange County Health Department	$390,978	
8	Consulting	$869,454	
9	Construction Intelligence & Analytics, Inc.	$869,454	
10	Entertainment	$60,299	
11	The Lab with Leo Crew	$60,299	
12	Retail	$613,514	
13	Hartville Marketplace & Flea Market	$613,514	
14	Software	$568,851	
15	F-Keys Ltd	$568,851	
16	Training	$704,359	
17	Cambia Factor	$704,359	
18	Grand Total	$3,957,618	
19			
20			

2. Open the Row Labels drop-down in cell A3. Open the Select Field drop-down and choose Customer.

3. Choose Value Filters and then Top 10.

4. In the Top 10 dialog, select Top 1 Items by Sum of Revenue. The pivot table now shows one customer per sector. As you can see in Figure 10.8, the grand total is only $3.96 million instead of the $6.7 million shown previously in Figure 10.6.

5. On the Design tab, open the Subtotals drop-down. Choose Include Filtered Items in Totals (see Figure 10.9). Each total is now marked with an asterisk, and the totals include all customers, not just the customers shown.

Figure 10.9
You can see detail about the top customer but the total revenue for all customers.

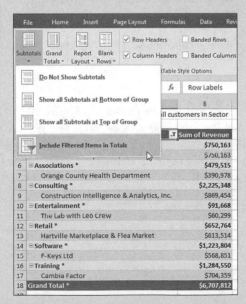

	Row Labels	
	B	
	all customers in Sector	
	Sum of Revenue	
	$750,163	
	$750,163	
6	Associations *	$479,515
7	Orange County Health Department	$390,978
8	Consulting *	$2,225,348
9	Construction Intelligence & Analytics, Inc.	$869,454
10	Entertainment *	$91,668
11	The Lab with Leo Crew	$60,299
12	Retail *	$652,764
13	Hartville Marketplace & Flea Market	$613,514
14	Software *	$1,223,804
15	F-Keys Ltd	$568,851
16	Training *	$1,284,550
17	Cambia Factor	$704,359
18	Grand Total *	$6,707,812

The report in Figure 10.9 is the type of report managers would like to see. It doesn't show hundreds of customers but would let the managers talk intelligently about who is the leading customer in each sector.

In fact, a manager just called and asked for the change shown in Figure 10.10. Therefore, add Revenue to the report a second time. Choose the second Revenue heading. Choose Field Settings. Change the calculation to Percent of Parent Row Total. You now have a report showing that Cambia Factor is 54.83% of the Training sector and that the Training sector is 19.15% of the total.

Figure 10.10
This will become the new favorite report of a manager for the next three days.

	A	B	C
1	Top Customer Per Sector, with Total from all customers in Sector		
2			
3	Row Labels	Sum of Revenue	% of Parent
4	⊟ Accounting *	$750,163	11.18%
5	Juliet Babcock-Hyde CPA, PLLC	$750,163	100.00%
6	⊟ Associations *	$479,515	7.15%
7	Orange County Health Department	$390,978	81.54%
8	⊟ Consulting *	$2,225,348	33.18%
9	Construction Intelligence & Analytics, Inc.	$869,454	39.07%
10	⊟ Entertainment *	$91,668	1.37%
11	The Lab with Leo Crew	$60,299	65.78%
12	⊟ Retail *	$652,764	9.73%
13	Hartville Marketplace & Flea Market	$613,514	93.99%
14	⊟ Software *	$1,223,804	18.24%
15	F-Keys Ltd	$568,851	46.48%
16	⊟ Training *	$1,284,550	19.15%
17	Cambia Factor	$704,359	54.83%
18	Grand Total *	$6,707,812	100.00%
19			

Creating a New Pivot Table from an Existing Data Model

As you go from example to example in this book, it is easy to delete the pivot table sheet and start over with a fresh pivot table. It is slightly more complicated to start over after you already have data in the Data Model. But you can do it by following these simple steps:

1. While in a blank cell in the grid, choose Insert, PivotTable.
2. In the Create Pivot Table dialog, choose Use This Workbook's Data Model.

Getting a Distinct Count

Excel pivot tables can count text values. The pivot table in Figure 10.11 is typical: Sector in the Rows area, Customer and Revenue in the Values area. You get a report showing that there are 563 customers. This is, of course, incorrect. There were 563 records that had non-blank customer names, but there were not 563 different customers. This is an ugly limitation of pivot tables that we have lived with.

Figure 10.11
Count of Customer does not mean there are 563 unique customers.

Row Labels	Count of Customer	Sum of Revenue
How Many Customers Per Sector?		
Accounting	60	$750,163
Associations	44	$479,515
Consulting	189	$2,225,348
Entertainment	8	$91,668
Retail	52	$652,764
Software	104	$1,223,804
Training	106	$1,284,550
Grand Total *	563	$6,707,812

If your pivot table is based on the Data Model, you can get a distinct count by following these steps:

1. Go to the Customer field at the bottom of the PivotTable Fields list. Open the drop-down and choose Value Field Settings. You now see the Value Field Settings dialog, where you could normally choose Sum, Average, Count, and so on.

2. Scroll to the bottom of the list in the Value Field Settings dialog. Along the way, you might or might not notice that Product and Index are missing from the list. Any sorrow over their loss will quickly be erased when you find a new item at the bottom called Distinct Count. Choose this and click OK.

3. The pivot table now shows that there are actually 27 unique customers in the database, 9 of which are in the consulting sector (see Figure 10.12).

Figure 10.12
Finally, an easy Distinct Count command.

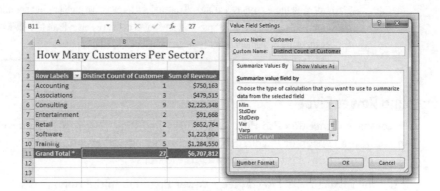

If I had a dollar for every time I needed a Distinct Count command in the past 10 years, I would easily have enough to afford the upgrade to Office Pro Plus. Speaking of that, the following section contrasts how to build a model if you are using the Power Pivot add-in.

Using the Power Pivot Add-in Excel 2016 Pro Plus

If your version of Excel 2016 includes the full Power Pivot add-in, you receive several benefits:

- You have more ways to get data into Power Pivot—more data sources, plus linked tables, copy and paste, and feeds.

- You can view, sort, and filter data in the Power Pivot grid.

- You can import many millions of rows into a single worksheet in the Power Pivot grid.

- You can use DAX formula calculations both in the grid and as new calculated fields called *measures*. DAX, which stands for Data Analysis Expressions and is discussed later in this chapter, is composed of 135 functions that let you to do two types of calculations. There are 81 typical Excel functions that you can use to add a calculated column to a table in the PowerPoint window. Then you can use 54 functions to create a new measure in the pivot table. These 54 functions add incredible power to pivot tables.

- You have more ways to create relationships, including a Diagram view to show relationships.

- You can hide or rename columns.

- You can set the numeric formatting for a column before you create a pivot table.

- You can assign categories such as Geography, Image URL, and Web URL to fields.

- You can define key performance indicators or hierarchies.

> **NOTE**
> If you plan to deal with millions of records, you should opt for the 64-bit versions of Office and Power Pivot. With those versions, you are still constrained by available memory, but because Power Pivot can compress data, you can fit 10 times that amount of data in a Power Pivot file. The 64-bit version of Office can make use of memory sizes beyond the 4GB limit in 32-bit Windows.

Enabling Power Pivot

If you have Office 365 Pro Plus, Office 2016 Pro Plus, Office 2016 Enterprise, or a stand-alone boxed version of Excel 2016, you probably have Power Pivot. With one of these versions, enable Power Pivot by following these steps:

1. Open Excel 2016. Do you see a Power Pivot tab in the ribbon? If so, you can skip the remaining steps.

2. Select File, Options and choose Add-ins from the left column. At the bottom, choose Manage: COM Add-ins. Click Go.

3. Look for Microsoft Office Power Pivot for Excel 2016 in the list of available COM add-ins. Check the box next to this option and click OK.

4. If the Power Pivot tab does not appear in the ribbon, close Excel 2016 and then restart it.

The next sections walk you through your first Power Pivot data mash-up. You'll create a report that merges a 1.8 million–row CSV file with a store identifying data in Excel.

Importing a Text File Using Power Query

Your main table in this example is a 1.8 million–record CSV file called 10-BigData.txt. It is important that you have column headings in row 1 of the CSV file. The file includes a StoreID field, but of course there are not 1.8 million store names, regions, and so on.

Create a workbook that has a StoreName lookup table. You will load the 1.8 million rows into this workbook.

> **NOTE** After Microsoft introduced the highly successful Power Query tool for Excel 2010 and Excel 2013, someone in marketing decided that the word *Power* in Power Query is too intimidating and started calling this feature Get and Transform. I am simply refusing to acknowledge the de-branding of this awesome feature. Throughout this chapter, I continue to refer to it as Power Query.

To import the 1.8 million–row file into Power Pivot, follow these steps:

1. Choose Data, New Query, From File, From CSV.
2. Browse to find your file. You will have to change Files of Type from CSV to All Files since your extension is .txt.
3. If you need to do any transformations using Power Query, make those changes.
4. On the Home tab of Power Query, open the Close and Load drop-down. Choose Close and Load To.
5. In the Load To pane, shown in Figure 10.13, choose Only Create Connection and check Add This Data to the Data Model. Click OK.

Figure 10.13
Load the data from Power Query to the Data Model.

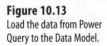

Load To

Select how you want to view this data in your workbook.
- ☐ ○ Table
- ☐ ⦿ Only Create Connection

Select where the data should be loaded.
- ⦿ New worksheet
- ○ Existing worksheet:
  - $A$3

☑ Add this data to the Data Model

Load Cancel

If you want to browse the 1.8 million rows of data, select Power Pivot, Manage. You are presented with a grid where you can scroll, sort, and filter the 1.8 million rows.

> **NOTE** Although this feels like Excel, it is not Excel. You cannot edit an individual cell. If you add a calculation in what amounts to cell E1, that calculation is automatically copied to all rows. If you format the revenue in one cell, all the cells in that column get formatted. You can change column widths by dragging the border between the column names just as in Excel.

The bottom line is that you have 1.8 million records you can sort, filter, and—later—pivot. This is going to be cool. Note that the entire 1.8 million rows from the text file are now stored in the Excel workbook. You can copy that one .xlsx file, move it to a new computer, and all of the rows will be there. You wouldn't believe this is happening when you look at the files in Windows Explorer. The original text file is 58MB, but the Excel file is only 4MB (because of the vertical compression).

Adding Excel Data by Linking

Although you can copy Excel data and paste in Power Pivot, it is not recommended. You should link the Excel data to Power Pivot. That way, if you change the data in Excel, a simple Refresh will get the changes into Power Pivot. You need to add the StoreInfo table to the Data Model. Here's how you do it:

1. If you start with an Excel worksheet, make sure you have single-row headings at the top, with no blank rows or blank columns.

2. Select one cell in the worksheet and press Ctrl+T. Excel asks you to confirm the extent of your table and whether your data has headers.

3. Go to the Table Tools Design tab. On the left side of the ribbon, you see that this table is called Table1. Type a new name, such as **StoreInfo**.

4. On the Power Pivot tab, in the Tables group, find the icon that says Add to Data Model. When you hover over it, the tooltip says that this icon will create a linked table. Click this icon to have a copy of the table appear in the Power Pivot grid.

Defining Relationships

Normally, in regular Excel you would be creating VLOOKUPs to match the two tables. Matching the tables is far easier in Power Pivot. Follow these steps:

1. In the Power Pivot window, go to the Home tab and choose Diagram View. Power Pivot shows your two tables, side by side.

2. Click the StoreID field in the main table and drag to the Store field in the lookup table. Excel draws arrows indicating the relationship (see Figure 10.14).

Figure 10.14
Drag from one field to another to define a relationship.

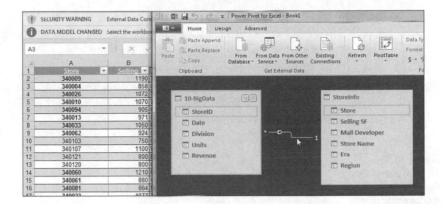

3. To return to the grid, click the Data View icon in the Home tab of the Power Pivot window.

10

Adding Calculated Columns Using DAX

You can add formulas in the Power Pivot grid. One common metric for retail stores is Sales per Square Foot. To enable this calculation, follow these steps:

1. Click the first worksheet tab at the bottom of the Power Pivot window. This is your 1.8 million–row data set.

2. Click in the first cell of the blank column to the right of Revenue, which has the heading Add Column.

3. Type an equal sign. Click on the Revenue column. The formula =[Revenue] appears in the formula bar.

4. Type a slash to denote division.

5. Start to type RELATED. Once it becomes the first item in AutoComplete, press Tab. (Note that RELATED is similar to VLOOKUP but far easier.)

6. AutoComplete now offers all the fields in the StoreInfo table. Double-click StoreInfo[Selling SF]. Type the final closing parenthesis. Press Enter. Excel fills the column with the calculation.

7. Right-click the column and select Rename Column. Type a name such as **SalesPerSF**.

At this point, you might be thinking of adding many more columns, but let's move on to using the pivot table.

Building a Pivot Table

Open the PivotTable drop-down on the Home tab of the Power Pivot ribbon. You have choices for a single pivot table, a single chart, a chart and a table, two charts, Power View, and so on. Follow these steps:

1. Select PivotTable. You now see the Power Pivot tab back in the Excel window.

2. Select to put the pivot table on a new worksheet and click OK. You are now back in Excel. The PivotTable Fields list shows both tables, although you have to use the triangle symbol next to each table to see the fields in the table.

3. Expand the 10-BigData table in the Power Pivot Fields list and select Revenue. Expand the StoreInfo table and select Region. Excel builds a pivot table that shows sales by region (see Figure 10.15). You now have a pivot table from 1.8 million rows of data with a virtual link to a lookup table.

Figure 10.15
This pivot table summarizes 1.8 million rows and data from two tables.

Row Labels	Sum of Revenue
Arizona	60782907
Atlanta	32638275
Colorado	11811315
Connecticut	19248377
Florida	102291967
Greater NYC	10350148
Hawaii	11813221
Illinois	45916862
Indiana	25148729
Massachusetts	19271177
MD	5913019
Michigan	23704144
Missouri	43000000
New Jersey	28121919
No California	72660342
Ohio	44414518
Other	173427185
So California	191277435
Texas	60663157
Upstate NY	2954238
Virginia	19282135
Washington State	26664635
xOutlets	19176437
Grand Total	1050532142

At this point, you might want to go to the PivotTable Tools tabs to further format the pivot table. You could apply a currency format and rename the Sum of Revenue field. You could also choose a format with banded rows and apply other formatting.

Understanding Differences Between Power Pivot and Regular Pivot Tables

If you have spent your whole Excel life building pivot tables out of regular Excel data, you are going to find some annoyances with Power Pivot pivot tables. Many of these issues are not because of Power Pivot. They are because any Power Pivot pivot table automatically is an OLAP pivot table. This means that it behaves like an OLAP pivot table.

Note the following differences between Power Pivot and regular pivot tables:

■ Days of the week do not automatically sort into the proper sequencein Power Pivot. You have to choose More Sort Options, Ascending, More Options. Uncheck the

AutoSort box. Open the First Key Sort Order drop-down and choose Sunday, Monday, Tuesday. Later in this chapter, you'll see how to solve this with a Calendar table.

■ There is a trick in regular Excel pivot tables that you can do instead of dragging field names where you want them. Say that you go to a cell that contains the word *Friday* and type **Monday** there. When you press Enter, the Monday data moves to that new column. This does not work in Power Pivot pivot tables!

■ When you enter a formula in the Excel interface, you can point to a cell to include that cell in the formula. You can do this by using the mouse or the arrow keys. Apparently, the Power Pivot team is made up of mouse people because they support building a formula using the mouse in the Power Pivot grid. Old-time Lotus 1-2-3 customers who build their formulas using arrow keys will be disappointed to find that the arrow-key method doesn't work.

■ The Refresh button on the Analyze tab forces Excel to update the data in the pivot table. Think before you do this in Excel 2016. In the current example, this forces Excel to go out and import the 1.8 million–row data set again.

Using DAX Calculations

Data Analysis Expressions is a relatively new formula language. In this chapter you've already seen an example of using a DAX function to add a calculated column to a table in the Power Pivot grid. The 81 DAX functions are mostly copied straight from Excel for doing these types of calculations. Most of the functions are identical to their Excel counterparts, with a few exceptions listed in the next section.

You can also use DAX to create new calculated fields in a pivot table. These functions do not calculate a single cell value. They are all aggregate functions that calculate a value for the filtered rows behind any cell in the pivot table. DAX offers 54 functions to enable these calculations. The real power is in these functions.

Using DAX Calculations for Calculated Columns

You've already seen one example of a calculated column. The DAX functions for calculated columns are remarkably similar to the same functions in Excel, and mostly don't require a lot of explanation. However, there are a few oddities where Excel functions were renamed in DAX:

■ The rarely documented DATEDIF function in Excel has been renamed YEARFRAC and was rewritten to actually work.

■ The TEXT function in Excel was renamed FORMAT.

■ The SUMIFS function was replaced and enhanced by CALCULATE.

■ The VLOOKUP function was simplified with the RELATED function.

■ DAX introduced the BLANK function. Because some of the aggregation functions can base a calculation on either ALLNONBLANKROW or FIRSTNONBLANK, you can use the BLANK function in an IF function to exclude certain rows from measure calculations.

■ The CHOOSE function was renamed SWITCH. Also, whereas CHOOSE must work with values from 1 to 255, the SWITCH function can be programmed to work with other values.

Using DAX to Create a Calculated Field in a Pivot Table

DAX calculated fields can run circles around traditional calculated fields. They are calculated only once per cell in the resultant pivot table. In Figure 10.16, the pivot table has numeric values in C4:C11. If you define a new DAX calculated field, it is calculated only for the 8 numeric cells in the pivot table. This is a lot faster than calculating 1.8 million cells and then summarizing. Before building your first calculated field, you need to understand filters, discussed next.

Figure 10.16
How many filters are on cell C4?

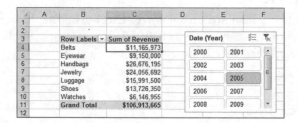

Filtering with DAX Calculated Fields

As you start to use DAX calculated fields, you have to realize that calculated fields automatically respect all filters applied to any particular cell in the pivot table. DAX filters first and then calculates. To understand this, consider cell C4 in Figure 10.16.

Think about how many filters are applied to cell C4. Would you say one? I think that the answer is two.

Everyone would agree that slicers are filtering the cell. Cell C4 is filtered to show only records that fall in the year 2005, based on the first slicer. That is one filter.

In addition, the Belts row header in B4 is really filtering C4 to include only records in the Belts division. That is the second filter.

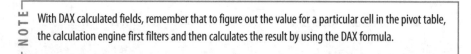

NOTE   With DAX calculated fields, remember that to figure out the value for a particular cell in the pivot table, the calculation engine first filters and then calculates the result by using the DAX formula.

Defining a DAX Calculated Field

To define a new calculated field, go to the Excel ribbon, click the Power Pivot tab, and choose Measures, New Measure.

> **NOTE** Microsoft used the term *measures* in Excel 2010 and then switched to *calculated fields* in Excel 2013. As this book goes to press, Microsoft has returned to calling them *measures*, but do not be surprised if it returns to using *calculated fields* in some future monthly release of Office 365.

You should specify your main table in the Table Name box. Give it a name like **StoreCount**. Type your formula in the formula box and use the fx icon to insert function names. For field names, start by typing a few characters of the table name and then use the AutoComplete list to select the field.

When you are done, click the Check Formula button to check the syntax. Note that the tooltip for the function still covers up the result of the Check Formula command. Click in the Description field to hide the tooltip so you can see the result of the Check Formula command. You should see "No errors in formula," as shown in Figure 10.17.

Figure 10.17
Define a new calculated field.

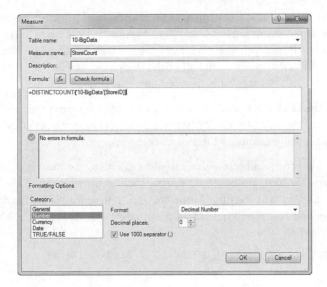

Click OK to add the new calculated field to the PivotTable Fields list.

After you define a calculated field, you can use that field in future calculations. The SalesPerStore field in Figure 10.18 is calculated as `=[Sum of Revenue]/ [StoreCount]`.

You do not have to display Sum of Revenue or StoreCount in the pivot table. You could simplify the pivot table to show only SalesPerStore.

10

Figure 10.18
SalesPerStore is calculated from a field in the data divided by a different DAX calculated field.

Row Labels	Sum of Revenue	StoreCount	SalesPerStore
2000	$13,434,145	9	$1,492,683
2001	$44,498,569	30	$1,483,286
2002	$60,664,358	41	$1,479,618
2003	$70,892,992	48	$1,476,937
2004	$78,744,311	53	$1,485,742
2005	$106,913,665	72	$1,484,912
2006	$116,096,650	78	$1,488,419
2007	$143,895,468	97	$1,483,458
2008	$202,661,884	137	$1,479,284
2009	$212,730,100	144	$1,477,292

Date (Year)

2000	2001
2002	2003
2004	2005
2006	2007
2008	2009

Using Time Intelligence

Typically, Excel stores dates as a serial number. When you enter 2/17/2018 in a cell, Excel only knows that this date is 43,148 days after December 31, 1899. Power Pivot adds time intelligence. When you have a date such as 2/17/2018 in Power Pivot, there are time intelligence functions that know that year-to-date means 1/1/2018 through 2/17/2018. The time intelligence functions know that month-to-date from the prior year is 2/1/2017 through 2/17/2017.

Remember that each value cell in a pivot table is a result of filters imposed by the slicers and by the row and column fields. Cell D28 in Figure 10.19 is being filtered to 2001 by the slicer and further filtered to January 25, 2001, by the row field in B28. But that cell needs to break free of the filter in order to add all of the sales from January 1, 2001, through January 25, 2001. The `CALCULATE` function helps you solve this problem.

In many ways, the DAX `CALCULATE` function is like a super-human version of the Excel `SUMIFS` function. `=CALCULATE(`*`Field,Filter,Filter,Filter,Filter`*`)` is the syntax. But any *`Filter`* argument could actually unapply a filter that's being imposed by a slicer or a row field.

`DATESMTD([Date])` returns all of the dates used to calculate the month-to-date total for the cell. For January 25, 2001, the `DATESMTD` function will return January 1 through 25, 2001. When you use `DATESMTD` as the filter in the `CALCULATE` function, it breaks the chains of the 1/25/2001 filter and reapplies a new filter of January 1–25, 2001. The DAX formula for MTDSales is

```
=CALCULATE([Sum of Revenue],DATESMTD('10-BigData'[Date]))
```

Figure 10.19
Time intelligence lets you calculate MTD or Prior Year sales.

	B	C	D	E
3	Row Labels	Sum of Revenue	MTDSales	LYSales
22	1/19/2001	$133,915	$1,741,562	$21,021
23	1/20/2001	$119,718	$1,861,280	$25,600
24	1/21/2001	$107,216	$1,968,496	$39,502
25	1/22/2001	$70,332	$2,038,828	$36,266
26	1/23/2001	$71,239	$2,110,067	$30,938
27	1/24/2001	$71,003	$2,181,070	$21,255
28	1/25/2001	$84,855	$2,265,925	$20,574
29	1/26/2001	$134,513	$2,400,438	$21,057
30	1/27/2001	$120,091	$2,520,529	$24,342
31	1/28/2001	$105,613	$2,626,142	$39,923
32	1/29/2001	$70,722	$2,696,864	$34,319
33	1/30/2001	$69,773	$2,766,637	$31,409
34	1/31/2001	$69,804	$2,836,441	$20,941
35	2/1/2001	$85,800	$85,800	$21,131
36	2/2/2001	$131,516	$217,316	$21,367

Date (Year)

2000	2001
2002	2003
2004	2005
2006	2007
2008	2009

The measure in column E requires two filter arguments. First, you need to tell DAX to ignore the Years filter. Use ALL([Years]) to do this. Then, you need to point to one year ago. Use DATEADD([Date],-1,YEAR) to move backward one year from January 25, 2002, to January 25, 2001. Therefore, this is the formula for LYSales:

```
CALCULATE([Sum of Revenue],
All('10-BigData'[Date (Year)]),
DATEADD('10-BigData'[Date],-1,YEAR))
```

Other time intelligence functions include DATESQTD and DATESYTD.

> **NOTE** To learn more about DAX, read *DAX Formulas for Power Pivot*, Second Edition, by Rob Collie and Avi Singh.

Next Steps

While Power Pivot lets you build pivot tables from complex models, the new Power View add-in for Excel 2016 Pro Plus customers lets you combine multiple Power Pivot charts in an animated, interactive dashboard within Excel. The 3D Map feature lets you animate your data on a globe. Chapter 11 introduces Power View and 3D Map.

Dashboarding with Power View and 3D Map

11

Chapter 10, "Mashing Up Data with Power Pivot," introduces the Power Pivot Data Model and the Vertipaq engine. If you have the Pro Plus edition of Excel 2016, you have the Power View add-in, which creates interactive dashboard elements from your Power Pivot data. You can combine pivot charts, maps, and pivot tables on an interactive canvas.

> **CAUTION**
>
> Power BI Desktop, which was introduced in Chapter 8, "Sharing Pivot Tables with Others," is a better implementation of the features introduced in Power View. The Excel team would love to replace Power View in Excel with Power BI Desktop. Consequently, they've removed the Insert Power View Sheet icon from the Excel 2016 ribbon. If you want to use Power View in Excel 2016, you will have to customize the Quick Access Toolbar or customize the ribbon to add the Insert Power View Sheet icon.

All editions of Excel 2016 include the 3D Map feature, which you can use to animate your pivot tables over time on a map. This feature was previously released as an add-in for Excel 2013 called Power Map.

Preparing Data for Power View

When you are adding data to the Data Model for Power Pivot, you simply need to add the data tables and create the relationships. Power View has a few extra features that require you to properly categorize certain data fields.

The data set for this chapter is 10 years of fictitious book sales data. The main Fact table reports quarterly sales data by city and title. There are more than 400,000 records in the Fact table. Three smaller lookup tables provide category information:

■ The Geography table provides City, State, and Region.

■ The Products table maps the ProdID to Title, List Price, Category, Version of Excel, Level, and other category information. Power View is particularly good at letting you visualize how one category relates to another category, hence the desire to add many categories.

■ You need to create a date table that converts daily dates to years and quarters. Yes, you could add 411,000 formulas in the Power Pivot grid with the =YEAR() function, but it is faster to use a date lookup table. To create the Dates table, copy the column of 411,000 dates in Excel to a new worksheet. Use Data, Remove Duplicates to get a unique list of daily dates. A new Year column comes from the =YEAR() function. The new Quarter column requires a VLOOKUP from MONTH() to convert to a quarter number. After you have the date columns, convert formulas to values and add this table to your model.

Consider adding a path to an image file for each product. If you store a link to a product image, you can add that image to your dashboard. This is a cool feature. If your company sells online, there is probably already a folder with a collection of image files. If you are lucky, there is a consistent naming convention where product 123 has an image called http://www.yourco.com/images/p123.jpg. In my sample data set, I learned we aren't very consistent at MrExcel.com. There were 28 products with 28 different naming conventions for the images. Note that the image files can be stored locally or on the Web. C:\Artwork\image.jpg works fine as an image URL. So does http://www.mrexcel.com/image.jpg.

You can also add a column for URL to the product page on your website. This is not as cool as showing images, however. Power View doesn't use a URL shortener, so the entire URL ends up showing in your report.

After adding your tables to Power Pivot and defining relationships, you should perform these extra steps to make your Power View experience better:

1. Format your numeric columns in Power Pivot. This matters in Power View. With a regular pivot table, if you format the underlying data and add it to the pivot table, you have to reformat it in the pivot table. The Power View people make it hard to change the numeric format in the dashboard, but they make up for it by respecting the numeric format that you define in Power Pivot. For the columns that you will be using in the report (such as Revenue and Profit), select the entire column. In the Power Pivot window, choose the Home tab and then Format as Currency. Select Decrease Decimal twice to get rid of the decimal places. Repeat for the numeric fields that you will likely include in the dashboard. For a Quantity field, use the Comma icon in the Formatting group to add commas. Even if all of your detail rows are in the 1–100 range, they will eventually total up to more than 1,000, so add the thousands separator now.

2. Select the DateTable tab in Power Pivot. On the Design tab, open the Mark as Date Table drop-down and then choose the redundant Mark as Date Table command. You have to specify which column contains a date field and contains only unique dates.

3. If you do not see an Advanced tab in the Power Pivot window, open the File drop-down and choose Switch to Advanced Mode. Note that the File drop-down does not

actually say File; it is a gray tab with a worksheet icon that appears to the left of the Home tab.

4. Go to the Advanced tab in the Power Pivot window. In the Data Category drop-down field, mark as many columns as you can with a data category. In Figure 11.1, select the entire ImagePath column and choose the data category Image URL. Starting in Excel 2016, Excel suggests data categories for certain fields. Make sure the suggestions are correct before accepting them. Here are examples of data categories you can use with the sample data set:

- Mark the web page column with the category Web URL.
- Mark the City column with the category City.

Figure 11.1
Assign a data category to a field that contains a link to an image.

- The data has both State and State Abbreviation columns. Mark both of these columns with the category State or Province.
- Mark the Product Name category with the category Product. Note that Product is not in the drop-down. You have to choose More Categories, All and then choose Product.

5. Select the Year field in the Dates table. On the Design tab, choose Summarize By and change from Default to Do Not Summarize. This prevents Power View from attempting to offer Sum of Year every time you add Year to a new element in Power View.

When you are done defining the relationships and the categories, close the Power Pivot window to return to Excel.

Creating a Power View Dashboard

A Power View dashboard looks like just another worksheet in a workbook. Go to the Insert tab in the ribbon and choose Power View. A new worksheet is inserted to the left of the current worksheet. The worksheet is given a name such as Power View1, Power View2, and so on. You can right-click the sheet tab to delete it just as you would a worksheet. You can drag to move it to a new location, just like a worksheet.

The Power View window contains a Power View Fields list, sort of like the PivotTable Fields list, on the right side. A large canvas appears on the left. This canvas initially contains a table element, which you will delete later. A collapsible Filters panel appears to the right of the canvas (see Figure 11.2).

Figure 11.2
A new Power View window.

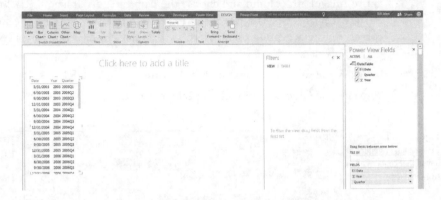

Perhaps having a completely blank canvas seems too intimidating, so Excel 2016 starts each Power View canvas with one table element. The data in the table seems to be based on which table was last active in Excel. You should delete this table before you go any further, by following these steps:

1. Click inside the table on the Power View canvas. Four angle brackets appear in each corner of the table.

2. Press the Delete key on the keyboard. The table is deleted. The Power View Fields list now shows all of the tables instead of the one selected table.

The Power View Fields list is far more flexible than the PivotTable Fields list. The top is similar, with an expandable list of tables that you can limit to just active tables or show all tables.

┌─ **C A U T I O N** ───┐
The areas at the bottom of the Fields list change dramatically as you change a dashboard element from a table to a chart to a map to a scatter chart. Expect areas to come and go.
└──┘

┌─ **C A U T I O N** ───┐
Be careful to watch for new contextual ribbon tabs that appear to the right of the Power View tab. Inexplicably, Microsoft did not group the related contextual tabs under a Power View Tools grouping, so you might not notice that tabs labeled Formatting, Text, and Analyze come and go as you select various items.
└──┘

When I first started working with Power View, I was hoping that formatting would appear on the Power View tab, but the command I needed was usually on a tab just to the right of the Power View tab in the ribbon. With Power Pivot, the usual action is to click the Power Pivot icon in the Excel ribbon to get to the Power Pivot window and more tabs. This does not work in Power View; instead, clicking the Power View icon inserts a new blank worksheet.

Every New Dashboard Element Starts as a Table

Expand the Geography table in the Fields list and choose Region. That field flies over to a new element on the canvas. Every new element starts as a table. This is just a starting point. After the table is on the canvas, you can use the Switch Visualization group on the Design tab to change to one of three kinds of tables, one of three kinds of bar charts, a columns chart, a pie chart, a line chart, a scatter chart, or a map.

You might build a dashboard with eight dashboard elements, but there will be only one Fields list and one Filters pane no matter what. The active element has four gray corner icons and four edge icons. Any changes that you make to the Fields list are applied to the active element. Right now, with your first table, this is a great feature. Check the Revenue box, and your one active element becomes a table showing revenue by region (see Figure 11.3).

With multiple elements on the dashboard, not paying attention to which element is the active element leads to the frequent use of Undo. I often think, "I am staring right at the element that I want to add the field to, but somehow, Power View can't read my mind."

11

Figure 11.3
A table element on a
Power View dashboard.

Region	Revenue
ArLaTxOk	$4,041,329.91
Midwest	$3,966,169.58
Northeast	$5,431,068.75
Plains	$1,148,393.89
Southeast	$2,723,915.99
Southwest	$2,285,514.80
West	$7,651,949.14
Total	**$27,248,342.06**

Subtlety Should Be Power View's Middle Name

I am frequently accused of being a control freak. When I look at the table in Figure 11.3, three things come screaming into my head: Where is the sort icon? Where is the Filter icon? How can I right-justify the Revenue heading? Here are some answers:

- First, there is no sort icon. To sort by Revenue, click the Revenue heading. The first click sorts smallest to largest. Click again to sort largest to smallest. A little blue triangle appears next to the Revenue heading to let you know that the report is sorted by that column.

- Second, the filter and pop-out icons are invisible until the mouse pointer is above the table. After you hover over the table, the icons appear above the table (see Figure 11.4).

■ You can't right-align a heading. The icons on the Home tab do not function in Power View. There are a lot of very basic settings that are still missing in Power View. There is a Power View tab with an icon where you can change the font, the text size, and the background.

Figure 11.4
Click a heading to sort or hover over it for more icons.

Region	Revenue
West	$7,651,949.14
Northeast	$5,431,068.75
ArLaTxOk	$4,041,329.91
Midwest	$3,966,169.58
Southeast	$2,723,915.99
Southwest	$2,285,514.80
Plains	$1,148,393.89
Total	**$27,248,342.06**

Converting a Table to a Chart

With the first table selected, you see a Design tab in the ribbon. The left group in this tab is called Switch Visualization. You have 13 choices in 4 drop-downs and the Map icon. The Column Chart drop-down offers Stacked, 100% Stacked, and Clustered Column options. The Other Chart drop-down offers Line, Scatter, and Pie options (see Figure 11.5).

Figure 11.5
Convert the default table to a chart or a map.

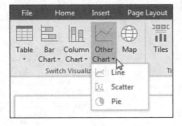

For now, choose a stacked bar chart. The element stays exactly the same size, and Power View tries to fit a chart in that small area. It doesn't fit, as you can see in Figure 11.6.

Figure 11.6
The converted chart doesn't fit in the previous space.

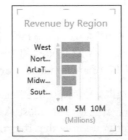

Click one of the eight resize handles and stretch the element frame until the chart looks good. As shown in Figure 11.7, you now have additional controls at the top left to control the sort order. The pop-out icon makes the element full screen temporarily. Say that you have 10 small elements on the dashboard. You can click the pop-out icon to make 1 of the small elements full screen. After the element is full screen, you can click a pop-out icon to return the element to the original size.

Figure 11.7
Resize the element to provide room for a chart.

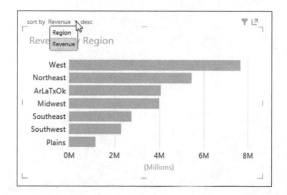

In the Fields list, drag the Channel field to the Legend area. The chart becomes a stacked bar chart showing book sales broken out as the channels Online, eBook, and Bricks (see Figure 11.8).

Figure 11.8
Add a field to the Legend area in the Fields list to create a stacked chart.

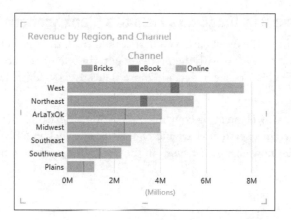

While a chart is selected, a Layout tab displays in the ribbon. Using the Layout tab, you can move the legend to the top, add data labels, or change the type of horizontal axis.

Adding Drill-down to a Chart

The current chart has Region as an Axis field. Drag the State field and drop it as a second Axis field. Optionally, add City as a third Axis field. After you make this change, nothing appears different in the chart. However, you've now created a hierarchy that you can drill into.

11

Double-click the bar for the Southwest region. The chart is replaced with a chart showing Arizona, Colorado, Utah, and New Mexico. Double-click the bar for Arizona to reveal a list of Arizona cities (see Figure 11.9). After you use drill-down, an arrow appears at the top right for drill-up.

Figure 11.9
Add a field to the Axis area in the Fields list to allow drill-down.

Beginning a New Element by Dragging a Field to a Blank Spot on the Canvas

To add a new element to the dashboard, you drag a field from the Fields list and drop it in a blank portion of the canvas. As with the first element, this element starts as a small table. You can switch it to a chart, resize it, and add more fields. Keep adding new elements as necessary.

You can also create a new element by copying and pasting an existing element. If you have designed one chart, right-click that chart and choose Copy. Click in a blank area of the canvas and paste. You can now change the fields in the Fields list to change the chart.

The next bit is magic.

Filtering One Chart with Another One

In Figure 11.10, two charts appear on the canvas. The right chart shows revenue by year. The left chart shows revenue by channel by region.

If you click on any part of any chart, all the other charts will be filtered to the same element. Click the 2013 column in the right chart, and the left chart is faded except for the 2013 revenue.

To return to the unfiltered report, click the 2013 column a second time.

Figure 11.10
All elements are connected. Click a column in one chart to filter the other chart.

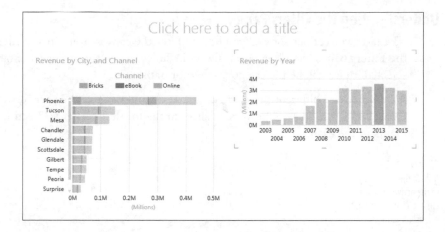

Adding a Real Slicer

The slicers in Power View look different from regular slicers, but they act the same way. To create a slicer, drag a field to a blank area of the canvas. That field starts out as a new table. Go to the Design tab of the ribbon and choose Slicer. The table is converted to a Power View slicer (see Figure 11.11).

Figure 11.11
A slicer on the canvas controls all elements on the canvas.

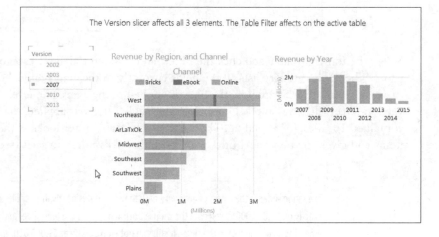

Notice these differences from a regular slicer:

- A colored square next to an item means the item is selected.
- You click an item to select that one item.
- To select multiple items, you have to Ctrl+click the other items.
- The slicer is always one column. You cannot rearrange the slicers in Power View as you can in a regular pivot table.
- An eraser icon appears in the top right of the slicer. This is the Clear Filter icon. It is equivalent to the Funnel with X icon in a regular slicer.

Understanding the Filters Pane

The last two sections showed you how to filter the canvas. You can also filter by using the Filters pane. The Filters pane always includes the category View. If a table or chart is selected, there will be the category Chart or Table.

Although these different filters are on the same Filters pane, they act very differently. Consider Figure 11.12. The Version slicer in the top-left corner is affecting all three elements in the dashboard.

Figure 11.12
A Table filter applies only to the active table and is applied to the aggregate values in the table.

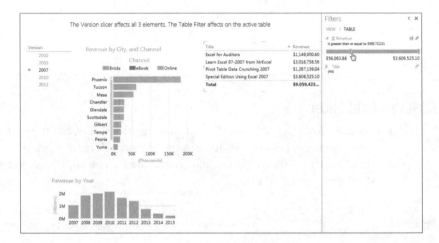

Select the top-right table and click the Filter icon to open the Table category in the Filters panel. The Table category lists all the fields currently in the active table. When you filter to ask for items over $1 million, the filter is applied at the aggregate level. After the 2007 version Slicer filter was applied but before the Table filter was applied, the top-right table contained 10 titles, for a total of $11.3 million. The Table filter looks at those 10 summary items and gives you only the 4 titles with more than $1 million in sales (see Figure11.12).

> **CAUTION**
>
> The range slider in the Filters pane is very easy to use, but it is nearly impossible to get it to stop exactly on $1,000,000. If you hold the mouse button down on the blue slider and use the left/right arrow keys, you can nudge the slider. It still will not stop exactly at $1,000,000. You can click the blue arrow to the right of the Revenue filter to open a form where you can type in the exact value 1,000,000.

Here are the differences between the Table filter and the View filter:

- The View filter affects all elements on the canvas.
- The View filter starts out blank. You have to drag a field from the Fields list onto the Filters pane.
- The View filter is applied to the individual detail records in the data set. By filtering for revenue greater than approximately $2,500, Power View goes back to the original

411,000 rows of data and looks for records where the revenue on the individual line item is greater than $2,500. It is tough to sell 100 computer books in one city in one quarter. The results here are likely tied to seminar or conference purchases (see Figure 11.13).

Figure 11.13
A View filter is applied to the underlying records and affects all elements on the canvas.

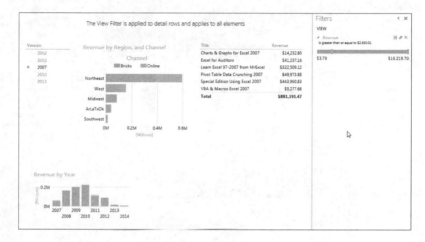

This last distinction of the filter applying at the detail level is not obvious.

Using Tile Boxes to Filter a Chart or a Group of Charts

The Power View Fields list offers a field called Tile By. Using it is another way to filter an element on the dashboard.

To use Tile By, select one chart or table element that you want to filter. Find the field you want to filter in the Fields list. You can drag the field to the Tile By area at the bottom of the Fields list. Alternatively, you can hover over the field, open the drop-down, and choose Add as Tile By.

If you choose a regular field, the tiles appear as words. In Figure 11.14, the Image field has been added as a file.

The filter appears as tiles across the top of the chart. Notice the thick blue lines above and below the chart. These lines tell you that only the one chart between the lines is affected by the tiles (see Figure 11.14).

Tiles are cool. They provide a way to filter one chart and not the other charts. But I can already hear what you're thinking: You want to have two charts controlled by Tile 1 and another chart controlled by Tile 2. Fortunately, you can do this.

In Figure 11.14, right-click an element that is outside the boundary and choose Cut. Click anywhere inside the tile boundary lines, right-click, and paste. The result will inevitably be messy, with two charts right on top of each other.

Drag the tile box up and drag the bottom boundary line to add some room. Then individually move the two charts so they fit. It is tricky to find the correct boundary box to drag. The result is shown in Figure 11.15. Both of these charts are within the boundary lines, so they are both controlled by the tiles at the top. The table outside the boundary lines is not affected by the tiles.

11

Figure 11.14
Only the elements between the tile boundary lines are filtered by the tile category filters.

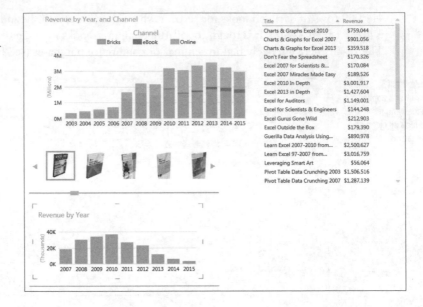

Figure 11.15
Both elements are within the boundary lines, and they are filtered together.

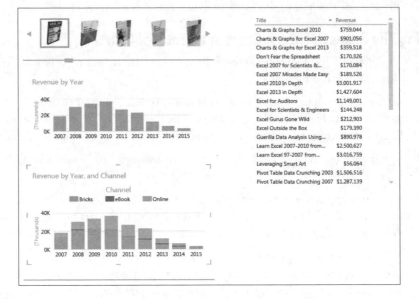

Replicating Charts Using Multiples

Say that you have a chart element that shows revenue by year. You could add a new field to the Legend area in order to create a stacked or clustered column chart. Alternatively, you could drag the new field to the Vertical Multiples or Horizontal Multiples field to cause Power View to replicate the chart for each value in that field. In Figure 11.16, the revenue chart appears as three charts based on the Channel field dropped in the Horizontal Multiples field.

Figure 11.16
Add a field to Horizontal
Multiples to replicate the
chart.

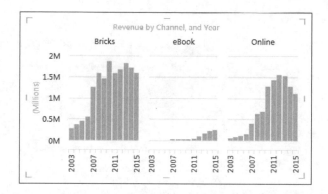

When you have only a few categories, there is no difference between dropping a field in Vertical
Multiples and dropping it in Horizontal Multiples. If you chose a field with nine values and a Vertical
Multiple, Power View uses three rows of three columns. In this example, both the horizontal multiple
and vertical multiple appear as one row by three columns. The Multiples group on the Layout tab offers
Grid Height and Grid Width settings where you can control the number of rows and columns used.

Showing Data on a Map

As you probably know, Microsoft owns Bing. Bing maps are pretty cool. Because Microsoft
owns Bing, Microsoft seems to have free rein to use the Bing API as much as it wants to,
and that is evident with the Map feature.

In a blank section of the Power View canvas, build a table showing revenue by state. With
the table active, go to the Design tab in the ribbon and choose Map from the Switch
Visualization category.

A warning appears that Excel has to send a list of states to Bing. I am trying to think of a
case where you would care. If you were working for a secret government agency and you
were mapping the location of where the Atomic Energy Commission stores the remains of
alien UFO crashes, and you think that some random person at Bing Maps is a UFO con-
spiracy theorist, then maybe you would care. However, I have to believe that Bing Maps
is getting a million requests a day, and the odds of anyone figuring out that your list is of
UFO storage sites instead of the location of Starbucks stores is slim.

After a few seconds of geocoding, a map displays. By default, the Revenue field becomes the
size of the bubble in each state. When you click the map, icons let you zoom in or zoom
out. Click the map and drag with the hand icon to center the map to a new position.

In Figure 11.17, the Channel field has been moved to the Color area. Excel creates a pie
chart in each state, showing the relative percentage of sales by channel. Apparently, eBooks
are doing better in California than in Arizona and New Mexico (though it's hard to see that
on the printed page).

11

Figure 11.17
Add Channel to the
Color area.

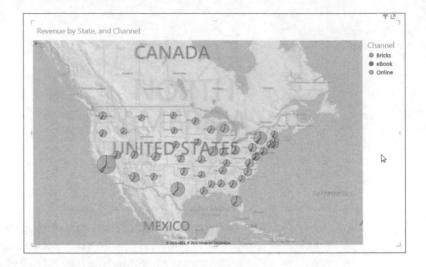

Using Images

What if you could populate a pivot table with pictures of the people or items? Tables in Power View allow the display of pictures. You can display pictures in all three types of tables: table, matrix, and card view.

To insert a picture, a column in your data needs to contain a URL that points to each image or a path and filename that point to the image on your computer.

Add the Image URL field to your table. After a quick warning that Excel is getting the pictures from external sources, the images show up in the table.

Pictures also work in Card View. To switch a table to Card View, go to Design, Switch Visualizations, Table, Card View. This view presents the field title for each field in every card. Figure 11.18 shows a Card View with a tile by category.

Figure 11.18
Card View adds heading
names to all the records.

Changing a Calculation

Multiple calculations are available for fields you add to an element. You can change numeric fields from Sum to Average, Min, Max, or Count. In addition, you can use Count Distinct and Count Non Blank for text fields.

In Figure 11.19, the table shows the states and then the number of distinct cities with sales in those states. Build a table like this with State, City, and Revenue. At the bottom of the Power View Fields list, open the drop-down for City and choose Count (Distinct).

Figure 11.19
Calculations include Count Distinct.

State	Count of City	Revenue
Alabama	5	$250,579.77
Alaska	1	$82,360.02
Arizona	11	$1,124,617.34
Arkansas	2	$81,444.63
California	100	$6,045,800.24
Colorado	13	$699,227.48
Connecticut	7	$231,313.32
District of Columbia	1	$167,671.19
Florida	29	$1,383,843.59
Georgia	7	$341,346.46
Hawaii	1	$106,791.79
Idaho	1	$58,593.69
Illinois	10	$1,122,721.45
Indiana	6	$402,285.48
Iowa	4	$151,516.51
Kansas	6	$201,215.19

Another useful calculation option occurs when Power View summarizes a field that should not be summarized. For example, the product table has a ProductTier field with numeric values from 1 to 5. If you add this to a report, Power View might try to sum the Tier field when you want it to categorize by that field. Hover over the field at the bottom of the Fields list. Choose Do Not Summarize as the calculation.

Animating a Scatter Chart over Time

To create a great scatter chart, you need three or four numeric fields that are related. Drag the first field to a blank section of the canvas. Choose Design, Switch Visualizations, Other Charts, Scatter.

Figure 11.20 shows the details of the choices available in the Fields list when you are creating a scatter chart:

- Any numeric field for the x-axis.
- Any numeric field for the y-axis.
- Optionally, an area to control the size of the data point.

11

- A Details area. For every unique value in the Details area, you get one point in the scatter chart.
- Optionally, a Color area. Each point is colored according to values in this field.
- A Play Axis area.

Figure 11.20
The scatter chart offers the most choices for areas.

If you add a field to the Play Axis area, a scrubber control appears along the bottom of the chart (see Figure 11.21). You can drag the marker left or right to see the chart at various points in time, or you can click the Play button to watch the chart animate.

The Play Axis area is the key to having the chart animate. Unfortunately, at this time, only the scatter chart offers a Play Axis area. You cannot animate column charts, bar charts, pie charts, or tables.

- To learn about using Power Map to animate data on maps, **see** "Analyzing Geographic Data with 3D Map," **p. 261**.

Figure 11.21
Use the scrubber at the bottom to see the points change over time.

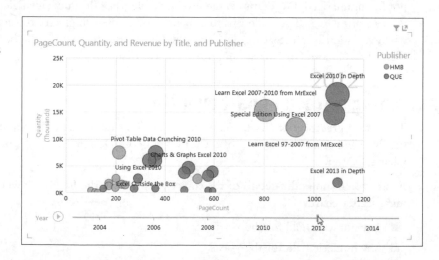

Some Closing Tips on Power View

As you experiment with Power View, keep these tips in mind:

- Be careful when clicking on charts. Click in the white space to select a chart. If you inadvertently click one of the chart columns, you've just filtered everything else on the canvas.

- The Fields list has headings for Active and All. If you just created a little chart with two fields, it is likely that the Fields list is now in Active mode, which means you see only the tables used in that chart. This is alarming because all your other tables and fields are missing. Don't be alarmed. Click All at the top of the Fields list, and they all come back.

- Don't be afraid to try new charts or tables. Create something. If it doesn't look good, right-click and select Cut. No harm. I am surprised how snappy and efficient Power View is. I have been demonstrating Power View using 411,000 records in five charts and animating over time for a few years and have not had one crash.

Analyzing Geographic Data with 3D Map

3D Map allows you to build a pivot table on a three-dimensional globe of the Earth. Provided that your data has any geographic field such as Street, City, State, or Zip Code, you can plot the data on a map.

Once the data is on the map, you can fly through the data, zooming in to study a city or zooming back out to a 50,000-foot view. You can either use 3D Map to interactively study the data or build a tour from various scenes and render that tour as a video for distribution to people who do not have 3D Map.

> **NOTE** The 3D Map feature was known as an add-in called Power Map in Excel 2013 and also formerly known as GeoFlow. If you have previously used Power Map or GeoFlow, you can find that functionality in Excel 2016 as 3D Map.

Preparing Data for 3D Map

Although 3D Map uses the Power Pivot Data Model, there is no need to load your data into Power Pivot. You can just select one cell from a data set with a geographic field such as Country, State, County, City, Street, or Zip Code. On the Insert tab, in the Tours group, choose 3D Map, as shown in Figure 11.22.

3D Map converts the current data set to a table and loads it to the Power Pivot Data Model before launching 3D Map. This step might take 10 to 20 seconds as Power Pivot is loaded in the background.

3D Map converts the data to latitude and longitude by using Bing Maps. If your data is outside the United States, you should include a field for country code. Otherwise, Paris will show up in Kentucky, and Melbourne will show up on the east coast of Florida.

There are three special types of geographic data that 3D Map can consume:

- 3D Map can deal with Latitude and Longitude as two separate fields. Note that west and south values should be negative.

- It is possible to plot the data not on a globe but on a custom map such as the floor plan for an airport or a store. In this case, you need to provide x and y data, remembering that x runs across the map, starting with 0 at the left edge, and y starts at 0 at the bottom edge.

- 3D Map now allows for custom shapes. You need to have a KML or SHP file describing the shapes. The names in your data set should match values in the KML file.

Although you don't have to preload the data into the Power Pivot Data Model, you can take that extra step if you need to define relationships between tables.

Figure 11.22
3D Map appears on the Insert tab.

Geocoding Data

The process of locating points on a map is called *geocoding*. When you first launch 3D Map, you have to choose the geographic fields. If you've used meaningful headings such as City or State, 3D Map auto-detects these fields.

In the Choose Geography section, place a check next to each geographic field. In the Geography and Map Level section, choose a field type for each of the geographic fields (see Figure 11.23).

> **TIP**
>
> Fields such as "123 Main Street" should be marked as Street. Fields such as "123 Main Street, Akron, OH" should be marked as Full Address. Marking "123 Main Street" as an address will lead to most of your data points placed in the wrong state.

Choose one of your geographic fields as the map level. If you choose State, you will get one point per state. If you choose Address, you will get one point for each unique address.

After you've chosen the geographic fields, click Next in the lower-right corner.

Figure 11.23
Choose geographic fields.

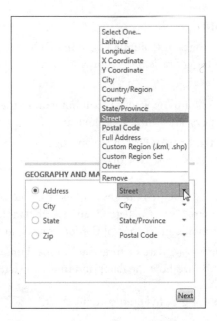

It takes a short while for 3D Map to complete the geocoding process. When it is finished, a percentage appears in the top of the PivotTable Fields list. Click this percentage to see a list of data points that could not be mapped (Figure 11.24). Items with a red X are not going to appear on the map. Items with a yellow ! are going to appear at the address shown.

11

Figure 11.24
3D Map indicates which addresses could not be found.

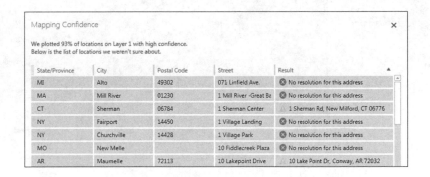

Mapping Confidence

We plotted 93% of locations on Layer 1 with high confidence.
Below is the list of locations we weren't sure about.

State/Province	City	Postal Code	Street	Result
MI	Alto	49302	071 Linfield Ave.	✖ No resolution for this address
MA	Mill River	01230	1 Mill River -Great Ba	✖ No resolution for this address
CT	Sherman	06784	1 Sherman Center	⚠ 1 Sherman Rd, New Milford, CT 06776
NY	Fairport	14450	1 Village Landing	✖ No resolution for this address
NY	Churchville	14428	1 Village Park	✖ No resolution for this address
MO	New Melle		10 Fiddlecreek Plaza	✖ No resolution for this address
AR	Maumelle	72113	10 Lakepoint Drive	⚠ 10 Lake Point Dr, Conway, AR 72032

NOTE

When an address is not found, there is currently no tool to place that data point on the map. Other mapping tools such as MapPoint would give you choices such as using a similar address or even adding the point to the center of the zip code. But 3D Map currently simply advises you to add more geographic fields to the original data set.

Building a Column Chart in 3D Map

3D Map offers five types of layers: Stacked Column, Clustered Column, Bubble, Heat Map, and Region. The processes for building Stacked Column and Clustered Column layers are similar:

1. Choose either the Clustered Column or Stacked Column icon in the bottom half of the Layer pane. Height, Category, and Time areas appear.

2. Drag a numeric field to the Height area. Use the drop-down arrow at the right edge of the field to choose Sum, Average, Count Not Blank, Count Distinct, Max, Min, or No Aggregation.

3. If you want the columns to be different colors, drag a field to the Category area. A large legend covers up the map. Click the legend, and resize handles appear. Right-click the legend and choose Edit to control the font, size, and color.

4. To animate the map over time, drag a date or time field to the Time area. Right-click the large time legend and customize how the dates and times appear.

Figure 11.25 shows an initial map using a clustered column chart.

Figure 11.25
One column appears for each street address in the data.

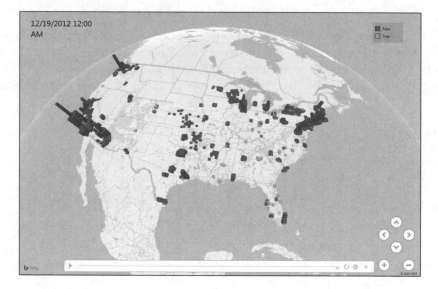

Navigating Through the Map

Initially, the zoom level is set to show all of your data points. You might discover that a few outliers cause the map to be zoomed out too far. For example, if you are analyzing customer data for an auto repair shop, you might find a few customers who stopped in for a repair while they were driving through on vacation. If 98% of your customers are near Charlotte, North Carolina, but three or four customers from New York and California are in the data set, the map will show everything from New York to California.

You can zoom in or out by using the + or − icons in the lower right of the map. You can use the mouse wheel to quickly zoom in or out.

As you start to zoom in, you might realize that you are zooming in on the wrong section of the map. Click and drag the map to re-center it. Or double-click any white space on the map to center the map at that point while zooming in.

Figure 11.26 shows a map zoomed in to show Florida.

Figure 11.26
Zoom in to show Florida.

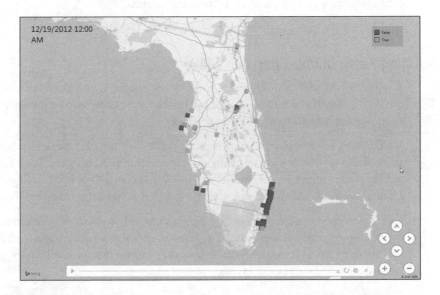

By default, you usually look straight down on the map, but it is easier to see the height of each column if you tip the map. Use the up arrow and down arrow icons on the map to tip the map up or down. Or use the Alt key and the mouse: Hold down Alt and drag the mouse straight up to tip the map so that you are viewing the map from a point closer to the ground.

Hold down Alt and drag the mouse straight down to move the vantage point higher. When you hold down Alt and drag the mouse left or right, you rotate the view left or right. Figure 11.27 shows Miami from a lower vantage point, as you would see the points from the Atlantic Ocean.

Figure 11.27
Alt+drag the mouse to tip or rotate the view.

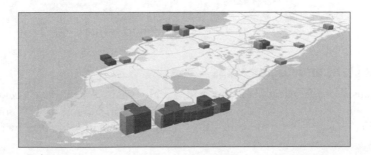

Labeling Individual Points

In many data sets, you see unusual data points. To see the details about a particular data point, hover over the point's column, and a tooltip appears, with identifiers for the data point. When you move away from the column, the tooltip is hidden.

If you are building a tour, you might want to display an annotation or a text box on a certain point. An annotation includes a custom title and the value of any fields you choose—or it can include a picture. A text box includes just text.

Right-click any point and choose Annotation or Text Box to build the label.

Building Pie or Bubble Charts on a Map

A bubble chart plots a single circle for each data point. The size of the circle tells you about the data point. If you add a Category field, the circle changes to a pie chart, with each category appearing as a wedge in the pie chart.

Unlike with column charts, you will likely want your bubble markers to be an aggregate of all points in a state or city. To change the level for a map, click the Pencil icon to the right of Geography at the top of the Layer pane. Then change the level to State and click Next. Drag a numeric field to the size area. Drag a text field to the category area.

You might need to adjust the size of the bubbles or pie charts. There are four symbols across the top of the Layer pane. The fourth symbol is a Settings gear-wheel icon. Click it and choose Layer Options. Slicers appear that let you change the opacity, size, thickness, and colors used (see Figure 11.28).

Figure 11.28
Use the Layer Options tab of the Layer pane to change the size of the bubbles.

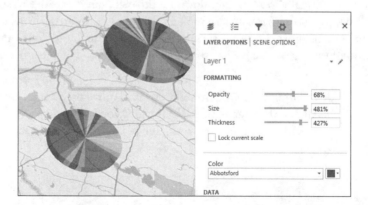

Using Heat Maps and Region Maps

3D Maps also offers heat maps and shaded region maps. A heat map is centered on an individual point and shows varying shades of green, yellow, and red to show intensity. A region map fills an outline with the same color and is useful for showing data by country, state, or county.

Figure 11.29 shows a map with two layers: One layer is a region map by state, and the other layer is a heat map by city.

Figure 11.29
Region maps and heat maps combined in a single map.

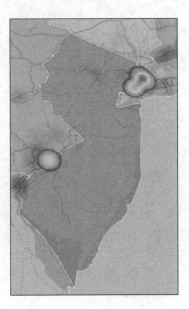

You might want to create region maps for shapes other than state or country. There are many free SHP or KML files available on the Internet. You can have 3D Map import these custom regions and then shade those areas on the map. To import a custom region, use Import Regions from the 3D Map ribbon.

Exploring 3D Map Settings

There are a number of useful settings in 3D Map. Here are some of my favorites:

- **Aerial Photography Map**—If you will be zooming in to the city level, you can show an aerial photograph over the map. Use the Themes drop-down in 3D Map and choose the second theme.

- **Add Map Labels**—Click the Map Labels icon in the ribbon to add labels to the map. If you are zoomed completely out, the labels will be country names. As you zoom in, the labels change to states, cities, and even street names. Note that labels are an all-or-nothing proposition. You cannot easily show some labels and not others.

- **Flat Map**—If you want to see the entire Earth at one time, use the Flat Map icon in the 3D Map ribbon.

Figure 11.30 shows a flat map with labels added and aerial photography.

Figure 11.30
See the whole Earth with a flat map.

Fine-Tuning 3D Map

There are situations where the defaults used by 3D Map are not the best. Here are trouble-shooting methods for various situations.

By default, each column in a column chart takes up a fair amount of space on the map. For example, if you plot every house on your street, each column takes up about one city block. You won't be able to make out the detail for each house. Click the Settings gear-wheel icon and then Layer Options. Change the Thickness setting to 5% or 10%. 3D Map makes each column very narrow (see Figure 11.31).

Figure 11.31
Change the thickness of individual columns to see more detail.

3D Map looks great on a huge 1080p monitor. If you are stuck on a tiny laptop, though, you should hide the Tour and Layer panes by using the icons in the 3D Map ribbon.

Most legends start out way to large. You can either resize them or right-click and choose Hide to remove them altogether.

The Funnel icon in the Layer pane allows you to add filters to any field. 3D Map cannot render 5,000 check boxes, so you might have to use the Search utility within the filters to find items to show or hide.

When you hover over a data point, the resulting tooltip is called a data card. You can customize what appears in the card by selecting Layer Options from the gear-wheel menu and then clicking the icon below Customize Data Card.

To combine different map types, add a layer using the Add Layer icon. Each layer can be shown at a different geography. You might have a column chart by city on Layer 1 and a region chart by state on Layer 2. The Layer Manager allows you to show and hide various layers.

Animating Data over Time

You can add a date or time field to any map layer. A time scrubber appears at the bottom of the map. Grab the scrubber and drag it left or right to show the data at any point in time. Use the Play button on the left side of the scrubber to have 3D Map animate the entire time period.

When you add the date or time field to the Time area, a small clock icon appears above the field. There are three choices in this drop-down menu:

- **Data Shows for an Instant**—The data appears when the time scrubber reaches this date, but then the data disappears once the scrubber passes the date.

- **Date Accumulates over Time**—This option is appropriate for showing how ticket sales happened. If you sold 10 tickets on Monday and then another 5 tickets on Tuesday, you would want the map to show 15 tickets on Tuesday.

- **Data Stays Until It Is Replaced**—Say that you have a list of housing sales for the past 30 years. If a house sold for $200,000 in 2001 and then for $225,000 in 2005, you would want to show $200,000 for all points from 2001 until the end of 2004.

To control the speed of the animation, click the gear-wheel icon in the Layer pane and choose Scene Options. The Speed slider in the Time section controls how fast the time will change. Watch the Scene Duration setting at the top of this panel to see how long it will take to animate through the entire period covered by the data set.

You can use the Start Date and End Date drop-downs to limit the animation to just a portion of the time period.

11

Building a Tour

You can use a tour in 3D Map to tell a story. Each scene in the tour can focus on a section of the map, and 3D Map will automatically fly from one scene to the next.

As you have been experimenting in 3D Map, you have been working on Scene 1 in the Tour pane. If you click the gear-wheel icon and then Scene Options, you will see that the default scene duration is 10 seconds, with a default transition duration of 3 seconds. Therefore, when you play a tour, this first scene lasts 10 seconds. The time to fly to the next scene takes 3 seconds.

Once you have the timing correct for the first scene, you can add a second scene by selecting Home, New Scene, Copy Scene 1. Customize the second scene to zoom in on a different section of the country or to show a different view of the map.

Say that you want to have the first scene show the data accumulate over time and then you want the next three scenes to zoom in to three interesting parts of the country. You have to remove the Time field from the Layer pane at the start of Scene 2, or the entire timeline will animate again.

Alternatively, perhaps you want to zoom in to an area at a particular part of the timeline. In this example, you might have these scenes:

■ You start with an establishing shot that shows the whole country at the beginning of the time period. Use the Scene Options and set both the start and end date to the earliest date in the data set. By using the same date for start and end, the opening scene will not animate over time.

■ You then have a scene that animates over part of the timeline, perhaps 1971 to 1995.

■ Next is a scene that zooms in to Florida in 1995. Use Scene Options to set the start and end date to December 31, 1995, to prevent the data from re-animating.

■ Finally, you have a scene that is a copy of Scene 2 but with the date range changed from 1996 to 2018.

 TIP Note that annotations and text boxes will appear throughout one scene and through the transition to the next scene. If you have a 6-second scene and a 20-second transition, the text box will appear for all 26 seconds. You might want to go to the extra effort to break this up as a 6-second scene with the text box and a 0-second transition, followed by a 1-second scene with no text box and a 20-second transition.

To have the map constantly moving, change the Effect drop-down to something other than No Effect. For example, with Circle or Figure 8, the camera flies in an arc above the scene. Depending on how long the scene lasts, you may not get a complete circle. Adjust the Effect speed to increase the chances of finishing the circle.

Click Play Tour to hide all panels and play the tour in full-screen mode. Drag the mouse over the tour to reveal Play and Pause buttons at the bottom of the screen. Press the Esc key to go back to 3D Map.

Creating a Video from 3D Map

To share a tour with others, you can use 3D Map to render a video. Build a tour first and then click Create Video. You can choose from three video resolutions and add a sound track.

> **NOTE**
>
> Note that rendering a several-minute tour in full HD resolution can take more than an hour on a fast PC.

CASE STUDY: USING A STORE MAP INSTEAD OF A GLOBE

Say that you have a database of sales in a retail mall. For each day, you have sales for each of several stores in the mall. You would like to animate how sales unfold during the business day in the mall. For example, items located near the coffee bar might sell best in the morning, while high-ticket items might sell best in the evening:

1. Find a drawing or an image of the store map. Figure out the height and width of the image. In this case, say that the image is 800 pixels wide and 366 pixels tall.

2. Build a table in Excel with a unique list of store names. (You could also use a unique list of departments or categories.)

3. Figure out an the x and y location for each unique store name. Remember that x measures the number of pixels across the image, starting at the left edge. In Figure 11.32, the image is inserted into Excel. It fills columns E:U. Since the total width is 800, each column represents about 47 pixels. Sears is around 620 pixels from the left edge. For the y value, remember to start at the bottom. Since the image is 366 pixels tall and fills 29 rows, each row is about 12.62 pixels tall. Cell C15 shows that the word Sears falls at about 176 pixels from the bottom edge.

> **CAUTION**
>
> The first time I tried finding x and y locations, I used the cursor location in Photoshop. It was fast and easy. But then I realized that Photoshop is measuring the y location starting at the top edge instead of the bottom edge. This initially seemed like a bad mistake, but since the data was keyed into Excel, a helper column with a formula of =366-F2 was able to quickly correct the Y values.

4. Create a table from your sales data by using Ctrl+T. Add the data to the Data Model.

5. Create a table from your location data by using Ctrl+T. Add the data to the Data Model.

6. In Power Pivot, create a relationship between the two tables.

7. From a blank cell in Excel, choose Insert, 3D Map. 3D Map shows you the fields from the Data Model.

11

Figure 11.32
Locate the X and Y coordinate for each store in the mall map.

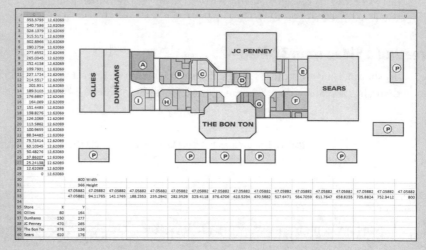

8. In the Choose Geography section of the Layer pane, choose X and Y.

9. In the Geography and Map Level section, assign X as X Coordinate. Assign Y as Y Coordinate. 3D Map now asks you a question: Change to a Custom Map? (see Figure 11.33).

Figure 11.33
When you choose X and Y, 3D Map asks about using a custom map.

10. Click Yes to choose a custom map. In the Change Map Type dialog, choose New Custom Map.

11. In the Custom Map Options dialog, click the Picture icon next to Browse for the Background Picture. Select the same picture used for step 3. As shown in Figure 11.34, the dialog starts out with Min and Max values for X and Y that represent the data in your data set. Because no data points are falling at the 0,0 coordinate nor at the 800,366 coordinate, these estimates will always be incorrect.

Figure 11.34
The Min and Max for X and Y will always be incorrect in real life.

12. Change the Min for X and the Min for Y to 0. Change the Max for X to the picture width. Change the Max for Y to the picture height. Click Apply to see your data on the picture. Click Done when everything looks correct.

13. In the 3D Map Layer pane, click Next.

Your data is now plotted on a custom map of the mall, as shown in Figure 11.35. You can use 3D Map navigation to tip, rotate, and zoom the map.

Figure 11.35
Sales plotted on a custom map.

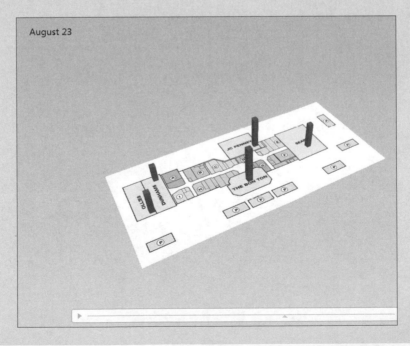

Next Steps

Chapter 12, "Enhancing Pivot Table Reports with Macros," introduces you to simple macros you can use to enhance your pivot table reports.

11

Enhancing Pivot Table Reports with Macros

12

Why Use Macros with Pivot Table Reports

Imagine that you could be in multiple locations at one time, with multiple clients at one time, helping them with their pivot table reports. Suppose you could help multiple clients refresh their data, extract top 20 records, group by months, or sort by revenue—all at the same time. The fact is you can do just that by using Excel macros.

In its broadest sense, a *macro* is a sequence of instructions that automates some aspect of Excel so that you can work more efficiently and with fewer errors. Macros can be created by recording and saving a series of keystrokes. Once saved, a macro can be played back on demand. In other words, you can record your actions in a macro, save the macro, and then allow your clients to play back your actions with the click of a button or press of a keyboard shortcut. It would be as though you were right there with them! This functionality is especially useful when you're distributing pivot table reports.

For example, suppose that you want to give your clients the option of grouping their pivot table report by month, by quarter, or by year. Although the process of grouping can be performed by anyone, some of your clients might not have a clue how to do it. In this case, you could record a macro to group by month, a macro to group by quarter, and a macro to group by year. Then you could create three buttons, one for each macro. In the end, your clients, having little experience with pivot tables, need only to click a button to group their pivot table report.

A major benefit of using macros with your pivot table reports is the power you can give your clients to easily perform pivot table actions that they would not normally be able to perform on their own, empowering them to more effectively analyze the data you provide.

Recording a Macro

Look at the pivot table in Figure 12.1. You know that you can refresh this pivot table by right-clicking inside the pivot table and selecting Refresh Data. Now, if you were to record your actions with a macro while you refreshed this pivot table, you or anyone else could replicate your actions and refresh this pivot table by running the macro.

Figure 12.1
You can easily refresh this basic pivot table by right-clicking and selecting Refresh, but if you recorded your actions with a macro, you could also refresh this pivot table simply by running the macro.

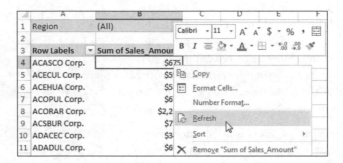

The first step in recording a macro is to initiate the Record Macro dialog. Select the Developer tab on the ribbon and then select Record Macro.

> **TIP**
> Can't find the Developer tab on the ribbon? Click the File tab on the ribbon and then choose Options. The Excel Options dialog opens; click Customize Ribbon. In the list box to the far right, place a check next to Developer. Placing a check next to this option enables the Developer tab.

12

When the Record Macro dialog activates, you can fill in a few key pieces of information about the macro:

- **Macro Name**—Enter a name for your macro. You should generally enter a name that describes the action being performed.

- **Shortcut Key**—You can enter any letter into this input box. That letter becomes part of a set of keys on your keyboard that can be pressed to play back the macro. This is optional.

- **Store Macro In**—Specify where you want the macro to be stored. If you are distributing your pivot table report, you should select This Workbook so that the macro is available to your clients.

- **Description**—In this input box, you can enter a few words that give more detail about the macro.

Because this macro refreshes your pivot table when it is played, name your macro **RefreshData**, as shown in Figure 12.2. Also assign the shortcut key **R**. Notice that, based on this, the dialog gives you the key combination Ctrl+Shift+R. Keep in mind that you use the key combination to play your macro after it is created. Be sure to store the macro in This Workbook. Click OK to continue.

Figure 12.2
Fill in the Record Macro dialog as shown here and then click OK to continue.

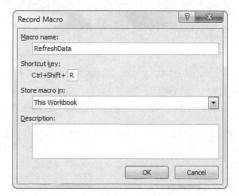

When you click OK in the Record Macro dialog, you initiate the recording process. At this point, any action you perform is recorded by Excel. In this case, you want to record the process of refreshing your pivot table.

Right-click anywhere inside the pivot table and select Refresh Data. After you have refreshed your pivot table, you can stop the recording process by going up to the Developer tab and selecting the Stop Recording button.

Congratulations! You have just recorded a macro. You can now play your macro by pressing Ctrl, Shift, and R on your keyboard at the same time.

12

A WORD ON MACRO SECURITY

You should be aware that when you record a macro yourself, your macro runs on your PC with no security restrictions. However, when you distribute workbooks that contain macros, your clients have to let Excel know that your workbook is not a security risk in order to allow your macros to run.

Indeed, you will note that the sample file that comes with this chapter does not run unless you tell Excel to enable the macros within.

The best way to do this is to use the workbook in a *trusted location*, a directory that is deemed a safe zone where only trusted workbooks are placed. A trusted location allows you and your clients to run a macro-enabled workbook with no security restrictions, as long as the workbook is in that location.

To set up a trusted location, follow these steps:

1. Select the Macro Security button on the Developer tab. This activates the Trust Center dialog.

2. Select the Trusted Locations button.

3. Select Add New Location.

4. Click Browse and then specify the directory to be considered a trusted location.

After you specify a trusted location, all workbooks opened from that location are, by default, opened with macros enabled.

> **NOTE**
>
> In Excel 2013, Microsoft enhanced the security model to remember files that you've deemed trustworthy. That is to say, when you open an Excel workbook and click the Enable button, Excel remembers that you trusted that file. Each time you open the workbook after that, Excel automatically trusts it.
>
> For information on macro security in Excel 2016, pick up Que Publishing's *Excel 2016 in Depth* by Bill Jelen.

Creating a User Interface with Form Controls

Allowing your clients to run your macro with shortcut keys such as Ctrl+Shift+R can be a satisfactory solution if you have only one macro in your pivot table report. However, suppose you want to allow your clients to perform several macro actions. In this case, you should give your clients a clear and easy way to run each macro without having to remember a gaggle of shortcut keys.

A basic user interface provides the perfect solution. A *user interface* is a set of controls such as buttons, scrollbars, and other devices that allow users to run macros with a simple click of the mouse. In fact, Excel offers a set of controls designed specifically for creating user interfaces directly on a spreadsheet. These controls are called *form controls*. The general idea behind form controls is that you can place one on a spreadsheet and then assign a macro to it—meaning a macro you have already recorded. After a macro is assigned to the control, that macro is executed, or played, when the control is clicked.

You can find form controls in the Controls group on the Developer tab. To get to the form controls, simply select the Insert icon in the Controls group, as shown in Figure 12.3.

Figure 12.3
To see the available form controls, click Insert in the Controls group on the Developer tab.

NOTE

Notice that there are form controls and ActiveX controls. Although they look similar, they are quite different. Form controls, with their limited overhead and easy configuration settings, are designed specifically for use on a spreadsheet. Meanwhile, ActiveX controls are typically used on Excel user forms. As a general rule, you should use form controls when working on a spreadsheet.

Here, you can select the control that best suits your needs. In this example, you want your clients to be able to refresh their pivot table with the click of a button. Click the Button control to select it and then drop the control onto your spreadsheet by clicking the location you would like to place the button.

After you drop the button control onto your spreadsheet, the Assign Macro dialog, shown in Figure 12.4, opens and asks you to assign a macro to this button. Select the macro you want to assign to the button, in this case RefreshData, and then click OK.

Figure 12.4
Select the macro you want to assign to the button, and then click OK. In this case, you want to select RefreshData.

12

NOTE

Keep in mind that all the controls in the Forms toolbar work in the same way as the command button, in that you assign a macro to run when the control is selected.

As you can see in Figure 12.5, you can assign each macro in your workbook to a different form control and then name the controls to distinguish between them.

Figure 12.5
You can create a different button for each one of your macros.

Region	(All)				
Row Labels	**Sum of Sales_Amount**			Refresh Pivot Table	
ACASCO Corp.	$675				
ACECUL Corp.	$593			See Top 20 Customers	
ACEHUA Corp.	$580			See Bottom 20 Customers	
ACOPUL Corp.	$675				
ACORAR Corp.	$2,232			Reset Pivot Table	
ACSBUR Corp.	$720				
ADACEC Corp.	$345				
ADADUL Corp.	$690				
ADANAS Corp.	$345				
ADCOMP Corp.	$553				

As you can see in Figure 12.6, when you have all the controls you need for your pivot table report, you can format the controls and surrounding spreadsheet to create a basic interface.

Figure 12.6
You can easily create the feeling of an interface by adding a handful of macros, a few form controls, and a little formatting.

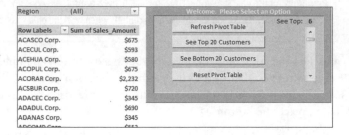

Altering a Recorded Macro to Add Functionality

When you record a macro, Excel creates a module that stores the recorded steps of your actions. These recorded steps are actually lines of VBA code that make up your macro. You can add some interesting functionality to pivot table reports by tweaking a macro's VBA code to achieve various effects.

To get a better understanding of how this process works, start by creating a new macro that extracts the top five records by customer. Go to the Developer tab and select Record Macro. Set up the Record Macro dialog as shown in Figure 12.7. Name your new macro **TopNthCusts**, and specify This Workbook as the place where you want to store the macro. Click OK to start recording.

Figure 12.7
Name your new macro and specify where you want to store it.

After you have started recording, right-click the Customer field and select Filter. Then select Top 10. Selecting this option opens the Filter dialog, where you specify that you want to see the top five customers by sales amount. Enter the settings shown in Figure 12.8 and then click OK.

Figure 12.8
Enter the settings you see here to get the top five customers by revenue.

After you record the steps to extract the top five customers by revenue, select Stop Recording from the Developer tab.

You now have a macro that, when played, filters your pivot table to the top five customers by revenue. The plan is to tweak this macro to respond to a scrollbar. That is, you force the macro to base the number used to filter the pivot table on the number represented by a scrollbar in your user interface. In other words, a user can get the top 5, top 8, or top 32 simply by moving a scrollbar up or down.

Inserting a Scrollbar Form Control

To get a scrollbar onto your spreadsheet, select the Insert icon on the Developer tab; then select the scrollbar control from the form controls. Place the scrollbar control onto your spreadsheet. You can change the dimensions of the scrollbar to an appropriate length and width by clicking and dragging the corners.

Right-click the scrollbar and select Format Control. This activates the Format Object dialog, in which you make the following setting changes: Set Minimum Level to 1 so the scrollbar cannot go below 1, set Maximum Level to 200 so the scrollbar cannot go above 200, and set Cell Link to $M$2 so that the number represented by the scrollbar will output to cell M2. After you have completed these steps, your dialog should look like the one shown in Figure 12.9.

12

Figure 12.9
After you have placed a scrollbar on your spreadsheet, configure the scrollbar as shown here.

Format Control

Size | Protection | Properties | Alt Text | Control

Current value: 0
Minimum value: 1
Maximum value: 200
Incremental change: 1
Page change: 10
Cell link: $M$2
☑ 3-D shading

OK | Cancel

Next, you need to assign the TopNthCusts macro you just recorded to your scrollbar. To do this, right-click the scrollbar and select Assign Macro. Select the TopNthCusts macro from the list shown in Figure 12.10 and then click OK. Assigning this macro ensures that it plays each time the scrollbar is clicked.

Figure 12.10
Select the macro from the list.

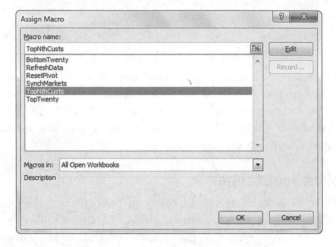

At this point, test your scrollbar by clicking it. When you click your scrollbar, two things should happen: The TopNthCusts macro should play, and the number in cell M2 should change to reflect your scrollbar's position. The number in cell M2 is important because that is the number you are going to reference in your TopNthCusts macro.

The only thing left to do is tweak your macro to respond to the number in cell M2, effectively tying it to your scrollbar. To do this, you have to get to the VBA code that makes up the macro. You have several ways to get there, but for the purposes of this example, go to the Developer tab and select Macros. Selecting this option opens the Macro dialog, exposing several options. From here, you can run, delete, step into, or edit a selected macro. To get to the VBA code that makes up your macro, select the macro and then click Edit, as demonstrated in Figure 12.11.

Figure 12.11
To get to the VBA code that makes up the TopNthCusts macro, select the macro and then select Edit.

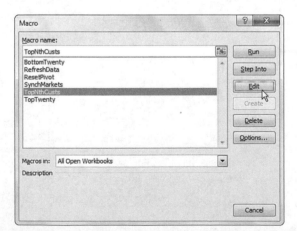

12

The Visual Basic Editor opens, with a detailed view of all the VBA code that makes up this macro (see Figure 12.12). Notice that the number 5 is hard-coded as part of your macro. The reason is that you originally recorded your macro to filter the top five customers by revenue. Your goal here is to replace the hard-coded number 5 with the value in cell M2, which is tied to your scrollbar. Therefore, you need to delete the number 5 and replace it with the following:

```
ActiveSheet.Range("M2").Value
```

Your macro's code should now look like the code shown in Figure 12.13.

Figure 12.12
Your goal is to replace the hard-coded number 5, as specified when you originally recorded your macro, with the value in cell M2.

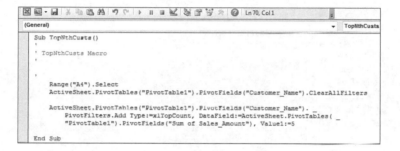

Figure 12.13
Simply delete the hard-coded number 5 and replace it with a reference to cell M2.

Close the Visual Basic Editor to get back to your pivot table report. Test your scrollbar by setting it to 11. Your macro should play and filter out the top 11 customers by revenue, as shown in Figure 12.14.

Figure 12.14
After a little formatting, you have a clear and easy way for your clients to get the top customers by revenue.

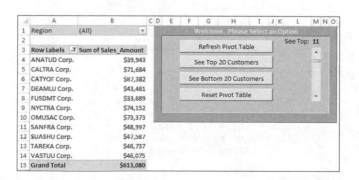

12

CASE STUDY: SYNCHRONIZING TWO PIVOT TABLES WITH ONE COMBO BOX

The report in Figure 12.15 contains two pivot tables. Each pivot table has a filter field for allowing you to select a market. The problem is that every time you select a market from the filter field in one pivot table, you have to select the same market from the filter field in the other pivot table to ensure that you are analyzing the correct units sold versus revenue.

Not only is it a bit of a hassle to have to synchronize both pivot tables every time you want to analyze a new market's data, but there is a chance that you or your clients might forget to do so.

Figure 12.15
This pivot table report contains two pivot tables with filter fields that filter out a market. The issue is that you have to synchronize the two pivot tables when analyzing data for a particular market.

	A	B	C	D	E
3					
4	**Revenue by Business Segment**				
5	Market	(All)			
6					
7	Sales_Amount	Quarters			
8	Business_Segment	Qtr1	Qtr2	Qtr3	Qtr4
9	Housekeeping and Organization	$257,218	$290,074	$297,251	$294,049
10	Landscaping and Area Beautification	$581,991	$635,946	$632,872	$616,890
11	Maintenance and Repair	$1,709,422	$1,880,546	$1,827,782	$1,750,130
12					
13					
14	**Contracted Hours by Business Segment**				
15	Market	(All)			
16					
17	Sum of Contracted Hours	Quarters			
18	Business_Segment	Qtr1	Qtr2	Qtr3	Qtr4
19	Housekeeping and Organization	4,254	4,847	4,985	4,953
20	Landscaping and Area Beautification	8,673	9,450	9,467	9,189
21	Maintenance and Repair	26,129	28,773	27,919	26,741

One way to synchronize these pivot tables is to use a combo box. The idea is to record a macro that selects a market from the Market field of both tables. Then you can create a combo box and fill it with the market names that exist in your two pivot tables. Finally, you can alter your macro to filter both pivot tables, using the value from your combo box. To do so, follow these steps:

1. Create a new macro and call it **SynchMarkets**. When recording starts, select the California market from the Market field in both pivot tables; then stop recording.

2. Activate the Forms toolbar and place a combo box onto your spreadsheet.

3. Create a hard-coded list of all the markets that exist in your pivot table. Note that the first entry in your list is (All). You must include this entry if you want to be able to select all markets with your combo box.

As you can see in Figure 12.16, you place the combo box and your list of markets directly in your spreadsheet.

Figure 12.16
At this point, you should have all the tools you need: a macro that changes the Market field of both pivot tables, a combo box on your spreadsheet, and a list of all the markets that exist in your pivot table.

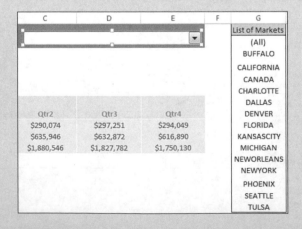

4. Right-click your combo box and select Format Control to perform the initial setup. First, specify an input range for the list you are using to fill your combo box—in this case, the market list you created in step 3. Next, specify a cell link—that is, the cell that shows the index number of the item you select (cell H1 in this example). After you have configured your combo box, your dialog should look like the one shown in Figure 12.17.

Figure 12.17
The settings for your combo box should reference your market list as the input range and specify a cell link close to your market list. In this case, the cell link is cell H1.

At this point, you should be able to select a market from your combo box and see the associated index number in cell H1. Why an index number instead of the name of the selected market? Well, the only output of a combo box form control is an index number. This is the position number of the selected item. For instance, in Figure 12.18, the selection of Charlotte from the combo box results in the number 5 in cell H1. This means that Charlotte is the fifth item in the combo box.

12

Figure 12.18
Your combo box, now filled with market names, will output an index number in cell H1 when a market is selected.

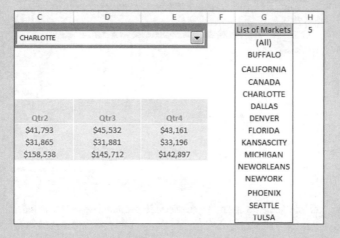

To make use of this index number, you have to pass it through the INDEX function. The INDEX function converts an index number to a value that can be recognized.

5. Enter an INDEX function (shown in Figure 12.19) that converts the index number in cell H1 to a value.

Figure 12.19
The INDEX function in cell I1 converts the index number in cell H1 to a value. You will eventually use the value in cell I1 to alter your macro.

⊿	F	G	H	I	J
1		List of Markets	5	=INDEX(G2:G16,H1)	
2		(All)			
3		BUFFALO			
4		CALIFORNIA			
5		CANADA			
6		CHARLOTTE			
7		DALLAS			
8		DENVER			
9		FLORIDA			
10		KANSASCITY			
11		MICHIGAN			
12		NEWORLEANS			
13		NEWYORK			
14		PHOENIX			
15		SEATTLE			
16		TULSA			

An INDEX function requires two arguments to work properly. The first argument is the range of the list you are working with. In most cases, you use the same range that is feeding your combo box. The second argument is the index number. If the index number is in a cell (for example, in cell H1), you can simply reference the cell.

6. Edit the SynchMarkets macro using the value in cell I1 instead of a hard-coded value.

To get to the VBA code that makes up your macro, click the Macros button on the Developer tab. This activates the Macro dialog, shown in Figure 12.20. From here, select the SynchMarkets macro and then click Edit.

Figure 12.20
In the Macro dialog, select the SynchMarkets macro and click Edit.

When you recorded your macro originally, you selected the California market from the Market field in both pivot tables. As you can see in Figure 12.21, California is hard-coded in your macro's VBA code.

Figure 12.21
The California market is hard-coded in your macro's VBA code.

Replace California with ActiveSheet.Range("I1").Value, as shown in Figure 12.22. This code references the value in cell I1. After you have edited the macro, close the Visual Basic Editor to get back to the spreadsheet.

Figure 12.22
Replace California with ActiveSheet.
Range("I1").
Value, and then close the Visual Basic Editor.

7. All that is left to do is ensure that the macro will play when you select a market from the combo box. Right-click the combo box and select Assign Macro. Select the SynchMarkets macro and then click OK.

8. Clean up the formatting on your newly created report by hiding the filter fields in your pivot tables, the market list you created, and any unseemly formulas.

As you can see in Figure 12.23, this setup provides your clients with an attractive interface that allows them to make selections in multiple pivot tables using one control.

Figure 12.23
Your pivot table report is ready to use!

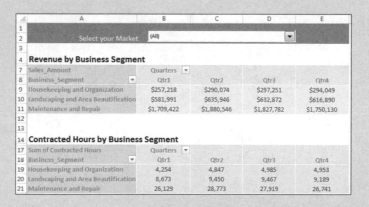

12

> **TIP**
>
> When you select a new item from the combo box you created here, the pivot tables automatically adjust the columns to fit the data. This behavior can be annoying when you have a formatted template. You can suppress this behavior by right-clicking each pivot table and selecting PivotTable Options. Selecting this option activates the PivotTable Options dialog, where you can remove the check next to the AutoFit Column Widths on Update selection.

Next Steps

In the next chapter, you'll go beyond recording macros. Chapter 13, "Using VBA to Create Pivot Tables," shows how to utilize Visual Basic for Applications to create powerful, behind-the-scenes processes and calculations using pivot tables.

12

Using VBA to Create Pivot Tables

13

Version 5 of Excel introduced a powerful new macro language called Visual Basic for Applications (VBA). Every copy of Excel shipped since 1993 has had a copy of the powerful VBA language hiding behind the worksheets. VBA enables you to perform steps that you normally perform in Excel quickly and flawlessly. I have seen a VBA program change a process that would take days each month into a single-click operation that now takes a minute of processing time.

Do not be intimidated by VBA. The VBA macro recorder tool gets you 90% of the way to a useful macro, and I get you the rest of the way, using examples in this chapter.

> **NOTE** Every example in this chapter is available for download from www.mrexcel.com/pivotbookdata2016.html.

Enabling VBA in Your Copy of Excel

By default, VBA is disabled in Office 2016. Before you can start using VBA, you need to enable macros in the Trust Center. Follow these steps:

1. Click the File menu to show the Backstage view.
2. In the left navigation pane, select Options. The Excel Options dialog displays.
3. In the left navigation pane of Excel Options, select Customize Ribbon.
4. In the list box on the right, choose the Developer tab from the list of main tabs available in Excel. Click OK to close Excel Options and include the Developer tab in the ribbon..
5. Click the Developer tab in the ribbon. As shown in Figure 13.1, the Code group on the left side of the ribbon includes icons for the Visual Basic Editor, Macros, Macro Recorder, and Macro Security.

Figure 13.1
Enable the Developer tab
to access the VBA tools.

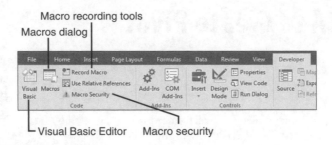

6. Click the Macro Security icon. Excel opens the Trust Center.

7. In the Trust Center, choose one of the four options:

■ **Disable All Macros with Notification**—When you open a workbook that contains macros, a message appears alerting you that macros are in the workbook. If you expect macros to be in the workbook, you can enable the macros. This is the safest setting because it forces you to explicitly enable macros in each workbook.

■ **Enable All Macros**—This setting is not recommended because potentially dangerous code can run. Because it can enable rogue macros to run in files that are sent to you by others, Microsoft recommends that you not use this setting.

■ **Disable All Macros Without Notification**—Your macros will not be able to run and, as the option says, you will not be notified that they're not running. You don't want to choose this option.

■ **Disable All Macros Except Digitally Signed Macros**—You would have to buy a digital code signing certificate from a third party in order to use this option. This is a waste of money if you are building macros for you and your co-workers.

Using a File Format That Enables Macros

The default Excel 2016 file format is initially the Excel Workbook (.xlsx). This workbook is defined to disallow macros. You can build a macro in an .xlsx workbook, but it won't be saved with the workbook.

You have several options for saving workbooks that enable macros:

■ **Excel Macro-Enabled Workbook (.xlsm)**—This uses the XML-based method for storing workbooks and enables macros. I prefer this file type because it is compact and less prone to becoming corrupt.

■ **Excel Binary Workbook (.xlsb)**—This is a binary format and always enables macros.

■ **Excel 97-2003 Workbook (.xls)**—While this legacy file type supports macros, it doesn't support a lot of handy newer features. You lose access to slicers, new filters, rows 65537 through 1048576, columns IX through XFD, and other pivot table improvements.

When you create a new workbook, you can use File, Save As to choose the appropriate file type.

Visual Basic Editor

From Excel, press Alt+F11 or select Developer, Visual Basic to open the Visual Basic Editor, as shown in Figure 13.2. The three main sections of the VBA Editor are described here. If this is your first time using VBA, some of these items might be disabled. Follow the instructions in the following list to make sure that each is enabled:

Figure 13.2
The Visual Basic Editor window is lurking behind every copy of Excel shipped since 1993.

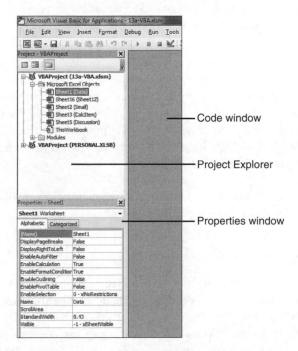

- Code window
- Project Explorer
- Properties window

- **Project Explorer**—This pane displays a hierarchical tree of all open workbooks. Expand the tree to see the worksheets, code modules, user forms, and class modules present in the workbook. If the Project Explorer is not visible, enable it by pressing Ctrl+R.

- **Properties window**—The Properties window is important when you begin to program user forms. It has some use when you are writing normal code, so enable it by pressing F4.

- **Code window**—This is the area where you write your code. Code is stored in one or more code modules attached to your workbook. To add a code module to a workbook, select Insert, Module from the VBA menu.

Visual Basic Tools

Visual Basic is a powerful development environment. Although this chapter cannot offer a complete course on VBA, if you are new to VBA, you should take advantage of these important tools:

13

- **AutoComplete**— As you begin to type code, Excel might offer a drop-down with valid choices. This feature, known as AutoComplete, enables you to type code faster and eliminate typing mistakes.

- **Excel Help**— For assistance on any keyword, put the cursor in the keyword and press F1. Excel Help displays a help topic regarding the keyword.

- **Comments**— Excel checks each line of code as you finish it. Lines in error appear in red. Comments appear in green. You can add a comment by typing a single apostrophe before the comment. Use lots of comments so you can remember what each section of code is doing.

- **Debugging**— Despite the aforementioned error checking, Excel might still encounter an error at runtime. If this happens, click the Debug button. The line that caused the error is highlighted in yellow. Hover your mouse cursor over any variable to see the current value of the variable. When you are in Debug mode, use the Debug menu to step line by line through code. If you have a wide monitor, try arranging the Excel window and the VBA window side by side. This way, you can see the effect of running a line of code on the worksheet.

Other great debugging tools are breakpoints, the Watch window, the Object Browser, and the Immediate window. Read about these tools in the Excel Help menu.

The Macro Recorder

Excel offers a macro recorder that is about 90% perfect. Unfortunately, the last 10% is frustrating. Code that you record to work with one data set is hard-coded to work only with that data set. This behavior might work fine if your transactional database occupies cells A1:L87601 every single day, but if you are pulling in a new invoice register every day, it is unlikely that you will have the same number of rows each day. Given that you might need to work with other data, it would be a lot better if Excel could record selecting cells using the End key. This is one of the shortcomings of the macro recorder.

In reality, Excel pros use the macro recorder to record code but then expect to have to clean up the recorded code.

Understanding Object-Oriented Code

VBA is an object-oriented language. Most lines of VBA code follow the *Noun.Verb* syntax. However, in VBA, it is called *Object.Method*. Examples of objects are workbooks, worksheets, cells, and ranges of cells. Methods can be typical Excel actions such as `.Copy`, `.Paste`, and `.PasteSpecial`.

Many methods allow adverbs—parameters you use to specify how to perform the method. If you see a construct with a colon and an equal sign (`:=`), you know that the macro recorder is describing how the method should work.

You also might see code in which you assign a value to the adjectives of an object. In VBA, adjectives are called *properties*. If you set `ActiveCell.Value = 3`, you are setting the value of the active cell to 3. Note that when you are dealing with properties, there is only an = (equal sign), not a := (colon and equal sign).

Learning Tricks of the Trade

This section explains a few simple techniques you need to master in order to write efficient VBA code. These techniques help you make the jump to writing effective code.

Writing Code to Handle a Data Range of Any Size

The macro recorder hard-codes the fact that your data is in a range, such as A1:L87601. Although this hard-coding works for today's data set, it might not work as you get new data sets. You need to write code that can deal with data sets of different sizes.

The macro recorder uses syntax such as `Range("H12")` to refer to a cell. However, it is more flexible to use `Cells(12, 8)` to refer to the cell in row 12, column 8. Similarly, the macro recorder refers to a rectangular range as `Range("A1:L87601")`. However, it is more flexible to use the `Cells` syntax to refer to the upper-left corner of the range and then use the `Resize()` syntax to refer to the number of rows and columns in the range. The equivalent way to describe the preceding range is `Cells(1, 1).Resize(87601,12)`. This approach is more flexible because you can replace any of the numbers with a variable.

In the Excel user interface, you can use Ctrl+any arrow on the keyboard to jump to the edge of a range of data. If you move the cell pointer to the final row on the worksheet and press the Ctrl+up arrow key, the cell pointer jumps to the last row with data. The equivalent of doing this in VBA is to use the following code:

```
Range("A1048576").End(xlUp).Select
```

> **CAUTION**
>
> The arguments for the End property are `XLUP`, `XLDOWN`, `XLTOLEFT`, and `XLTORIGHT`. Using these properties is equivalent to pressing Ctrl plus the up, down, left, or right arrow keys. Since the VBA Editor shows `XLUP` as `xlUp`, many people think the argument contains the number one instead of the letter *L*. Think of how "XL" sounds like "Excel." There is also no logical explanation for why Microsoft added the word `To` in `XLToLeft` and `XLToRight`.

You do not need to select this cell; you just need to find the row number that contains the last row. The following code locates this row and saves the row number to a variable named `FinalRow`:

```
FinalRow = Range("A1048576").End(xlUp).Row
```

13

There is nothing magical about the variable name `FinalRow`. You could call this variable `x`, `y`, or even your dog's name. However, because VBA enables you to use meaningful variable names, you should use something such as `FinalRow` to describe the final row.

```
FinalRow = Cells(Rows.Count, 1).End(xlUp).Row
```

> **NOTE** Excel 2016 offers 1,048,576 rows and 16,384 columns for a regular workbook. If the workbook opens in Compatibility mode, you have only 65,536 rows and 256 columns. To make your code flexible enough to handle either situation, you can use `Rows.Count` to learn the total number of rows in the current workbook. The preceding code can then be generalized like so:
>
> ```
> FinalRow = Cells(Rows.Count, 1).End(x1Up).Row
> ```

You can also find the final column in a data set. If you are relatively sure that the data set begins in row 1, you can use the End key in combination with the left-arrow key to jump from cell XFD1 to the last column with data. To generalize for the possibility that the code is running in legacy versions of Excel, you can use the following code:

```
FinalCol = Cells(1, Columns.Count).End(xlToLeft).Column
```

END+DOWN ARROW VERSUS END+UP ARROW

You might be tempted to find the final row by starting in cell A1 and using the End key in conjunction with the down-arrow key. Avoid this approach. Data coming from another system is imperfect. If your program imports 500,000 rows from a legacy computer system every day for the next five years, a day will come when someone manages to key a null value into the data set. This value will cause a blank cell or even a blank row to appear in the middle of the data set. Using `Range("A1").End(xlDown)` stops prematurely just above the blank cell instead of including all the data. This blank cell causes that day's report to miss thousands of rows of data, which is a potential disaster that calls into question the credibility of your report. Take the extra step of starting at the last row in the worksheet to greatly reduce the risk of problems.

Using Super-Variables: Object Variables

In typical programming languages, a variable holds a single value. You might use `x = 4` to assign the value 4 to the variable `x`.

Think about a single cell in Excel. Many properties describe a cell. A cell might contain a value such as 4, but the cell also has a font size, a font color, a row, a column, possibly a formula, possibly a comment, a list of precedents, and more. It is possible in VBA to create a super-variable that contains all the information about a cell or about any object. A statement to create a typical variable such as `x = Range("A1")` assigns the current value of A1 to the variable `x`.

However, you can use the `Set` keyword to create an object variable:

```
Set x = Range("A1")
```

You have now created a super-variable that contains all the properties of the cell. Instead of having a variable with only one value, you have a variable in which you can access the values of many properties associated with that variable. You can reference x.Formula to learn the formula in A1 or x.Font.ColorIndex to learn the color of the cell.

> **NOTE** The examples in this chapter frequently set up an object variable called PT to refer to the entire pivot table. This way, any time the code would generally refer to ActiveSheet.PivotTables("PivotTable1"), you can specify PT to avoid typing the longer text.

Using With and End With to Shorten Code

You will frequently find that you repeatedly make certain changes to a pivot table. Although the following code is explained later in this chapter, all these lines of code are for changing settings in a pivot table:

```
PT.NullString = 0
PT.RepeatAllLabels xlRepeatLabels
PT.ColumnGrand = False
PT.RowGrand = False
PT.RowAxisLayout xlTabularRow
PT.TableStyle2 = "PivotStyleMedium10"
PT.TableStyleRowStripes = True
```

For all these lines of code, the VBA engine has to figure out what you mean by PT. Your code executes faster if you refer to PT only once. Add the initial line With PT. Then all the remaining lines do not need to start with PT. Any line that starts with a period is assumed to be referring to the object in the With statement. Finish the code block by using an End With statement:

```
With PT
        .NullString = 0
        .RepeatAllLabels xlRepeatLabels
        .ColumnGrand = False
        .RowGrand = False
        .RowAxisLayout xlTabularRow
        .TableStyle2 = "PivotStyleMedium10"
        .TableStyleRowStripes = True
End With
```

Understanding Versions

Pivot tables have been evolving. They were introduced in Excel 5 and perfected in Excel 97. In Excel 2000, pivot table creation in VBA was dramatically altered. Some new parameters were added in Excel 2002. A few new properties, such as PivotFilters and TableStyle2, were added in Excel 2007. Slicers and new choices for Show Values As were added in Excel 2010. Timelines and the Power Pivot Data Model were added in Excel 2013. The AutoGroup method was added in Excel 2016. Because of all the changes over the years, you

13

need to be extremely careful when writing code in Excel 2016 that might be run in older versions of Excel.

Each of the last four versions of Excel offered many new features in pivot tables. If you use code for a new feature, the code works in the current version, but it crashes in previous versions of Excel:

- Excel 2016 introduced the AutoGroup functionality for dates in the Excel interface, but not with pivot tables created in VBA. Thus, the `AutoGroup` method is new in Excel 2016.

- Excel 2013 introduced the Power Pivot Data Model. You can add tables to the Data Model, create a relationship, and produce a pivot table. This code does not run in Excel 2010 or earlier. The function `xlDistinctCount` was new in Excel 2013, as were timelines.

- Excel 2010 introduced slicers, Repeat All Item Labels, named sets, and several new calculation options: `xlPercentOfParentColumn`, `xlPercentOfParentRow`, `xlPercentRunningTotal`, `xlRankAscending`, and `xlRankDescending`. These do not work in Excel 2007 or earlier.

- Excel 2007 introduced `ConvertToFormulas`, `xlCompactRow` layout, `xlAtTop` for the subtotal location, `TableStyles`, and `SortUsingCustomLists`. Macros that include this code fail in previous versions.

Building a Pivot Table in Excel VBA

This chapter does not mean to imply that you use VBA to build pivot tables to give to your clients. Instead, the purpose of this chapter is to remind you that you can use pivot tables as a means to an end. You can use a pivot table to extract a summary of data and then use that summary elsewhere.

> **NOTE**
> This chapter's code listings are available for download at www.mrexcel.com/ pivotbookdata2016.html.

> **CAUTION**
> Beginning with Excel 2007, the user interface has new names for the various sections of a pivot table. Even so, VBA code continues to refer to the old names. Although the four sections of a pivot table in the Excel user interface are Filters, Columns, Rows, and Values, VBA continues to use the old terms of page fields, column fields, row fields, and data fields. If Microsoft hadn't made this decision, millions of lines of code would have stopped working in Excel 2007 when they referred to a page field instead of a filter field.

In Excel 2000 and newer, you first build a pivot cache object to describe the input area of the data:

```
Dim WSD As Worksheet
Dim PTCache As PivotCache
Dim PT As PivotTable
Dim PRange As Range
Dim FinalRow As Long
Dim FinalCol As Long
Set WSD = Worksheets("Data")

' Delete any prior pivot tables
For Each PT In WSD.PivotTables
        PT.TableRange2.Clear
Next PT

' Define input area and set up a Pivot Cache
FinalRow = WSD.Cells(Rows.Count, 1).End(xlUp).Row
FinalCol = WSD.Cells(1, Columns.Count).End(xlToLeft).Column
Set PRange = WSD.Cells(1, 1).Resize(FinalRow, FinalCol)
Set PTCache = ActiveWorkbook.PivotCaches.Add(SourceType:=xlDatabase, _
        SourceData:=PRange)
```

After defining the pivot cache, use the `CreatePivotTable` method to create a blank pivot table based on the defined pivot cache:

```
Set PT = PTCache.CreatePivotTable(TableDestination:=WSD.Cells(2, _
        FinalCol + 2), TableName:="PivotTable1")
```

In the `CreatePivotTable` method, you specify the output location and optionally give the table a name. After running this line of code, you have a strange-looking blank pivot table, like the one shown in Figure 13.3. You now have to use code to drop fields onto the table.

Figure 13.3
Immediately after you use the `CreatePivotTable` method, Excel gives you a four-cell blank pivot table that is not useful.

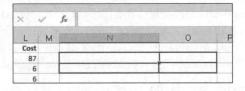

CAUTION

If you choose the Defer Layout Update setting in the user interface to build the pivot table, Excel does not recalculate the pivot table after you drop each field onto the table. By default in VBA, Excel calculates the pivot table as you execute each step of building the table. This could require the pivot table to be executed a half-dozen times before you get to the final result.

To speed up your code execution, you can temporarily turn off calculation of the pivot table by using the `ManualUpdate` property:

```
PT.ManualUpdate = True
```

13

You can now run through the steps needed to lay out the pivot table. In the `AddFields` method, you can specify one or more fields that should be in the row, column, or filter area of the pivot table.

The `RowFields` parameter enables you to define fields that appear in the Rows area of the PivotTable Fields list. The `ColumnFields` parameter corresponds to the Columns layout area. The `PageFields` parameter corresponds to the Filters layout area.

The following line of code populates a pivot table with two fields in the Rows area and one field in the Columns area:

```
' Set up the row & column fields
PT.AddFields RowFields:=Array("Category", "Product"), _
     ColumnFields:="Region"
```

> **NOTE** If you are adding a single field such as Region to the Columns area, you only need to specify the name of the field in quotes. If you are adding two or more fields, you have to include that list inside the array function.

Although the row, column, and filter fields of the pivot table can be handled with the `AddFields` method, it is best to add fields to the data area using the code described in the next section.

Adding Fields to the Data Area

When you are adding fields to the data area of a pivot table, for many settings it is better for you to have control than to let Excel's IntelliSense decide.

Say that you are building a report with revenue. You likely want to sum the revenue. If you do not explicitly specify the calculation, Excel scans through the values in the underlying data. If 100% of the revenue cells are numeric, Excel sums. If one cell is blank or contains text, Excel decides to count the revenue. This produces confusing results.

Because of this possible variability, you should never use the `DataFields` argument in the `AddFields` method. Instead, change the property of the field to `xlDataField`. You can then specify the function to be `xlSum`.

While you are setting up the data field, you can change several other properties within the same `With...End With` block.

The `Position` property is useful when adding multiple fields to the data area. Specify `1` for the first field, `2` for the second field, and so on.

By default, Excel renames a Revenue field to something strange like Sum of Revenue. You can use the `Name` property to change that heading back to something normal. Note that you cannot reuse the word Revenue as a name, but you can use "Revenue " (with a trailing space).

You are not required to specify a number format, but doing so can make the resulting pivot table easier to understand and takes only one extra line of code:

```
' Set up the data fields
With PT.PivotFields("Revenue")
        .Orientation = xlDataField
        .Function = xlSum
        .Position = 1
        .NumberFormat = "#,##0"
        .Name = "Revenue "
End With
```

The preceeding block of code adds the Revenue field to the values area of the pivot table with a new name and a number format.

Formatting the Pivot Table

Microsoft introduced the Compact layout for pivot tables in Excel 2007. This means that three layouts are available in Excel 2016 (Compact, Tabular, and Outline). When a pivot table is created with VBA, Excel usually defaults to using the Tabular layout, which is good because Tabular view is the one that makes the most sense. It cannot hurt, though, to add one line of code to ensure that you get the desired layout:

```
PT.RowAxisLayout xlTabularRow
```

In Tabular layout, each field in the row area is in a different column. Subtotals always appear at the bottom of each group. This is the layout that has been around the longest and is most conducive to reusing a pivot table report for further analysis.

The Excel user interface frequently defaults to Compact layout. In this layout, multiple column fields are stacked up into a single column on the left side of the pivot table. To create this layout, use the following code:

```
PT.RowAxisLayout xlCompactRow
```

> **TIP** The one limitation of Tabular layout is that you cannot show the totals at the top of each group. If you need to do this, you'll want to switch to the Outline layout and show totals at the top of the group:
>
> ```
> PT.RowAxisLayout xlOutlineRow
> PT.SubtotalLocation xlAtTop
> ```

Your pivot table inherits the table style settings selected as the default on whatever computer happens to run the code. If you would like control over the final format, you can explicitly choose a table style. The following code applies banded rows and a medium table style:

```
' Format the pivot table
PT.ShowTableStyleRowStripes = True
PT.TableStyle2 = "PivotStyleMedium10"
```

At this point, you have given VBA all the settings required to correctly generate the pivot table. If you set `ManualUpdate` to `False`, Excel calculates and draws the pivot table. Thereafter, you can immediately set this back to `True` by using this code:

```
' Calc the pivot table
PT.ManualUpdate = False
PT.ManualUpdate = True
```

At this point, you have a complete pivot table, like the one shown in Figure 13.4.

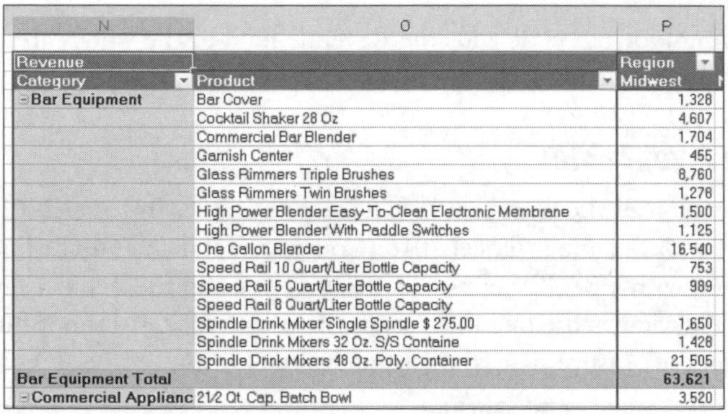

N	O	P
Revenue		Region
Category	Product	Midwest
Bar Equipment	Bar Cover	1,328
	Cocktail Shaker 28 Oz	4,607
	Commercial Bar Blender	1,704
	Garnish Center	455
	Glass Rimmers Triple Brushes	8,760
	Glass Rimmers Twin Brushes	1,276
	High Power Blender Easy-To-Clean Electronic Membrane	1,500
	High Power Blender With Paddle Switches	1,125
	One Gallon Blender	16,540
	Speed Rail 10 Quart/Liter Bottle Capacity	753
	Speed Rail 5 Quart/Liter Bottle Capacity	989
	Speed Rail 8 Quart/Liter Bottle Capacity	
	Spindle Drink Mixer Single Spindle $ 275.00	1,650
	Spindle Drink Mixers 32 Oz. S/S Containe	1,428
	Spindle Drink Mixers 48 Oz. Poly. Container	21,505
Bar Equipment Total		63,621
Commercial Applianc	21/2 Qt. Cap. Batch Bowl	3,520

Figure 13.4
Fewer than 50 lines of code create this pivot table in less than a second.

Listing 13.1 shows the complete code used to generate this pivot table.

Listing 13.1 Code to Generate the Pivot Table Shown in Figure 13.4

```
Sub CreatePivot()
        '
        Dim WSD As Worksheet
        Dim PTCache As PivotCache
        Dim PT As PivotTable
        Dim PRange As Range
        Dim FinalRow As Long
        Set WSD = Worksheets("Data")

        ' Delete any prior pivot tables
        For Each PT In WSD.PivotTables
                PT.TableRange2.Clear
        Next PT
        WSD.Range("N1:AZ1").EntireColumn.Clear

        ' Define input area and set up a Pivot Cache
        FinalRow = WSD.Cells(Application.Rows.Count, 1).End(xlUp).Row
        FinalCol = WSD.Cells(1, Application.Columns.Count). _
                End(xlToLeft).Column
        Set PRange = WSD.Cells(1, 1).Resize(FinalRow, FinalCol)
        Set PTCache = ActiveWorkbook.PivotCaches.Add(SourceType:= _
                xlDatabase, SourceData:=PRange.Address)

        ' Create the Pivot Table from the Pivot Cache
        Set PT = PTCache.CreatePivotTable(TableDestination:=WSD. _
                Cells(2, FinalCol + 2), TableName:="PivotTable1")
```

```
' Turn off updating while building the table
PT.ManualUpdate = True

' Set up the row & column fields
PT.AddFields RowFields:=Array("Category", "Product"), _
        ColumnFields:="Region"

' Set up the data fields
With PT.PivotFields("Revenue")
        .Orientation = xlDataField
        .Function = xlSum
        .Position = 1
        .NumberFormat = "#,##0"
End With

' Format the pivot table
PT.RowAxisLayout xlTabularRow
PT.ShowTableStyleRowStripes = True
PT.TableStyle2 = "PivotStyleMedium10"

' Calc the pivot table
PT.ManualUpdate = False
PT.ManualUpdate = True

WSD.Activate
Cells(2, FinalCol + 2).Select

End Sub
```

Dealing with Limitations of Pivot Tables

As with pivot tables in the user interface, Microsoft maintains tight control over a live pivot table. You need to be aware of these issues as your code is running on a sheet with a live pivot table.

Filling Blank Cells in the Data Area

It is a bit annoying that Excel puts blank cells in the data area of a pivot table. For example, in Figure 13.4, the North region had no sales of a Bar Cover, so that cell (Q4) appears blank instead of containing a zero.

You can override this in the Excel interface by using the For Empty Cells Show setting in the PivotTable Options dialog. The equivalent code is shown here:

```
PT.NullString = "0"
```

13

> **NOTE**
> Note that the Excel macro recorder always wraps that zero in quotation marks. No matter whether you specify "0" or just 0, the blank cells in the data area of the pivot table have numeric zeros.

Filling Blank Cells in the Row Area

Excel 2010 added a much-needed setting to fill in the blank cells along the left columns of a pivot table. This problem happens any time that you have two or more fields in the row area of a pivot table. Rather than repeat a label such as "Bar Equipment" in cells N5:N18 in the pivot table shown in Figure 13.4, Microsoft traditionally has left those cells blank. To solve this problem in Excel 2016, use the following line of code:

```
PT.RepeatAllLabels xlRepeatLabels
```

Preventing Errors from Inserting or Deleting Cells

You cannot use many Excel commands inside a pivot table. Inserting rows, deleting rows, and cutting and pasting parts of a pivot table are all against the rules.

Say that you tried to delete the Grand Total column from column W in a pivot table. If you try to delete or clear column W, the macro comes to a screeching halt with a 1004 error, as shown in Figure 13.5.

Figure 13.5
You cannot delete just part of a pivot table.

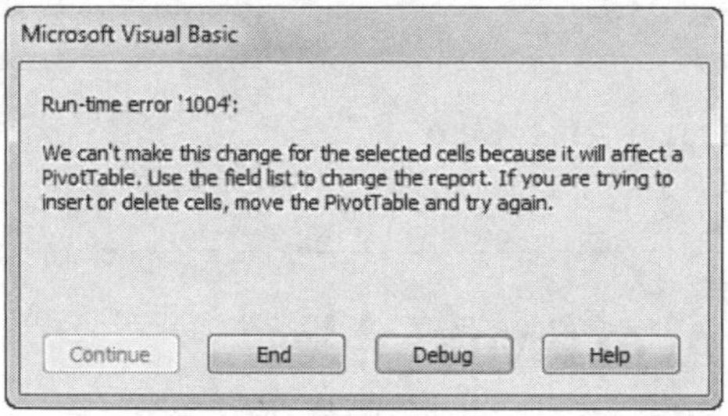

Microsoft Visual Basic

Run-time error '1004':

We can't make this change for the selected cells because it will affect a PivotTable. Use the field list to change the report. If you are trying to insert or delete cells, move the PivotTable and try again.

| Continue | End | Debug | Help |

There are two strategies for getting around this limitation. The first strategy is to find if there is already an equivalent command in the pivot table interface. For example, you want to determine whether there is code to perform any of these actions:

- Remove the grand total column.
- Remove the grand total row.
- Add blank rows between each section.
- Suppress subtotals for outer row fields.

The second strategy is to convert the pivot table to values. You can then insert, cut, and clear as necessary.

Both strategies are discussed in the following sections.

Controlling Totals

The default pivot table includes a grand total row and a grand total column. You can choose to hide one or both of these elements.

To remove the grand total column from the right side of the pivot table, use this:

```
PT.ColumnGrand = False
```

To remove the grand total row from the bottom of the pivot table, use this:

```
PT.RowGrand = False
```

Turning off the subtotals rows is surprisingly complex. This issue comes up when you have multiple fields in the row area. Excel automatically turns on subtotals for the outermost row fields.

Figure 13.6
is the Custom setting is rarely used, but the fact that you can specify multiple types of subtotals for a single field complicates the VBA code for suppressing subtotals.

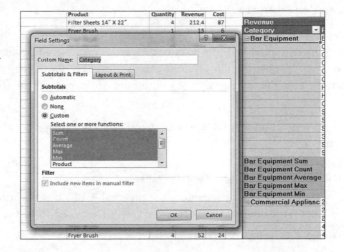

To suppress the subtotals for a field, you must set the `Subtotals` property equal to an array of 12 `False` values. The first `False` turns off automatic subtotals, the second `False` turns off the `Sum` subtotal, the third `False` turns off the `Count` subtotal, and so on. This line of code suppresses the `Category` subtotal:

```
PT.PivotFields("Category").Subtotals = Array(False, False, False, False, _
    False, False, False, False, False, False, False, False)
```

A different technique is to turn on the first subtotal. This method automatically turns off the other 11 subtotals. You can then turn off the first subtotal to make sure all subtotals are suppressed:

```
PT.PivotFields("Category").Subtotals(1) = True
PT.PivotFields("Category").Subtotals(1) = False
```

13

NOTE You might be wondering about the Distinct Count option introduced in Excel 2013. Does it force a 12th position in the array? No. The Custom subtotals option is grayed out for pivot tables that use the Data Model, so you won't ever be able to choose Sum and Distinct Count together.

■ **See** "Using the Data Model in Excel 2016," **p. 345**, for an example of using Distinct Count.

Converting a Pivot Table to Values

If you plan on converting a live pivot table to values, you need to copy the entire pivot table. How much space it will take might be tough to predict. If you summarize transactional data every day, you might find that on any given day you do not have sales from one region. This can cause your table to be perhaps seven columns wide on some days and only six columns wide on other days.

Excel provides two range properties that you can use to refer to a pivot table. The TableRange2 property includes all the rows of the pivot table, including any Filter dropdowns at the top of the pivot table. The TableRange1 property starts just below the filter fields. It often includes the unnecessary row with Sum of Revenue at the top of the pivot table.

If your goal is to convert a pivot table to values and not move the pivot table to a new place, you can use this code:

```
PT.TableRange2.Copy
PT.TableRange2.PasteSpecial xlPasteValues
```

If you want to copy only the data section of the pivot table to a new location, you frequently use the Offset property to start one row lower than the top of TableRange2, like so:

```
PT.TableRange2.Offset(1,0).Copy
```

This reference copies the data area plus one row of headings.

Notice in Figure 13.7 that using Offset without .Resize causes one extra row to be copied. However, because that row is always blank, there is no need to use Resize to not copy the extra blank row.

The code copies PT.TableRange2 and uses PasteSpecial on a cell six rows below the current pivot table. At that point in the code, your worksheet looks as shown in Figure 13.7. The table in cell N2 is a live pivot table, and the table in cell N57 contains the copied results.

13

Figure 13.7
An intermediate result of the macro. The data in cell N58 has been converted to values.

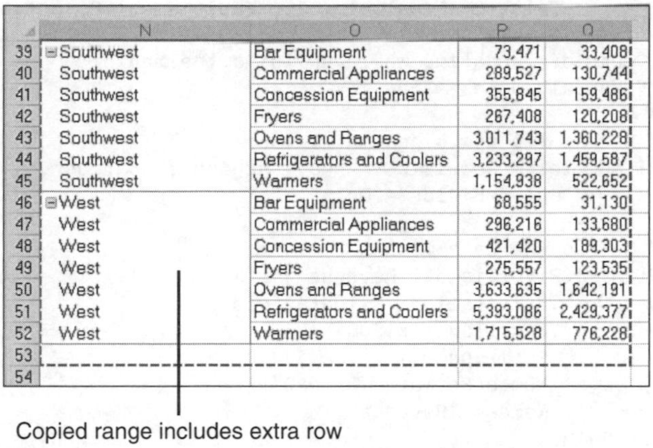

	N	O	P	Q
39	⊟ Southwest	Bar Equipment	73,471	33,408
40	Southwest	Commercial Appliances	289,527	130,744
41	Southwest	Concession Equipment	355,845	159,486
42	Southwest	Fryers	267,408	120,208
43	Southwest	Ovens and Ranges	3,011,743	1,360,228
44	Southwest	Refrigerators and Coolers	3,233,297	1,459,587
45	Southwest	Warmers	1,154,938	522,652
46	⊟ West	Bar Equipment	68,555	31,130
47	West	Commercial Appliances	296,216	133,680
48	West	Concession Equipment	421,420	189,303
49	West	Fryers	275,557	123,535
50	West	Ovens and Ranges	3,633,635	1,642,191
51	West	Refrigerators and Coolers	5,393,086	2,429,377
52	West	Warmers	1,715,528	776,228
53				
54				

Copied range includes extra row

You can then eliminate the pivot table by applying the Clear method to the entire table. If your code is then going on to do additional formatting, you should remove the pivot cache from memory by setting PTCache equal to Nothing.

The code in Listing 13.2 uses a pivot table to produce a summary from the underlying data. More than 80,000 rows are reduced to a tight 50-row summary. The resulting data is properly formatted for additional filtering, sorting, and so on. At the end of the code, the pivot table is copied to static values, and the pivot table is cleared.

Listing 13.2   Code to Produce a Static Summary from a Pivot Table

```
Sub UsePivotToCreateValues()
    '
        Dim WSD As Worksheet
        Dim PTCache As PivotCache
        Dim PT As PivotTable
        Dim PRange As Range
        Dim FinalRow As Long
        Set WSD = Worksheets("Data")

        ' Delete any prior pivot tables
        For Each PT In WSD.PivotTables
                PT.TableRange2.Clear
        Next PT
        WSD.Range("N1:AZ1").EntireColumn.Clear

        ' Define input area and set up a Pivot Cache
        FinalRow = WSD.Cells(Application.Rows.Count, 1).End(xlUp).Row
        FinalCol = WSD.Cells(1, Application.Columns.Count). _
                End(xlToLeft).Column
        Set PRange = WSD.Cells(1, 1).Resize(FinalRow, FinalCol)
        Set PTCache = ActiveWorkbook.PivotCaches.Add(SourceType:= _
                xlDatabase, SourceData:=PRange.Address)

        ' Create the Pivot Table from the Pivot Cache
        Set PT = PTCache.CreatePivotTable(TableDestination:=WSD. _
```

13

```
                          Cells(2, FinalCol + 2), TableName:="PivotTable1")

        ' Turn off updating while building the table
        PT.ManualUpdate = True

        ' Set up the row & column fields
        PT.AddFields RowFields:=Array("Region", "Category"), _
                ColumnFields:="Data"

        ' Set up the data fields
        With PT.PivotFields("Revenue")
                .Orientation = xlDataField
                .Function = xlSum
                .Position = 1
                .NumberFormat = "#,##0"
                .Name = "Revenue "
        End With
        With PT.PivotFields("Cost")
                .Orientation = xlDataField
                .Function = xlSum
                .Position = 2
                .NumberFormat = "#,##0"
                .Name = "COGS"
        End With

        ' Settings to create a solid block of data
        With PT
                .NullString = 0
                .RepeatAllLabels Repeat:=xlRepeatLabels
                .ColumnGrand = False
                .RowGrand = 0
                .PivotFields("Region").Subtotals(1) = True
                .PivotFields("Region").Subtotals(1) = False
        End With

        ' Calc the pivot table
        PT.ManualUpdate = False
        PT.ManualUpdate = True

        ' Copy the pivot table as values below the pivot table
        PT.TableRange2.Offset(1, 0).Copy
        PT.TableRange1.Cells(1, 1).Offset(PT.TableRange1.Rows.Count + 4, 0). _
            StartRow = PT.TableRange1.Cells(1, 1).Offset( _
                PT.TableRange1.Rows.Count+ 5, 0).Row
            + 5, 0).Row

                '       Figure 13.7 at this point

        PT.TableRange1.Clear
        Set PTCache = Nothing

        WSD.Activate
        Cells(StartRow, FinalCol + 2).Select

End Sub
```

The code in Listing 13.2 creates the pivot table. It then copies the results as values and pastes them below the original pivot table. In reality, you probably want to copy this report to another worksheet or another workbook. Examples later in this chapter introduce the code necessary for this.

So far, this chapter has walked you through building the simplest of pivot table reports. Pivot tables offer far more flexibility, though. Read on for more complex reporting examples.

Pivot Table 201: Creating a Report Showing Revenue by Category

A typical report might provide a list of markets by category with revenue by year. This report could be given to product line managers to show them which markets are selling well. The report in Figure 13.8 is not a pivot table, but the macro to create the report used a pivot table to summarize the data. Regular Excel commands such as Subtotal then finish off the report.

C11 =SUBTOTAL(9,C4:C10)

	A	B	C	D	E	F
1	Revenue by Category & Region					
2						
3	Category	Region	2017	2018	2019	Grand Total
4	Ovens and Ranges	South	15,672K	13,796K	8,284K	37,752K
5	Ovens and Ranges	Southeast	2,639K	2,745K	1,418K	6,802K
6	Ovens and Ranges	West	519K	1,520K	1,594K	3,634K
7	Ovens and Ranges	Southwest	572K	1,335K	1,104K	3,012K
8	Ovens and Ranges	Northeast	662K	1,146K	801K	2,609K
9	Ovens and Ranges	Midwest	290K	1,379K	760K	2,429K
10	Ovens and Ranges	North	247K	421K	263K	931K
11	**Ovens and Ranges Total**		20,602K	22,342K	14,225K	57,169K
12	Refrigerators and Coolers	South	4,855K	4,659K	12,093K	21,606K

Figure 13.8
This report started as a pivot table but finished as a regular data set.

In this example, you want to show the markets in descending order by revenue, with years going across the columns. A sample pivot table report is shown in Figure 13.9.

Sum of Revenue		Date			
Category	Region	2017	2018	2019	Grand Total
Ovens and Ranges	South	15,672K	13,796K	8,284K	37,752K
Ovens and Ranges	Southeast	2,639K	2,745K	1,418K	6,002K
Ovens and Ranges	West	519K	1,520K	1,594K	3,634K
Ovens and Ranges	Southwest	572K	1,335K	1,104K	3,012K
Ovens and Ranges	Northeast	662K	1,146K	801K	2,609K
Ovens and Ranges	Midwest	290K	1,379K	760K	2,429K
Ovens and Ranges	North	247K	421K	263K	931K
Refrigerators and Cooler	South	4,855K	4,659K	12,093K	21,606K
Refrigerators and Cooler	West	1,957K	348K	3,088K	5,393K
Refrigerators and Cooler	Southeast	929K	1,311K	2,062K	4,302K
Refrigerators and Cooler	Midwest	882K	544K	1,810K	3,236K
Refrigerators and Cooler	Southwest	1,071K	443K	1,720K	3,233K
Refrigerators and Cooler	Northeast	1,043K	427K	1,591K	3,061K
Refrigerators and Cooler	North	369K	100K	492K	961K
Warmers	South	456K	5,161K	20,044K	25,661K
Warmers	Southeast	149K	1,556K	4,938K	6,643K
Warmers	West	14K	82K	1,619K	1,716K
Warmers	Southwest	6K	316K	833K	1,155K
Warmers	Northeast	45K	255K	854K	1,154K
Warmers	Midwest	45K	351K	523K	919K
Warmers	North	8K	4K	223K	235K
Concession Equipment	South	779K	3,039K	3,154K	6,972K

Figure 13.9
A typical request is to take transactional data and produce a summary by product for product line managers.

There are some tricky issues involved in creating this pivot table:

- You have to roll the daily dates in the original data set up to years. Although changes to the Excel 2016 user interface make this happen automatically, the Excel team thankfully chose not to break VBA by leaving daily dates as daily dates.

- You want to control the sort order of the row fields.

- You want to fill in blanks throughout the pivot table, use a better number format, and suppress the subtotals for the Category field.

The key to producing this data quickly is to use a pivot table. The default pivot table has a number of quirky problems that you can correct in the macro. To start, use VBA to build a pivot table with Category and Region as the row fields. Add Date as a column field. Add Revenue as a data field. Here's the code to do all this:

```
PT.AddFields RowFields:=Array("Category", _
        "Region"), ColumnFields:="Date"

' Set up the data fields
With PT.PivotFields("Revenue")
        .Orientation = xlDataField
        .Function = xlSum
        .Position = 1
        .NumberFormat = "#,##0"
End With
```

Figure 13.10 shows the default pivot table created with these settings.

Figure 13.10
By default, the initial report has many problems.

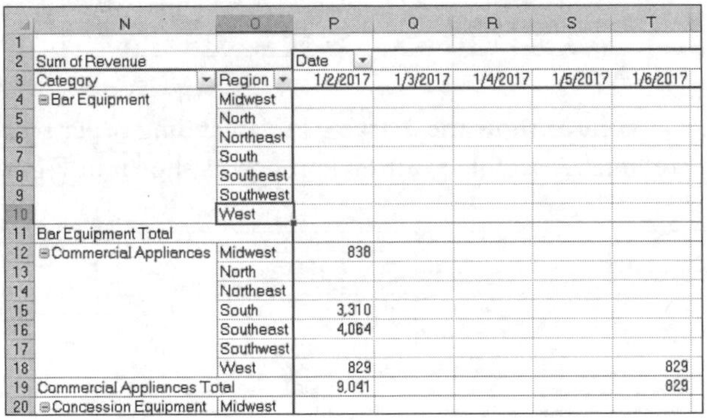

	N	O	P	Q	R	S	T
1							
2	Sum of Revenue		Date				
3	Category	Region	1/2/2017	1/3/2017	1/4/2017	1/5/2017	1/6/2017
4	Bar Equipment	Midwest					
5		North					
6		Northeast					
7		South					
8		Southeast					
9		Southwest					
10		West					
11	Bar Equipment Total						
12	Commercial Appliances	Midwest	838				
13		North					
14		Northeast					
15		South	3,310				
16		Southeast	4,064				
17		Southwest					
18		West	829				829
19	Commercial Appliances Total		9,041				829
20	Concession Equipment	Midwest					

Here are just a few of the annoyances that most pivot tables present in their default state:

- **The outline view is horrible.** In Figure 13.10, the value Bar Equipment appears in the product column only once and is followed by six blank cells. Thankfully, Excel 2016 offers the RepeatAllLabels method to correct this problem. If you intend to repurpose the data, you need the row labels to be repeated on every row.

- Because the original data set contains daily dates, the default pivot table has more than 1,000 columns of daily data. No one is able to process this report. You need to roll those daily dates up to years. Pivot tables make this easy.

- The report contains blank cells instead of zeros. In Figure 13.10, the entire visible range of Bar Equipment is blank. These cells should contain zeros instead of blanks.

- The title is boring. Most people would agree that Sum of Revenue is an annoying title.

- Some captions are extraneous. Date floating in cell P2 of Figure 13.10 does not belong in a report.

- The default alphabetical sort order is rarely useful. Product line managers are going to want the top markets at the top of the list. It would be helpful to have the report sorted in descending order by revenue.

- The borders are ugly. Excel draws in myriad borders that make the report look awful.

- Pivot tables offer no intelligent page break logic. If you want to produce one report for each product line manager, there is no fast method for indicating that each product should be on a new page.

- Because of the page break problem, you might find that it is easier to do away with the pivot table's subtotal rows and have the Subtotal method add subtotal rows with page breaks. You need a way to turn off the pivot table subtotal rows offered for Category in Figure 13.10. These rows show up automatically whenever you have two or more row fields. If you had four row fields, you would want to turn off the automatic subtotals for the three outermost row fields.

Even with all these problems in default pivot tables, default pivot tables are still the way to go. You can overcome each complaint either by using special settings within the pivot table or by entering a few lines of code after the pivot table is created and then copied to a regular data set.

Ensuring That Tabular Layout Is Utilized

In legacy versions of Excel, multiple row fields appeared in multiple columns. Three layouts are now available. The Compact layout squeezes all the row fields into a single column. Compact layout is the default when a pivot table is created in the Excel interface. Currently, when you create a pivot table in VBA, the default is the Tabular layout. However, in some future version, Microsoft will correct this discrepancy, so get in the habit of explicitly changing the layout to a Tabular layout with this code:

```
PT.RowAxisLayout xlTabularRow
```

Rolling Daily Dates Up to Years

With transactional data, you often find your date-based summaries having one row per day. Although daily data might be useful to a plant manager, many people in the company want to see totals by month or quarter and year.

13

The great news is that Excel handles the summarization of dates in a pivot table with ease. If you have ever had to use the arcane formula =A2+1-Day(A2) to change daily dates into monthly dates, you will appreciate the ease with which you can group transactional data into months or quarters.

> **TIP**
>
> Although the Excel 2016 user interface automatically groups daily dates up to months, quarters, and years, pivot tables created with VBA do not automatically group the dates. If you are sure that your code will never have to run in Excel 2013 or earlier, you could use the following code to automatically group dates as in the Excel 2016 interface:
>
> ```
> PT.PivotFields("Date").AutoGroup
> ```

Creating a date group with VBA is a bit quirky. The Group method can be applied to only a single cell in the pivot table, and that cell must contain a date or the Date field label.

In Figure 13.10, you would have to select either the Date heading in cell P2 or one of the dates in cells P3:APM3. Selecting one of these specific cells is risky, particularly if the pivot table later starts being created in a new column. Two other options are more reliable.

First, if you will never use a different number of row fields, then you can assume that the Date heading is in row 1, column 3 of the area known as TableRange2. The following line of code selects this cell:

```
PT.TableRange2.Cells(1, 3).Select
```

You should probably add a comment that you need to edit the 3 in that line to another number any time that you change the number of row fields.

Another solution is to use the LabelRange property for the Date field. The following code always selects the cell containing the Date heading:

```
PT.PivotFields("Date").LabelRange.Select
```

To group the daily dates up to yearly dates, you should define a pivot table with Date in the row field. Turn off ManualUpdate to enable the pivot table to be drawn. You can then use the LabelRange property to locate the date label.

You use the Group method on the date label cell. You specify an array of seven Boolean values for the Periods argument. The seven values correspond to seconds, minutes, hours, days, months, quarters, and years. For example, to group by years, you would use this:

```
PT.PivotFields("Date"),LabelRange.Group _
       Periods:=(False, False, False, False, False, False, True)
```

After you have grouped by years, the field is still called Date. This differs from the results when you group by multiple fields. To group by months, quarters, and years, you would use this:

```
PT.PivotFields("Date"),LabelRange.Group _
       Periods:=(False, False, False, False, True, True, True)
```

After you have grouped up to months, quarters, and years, the Date field starts referring to months. Two new virtual fields are available in the pivot table: Quarters and Years.

To group by weeks, you choose only the Day period and then use the By argument to group into seven-day periods:

```
PT.PivotFields("Date"),LabelRange.Group By:=7_
        Periods:=(False, False, False, True, False, False, False)
```

In Figure 13.10, the goal is to group the daily dates up to years, so the following code is used:

```
PT.PivotFields("Date"),LabelRange.Group _
        Periods:=(False, False, False, False, False, False, True)
```

Figure 13.11 shows the pivot table after grouping daily dates up to years.

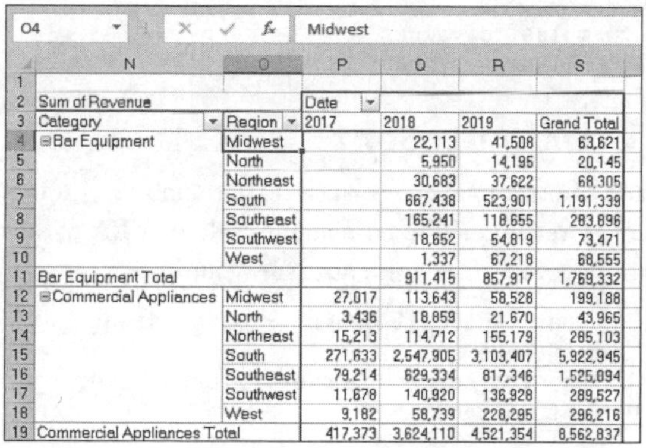

Figure 13.11
Daily dates have been rolled up to years by using the `Group` method.

	N	O	P	Q	R	S
O4		Midwest				
1						
2	Sum of Revenue		Date			
3	Category	Region	2017	2018	2019	Grand Total
4	Bar Equipment	Midwest		22,113	41,508	63,621
5		North		5,950	14,195	20,145
6		Northeast		30,683	37,622	68,305
7		South		667,438	523,901	1,191,339
8		Southeast		165,241	118,655	283,896
9		Southwest		18,652	54,819	73,471
10		West		1,337	67,218	68,555
11	Bar Equipment Total			911,415	857,917	1,769,332
12	Commercial Appliances	Midwest	27,017	113,643	58,528	199,188
13		North	3,436	18,859	21,670	43,965
14		Northeast	15,213	114,712	155,179	285,103
15		South	271,633	2,547,905	3,103,407	5,922,945
16		Southeast	79,214	629,334	817,346	1,525,094
17		Southwest	11,678	140,920	136,928	289,527
18		West	9,182	58,739	228,295	296,216
19	Commercial Appliances Total		417,373	3,624,110	4,521,354	8,562,837

Eliminating Blank Cells

The blank cells in a pivot table are annoying. You will want to fix two kinds of blank cells. Blank cells occur in the Values area when there were no records for a particular combination. For example, in Figure 13.11, the company did not sell bar equipment in 2017, so all of cells P4:P11 are blank. Most people would prefer to have zeros instead of those blank cells.

Blank cells also occur in the Row Labels area when you have multiple row fields. The words Bar Equipment appear in cell N4, but then cells N5:N10 are blank.

To replace blanks in the Values area with zeros, use this:

```
PT.NullString = "0"
```

> **NOTE**
> Although the preceeding code appears to use a zero inside of quotation marks, Excel actually puts a numeric zero in the empty cells.

13

To fill in the blanks in the label area in Excel 2016, use this:

```
PT.RepeatAllLabels xlRepeatLabels
```

The `RepeatAllLabels` code fails in Excel 2007 and earlier. The only solution in legacy versions of Excel is to convert the pivot table to values and then set the blank cells to a formula that grabs the value from the row above, like this:

```
Dim FillRange As Range
Set PT = ActiveSheet.PivotTables("PivotTable1")
' Locate outer row column
Set FillRange = PT.TableRange1.Resize(, 1)
' Convert entire table to values
PT.TableRange2.Copy
PT.TableRange2.PasteSpecial xlPasteValues
' Fill Special Cells Blanks with the value from above
FillRange.SpecialCells(xlCellTypeBlanks).FormulaR1C1 = _
        "=R[-1]C"
' Convert those formulas to values
FillRange.Value = FillRange.Value
```

Controlling the Sort Order with `AutoSort`

The Excel user interface offers an `AutoSort` option that enables you to sort a field in descending order based on revenue. The equivalent code in VBA to sort the region and category fields by descending revenue uses the `AutoSort` method:

```
PT.PivotFields("Region").AutoSort Order:=xlDescending, _
        Field:="Sum of Revenue"
PT.PivotFields("Category").AutoSort Order:=xlDescending, _
        Field:="Sum of Revenue"
```

Changing the Default Number Format

Numbers in the Values area of a pivot table need to have a suitable number format applied. You cannot count on the numeric format of the underlying field carrying over to the pivot table.

To show the Revenue values with zero decimal places and a comma, use this:

```
PT.PivotFields("Sum of Revenue").NumberFormat = "#,##0"
```

Some companies have customers who typically buy thousands or millions of dollars' worth of goods. You can display numbers in thousands by using a single comma after the number format. To do this, you need to include a K abbreviation to indicate that the numbers are in thousands:

```
PT.PivotFields("Sum of Revenue").NumberFormat = "#,##0,K"
```

Local custom dictates the thousands abbreviation. If you are working for a relatively young computer company where everyone uses K for the thousands separator, you are in luck because Microsoft makes it easy to use this abbreviation. However, if you work at a more than 100-year-old soap company where you use M for thousands and MM for millions, you have a few more hurdles to jump. You must prefix the M character with a backslash to have it work:

```
PT.PivotFields("Sum of Revenue").NumberFormat = "#,##0,\M"
```

Alternatively, you can surround the M character with double quotation marks. To put double quotation marks inside a quoted string in VBA, you must use two sequential quotation marks. To set up a format in tenths of millions that uses the #,##0.0,,"MM" format, you would use this line of code:

```
PT.PivotFields("Sum of Revenue").NumberFormat = "#,##0.0,,""M"""
```

Here, the format is quotation mark, pound, comma, pound, pound, zero, period, zero, comma, comma, quotation mark, quotation mark, M, quotation mark, quotation mark, quotation mark. The three quotation marks at the end are correct. You use two quotation marks to simulate typing one quotation mark in the custom number format box and a final quotation mark to close the string in VBA.

Figure 13.12 shows the pivot table blanks filled in, numbers shown in thousands, and category and region sorted in descending order.

Figure 13.12
After filling in blanks and sorting, you have only a few extraneous totals and labels to remove.

	N	O	P	Q	R	S
1						
2	Sum of Revenue		Date			
3	Category	Region	2017	2018	2019	Grand Total
4	⊟ Ovens and Ranges	South	15,672K	13,796K	8,284K	37,752K
5	Ovens and Ranges	Southeast	2,639K	2,745K	1,418K	6,802K
6	Ovens and Ranges	West	519K	1,520K	1,594K	3,634K
7	Ovens and Ranges	Southwest	572K	1,335K	1,104K	3,012K
8	Ovens and Ranges	Northeast	662K	1,146K	801K	2,609K
9	Ovens and Ranges	Midwest	290K	1,379K	760K	2,429K
10	Ovens and Ranges	North	247K	421K	283K	931K
11	Ovens and Ranges Total		20,602K	22,342K	14,225K	57,169K
12	⊟ Refrigerators and Cooler	South	4,855K	4,659K	12,093K	21,606K
13	Refrigerators and Cooler	West	1,957K	348K	3,088K	5,393K

(O4 / South)

Suppressing Subtotals for Multiple Row Fields

As soon as you have more than one row field, Excel automatically adds subtotals for all but the innermost row field. That extra row field can get in the way if you plan on reusing the results of the pivot table as a new data set for some other purpose.

In the current example, you have taken 87,000 rows of data and produced a tight 50-row summary of yearly sales by category and region. That new data set would be interesting for sorting, filtering, and charting if you could remove the total row and the category subtotals.

To remove the subtotal, you first set the Subtotals(1) property to True to turn off the other 10 possible subtotals. You can then turn off the first subtotal to make sure that all subtotals are suppressed:

```
PT.PivotFields("Category").Subtotals(1) = True
PT.PivotFields("Category").Subtotals(1) = False
```

To remove the grand total row, use this:

```
PT.ColumnGrand = False
```

13

Figure 13.13 shows the first section of the pivot table with the subtotals removed.

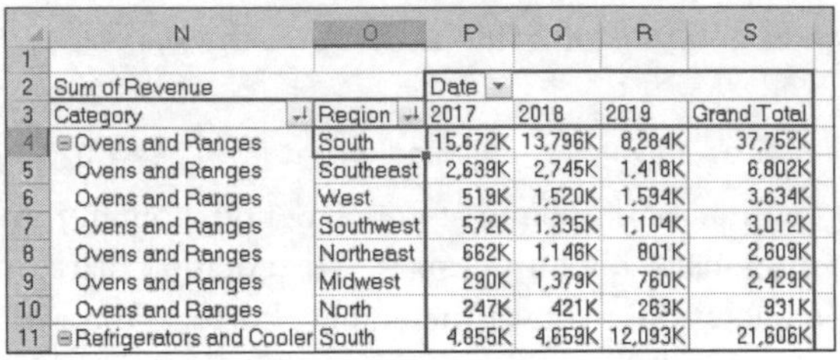

Figure 13.13
Remove the subtotal rows from column A.

	N	O	P	Q	R	S
1						
2	Sum of Revenue		Date			
3	Category	Region	2017	2018	2019	Grand Total
4	⊟Ovens and Ranges	South	15,672K	13,796K	8,284K	37,752K
5	Ovens and Ranges	Southeast	2,639K	2,745K	1,418K	6,802K
6	Ovens and Ranges	West	519K	1,520K	1,594K	3,634K
7	Ovens and Ranges	Southwest	572K	1,335K	1,104K	3,012K
8	Ovens and Ranges	Northeast	662K	1,146K	801K	2,609K
9	Ovens and Ranges	Midwest	290K	1,379K	760K	2,429K
10	Ovens and Ranges	North	247K	421K	263K	931K
11	⊟Refrigerators and Cooler	South	4,855K	4,659K	12,093K	21,606K

Copying a Finished Pivot Table as Values to a New Workbook

If you plan to repurpose the results of a pivot table, you need to convert the table to values. This section shows you how to copy a pivot table to a brand-new workbook.

To make the code more portable, assign object variables to the original workbook, new workbook, and first worksheet in the new workbook. At the top of the procedure, add these statements:

```
Dim WSR As Worksheet
Dim WSD As Worksheet
Dim WBO As Workbook
Dim WBN As Workbook
Set WBO = ActiveWorkbook
Set WSD = Worksheets("Data")
```

After the pivot table has been successfully created, build a blank Report workbook with this code:

```
' Create a New Blank Workbook with one Worksheet
Set WBN = Workbooks.Add(xlWorksheet)
Set WSR = WBN.Worksheets(1)
WSR.Name = "Report"
' Set up Title for Report
With WSR.Range("A1")
        .Value = "Revenue by Category, Region and Year"
        .Style = "Title"
End With
```

There are a few remaining annoyances in the pivot table. The borders are annoying, and there are stray labels such as Sum of Revenue and Date in the first row of the pivot table. You can solve these problems by excluding the first row(s) of `PT.TableRange2` from the `Copy` method and then using `PasteSpecial(xlPasteValuesAndNumberFormats)` to copy the data to the report sheet.

In the current example, the `TableRange2` property includes only one row to eliminate, row 2, as shown in Figure 13.13. If you had a more complex pivot table with several column fields and/or one or more page fields, you would have to eliminate more than just the first row of the report. It helps to run your macro to this point, look at the result, and figure out how many rows you need to delete. You can effectively not copy these rows to the report by using the `Offset` property. Then copy the `TableRange2` property, offset by one row.

Purists will note that this code copies one extra blank row from below the pivot table, but this really does not matter because the row is blank. After copying, you can erase the original pivot table and destroy the pivot cache, like this:

```
' Copy the Pivot Table data to row 3 of the Report sheet
' Use Offset to eliminate the title row of the pivot table
PT.TableRange2.Offset(1, 0).Copy
WSR. Range("A3").PasteSpecial Paste:=xlPasteValuesAndNumberFormats
PT.TableRange1.Clear

Set PTCache = Nothing
```

> **TIP**
>
> Note that you use the Paste Special option to paste just values and number formats. This gets rid of both borders and the pivot nature of the table. You might be tempted to use the All Except Borders option under Paste, but that keeps the data in a pivot table, and you will not be able to insert new rows in the middle of the data.

Handling Final Formatting

The last steps for the report involve some basic formatting tasks and addition of the subtotals. You can bold and right-justify the headings in row 3. Set up rows 1–3 so that the top three rows print on each page:

```
' Do some basic formatting
' Autofit columns, format the headings , right-align
Range("A3").EntireRow.Style = "Heading 4"
Range("A3").CurrentRegion.Columns.AutoFit
Range("A3").EntireRow.HorizontalAlignment = xlRight
Range("A3:B3").HorizontalAlignment = xlLeft
    ' Repeat rows 1-3 at the top of each page
WSR.PageSetup.PrintTitleRows = "$1:$3"
```

Adding Subtotals to Get Page Breaks

The Data tab offers a powerful feature: subtotals. Figure 13.14 shows the Subtotal dialog. Note the option Page Break Between Groups. Rather than looping through records to manually add a page break after each category, you can apply them in one command using the `Subtotal` method.

13

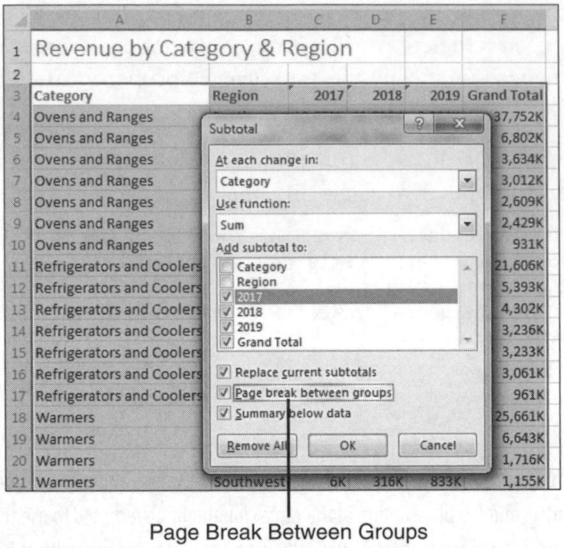

Figure 13.14
Using automatic subtotals enables you to add a page break after each category. Using this feature ensures that each category manager has a clean report with only her data on it.

Page Break Between Groups

If you were sure that you would always have three years and a total, you could use the following code to add subtotals for each line of business group:

```
' Add Subtotals by Category.
' Be sure to add a page break at each change in category
Selection.Subtotal GroupBy:=1, Function:=xlSum, _
        TotalList:=Array(3, 4, 5, 6), PageBreaks:=True
```

However, this code fails if you have more or less than three years. The solution is to use the following convoluted code to dynamically build a list of the columns to total, based on the number of columns in the report:

```
Dim TotColumns()
Dim I as Integer
FinalCol = Cells(3, Columns.Count).End(xlToLeft).Column
ReDim Preserve TotColumns(1 To FinalCol - 2)
For i = 3 To FinalCol
        TotColumns(i - 2) = i
Next i
Selection.Subtotal GroupBy:=1, Function:=xlSum, TotalList:=TotColumns,_
        Replace:=True, PageBreaks:=True, SummaryBelowData:=True
```

Finally, with the new totals added to the report, you need to AutoFit the numeric columns again with this code:

```
Dim GrandRow as Long
' Make sure the columns are wide enough for totals
GrandRow = Cells(Rows.Count, 1).End(xlUp).Row
Cells(3, 3).Resize(GrandRow - 2, FinalCol - 2).Columns.AutoFit
Cells(GrandRow, 3).Resize(1, FinalCol - 2).NumberFormat = "#,##0,K"
' Add a page break before the Grand Total row, otherwise
' the    manager for the final category will have two totals
WSR.HPageBreaks.Add Before:=Cells(GrandRow, 1)
```

Putting It All Together

Listing 13.3 produces the product line manager reports in a few seconds. Figure 13.15 shows the report produced by this code.

Listing 13.3   Code That Produces the Category Report in Figure 13.15

```vba
Sub CategoryRegionReport()
    ' Category and Region as Row
    ' Years as Column
    Dim WSD As Worksheet
    Dim PTCache As PivotCache
    Dim PT As PivotTable
    Dim PRange As Range
    Dim FinalRow As Long
    Dim TotColumns()

    Set WSD = Worksheets("Data")
    Dim WSR As Worksheet
    Dim WBO As Workbook
    Dim WBN As Workbook
    Set WBO = ActiveWorkbook

    ' Delete any prior pivot tables
    For Each PT In WSD.PivotTables
            PT.TableRange2.Clear
    Next PT
    WSD.Range("N1:XFD1").EntireColumn.Clear

    ' Define input area and set up a Pivot Cache
    FinalRow = WSD.Cells(Application.Rows.Count, 1).End(xlUp).Row
    FinalCol = WSD.Cells(1, Application.Columns.Count). _
            End(xlToLeft).Column
    Set PRange = WSD.Cells(1, 1).Resize(FinalRow, FinalCol)
    Set PTCache = ActiveWorkbook.PivotCaches.Add(SourceType:= _
            xlDatabase, SourceData:=PRange.Address)

    ' Create the Pivot Table from the Pivot Cache
    Set PT = PTCache.CreatePivotTable(TableDestination:=WSD. _
            Cells(2, FinalCol + 2), TableName:="PivotTable1")

    ' Turn off updating while building the table
    PT.ManualUpdate = True

    ' Set up the row fields
    PT.AddFields RowFields:=Array("Category", _
            "Region"), ColumnFields:="Date"

    ' Set up the data fields
    With PT.PivotFields("Revenue")
            .Orientation = xlDataField
            .Function = xlSum
            .Position = 1
            .NumberFormat = "#,##0"
    End With
```

13

```
' Ensure tabular layout is used
PT.RowAxisLayout xlTabularRow

' Calc the pivot table before grouping dates
PT.ManualUpdate = False
PT.ManualUpdate = True
 PT.PivotFields("Date").LabelRange.Group _
        Periods:=Array(False, False, False, False, False, False, True)

' Change number format of Revenue
PT.PivotFields("Sum of Revenue").NumberFormat = "#,##0,K"

' Fill in blank cells
PT.NullString = "0"
PT.RepeatAllLabels xlRepeatLabels

' Sort both label fields by descending revenue
PT.PivotFields("Category").AutoSort Order:=xlDescending, _
        field:="Sum of Revenue"
PT.PivotFields("Region").AutoSort Order:=xlDescending, _
        field:="Sum of Revenue"

' Suppress Category totals
PT.PivotFields("Category").Subtotals(1) = True
PT.PivotFields("Category").Subtotals(1) = False
PT.ColumnGrand = False

' Calc the pivot table
PT.ManualUpdate = False
PT.ManualUpdate = True

' Create a New Blank Workbook with one Worksheet
Set WBN = Workbooks.Add(xlWBATWorksheet)
Set WSR = WBN.Worksheets(1)
WSR.Name = "Report"
' Set up Title for Report
With WSR.[A1]
        .Value = "Revenue by Category & Region"
        .Style = "Title"
End With

' Copy the Pivot Table data to row 3 of the Report sheet
' Use Offset to eliminate the title row of the pivot table
PT.TableRange1.Offset(1, 0).Copy
WSR.[A3].PasteSpecial Paste:=xlPasteValuesAndNumberFormats
PT.TableRange2.Clear
Set PTCache = Nothing

' Do some basic formatting
' Autofit columns, bold the headings, right-align
Range("A3").EntireRow.Style = "Heading 4"
Range("A3").CurrentRegion.Columns.AutoFit
Range("A3").EntireRow.HorizontalAlignment = xlRight
Range("A3:B3").HorizontalAlignment = xlLeft

' Repeat rows 1-3 at the top of each page
WSR.PageSetup.PrintTitleRows = "$1:$3"
```

13

```
    ' Add subtotals
    FinalCol = Cells(3, 255).End(xlToLeft).Column
    ReDim Preserve TotColumns(1 To FinalCol - 2)
    For i = 3 To FinalCol
            TotColumns(i - 2) = i
    Next i
    Range("A3").CurrentRegion.Subtotal GroupBy:=1, Function:=xlSum, _
            TotalList:=TotColumns, Replace:=True, _
            PageBreaks:=True, SummaryBelowData:=True

    ' Make sure the columns are wide enough for totals
    GrandRow = Cells(Rows.Count, 1).End(xlUp).Row
    Cells(3, 3).Resize(GrandRow - 2, FinalCol - 2).Columns.AutoFit
    Cells(GrandRow, 3).Resize(1, FinalCol - 2).NumberFormat = "#,##0,K"
    ' Add a page break before the Grand Total row, otherwise
    ' the product manager for the final Line will have two totals
    WSR.HPageBreaks.Add Before:=Cells(GrandRow, 1)

End Sub
```

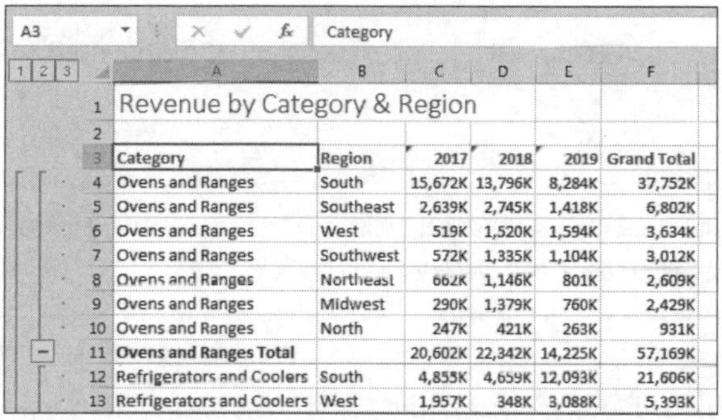

Revenue by Category & Region

Category	Region	2017	2018	2019	Grand Total
Ovens and Ranges	South	15,672K	13,796K	8,284K	37,752K
Ovens and Ranges	Southeast	2,639K	2,745K	1,418K	6,802K
Ovens and Ranges	West	519K	1,520K	1,594K	3,634K
Ovens and Ranges	Southwest	572K	1,335K	1,104K	3,012K
Ovens and Ranges	Northeast	662K	1,146K	801K	2,609K
Ovens and Ranges	Midwest	290K	1,379K	760K	2,429K
Ovens and Ranges	North	247K	421K	263K	931K
Ovens and Ranges Total		20,602K	22,342K	14,225K	57,169K
Refrigerators and Coolers	South	4,855K	4,659K	12,093K	21,606K
Refrigerators and Coolers	West	1,957K	348K	3,088K	5,393K

Figure 13.15 Converting 80,000 rows of transactional data to this useful report takes less than two seconds if you use the code that produced this example. Without pivot tables, the code would be far more complex.

You have now seen the VBA code to produce useful summary reports from transactional data. The next section deals with additional features in pivot tables.

Calculating with a Pivot Table

So far in this chapter, the pivot tables have presented a single field in the Values area, and that field has always shown as a Sum calculation. You can add more fields to the Values area. You can change from Sum to any of 11 functions or alter the Sum calculation to display running totals, percentage of total, and more. You can also add new calculated fields or calculated items to the pivot table.

Addressing Issues with Two or More Data Fields

It is possible to have multiple fields in the Values section of a pivot report. For example, you might have Quantity, Revenue, and Cost in the same pivot table.

When you have two or more data fields in an Excel 2016 pivot table that you built in the Excel interface, the value fields go across the columns. However, VBA builds the pivot table with the Values fields going down the innermost row field. This creates a bizarre-looking table like the one shown in Figure 13.16.

Figure 13.16
This ugly view was banished in the Excel interface after Excel 2003, but VBA still produces it by default.

	N	O	P
1			
2	State ▼	Data	Total
3	AL	Sum of Revenue	752,789.55
4		Sum of Cost	337,502.00
5		Sum of Quantity	1,890
6	AR	Sum of Revenue	134,244.75
7		Sum of Cost	59,499.00
8		Sum of Quantity	130
9	AZ	Sum of Revenue	3,687,831.25
10		Sum of Cost	1,665,417.00
11		Sum of Quantity	6,950
12	CA	Sum of Revenue	11,322,124.25
13		Sum of Cost	5,108,375.00

To correct this problem, you should specify that a virtual field called Data is one of the column fields.

> **NOTE**
> In this instance, note that Data is not a column in your original data; it is a special name used to indicate the orientation of the multiple Values fields.

To have multiple Values fields go across the report, use this code:

```
PT.AddFields RowFields:="State", ColumnFields:="Data"
```

After adding a column field called Data, you then define multiple data fields:

```
' Set up the data fields
With PT.PivotFields("Revenue")
        .Orientation = xlDataField
        .Function = xlSum
        .Position = 1
        .NumberFormat = "#,##0.00"
End With

With PT.PivotFields("Cost")
        .Orientation = xlDataField
        .Function = xlSum
        .Position = 2
        .NumberFormat = "#,##0.00"
End With

With PT.PivotFields("Quantity")
        .Orientation = xlDataField
        .Function = xlSum
        .Position = 3
```

13

```
            .NumberFormat = "#,##0"
        End With
```

This code produces the pivot table shown in Figure 13.17.

Figure 13.17
When you specify the
virtual field Data as a
column field, multiple
values go across the
report.

	N	O	P	Q
1				
2		Data		
3	State ▾	Sum of Revenue	Sum of Cost	Sum of Quantity
4	AL	752,789.55	337,502.00	1,890
5	AR	134,244.75	59,499.00	130
6	AZ	3,687,831.25	1,665,417.00	6,950
7	CA	11,322,124.25	5,108,375.00	14,585
8	CO	1,280,417.15	580,449.00	1,730
9	FL	65,272,493.30	29,399,753.00	103,763
10	GA	27,955,642.10	12,582,085.00	48,897
11	IA	816,462.00	368,449.00	950

Using Calculations Other Than Sum

So far, all the pivot tables in this chapter have used the Sum function to calculate. There are 11 functions available, including Sum. To specify a different calculation, specify one of these values as the `Function` property:

- **`xlAverage`**—Average
- **`xlCount`**—Count
- **`xlCountNums`**—Count numeric values only
- **`xlMax`**—Maximum
- **`xlMin`**—Minimum
- **`xlProduct`**—Multiply
- **`xlStDev`**—Standard deviation, based on a sample
- **`xlStDevP`**—Standard deviation, based on the whole population
- **`xlSum`**—Sum
- **`xlVar`**—Variation, based on a sample
- **`xlVarP`**—Variation, based on the whole population

Although Count Distinct was added in Excel 2013, you cannot create Count Distinct in a regular pivot-cache pivot table. See "Using the Data Model in Excel 2016" at the end of this chapter.

> **TIP**
> Note that when you add a field to the Values area of the pivot table, Excel modifies the field name with the function name and the word *of*. For example, "Revenue" becomes "Sum of Revenue." "Cost" might become "StdDev of Cost." If you later need to refer to those fields in your code, you need to do so using the new name, such as Average of Quantity.

13

You can improve the look of your pivot table by changing the Name property of the field. If you do not want Sum of Revenue appearing in the pivot table, change the Caption property to something like Total Revenue. This sounds less awkward than Sum of Revenue. Remember that you cannot have a name that exactly matches an existing field name in the pivot table, so "Revenue" is not suitable as a name. However, " Revenue" (with a leading space) is fine to use as a name.

For text fields, the only function that makes sense is a count. You will frequently count the number of records by adding a text field to the pivot table and using the Count function.

The following code fragment calculates total revenue, a count of records by counting a text field, and average quantity:

```
With PT.PivotFields("Revenue")
        .Orientation = xlDataField
        .Function = xlSum
        .Position = 1
        .NumberFormat = "$#,##0.00"
        .Name = " Revenue"
End With

With PT.PivotFields("Customer")
        .Orientation = xlDataField
        .Function = xlCount
        .Position = 2
        .NumberFormat = "#,##0"
        .Name = "# of Records"
End With

With PT.PivotFields("Revenue")
        .Orientation = xlDataField
        .Function = xlAverage
        .Position = 3
        .NumberFormat = "#,##0.00"
        .Name = "Average Revenue"
End With
' Ensure that we get zeros instead of blanks in the data area
PT.NullString = "0"
PT.TableStyle2 = "PivotStyleMedium3"
```

Figure 13.18 shows the pivot table this code creates.

Figure 13.18

You can change the function used to summarize columns in the Values area of the pivot table.

	N	O	P	Q
1				
2		Data		
3	Rep	Revenue	# of Records	Average Revenue
4	Anne Troy	$5,582,120	2,910	1,918.3
5	Jade Miller	$2,225,244	799	2,785.0
6	James Tallman	$3,045,306	1,192	2,554.8
7	Jeffrey P. Coulson	$1,308,212	1,059	1,235.3
8	John Cockerill	$173,245	182	951.9
9	John Durran	$331,932	396	838.2
10	Larry Vance	$575,548	385	1,494.9
11	Michael Karpfen	$848,890	466	1,821.7
12	Mike Mann	$282,422	159	1,776.2
13	Pauline Mccollum	$292,028	262	1,114.6

Using Calculated Data Fields

Pivot tables offer two types of formulas. The most useful type defines a formula for a calculated field. This adds a new field to the pivot table. Calculations for calculated fields are always done at the summary level.

To set up a calculated field, use the `Add` method with the `CalculatedFields` object. You have to specify a field name and a formula, like so:

```
PT.CalculatedFields.Add Name:="GrossProfit", Formula:="=Revenue-Cost"
PT.CalculatedFields.Add "GP_Pct", "=GrossProfit/Revenue"
```

After you define the field, add it as a data field:

```
With PT.PivotFields("GrossProfit")
        .Orientation = xlDataField
        .Function = xlSum
        .Position = 3
        .NumberFormat = "$#,##0"
        .Caption = "Gross Profit"
End With
With PT.PivotFields("GP_Pct")
        .Orientation = xlDataField
        .Function = xlSum
        .Position = 4
        .NumberFormat = "0.0%"
        .Caption = "GP%"
End With
```

Figure 13.19 shows the Gross Profit calculated field.

Figure 13.19
A calculated field adds Gross Profit to the pivot table.

Category	Data Sum of Revenue	Sum of Cost	Gross Profit
Bar Equipment	$1,769,332	$799,967	$969,365
Commercial Appliances	$8,562,837	$3,848,608	$4,714,229
Concession Equipment	$9,876,342	$4,436,685	$5,439,657
Fryers	$3,835,963	$1,723,930	$2,112,033
Ovens and Ranges	$57,168,593	$25,787,407	$31,381,186
Refrigerators and Coolers	$41,793,565	$18,828,219	$22,965,346
Warmers	$37,482,133	$16,876,630	$20,605,503
Grand Total	$160,488,764	$72,301,446	$88,187,318

A calculated field can be referenced in subsequent calculated fields. The following code uses the Gross Profit field to calculate Gross Profit Percent. Although the `Caption` property renamed the field to "Gross Profit" (with a space in the middle), the field name in the preceding code is "GrossProfit" (without a space). Use the field name in the following calculation:

```
PT.CalculatedFields.Add "GP_Pct", "=GrossProfit/Revenue", True
With PT.PivotFields("GP_Pct")
        .Orientation = xlDataField
        .Function = xlSum
        .Position = 4
        .NumberFormat = "0.0%"
        .Caption = "GP%"
End With
```

13

Figure 13.20 shows a report with GP%.

Figure 13.20
GP% is based on a field in the data set and another calculated field.

Category	Data			
	Sum of Revenue	Sum of Cost	Gross Profit	GP%
Bar Equipment	$1,769,332	$799,967	$969,365	54.8%
Commercial Appliances	$8,562,837	$3,848,608	$4,714,229	55.1%
Concession Equipment	$9,876,342	$4,436,685	$5,439,657	55.1%
Fryers	$3,835,963	$1,723,930	$2,112,033	55.1%
Ovens and Ranges	$57,168,593	$25,787,407	$31,381,186	54.9%
Refrigerators and Coolers	$41,793,565	$18,828,219	$22,965,346	54.9%
Warmers	$37,482,133	$16,876,630	$20,605,503	55.0%
Grand Total	$160,488,764	$72,301,446	$88,187,318	54.9%

Using Calculated Items

Calculated items have the potential to produce incorrect results in a pivot table. Say that you have a report of sales by nine states. You want to show a subtotal of four of the states. A calculated item would add a ninth item to the state column. Although the pivot table gladly calculates this new item, it causes the grand total to appear overstated.

Figure 13.21 shows a pivot table with these nine states. The total revenue is $10 million. When a calculated item provides a subtotal of four states (see Figure 13.22), the grand total increases to $15 million. This means that the items that make up the calculated item are included in the total twice. If you like restating numbers to the Securities and Exchange Commission, feel free to use calculated items.

Figure 13.21
This pivot table adds up to $10 million

Revenue	
State	Total
Arizona	$550,550
California	$3,165,104
Colorado	$616,097
Louisiana	$814,431
Nevada	$1,170,320
New Mexico	$322,168
Oklahoma	$186,715
Texas	$2,559,021
Utah	$632,897
Grand Total	**$10,017,303**

Figure 13.22
Add a calculated item, and the total is overstated.

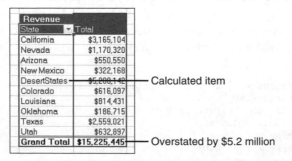

Revenue	
State	Total
California	$3,165,104
Nevada	$1,170,320
Arizona	$550,550
New Mexico	$322,168
DesertStates	$5,208,142	── Calculated item
Colorado	$616,097
Louisiana	$814,431
Oklahoma	$186,715
Texas	$2,559,021
Utah	$632,897
Grand Total	**$15,225,445**	── Overstated by $5.2 million

The code to produce the calculated item is shown here. Calculated items are added as the final position along the field, so this code changes the Position property to move the Desert States item to the proper position:

```
PT.PivotFields("State").CalculatedItems.Add _
      Name:="DesertStates", _
      Formula:="=California +Nevada +Arizona +'New Mexico'"
PT.PivotFields("State").PivotItems("California").Position = 1
PT.PivotFields("State").PivotItems("Nevada").Position = 2
PT.PivotFields("State").PivotItems("Arizona").Position = 3
PT.PivotFields("State").PivotItems("New Mexico").Position = 4
PT.PivotFields("State").PivotItems("DesertStates").Position = 5
```

If you hope to use a calculated item, you should either remove the grand total row or remove the four states that go into the calculated item. This code hides the four states, and the resulting pivot table returns to the correct total, as shown in Figure 13.23:

```
PT.PivotFields("State").CalculatedItems.Add _
      Name:="DesertStates", _
      Formula:="=California +Nevada +Arizona +'New Mexico'"
' Hide the items included in the new subtotal
With PT.PivotFields("State")
      .PivotItems("California").Visible = False
      .PivotItems("Nevada").Visible = False
      .PivotItems("Arizona").Visible = False
      .PivotItems("New Mexico").Visible = False
End With
```

Figure 13.23
One way to use a calculated item is to remove any elements that went into it.

Revenue	
State ▾	Total
DesertStates	$5,208,142
Colorado	$616,097
Louisiana	$814,431
Oklahoma	$186,715
Texas	$2,559,021
Utah	$632,897
Grand Total	**$10,017,303**

A better solution, which is discussed in the next section, is to skip calculated items and use text grouping.

Calculating Groups

If you need to calculate subtotals for certain regions, a better solution is to use text grouping to define the groups. If you group the four states, Excel adds a new field to the row area of the pivot table. Although this process requires some special handling, it is worthwhile and creates a nice-looking report.

13

To group four states in the Excel interface, you select the cells that contain those four states and select Group Selection from the PivotTable Tools Options tab. This immediately does several things:

- The items in the group are moved together in the row area.

- A new field is added to the left of the state field. If the original field was called State, the new field is called State2.

- Annoyingly, the subtotals property for the new State2 field is set to None instead of Automatic.

- A subtotal for the selected items is added with the name of Group1.

- Any items that are not in a group have a new subtotal added to State2 with the state name repeated.

In VBA, it is somewhat tricky to select the cells that contain the proper states. The following code uses the LabelRange property to point to the cells and then uses the Union method to refer to the four noncontiguous cells:

```
Set R1 = PT.PivotFields("State").PivotItems("California").LabelRange
Set R2 = PT.PivotFields("State").PivotItems("Arizona").LabelRange
Set R3 = PT.PivotFields("State").PivotItems("New Mexico").LabelRange
Set R4 = PT.PivotFields("State").PivotItems("Nevada").LabelRange
Union(R1, R2, R3, R4).Group
```

After setting up the first group, rename the newly created States2 field to have a suitable name:

```
PT.PivotFields("State2").Caption = "State Group"
```

Then change the name of this region from Group1 to the desired group name:

```
PT.PivotFields("State Group").PivotItems("Group1").Caption = "Desert States"
```

Change the Subtotals property from None to Automatic:

```
PT.PivotFields("State Group").Subtotals(1) = True
```

After you have set up the first group, you can define the remaining groups with this code:

```
Set R1 = PT.PivotFields("State").PivotItems("Utah").LabelRange
Set R2 = PT.PivotFields("State").PivotItems("Colorado").LabelRange
Union(R1, R2).Group
PT.PivotFields("State Group").PivotItems("Group2").Caption = "Rockies"

Set R1 = PT.PivotFields("State").PivotItems("Texas").LabelRange
Set R2 = PT.PivotFields("State").PivotItems("Louisiana").LabelRange
Set R3 = PT.PivotFields("State").PivotItems("Oklahoma").LabelRange
Union(R1, R2, R3).Group
PT.PivotFields("State Group").PivotItems("Group3").Caption = "Oil States"
```

The result is a pivot table with new virtual groups, as shown in Figure 13.24.

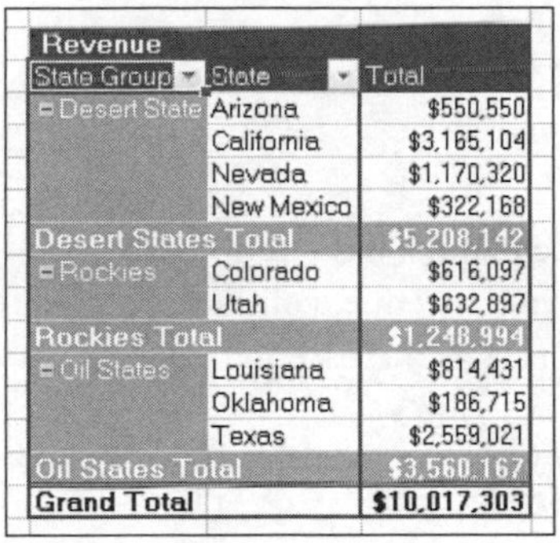

Figure 13.24
Grouping text fields allows for reporting by territories that are not in the original data.

Revenue		
State Group ▾	State ▾	Total
⊟ Desert State	Arizona	$550,550
	California	$3,165,104
	Nevada	$1,170,320
	New Mexico	$322,168
Desert States Total		$5,208,142
⊟ Rockies	Colorado	$616,097
	Utah	$632,897
Rockies Total		$1,248,994
⊟ Oil States	Louisiana	$814,431
	Oklahoma	$186,715
	Texas	$2,559,021
Oil States Total		$3,560,167
Grand Total		$10,017,303

Using Show Values As to Perform Other Calculations

The Show Values As tab in the Value Field Settings dialog offers 15 different calculations. These calculations enable you to change from numbers to percentage of total, running totals, ranks, and more.

You change the calculation by using the `Calculation` option for the pivot field.

> **NOTE**
> Note that the `Calculation` property works with the `BaseField` and `BaseItem` properties. Depending on the selected calculation, you might be required to specify a base field and base item, or sometimes only a base field, or sometimes neither of them.

Some calculations, such as % of Column and % of Row, need no further definition; you do not have to specify a base field. Here is code that shows revenue as a percentage of total revenue:

```
With PT.PivotFields("Revenue")
        .Orientation = xlDataField
        .Function = xlSum
        .Calculation = xlPercentOfTotal
        .Position = 2
        .NumberFormat = "0.0%"
        .Name = "% of Total"
    End With
```

Other calculations need a base field. If you are showing revenue and ask for the descending rank, you can specify that the base field is the State field. In this case, you are asking for this state's rank based on revenue:

```
With PT.PivotFields("Revenue")
        .Orientation = xlDataField
        .Calculation = xlRankDescending
```

13

```
            .BaseField = "State"
            .Position = 3
            .NumberFormat = "0%"
            .Name = "RankD"
    End With
```

A few calculations require both a base field and a base item. If you want to show every state's revenue as a percentage of California revenue, you have to specify % Of as the calculation, State as the base field, and California as the base item:

```
With PT.PivotFields("Revenue")
            .Orientation = xlDataField
            .Calculation = xlPercentOf
            .BaseField = "State"
            .BaseItem = "California"
            .Position = 4
            .NumberFormat = "0%"
            .Name = "% of CA"
    End With
```

Some of the calculation fields were new in Excel 2010. In Figure 13.25, column I uses the new % of Parent calculation and column H uses the old % of Total calculation. In both columns, Desert States is 52% of the Grand Total (cells H8 and I8). However, cell I5 shows that California is 60.8% of Desert States, whereas cell H5 shows that California is 31.6% of the grand total.

Table 13.1 shows the complete list of `Calculation` options. The second column indicates whether the calculations are compatible with previous versions of Excel. The third column indicates whether you need a base field and base item.

Figure 13.25
% of Parent in column I
was new in Excel 2010.

State Group	State	Data Revenue	% of Total	% of Parent	RankD
= Desert State	Arizona	$550,550	5.5%	10.6%	3
	California	$3,165,104	31.6%	60.8%	1
	Nevada	$1,170,320	11.7%	22.5%	2
	New Mexico	$322,168	3.2%	6.2%	4
Desert States Total		$5,208,142	52.0%	52.0%	
= Rockies	Colorado	$616,097	6.2%	49.3%	2
	Utah	$632,897	6.3%	50.7%	1
Rockies Total		$1,248,994	12.5%	12.5%	
= Oil States	Louisiana	$814,431	8.1%	22.9%	2
	Oklahoma	$186,715	1.9%	5.2%	3
	Texas	$2,559,021	25.5%	71.9%	1
Oil States Total		$3,560,167	35.5%	35.5%	
Grand Total		$10,017,303	100.0%	100.0%	

Table 13.1   Calculation Options Available in Excel 2016 VBA

Calculation	Version	Base Field/Base Item?
xlDifferenceFrom	All	Both required
xlIndex	All	Neither
xlNoAdditionalCalculation	All	Neither
xlPercentDifferenceFrom	All	Both required
xlPercentOf	All	Both required
xlPercentOfColumn	All	Neither
xlPercentOfParent	2010 and later	Base field only
xlPercentOfParentColumn	2010 and later	Both required
xlPercentOfParentRow	2010 and later	Both required
xlPercentOfRow	All	Neither
xlPercentOfTotal	All	Neither
xlPercentRunningTotal	2010 and later	Base field only
xlRankAscending	2010 and later	Base field only
xlRankDescending	2010 and later	Base field only
xlRunningTotal	All	Base field only

Using Advanced Pivot Table Techniques

Even if you are a pivot table pro, you might never have run into some of the really advanced techniques available with pivot tables. The following sections discuss such techniques.

Using AutoShow to Produce Executive Overviews

If you are designing an executive dashboard utility, you might want to spotlight the top five markets. This setting lets you select either the top or bottom *n* records, based on any data field in the report.

The code to use AutoShow in VBA uses the AutoShow method:

```
' Show only the top 5 Markets
PT.PivotFields("Market").AutoShow Top:=xlAutomatic, Range:=xlTop, _
        Count:=5, Field:= "Sum of Revenue"
```

When you create a report using the AutoShow method, it is often helpful to copy the data and then go back to the original pivot report to get the totals for all markets. In the code in Listing 13.4, this is achieved by removing the Market field from the pivot table and copying the grand total to the report. The code in Listing 13.4 produces the report shown in Figure 13.26.

13

Figure 13.26
The Top 5 Markets report contains two pivot tables.

	A	B	C
1	Top 5 Markets		
2			
3	**Market**	**Bar Equipment**	**Commercial Appliances**
4	Florida	1,131,779	5,667,799
5	Charlotte	283,676	1,525,742
6	California	66,233	294,080
7	Dallas	59,560	255,146
8	Buffalo	37,366	237,298
9	Top 5 Total	1,578,614	7,980,064
10			
11	Total Company	1,769,332	8,562,837
12			

Listing 13.4   Code Used to Create the Top 5 Markets Report

```
Sub Top5Markets()
        ' Produce a report of the top 5 markets
        Dim WSD As Worksheet
        Dim WSR As Worksheet
        Dim WBN As Workbook
        Dim PTCache As PivotCache
        Dim PT As PivotTable
        Dim PRange As Range
        Dim FinalRow As Long
        Set WSD = Worksheets("Data")

        ' Delete any prior pivot tables
        For Each PT In WSD.PivotTables
                PT.TableRange2.Clear
        Next PT
        WSD.Range("M1:Z1").EntireColumn.Clear

        ' Define input area and set up a Pivot Cache
        FinalRow = WSD.Cells(Application.Rows.Count, 1).End(xlUp).Row
        FinalCol = WSD.Cells(1, Application.Columns.Count). _
                End(xlToLeft).Column
        Set PRange = WSD.Cells(1, 1).Resize(FinalRow, FinalCol)
        Set PTCache = ActiveWorkbook.PivotCaches.Add(SourceType:= _
                xlDatabase, SourceData:=PRange.Address)

        ' Create the Pivot Table from the Pivot Cache
        Set PT = PTCache.CreatePivotTable(TableDestination:=WSD. _
                Cells(2, FinalCol + 2), TableName:="PivotTable1")

        ' Turn off updating while building the table
        PT.ManualUpdate = True

        ' Set up the row fields
        PT.AddFields RowFields:="Market", ColumnFields:="Category"

        ' Set up the data fields
        With PT.PivotFields("Revenue")
```

```
                    .Orientation = xlDataField
                    .Function = xlSum
                    .Position = 1
                    .NumberFormat = "#,##0"
                    .Name = "Total Revenue"
End With

' Ensure that we get zeros instead of blanks in the data area
PT.NullString = "0"

' Sort markets descending by sum of revenue
PT.PivotFields("Market").AutoSort Order:=xlDescending, _
        field:="Total Revenue"

' Show only the top 5 markets
PT.PivotFields("Market").AutoShow Type:=xlAutomatic, Range:=xlTop, _
        Count:=5, field:="Total Revenue"

' Calc the pivot table to allow the date label to be drawn
PT.ManualUpdate = False
PT.ManualUpdate = True

' Create a new blank workbook with one worksheet
Set WBN = Workbooks.Add(xlWBATWorksheet)
Set WSR = WBN.Worksheets(1)
WSR.Name = "Report"
' Set up title for report
With WSR.[A1]
        .Value = "Top 5 Markets"
        .Font.Size = 14
End With

' Copy the pivot table data to row 3 of the report sheet
' Use offset to eliminate the title row of the pivot table
PT.TableRange2.Offset(1, 0).Copy
WSR.[A3].PasteSpecial Paste:=xlPasteValuesAndNumberFormats
LastRow = WSR.Cells(Rows.Count, 1).End(xlUp).Row
WSR.Cells(LastRow, 1).Value = "Top 5 Total"

' Go back to the pivot table to get totals without the AutoShow
PT.PivotFields("Market").Orientation = xlHidden
PT.ManualUpdate = False
PT.ManualUpdate = True
PT.TableRange2.Offset(2, 0).Copy
WSR.Cells(LastRow + 2, 1).PasteSpecial _
        Paste:=xlPasteValuesAndNumberFormats

' Clear the pivot table
PT.TableRange2.Clear
Set PTCache = Nothing

' Do some basic formatting
' Autofit columns, bold the headings, right-align
WSR.Range(WSR.Range("A3"), WSR.Cells(LastRow + 2, 9)).Columns.AutoFit
Range("A3").EntireRow.Font.Bold = True
Range("A3").EntireRow.HorizontalAlignment = xlRight
Range("A3").HorizontalAlignment = xlLeft
```

```
        Range("A2").Select
        MsgBox "CEO Report has been Created"

End Sub
```

The Top 5 Markets report actually contains two snapshots of a pivot table. After using the AutoShow feature to grab the top five markets with their totals, the macro goes back to the pivot table, removes the AutoShow option, and grabs the total of all markets to produce the Total Company row.

Using `ShowDetail` to Filter a Recordset

Open any pivot table in the Excel user interface. Double-click any number in the pivot table. Excel inserts a new sheet in the workbook and copies all the source records that represent that number. In the Excel user interface, this is a great way to perform a drill-down query into a data set.

The equivalent VBA property is `ShowDetail`. By setting this property to `True` for any cell in a pivot table, you generate a new worksheet with all the records that make up that cell:

```
    PT.TableRange1.Offset(2, 1).Resize(1, 1).ShowDetail = True
```

Listing 13.5 produces a pivot table with the total revenue for the top three stores and `ShowDetail` for each of those stores. This is an alternative method to using the Advanced Filter report. The results of this macro are three new sheets. Figure 13.27 shows the first sheet created.

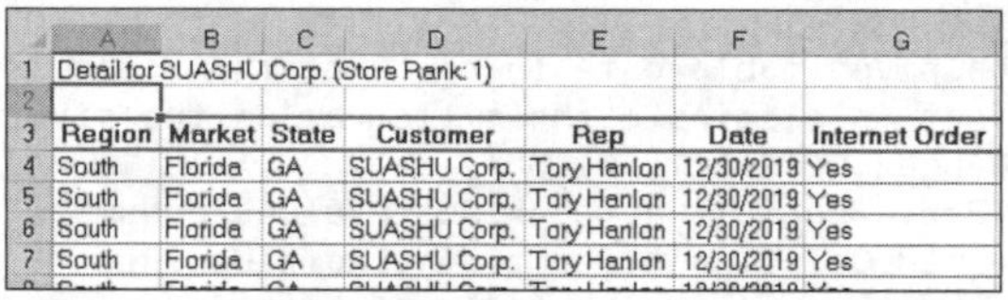

Figure 13.27
Pivot table applications are incredibly diverse. This macro created a pivot table of the top three stores and then used the `ShowDetail` property to retrieve the records for each of those stores.

	A	B	C	D	E	F	G
1	Detail for SUASHU Corp. (Store Rank: 1)						
2							
3	Region	Market	State	Customer	Rep	Date	Internet Order
4	South	Florida	GA	SUASHU Corp.	Tory Hanlon	12/30/2019	Yes
5	South	Florida	GA	SUASHU Corp.	Tory Hanlon	12/30/2019	Yes
6	South	Florida	GA	SUASHU Corp.	Tory Hanlon	12/30/2019	Yes
7	South	Florida	GA	SUASHU Corp.	Tory Hanlon	12/30/2019	Yes

Listing 13.5   Code Used to Create a Report for Each of the Top Three Customers

```
Sub RetrieveTop3CustomerDetail()
        ' Retrieve Details from Top 3 Customers
        Dim WSD As Worksheet
        Dim WSR As Worksheet
        Dim WBN As Workbook
        Dim PTCache As PivotCache
        Dim PT As PivotTable
        Dim PRange As Range
        Dim FinalRow As Long
        Set WSD = Worksheets("Data")
```

```vba
' Delete any prior pivot tables
For Each PT In WSD.PivotTables
        PT.TableRange2.Clear
Next PT
WSD.Range("M1:Z1").EntireColumn.Clear

' Define input area and set up a Pivot Cache
FinalRow = WSD.Cells(Application.Rows.Count, 1).End(xlUp).Row
FinalCol = WSD.Cells(1, Application.Columns.Count). _
        End(xlToLeft).Column
Set PRange = WSD.Cells(1, 1).Resize(FinalRow, FinalCol)
Set PTCache = ActiveWorkbook.PivotCaches.Add(SourceType:= _
        xlDatabase, SourceData:=PRange.Address)

' Create the Pivot Table from the Pivot Cache
Set PT = PTCache.CreatePivotTable(TableDestination:=WSD. _
        Cells(2, FinalCol + 2), TableName:="PivotTable1")

' Turn off updating while building the table
PT.ManualUpdate = True

' Set up the row fields
PT.AddFields RowFields:="Customer", ColumnFields:="Data"

' Set up the data fields
With PT.PivotFields("Revenue")
        .Orientation = xlDataField
        .Function = xlSum
        .Position = 1
        .NumberFormat = "#,##0"
        .Name = "Total Revenue"
End With

' Sort Stores descending by sum of revenue
PT.PivotFields("Customer").AutoSort Order:=xlDescending, _
        field:="Total Revenue"

' Show only the top 3 stores
PT.PivotFields("Customer").AutoShow Type:=xlAutomatic, Range:=xlTop, _
        Count:=3, field:="Total Revenue"

' Ensure that we get zeros instead of blanks in the data area
PT.NullString = "0"

' Calc the pivot table to allow the date label to be drawn
PT.ManualUpdate = False
PT.ManualUpdate = True

' Produce summary reports for each customer
For i = 1 To 3
        PT.TableRange2.Offset(i + 1, 1).Resize(1, 1).ShowDetail = True
        ' The active sheet has changed to the new detail report
        ' Add a title
        Range("A1:A2").EntireRow.Insert
        Range("A1").Value = "Detail for " & _
                PT.TableRange2.Offset(i + 1, 0).Resize(1, 1).Value & _
```

13

```
                        " (Store Rank: " & i & ")"
        Next i

        MsgBox "Detail reports for top 3 stores have been created."

End Sub
```

Creating Reports for Each Region or Model

A pivot table can have one or more filter fields. A filter field goes in a separate set of rows above the pivot report. It can serve to filter the report to a certain region, certain model, or certain combination of region and model. In VBA, filter fields are called *page fields*.

You might create a pivot table with several filter fields to allow someone to do ad hoc analyses. However, it is more likely that you will use the filter fields in order to produce reports for each region.

To set up a filter in VBA, add the `PageFields` parameter to the `AddFields` method. The following line of code creates a pivot table with Region in the Filters area:

```
PT.AddFields RowFields:= "Product", ColumnFields:= "Data", PageFields:=
➥"Region"
```

The preceding line of code sets up the Region filter with the value (All), which returns all regions. To limit the report to just the North region, use the `CurrentPage` property:

```
PT.PivotFields("Region").CurrentPage = "North"
```

One use of a filter is to build a user form in which someone can select a particular region or particular product. You then use this information to set the `CurrentPage` property and display the results of the user form.

One amazing trick is to use the Show Pages feature to replicate a pivot table for every item in one filter field drop-down. After creating and formatting a pivot table, you can run this single line of code. If you have eight regions in the data set, eight new worksheets are inserted in the workbook, one for each region. The pivot table appears on each worksheet, with the appropriate region chosen from the drop-down:

```
PT.ShowPages PageField:=Region
```

CAUTION

Be careful with `ShowPages`. If you use `ShowPages` on the Customer field and you have 1,000 customers, Excel attempts to insert 1,000 worksheets in the workbook, each with a pivot table. All of those pivot tables share the same pivot cache in order to minimize memory usage. However, you will eventually run out of memory, and the program will end with a debug error when no additional worksheets will fit in available memory.

The other problem with `ShowPages` is that it creates the individual reports as worksheets in a single workbook. In real life, you probably want separate workbooks for each region so that you can email the reports to the appropriate office. You can loop through all `PivotItems` and display them one at a time in the page field. You can quickly produce top 10 reports for each region using this method.

13

To determine how many regions are available in the data, use `PT.PivotFields("Region")`. `PivotItems.Count`. Either of these loops would work:

```
For i = 1 To PT.PivotFields("Region").PivotItems.Count
        PT.PivotFields("Region").CurrentPage = _
                     PT.PivotFields("Region").PivotItems(i).Name
        PT.ManualUpdate = False
        PT.ManualUpdate = True
Next i

For Each PivItem In PT.PivotFields("Region").PivotItems
        PT.PivotFields("Region").CurrentPage = PivItem.Name
        PT.ManualUpdate = False
        PT.ManualUpdate = True
Next PivItem
```

Of course, in both of these loops, the three region reports fly by too quickly to see. In practice, you would want to save each report while it is displayed.

So far in this chapter, you have been using `PT.TableRange2` when copying the data from the pivot table. The `TableRange2` property includes all rows of the pivot table, including the page fields.

There is also a `TableRange1` property, which excludes the page fields. You can use either of these statements to get the detail rows:

```
PT.TableRange2.Offset(3, 0)
PT.TableRange1.Offset(1, 0)
```

> **CAUTION**
> Which statement you use is your preference, but if you use `TableRange2`, you will not have problems when you try to delete the pivot table with `PT.TableRange2.Clear`. If you were to accidentally attempt to clear `TableRange1` when there are page fields, you would end up with the dreaded "Cannot move or change part of a pivot table" error.

Listing 13.6 produces a new workbook for each region, as shown in Figure 13.28.

Figure 13.28
By looping through all items found in the Region page field, the macro produced one workbook for each regional manager.

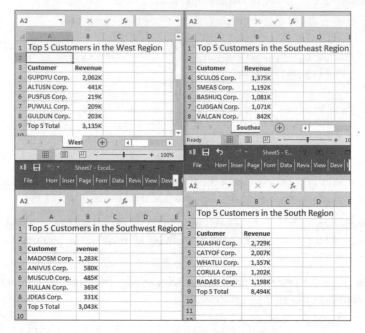

Listing 13.6   Code That Creates a New Workbook for Each Region

```
Sub Top5ByRegionReport()
        ' Produce a report of top 5 customers for each region
        Dim WSD As Worksheet
        Dim WSR As Worksheet
        Dim WBN As Workbook
        Dim PTCache As PivotCache
        Dim PT As PivotTable
        Dim PRange As Range
        Dim FinalRow As Long

        Set WSD = Worksheets("Data")

        ' Delete any prior pivot tables
        For Each PT In WSD.PivotTables
                PT.TableRange2.Clear
        Next PT
        WSD.Range("M1:Z1").EntireColumn.Clear

        ' Define input area and set up a Pivot Cache
        FinalRow = WSD.Cells(Application.Rows.Count, 1).End(xlUp).Row
        FinalCol = WSD.Cells(1, Application.Columns.Count). _
                End(xlToLeft).Column
        Set PRange = WSD.Cells(1, 1).Resize(FinalRow, FinalCol)
        Set PTCache = ActiveWorkbook.PivotCaches.Add(SourceType:= _
                xlDatabase, SourceData:=PRange.Address)
```

```
' Create the Pivot Table from the Pivot Cache
Set PT = PTCache.CreatePivotTable(TableDestination:=WSD. _
        Cells(2, FinalCol + 2), TableName:="PivotTable1")

' Turn off updating while building the table
PT.ManualUpdate = True

' Set up the row fields
PT.AddFields RowFields:="Customer", ColumnFields:="Data", _
        PageFields:="Region"

' Set up the data fields
With PT.PivotFields("Revenue")
        .Orientation = xlDataField
        .Function = xlSum
        .Position = 1
        .NumberFormat = "#,##0,K"
        .Name = "Total Revenue"
End With

' Sort stores descending by sum of revenue
PT.PivotFields("Customer").AutoSort Order:=xlDescending, _
        field:="Total Revenue"

' Show only the top 5 stores
PT.PivotFields("Customer").AutoShow Type:=xlAutomatic, Range:=xlTop, _
        Count:=5, field:="Total Revenue"

' Ensure that we get zeros instead of blanks in the data area
PT.NullString = "0"

' Calc the pivot table
PT.ManualUpdate = False
PT.ManualUpdate = True
 Ctr = 0

' Loop through each region
For Each PivItem In PT.PivotFields("Region").PivotItems
        Ctr = Ctr + 1
        PT.PivotFields("Region").CurrentPage = PivItem.Name
        PT.ManualUpdate = False
        PT.ManualUpdate = True

        ' Create a new blank workbook with one worksheet
        Set WBN = Workbooks.Add(xlWBATWorksheet)
        Set WSR = WBN.Worksheets(1)
        WSR.Name = PivItem.Name
        ' Set up Title for Report
        With WSR.[A1]
        .Value = "Top 5 Customers in the " & _
                PivItem.Name & " Region"
         End With

        ' Copy the pivot table data to row 3 of the report sheet
        ' Use offset to drop the page & title rows
        PT.TableRange2.Offset(3, 0).Copy
```

13

```
                         WSR.[A3].PasteSpecial Paste:=xlPasteValuesAndNumberFormats
                         LastRow = WSR.Cells(65536, 1).End(xlUp).Row
                         WSR.Cells(LastRow, 1).Value = "Top 5 Total"

                         ' Do some basic formatting
                         ' Autofit columns, bold the headings, right-align
                         WSR.Range(WSR.Range("A2"), WSR.Cells(LastRow, 3)) _
                                 .Columns.AutoFit
                         Range("A3").EntireRow.Font.Bold = True
                         Range("A3").EntireRow.HorizontalAlignment = xlRight
                         Range("A3").HorizontalAlignment = xlLeft
                         Range("B3").Value = "Revenue"

                         Range("A2").Select

                 Next PivItem

                 ' Clear the pivot table
                 PT.TableRange2.Clear
                 Set PTCache = Nothing

                 MsgBox Ctr & " Region reports have been created"

         End Sub
```

Manually Filtering Two or More Items in a Pivot Field

In addition to setting up a calculated pivot item to display the total of a couple products that make up a dimension, you can manually filter a particular pivot field.

For example, say that you have one client who sells shoes. In the report showing sales of sandals, he wants to see just the stores that are in warm-weather states. This is the code to hide a particular store:

```
PT.PivotFields("Store").PivotItems("Minneapolis").Visible = False
```

> **CAUTION**
>
> You must be very careful never to set all items to `False` because doing so causes the macro to end with an error. This tends to happen more than you would expect. An application may first show products A and B and then on the next loop show products C and D. If you attempt to make A and B not visible before making C and D visible, no products will be visible along the pivot field, which causes an error. To correct this, always loop through all pivot items and make sure to turn them back to visible before the second pass through the loop.

This process is easy in VBA. After building the table with `Product` in the page field, loop through to change the `Visible` property to show only the total of certain products:

```
' Make sure all PivotItems along line are visible
For Each PivItem In _
        PT.PivotFields("Product").PivotItems
        PivItem.Visible = True
Next PivItem
```

```
' Now - loop through and keep only certain items visible
For Each PivItem In _
        PT.PivotFields("Product").PivotItems
        Select Case PivItem.Name
                Case "Landscaping/Grounds Care", _
                        "Green Plants and Foliage Care"
                        PivItem.Visible = True
                Case Else
                        PivItem.Visible = False
        End Select
Next PivItem
```

Using the Conceptual Filters

Beginning with Excel 2007, conceptual filters for date fields, numeric fields, and text fields are provided. In the PivotTable Fields list, hover the mouse cursor over any active field in the field list portion of the pane. In the drop-down that appears, you can choose Label Filters, Date Filters, or Value Filters.

To apply a label filter in VBA, use the PivotFilters.Add method. The following code filters to the customers that start with 1:

```
PT.PivotFields("Customer").PivotFilters.Add _
        Type:=xlCaptionBeginsWith, Value1:="1"
```

To clear the filter from the Customer field, use the ClearAllFilters method:

```
PT.PivotFields("Customer").ClearAllFilters
```

To apply a date filter to the date field to find records from this week, use this code:

```
PT.PivotFields("Date").PivotFilters.Add Type:=xlThisWeek
```

A value filters allow you to filter one field based on the value of another field. For example, to find all the markets where the total revenue is more than $100,000, you would use this code:

```
PT.PivotFields("Market").PivotFilters.Add _
        Type:=xlValueIsGreaterThan, _
        DataField:=PT.PivotFields("Sum of Revenue"), _
        Value1:=100000
```

Other value filters might allow you to specify that you want branches where the revenue is between $50,000 and $100,000. In this case, you would specify one limit as Value1 and the second limit as Value2:

```
PT.PivotFields("Market").PivotFilters.Add _
        Type:=xlValueIsBetween, _
        DataField:=PT.PivotFields("Sum of Revenue"), _
        Value1:=50000, Value2:=100000
```

Table 13.2 lists all the possible filter types.

13

Table 13.2   Filter Types in VBA

Filter Type	Description
`xlBefore`	Filters for all dates before a specified date
`xlBeforeOrEqualTo`	Filters for all dates on or before a specified date
`xlAfter`	Filters for all dates after a specified date
`xlAfterOrEqualTo`	Filters for all dates on or after a specified date
`xlAllDatesInPeriodJanuary`	Filters for all dates in January
`xlAllDatesInPeriodFebruary`	Filters for all dates in February
`xlAllDatesInPeriodMarch`	Filters for all dates in March
`xlAllDatesInPeriodApril`	Filters for all dates in April
`xlAllDatesInPeriodMay`	Filters for all dates in May
`xlAllDatesInPeriodJune`	Filters for all dates in June
`xlAllDatesInPeriodJuly`	Filters for all dates in July
`xlAllDatesInPeriodAugust`	Filters for all dates in August
`xlAllDatesInPeriodSeptember`	Filters for all dates in September
`xlAllDatesInPeriodOctober`	Filters for all dates in October
`xlAllDatesInPeriodNovember`	Filters for all dates in November
`xlAllDatesInPeriodDecember`	Filters for all dates in December
`xlAllDatesInPeriodQuarter1`	Filters for all dates in Quarter 1
`xlAllDatesInPeriodQuarter2`	Filters for all dates in Quarter 2
`xlAllDatesInPeriodQuarter3`	Filters for all dates in Quarter 3
`xlAllDatesInPeriodQuarter4`	Filters for all dates in Quarter 4
`xlBottomCount`	Filters for the specified number of values from the bottom of a list
`xlBottomPercent`	Filters for the specified percentage of values from the bottom of a list
`xlBottomSum`	Sums the values from the bottom of the list
`xlCaptionBeginsWith`	Filters for all captions beginning with the specified string
`xlCaptionContains`	Filters for all captions that contain the specified string
`xlCaptionDoesNotBeginWith`	Filters for all captions that do not begin with the specified string
`xlCaptionDoesNotContain`	Filters for all captions that do not contain the specified string
`xlCaptionDoesNotEndWith`	Filters for all captions that do not end with the specified string
`xlCaptionDoesNotEqual`	Filters for all captions that do not match the specified string

13

Filter Type	Description
xlCaptionEndsWith	Filters for all captions that end with the specified string
xlCaptionEquals	Filters for all captions that match the specified string
xlCaptionIsBetween	Filters for all captions that are between a specified range of values
xlCaptionIsGreaterThan	Filters for all captions that are greater than the specified value
xlCaptionIsGreaterThan-OrEqualTo	Filters for all captions that are greater than or match the specified value
xlCaptionIsLessThan	Filters for all captions that are less than the specified value
xlCaptionIsLessThanOrEqualTo	Filters for all captions that are less than or match the specified value
xlCaptionIsNotBetween	Filters for all captions that are not between a specified range of values
xlDateBetween	Filters for all dates that are between a specified range of dates
xlDateLastMonth	Filters for all dates that apply to the previous month
xlDateLastQuarter	Filters for all dates that apply to the previous quarter
xlDateLastWeek	Filters for all dates that apply to the previous week
xlDateLastYear	Filters for all dates that apply to the previous year
xlDateNextMonth	Filters for all dates that apply to the next month
xlDateNextQuarter	Filters for all dates that apply to the next quarter
xlDateNextWeek	Filters for all dates that apply to the next week
xlDateNextYear	Filters for all dates that apply to the next year
xlDateThisMonth	Filters for all dates that apply to the current month
xlDateThisQuarter	Filters for all dates that apply to the current quarter
xlDateThisWeek	Filters for all dates that apply to the current week
xlDateThisYear	Filters for all dates that apply to the current year
xlDateToday	Filters for all dates that apply to the current date
xlDateTomorrow	Filters for all dates that apply to the next day
xlDateYesterday	Filters for all dates that apply to the previous day
xlNotSpecificDate	Filters for all dates that do not match a specified date
xlSpecificDate	Filters for all dates that match a specified date

13

Table 13.2   Filter Types in VBA

Filter Type	Description
xlTopCount	Filters for the specified number of values from the top of a list
xlTopPercent	Filters for the specified percentage of values from a list
xlTopSum	Sums the values from the top of the list
xlValueDoesNotEqual	Filters for all values that do not match the specified value
xlValueEquals	Filters for all values that match the specified value
xlValueIsBetween	Filters for all values that are between a specified range of values
xlValueIsGreaterThan	Filters for all values that are greater than the specified value
xlValueIsGreaterThanOrEqualTo	Filters for all values that are greater than or match the specified value
xlValueIsLessThan	Filters for all values that are less than the specified value
xlValueIsLessThanOrEqualTo	Filters for all values that are less than or match the specified value
xlValueIsNotBetween	Filters for all values that are not between a specified range of values
xlYearToDate	Filters for all values that are within one year of a specified date

Using the Search Filter

Excel 2010 added a search box to the filter drop-down. Although this is a slick feature in the Excel interface, there is no equivalent magic in VBA. Figure 13.29 shows the (Select All Search Results) check box checked after the search for "ce." Using the macro recorder during this process creates a 5,876-line macro that goes through and turns all customers without "ce" to invisible:

```
With ActiveSheet.PivotTables("PivotTable3").PivotFields("Customer")
        .PivotItems("ACASCO Corp.").Visible = False
        .PivotItems("ACECUL Corp.").Visible = False
        .PivotItems("ACEHUA Corp.").Visible = False
' snipped 587_ similar lines
        .PivotItems("ZUQHYR Corp.").Visible = False
        .PivotItems("ZUSOEA Corp.").Visible = False
        .PivotItems("ZYLSTR Corp.").Visible = False
End With
```

There is nothing new in Excel 2016 VBA to emulate the search box. To achieve the same results in VBA, you use the xlCaptionContains filter described in Table 13.2.

Figure 13.29
The Excel 2016 interface offers a search box. In VBA, you can emulate this by using the old `xlCaptionContains` filter.

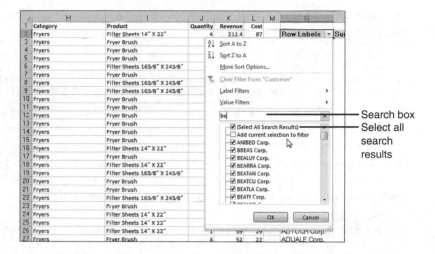

Search box
Select all search results

Setting Up Slicers to Filter a Pivot Table

Excel 2010 introduced the concept of slicers for filtering pivot tables. A slicer is a visual filter. You can resize and reposition slicers. You can control the color of the slicer and control the number of columns in a slicer. You can also select or clear items from a slicer by using VBA.

Figure 13.30 shows a pivot table with two slicers. The State slicer has been modified to have five columns. The slicer with the caption "Territory" is actually based on the Region field. You can give slicers friendlier captions, which might be helpful when the underlying field is called IDKTxtReg or some other bizarre name invented by the IT department.

Figure 13.30
Slicers provide a visual filter for State and Region.

Region caption changed to Territory

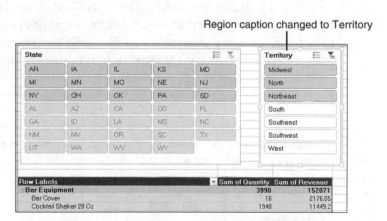

13

A slicer is composed of `SlicerCache` and `Slicer`. To define a slicer cache, you need to specify a pivot table as the source and a field name as `SourceField`. `SlicerCache` is defined at the workbook level. This enables you to have the slicer on a different worksheet than the actual pivot table. Here's the code to do all this:

```
Dim SCS as SlicerCache
Dim SCR as SlicerCache
Set SCS = ActiveWorkbook.SlicerCaches.Add(Source:=PT, SourceField:="State")
Set SCR = ActiveWorkbook.SlicerCaches.Add(Source:=PT, SourceField:="Region")
```

After you have defined `SlicerCache`, you can add `Slicer`, which is defined as an object of the slicer cache. Specify a worksheet as the destination. The `Name` argument controls the internal name for the slicer. The `Caption` argument is the heading that will be visible in the slicer. Specify the size of the slicer using height and width in points. Specify the location using top and left in points. In the following code, the values for top, left, height, and width are assigned to be equal to the location or size of certain cell ranges:

```
Dim SLS as Slicer
Set SLS = SCS.Slicers.Add(SlicerDestination:=WSD, Name:="State", _
        Caption:="State", _
        Top:=WSD.Range("O2").Top, _
        Left:=WSD.Range("O2").Left, _
        Width:=WSR.Range("O2:U2").Width, _
        Height:=WSD.Range("O2:O17").Height)
' Format the color and number of columns
```

Every slicer starts out as one column. You can change the style and number of columns with this code:

```
With SLS
        .Style = "SlicerStyleLight6"
        .NumberOfColumns = 5
End With
```

> **NOTE**
> I find that when I create slicers in the Excel interface, I spend many mouse clicks making adjustments to them. After adding two or three slicers, I position them in an overlapping tile arrangement. I always tweak the location, size, number of columns, and so on. For many years in my seminars, I bragged that I could create a pivot table in 6 mouse clicks. That was before slicers were introduced. Slicers are admittedly powerful, but they seem to take 20 mouse clicks before they look right. Having a macro make all of these adjustments at once is a time-saver.

After a slicer is defined, you can use VBA to choose which items are activated in the slicer. It seems counterintuitive, but to choose items in the slicer, you have to change `SlicerItem`, which is a member of `SlicerCache`, not a member of `Slicer`:

```
With SCR
        .SlicerItems("Midwest").Selected = True
        .SlicerItems("North").Selected = True
        .SlicerItems("Northeast").Selected = True
        .SlicerItems("South").Selected = False
        .SlicerItems("Southeast").Selected = False
        .SlicerItems("Southwest").Selected = False
        .SlicerItems("West").Selected = False
End With
```

You might need to deal with slicers that already exist. If a slicer is created for the State field, the slicer cache is named "Slicer_State". The following code is used to format the slicers shown in Figure 13.30:

```
Sub MoveAndFormatSlicer()
        Dim SCS As SlicerCache
        Dim SLS As Slicer
        Dim SCR As SlicerCache
        Dim SLR As Slicer
        Dim WSD As Worksheet
        Set WSD = ActiveSheet

        Set SCS = ActiveWorkbook.SlicerCaches("Slicer_State")
        Set SLS = SCS.Slicers("State")
        With SLS
                .Style = "SlicerStyleLight6"
                .NumberOfColumns = 5
                .Top = WSD.Range("A1").Top + 5
                .Left = WSD.Range("A1").Left + 5
                .Width = WSD.Range("A1:B14").Width - 60
                .Height = WSD.Range("A1:B14").Height
        End With

        Set SCR = ActiveWorkbook.SlicerCaches("Slicer_Region")
        Set SLR = SCR.Slicers("Region")
        With SLR
                .Style = "SlicerStyleLight3"
                .NumberOfColumns = 1
                .Top = WSD.Range("C1").Top + 5
                .Left = WSD.Range("C1").Left - 20
                .Width = WSD.Range("C1").Width
                .Height = WSD.Range("C1:C14").Height
                .Caption = "Territory"
        End With

        ' Choose three regions
        With SCR
                .SlicerItems("Midwest").Selected = True
                .SlicerItems("North").Selected = True
                .SlicerItems("Northeast").Selected = True
                .SlicerItems("South").Selected = False
                .SlicerItems("Southeast").Selected = False
                .SlicerItems("Southwest").Selected = False
                .SlicerItems("West").Selected = False
        End With

    End Sub
```

Using the Data Model in Excel 2016

Excel 2016 incorporates parts of Power Pivot into the core Excel product. Items in the Excel ribbon are incorporated into the Data Model; items in the Power Pivot ribbon are not. This means you can add two tables to the Data Model, create a relationship, and then build a pivot table from the Data Model.

To follow along with the example in this section, open the 13-BeforeDataModel.xlsm file from the sample download files. This workbook has two tables: Sales and Sector. Sector is a lookup table that is related to the Sales table via a customer field. To build the pivot table, you follow these general steps in the macro:

1. Add the main table to the model.
2. Add the lookup table to the model.
3. Link the two tables with a relationship.
4. Create a pivot cache from `ThisWorkbookDataModel`.
5. Create a pivot table from the cache.
6. Add row fields.
7. Define a measure. Add the measure to the pivot table.

Adding Both Tables to the Data Model

You should already have a data set in the workbook that has been converted to a table using the Ctrl+T shortcut. On the Table Tools Design tab, change the table name to Sales. To link this table to the Data Model, use this code:

```
' Build Connection to the main Sales table
Set WBT = ActiveWorkbook
TableName = "Sales"
WBT.Connections.Add2 Name:="LinkedTable_" & TableName, _
        Description:="", _
        ConnectionString:="WORKSHEET;" & WBT.FullName, _
        CommandText:=WBT.Name & "!" & TableName, _
        lCmdType:=7, _
        CreateModelConnection:=True, _
        ImportRelationships:=False
```

Several variables in this code use the table name, the workbook path, and/or the workbook name. By storing the table name in a variable at the top of the code, you can build the connection name, connection string, and command text using the variables.

Adapting the preceding code to link to the lookup table then requires only changing the `TableName` variable:

```
TableName = "Sector"
WBT.Connections.Add2 Name:="LinkedTable_" & TableName, _
        Description:="", _
        ConnectionString:="WORKSHEET;" & WBT.FullName, _
        CommandText:=WBT.Name & "!" & TableName, _
        lCmdType:=7, _
        CreateModelConnection:=True, _
        ImportRelationships:=False
```

Creating a Relationship Between the Two Tables

When you create a relationship in the Excel interface, you specify the following four items in the Create Relationship dialog (see Figure 13.31):

- Table 1 is Sector
- Columns is Customer
- Table 2 is Sales
- Columns is Customer

Figure 13.31
To create a relationship, specify a field in both tables.

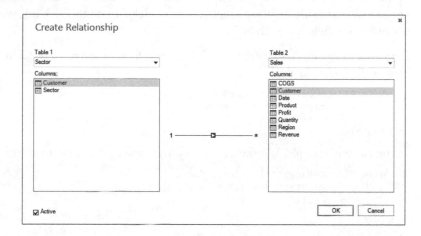

The code to create the relationship is more streamlined. There can be only one Data Model per workbook. Set an object variable named MO to refer to the model in this workbook. Use the ModelRelationships.Add method and specify the two fields that are linked.

```
' Relate the two tables
Dim MO As Model
Set MO = ActiveWorkbook.Model
MO.ModelRelationships.Add _
        ForeignKeyColumn:=MO.ModelTables("Sales").
ModelTableColumns("Customer"), PrimaryKeyColumn:= _
        MO.ModelTables("Sector").ModelTableColumns("Customer")
```

Defining the Pivot Cache and Building the Pivot Table

The code to define the pivot cache specifies that the data is external. Even though the linked tables are in your workbook, and even though the Data Model is stored as a binary large object within the workbook, this is still considered an external data connection. The connection is always called ThisWorkbookDataModel. Here's the code for defining the pivot cache and building the pivot table:

```
' Define the PivotCache
Set PTCache = WBT.PivotCaches.Create(SourceType:=xlExternal, _
        SourceData:=WBT.Connections("ThisWorkbookDataModel"), _
        Version:=xlPivotTableVersion15)

' Create the Pivot Table from the Pivot Cache
Set PT = PTCache.CreatePivotTable( _
        TableDestination:=WSD.Cells(1, 1), TableName:="PivotTable1")
```

13

Adding Model Fields to the Pivot Table

You need to add two types of fields to the pivot table. Text fields such as Customer, Sector, and Product are simply fields that can be added to the row or column area of the pivot table. No calculation has to happen for these fields. The code for adding text fields is shown in this section. When you add a numeric field to the Values area in the Excel interface, you are actually implicitly defining a new calculated field. To do this in VBA, you have to explicitly define the field and then add it.

Let's look at the simpler example of adding a text field to the row area. The VBA code generically looks like this:

```
With PT.CubeFields("[TableName].[FieldName]")
        .Orientation = xlRowField
        .Position = 1
End With
```

In the current example, add the Sector field from the Sector table by using this code:

```
With PT.CubeFields("[Sector].[Sector]")
        .Orientation = xlRowField
        .Position = 1
End With
```

Adding Numeric Fields to the Values Area

In Excel 2010, Power Pivot calculated fields were called *measures*. In Excel 2016, the Excel interface calls them *calculations*. However, the underlying VBA code still calls them *measures*.

If you have a Data Model pivot table and you check the Revenue field, you see the Revenue field move to the Values area. Behind the scenes, though, Excel is implicitly defining a new measure called Sum of Revenue. (You can see the implicit measures in the Power Pivot window if you use Excel 2016 Pro Plus.) In VBA, the first step is to define a new measure for Sum of Revenue. To make it easier to refer to this measure later, assign the new measure to an object variable:

```
' Before you can add Revenue to the pivot table,
' you have to define the measure.
' This happens using the GetMeasure method.
' Assign the cube field to CFRevenue object
Dim CFRevenue As CubeField
Set CFRevenue = PT.CubeFields.GetMeasure( _
        AttributeHierarchy:="[Sales].[Revenue]", _
        Function:=xlSum, _
        Caption:="Sum of Revenue")
' Add the newly created cube field to the pivot table
PT.AddDataField Field:=CFRevenue, _
        Caption:="Total Revenue"
PT.PivotFields("[Measures].[Sum of Revenue]").NumberFormat = "$#,##0,K"
```

You can use the sample code to create a new measure. The following measure uses the Distinct Count function to count the number of unique customers in each sector:

```
' Add Distinct Count of Customer as a Cube Field
Dim CFCustCount As CubeField
Set CFCustCount = PT.CubeFields.GetMeasure( _
```

```
        AttributeHierarchy:="[Sales].[Customer]", _
        Function:=xlDistinctCount, _
        Caption:="Customer Count")
' Add the newly created cube field to the pivot table
PT.AddDataField Field:=CFCustCount, _
        Caption:="Customer Count"
```

CAUTION

Before you get too excited, you need to know that the Excel team drew an interesting line in the sand with regard to what parts of Power Pivot are available via VBA. Any functionality that is available in Office 2016 Standard is available in VBA. If you try to define a new calculated field that uses the DAX language, it does not work in VBA.

Putting It All Together

Figure 13.32 shows the Data Model pivot table created using the code in Listing 13.7.

Figure 13.32
Two tables linked with a pivot table and two measures, all via a macro.

	A	B	C
1	Row Labels	Total Revenue	Customer Count
2	Apparel	$758K	2
3	Chemical	$569K	1
4	Consumer	$2,195K	7
5	Electronics	$222K	4
6	Food	$750K	1
7	Hardware	$2,179K	11
8	Textiles	$35K	1
9	**Grand Total**	**$6,708K**	**27**
10			

Listing 13.7   Code to Create the Data Model Pivot Table in Figure 13.32

```
Sub BuildModelPivotTable()
        Dim WBT As Workbook
        Dim WC As WorkbookConnection
        Dim MO As Model
        Dim PTCache As PivotCache
        Dim PT As PivotTable
        Dim WSD As Worksheet
        Dim CFRevenue As CubeField
        Dim CFCustCount As CubeField

        Set WBT = ActiveWorkbook
        Set WSD = WBT.Worksheets("Report")

        ' Build Connection to the main Sales table
        TableName = "Sales"
        WBT.Connections.Add2 Name:="LinkedTable_" & TableName, _
                Description:="MainTable", _
                ConnectionString:="WORKSHEET;" & WBT.FullName, _
                CommandText:=WBT.Name & "!" & TableName, _
                lCmdType:=7, _
```

13

```
            CreateModelConnection:=True, _
            ImportRelationships:=False

    ' Build Connection to the Sector lookup table
    TableName = "Sector"
    WBT.Connections.Add2 Name:="LinkedTable_" & TableName, _
            Description:="LookupTable", _
            ConnectionString:="WORKSHEET;" & WBT.FullName, _
            CommandText:=WBT.Name & "!" & TableName, _
            lCmdType:=7, _
            CreateModelConnection:=True, _
            ImportRelationships:=False


    ' Relate the two tables
    Set MO = ActiveWorkbook.Model
    MO.ModelRelationships.Add ForeignKeyColumn:= _
            MO.ModelTables("Sales").ModelTableColumns("Customer"), _
            PrimaryKeyColumn:=MO.ModelTables("Sector"). _
            ModelTableColumns("Customer")

    ' Delete any prior pivot tables
    For Each PT In WSD.PivotTables
            PT.TableRange2.Clear
    Next PT

    ' Define the PivotCache
    Set PTCache = WBT.PivotCaches.Create(SourceType:=xlExternal, _
            SourceData:=WBT.Connections("ThisWorkbookDataModel"), _
            Version:=xlPivotTableVersion15)

    ' Create the Pivot Table from the Pivot Cache
    Set PT = PTCache.CreatePivotTable( _
            TableDestination:=WSD.Cells(1, 1), TableName:="PivotTable1")

    ' Add the Sector field from the Sector table to the Row areas
    With PT.CubeFields("[Sector].[Sector]")
            .Orientation = xlRowField
            .Position = 1
    End With

    ' Before you can add Revenue to the pivot table,
    ' you have to define the measure.
    ' This happens using the GetMeasure method
    ' Assign the cube field to CFRevenue object
    Set CFRevenue = PT.CubeFields.GetMeasure( _
            AttributeHierarchy:="[Sales].[Revenue]", _
            Function:=xlSum, _
            Caption:="Sum of Revenue")
    ' Add the newly created cube field to the pivot table
    PT.AddDataField Field:=CFRevenue, _
            Caption:="Total Revenue"
    PT.PivotFields("[Measures].[Sum of Revenue]"). _
            NumberFormat = "$#,##0,K"
    ' Add Distinct Count of Customer as a Cube Field
    Set CFCustCount = PT.CubeFields.GetMeasure( _
            AttributeHierarchy:="[Sales].[Customer]", _
```

```
            Function:=xlDistinctCount, _
            Caption:="Customer Count")
    ' Add the newly created cube field to the pivot table
    PT.AddDataField Field:=CFCustCount, _
            Caption:="Customer Count"

End Sub
```

Next Steps

In Chapter 14, "Advanced Pivot Table Tips and Techniques," you'll learn many techniques for handling common questions and issues related to pivot tables.

Advanced Pivot Table Tips and Techniques

14

In this chapter, you'll discover some techniques that provide unique solutions to some of the most common pivot table problems. Take some time to glance at the topics covered here. Who knows? You might find a few unique tips that can help you tackle some of your pivot table conundrums!

Tip 1: Force Pivot Tables to Refresh Automatically

In some situations you might need to have pivot tables refresh themselves automatically. For instance, suppose you create a pivot table report for your manager. You might not be able to trust that he will refresh the pivot table when needed.

You can force each pivot table to automatically refresh when the workbook opens by following these steps:

1. Right-click the pivot table and select PivotTable Options.
2. In the PivotTable Options dialog that appears, select the Data tab.
3. Place a check next to Refresh Data When Opening the File property.

When this property is activated, the pivot table refreshes itself each time the workbook in which it's located is opened.

> **TIP**
>
> The Refresh Data When Opening the File property must be set for each pivot table individually.

Tip 2: Refresh All Pivot Tables in a Workbook at the Same Time

When you have multiple pivot tables in a workbook, refreshing all of them can be bothersome. There are several ways to avoid the hassle of manually refreshing multiple pivot tables. Here are a few options:

- **Option 1**—You can configure each pivot table in a workbook to automatically refresh when the workbook opens. To do so, right-click the pivot table and select PivotTable Options. This activates the PivotTable Options dialog. Here, select the Data tab and place a check next to Refresh Data When Opening the File property. After you have configured all pivot tables in the workbook, they will automatically refresh when the workbook is opened.

- **Option 2**—You can create a macro to refresh each pivot table in the workbook. This option is ideal when you need to refresh pivot tables on demand rather than only when the workbook opens. To do this, start recording a macro, and while the macro is recording, go to each pivot table in your workbook and refresh. After all pivot tables are refreshed, stop recording. The result is a macro that can be fired any time you need to refresh all pivot tables.

→ Revisit Chapter 12, "Enhancing Pivot Table Reports with Macros," to get more detail on using macros with pivot tables.

- **Option 3**—You can use VBA to refresh all pivot tables in a workbook on demand. This option can be used when it is impractical to record and maintain macros that refresh all pivot tables. This approach entails the use of the `RefreshAll` method of the `Workbook` object. To employ this technique, start a new module and enter the following code:

```
Sub RefreshAll ()
ThisWorkbook.RefreshAll
End Sub
```

You can now call this procedure any time you want to refresh all pivot tables within the workbook.

> **NOTE**
>
> Keep in mind that the `RefreshAll` method refreshes all external data ranges along with pivot tables. This means that if your workbook contains data from external sources, such as databases and external files, that data is refreshed along with your pivot tables.

Tip 3: Sort Data Items in a Unique Order, Not Ascending or Descending

Figure 14.1 shows the default sequence of regions in a pivot table report. Alphabetically, the regions are shown in the sequence Midwest, North, South, West. If your company is based in California, company tradition might dictate that the West region be shown first, followed by Midwest, North, and South. Unfortunately, neither an ascending sort order nor a descending sort order can help you with this.

Figure 14.1
Company tradition dictates that the Region field should be in West–Midwest–North–South sequence.

◢	A	B	C	D	E	F
1						
2						
3	Sum of Sales_Amount	Column Labels ▾				
4	Row Labels ▾	MIDWEST	NORTH	SOUTH	WEST	Grand Total
5	Cleaning & Housekeeping Services	$174,518	$534,282	$283,170	$146,623	$1,138,593
6	Facility Maintenance and Repair	$463,077	$606,747	$846,515	$444,820	$2,361,158
7	Fleet Maintenance	$448,800	$610,791	$1,046,231	$521,976	$2,627,798
8	Green Plants and Foliage Care	$93,562	$155,021	$157,821	$870,379	$1,276,783
9	Landscaping/Grounds Care	$190,003	$299,309	$335,676	$365,928	$1,190,915
10	Predictive Maintenance/Preventative Maintenance	$478,928	$572,860	$472,045	$655,092	$2,178,925
11	Grand Total	$1,848,887	$2,779,009	$3,141,458	$3,004,818	$10,774,172

You can rearrange data items in your pivot table manually by simply typing the exact name of the data item where you would like to see its data. You can also drag the data item where you want it.

To solve the problem in this example, you simply type **West** in cell B4 and then press Enter. The pivot table responds by resequencing the regions. The $3 million in sales for the West region automatically moves from column E to column B. The remaining regions move over to the next three columns.

Tip 4: Turn Pivot Tables into Hard Data

Say that you created a pivot table in order to summarize and shape data. You do not want to keep the source data, nor do you want to keep the pivot table with all its overhead.

Turning a pivot table into hard data enables you to utilize the results of the pivot table without having to deal with the source data or a pivot cache. How you turn the pivot table into hard data depends on how much of the pivot table you are going to copy.

If you are copying just a portion of a pivot table, do the following:

1. Select the data you want to copy from the pivot table, right-click, and select Copy.
2. Right-click anywhere on a spreadsheet and select Paste.

If you are copying an entire pivot table, follow these steps:

1. Select the entire pivot table, right-click, and select Copy. Alternatively, you can choose the Analyze tab, click Select, and then click Entire PivotTable.
2. Right-click anywhere on a spreadsheet and select Paste Special.
3. Select Values and then click OK.

14

TIP

> You might want to consider removing any subtotals before turning a pivot table into hard data. Subtotals typically aren't very useful when you are creating a stand-alone data set.
>
> To remove the subtotals from a pivot table, first identify the field for which subtotals are being calculated. Then right-click the field's header (either in the pivot table itself or in the PivotTable Fields list), and select Field Settings. Selecting this option opens the Field Settings dialog. Here, you change the Subtotals option to None. After you click OK, your subtotals are removed.

Tip 5: Fill the Empty Cells Left by Row Fields

When you turn a pivot table into hard data, you are left not only with the values created by the pivot table but also the pivot table's data structure. For example, the data in Figure 14.2 came from a pivot table that had a tabular layout.

Figure 14.2

It would be impractical to use this data anywhere else without filling in the empty cells left by the row field.

	A	B	C	D
3	Region	Market	Product_Description	Sum of Sales_Amount
4	⊟MIDWEST	⊟DENVER	Cleaning & Housekeeping Services	$12,564
5			Facility Maintenance and Repair	$160,324
6			Fleet Maintenance	$170,190
7			Green Plants and Foliage Care	$42,409
8			Landscaping/Grounds Care	$73,622
9			Predictive Maintenance/Preventative Maintenance	$186,475
10		DENVER Total		$645,583
11		⊟KANSASCITY	Cleaning & Housekeeping Services	$65,439
12			Facility Maintenance and Repair	$132,120
13			Fleet Maintenance	$133,170
14			Green Plants and Foliage Care	$35,315
15			Landscaping/Grounds Care	$52,442
16			Predictive Maintenance/Preventative Maintenance	$156,412
17		KANSASCITY Total		$574,899
18		⊟TULSA	Cleaning & Housekeeping Services	$96,515
19			Facility Maintenance and Repair	$170,632
20			Fleet Maintenance	$145,440
21			Green Plants and Foliage Care	$15,838
22			Landscaping/Grounds Care	$63,939
23			Predictive Maintenance/Preventative Maintenance	$136,041
24		TULSA Total		$628,405
25	MIDWEST Total			$1,848,887

Notice that the Market field kept the same row structure it had when this data was in the row area of the pivot table. It would be unwise to use this table anywhere else without filling in the empty cells left by the row field, but how do you easily fill these empty cells?

The next sections discuss two options provided by Excel 2016 to fix this problem effectively.

Option 1: Implement the Repeat All Data Items Feature

The first option for easily filling the empty cells left by row fields is to apply the Repeat Item Labels functionality. This feature ensures that all item labels are repeated to create a solid block of contiguous cells. To implement this feature, place your cursor anywhere in your pivot table. Then go to the ribbon and select Design, Report Layout, Repeat All Item Labels (see Figure 14.3).

Figure 14.3
The Repeat All Item Labels option enables you to show your pivot data in one contiguous block of data.

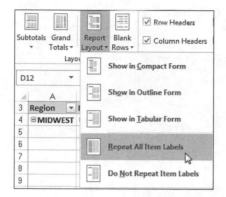

Figure 14.4 shows what a pivot table with this feature applied looks like.

Now you can turn this pivot table into hard values, and you will end up with a contiguous table of data without gaps.

Figure 14.4
The Repeat All Item Labels option fills all cells with data items.

Region	Market	Product_Description	Sum of Sales_Amount
⊟MIDWEST	⊟DENVER	Cleaning & Housekeeping Services	$12,564
MIDWEST	DENVER	Facility Maintenance and Repair	$160,324
MIDWEST	DENVER	Fleet Maintenance	$170,190
MIDWEST	DENVER	Green Plants and Foliage Care	$42,409
MIDWEST	DENVER	Landscaping/Grounds Care	$73,622
MIDWEST	DENVER	Predictive Maintenance/Preventative Maintenance	$186,475
MIDWEST	DENVER Total		$645,583
MIDWEST	⊟KANSASCITY	Cleaning & Housekeeping Services	$65,439
MIDWEST	KANSASCITY	Facility Maintenance and Repair	$132,120
MIDWEST	KANSASCITY	Fleet Maintenance	$133,170
MIDWEST	KANSASCITY	Green Plants and Foliage Care	$35,315
MIDWEST	KANSASCITY	Landscaping/Grounds Care	$52,442
MIDWEST	KANSASCITY	Predictive Maintenance/Preventative Maintenance	$156,412
MIDWEST	KANSASCITY Total		$574,899
MIDWEST	⊟TULSA	Cleaning & Housekeeping Services	$96,515
MIDWEST	TULSA	Facility Maintenance and Repair	$170,632
MIDWEST	TULSA	Fleet Maintenance	$145,440
MIDWEST	TULSA	Green Plants and Foliage Care	$15,838
MIDWEST	TULSA	Landscaping/Grounds Care	$63,939
MIDWEST	TULSA	Predictive Maintenance/Preventative Maintenance	$136,041
MIDWEST	TULSA Total		$628,405
MIDWEST Total			$1,848,887

Option 2: Use Excel's Go To Special Functionality

The other way to easily fill the empty cells left by row fields involves using Excel's Go To Special functionality.

You start by converting your pivot table into hard data as explained in Tip 4. Next, select the range in columns A and B that extends from the first row with blanks to the row just above the grand total. In the present example, this is A4:B100. Press the F5 key to activate the Go To dialog. In the lower-left corner of the Go To dialog, choose the Special button. This activates the Go To Special dialog, which is a powerful feature that enables you to modify your selection based on various conditions (see Figure 14.5). In this dialog, choose the Blanks option and click OK. Now only the blank cells in the selection are selected.

14

Figure 14.5
Using the Go To Special dialog enables you to select all the blank cells to be filled.

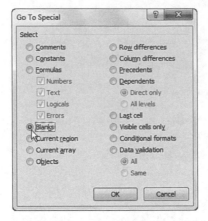

Enter a formula to copy the pivot item values from the cell above to the blank cells. You can do this with four keystrokes: Type an equal sign, press the up arrow key, and hold down the Ctrl key while pressing Enter. The equal sign tells Excel that you are entering a formula in the active cell. Pressing the up arrow key points to the cell above the active cell. Pressing Ctrl+Enter tells Excel to enter a similar formula in all the selected cells instead of just the active cell. As Figure 14.6 shows, with these few keystrokes, you enter a formula to fill in all the blank cells at once.

Figure 14.6
Pressing Ctrl+Enter enters the formula in all selected cells.

	A	B	C	D
3	Region	Market	Product_Description	Sum of Sales_Amount
4	MIDWEST	DENVER	Cleaning & Housekeeping Services	$12,564
5	MIDWEST	DENVER	Facility Maintenance and Repair	$160,324
6	MIDWEST	DENVER	Fleet Maintenance	$170,190
7	MIDWEST	DENVER	Green Plants and Foliage Care	$42,409
8	MIDWEST	DENVER	Landscaping/Grounds Care	$73,622
9	MIDWEST	DENVER	Predictive Maintenance/Preventative Maintenance	$186,475
10	MIDWEST	DENVER Total		$645,583
11	MIDWEST	KANSASCITY	Cleaning & Housekeeping Services	$65,439
12	MIDWEST	KANSASCITY	Facility Maintenance and Repair	$132,120
13	MIDWEST	KANSASCITY	Fleet Maintenance	$133,170
14	MIDWEST	KANSASCITY	Green Plants and Foliage Care	$35,315
15	MIDWEST	KANSASCITY	Landscaping/Grounds Care	$52,442
16	MIDWEST	KANSASCITY	Predictive Maintenance/Preventative Maintenance	$156,412
17	MIDWEST	KANSASCITY Total		$574,899
18	MIDWEST	TULSA	Cleaning & Housekeeping Services	$96,515
19	MIDWEST	TULSA	Facility Maintenance and Repair	$170,632
20	MIDWEST	TULSA	Fleet Maintenance	$145,440
21	MIDWEST	TULSA	Green Plants and Foliage Care	$15,838
22	MIDWEST	TULSA	Landscaping/Grounds Care	$63,939
23	MIDWEST	TULSA	Predictive Maintenance/Preventative Maintenance	$136,041
24	MIDWEST	TULSA Total		$628,405

At this point, there is no need to the formulas. You can will want to convert those formulas to values. Reselect the original range A4:B100. You can then press Ctrl+C to copy and choose Edit, Paste Special, Values to convert the formulas to values. This method provides a quick way to easily fill in the Outline view provided by the pivot table.

14

Tip 6: Add a Rank Number Field to a Pivot Table

When you are sorting and ranking a field with a large number of data items, it can be difficult to determine the number ranking of the data item you are currently analyzing. Furthermore, you might want to turn your pivot table into hard values for further analysis. An integer field that contains the actual rank number of each data item could be helpful in analysis outside the pivot table.

Start with a pivot table like the one shown in Figure 14.7. Notice in Figure 14.7 that the same data measure, Sum of Sales_Amount, is shown twice.

Figure 14.7
Start with a pivot table where the data value is listed twice.

	A	B	C
1			
2			
3	**Market** ▾	**Sum of Sales_Amount**	**Sum of Sales_Amount2**
4	BUFFALO	450478.27	450478.27
5	CALIFORNIA	2254735.38	2254735.38
6	CANADA	776245.27	776245.27
7	CHARLOTTE	890522.49	890522.49
8	DALLAS	467089.47	467089.47
9	DENVER	645583.29	645583.29
10	FLORIDA	1450392	1450392
11	KANSASCITY	574898.97	574898.97
12	MICHIGAN	678704.95	678704.95
13	NEWORLEANS	333453.65	333453.65
14	NEWYORK	873580.91	873580.91
15	PHOENIX	570255.09	570255.09
16	SEATTLE	179827.21	179827.21
17	TULSA	628404.83	628404.83
18	**Grand Total**	**10774171.78**	**10774171.78**

Right-click the second instance of the data measure, select Show Values As, and then select Rank Largest to Smallest (see Figure 14.8).

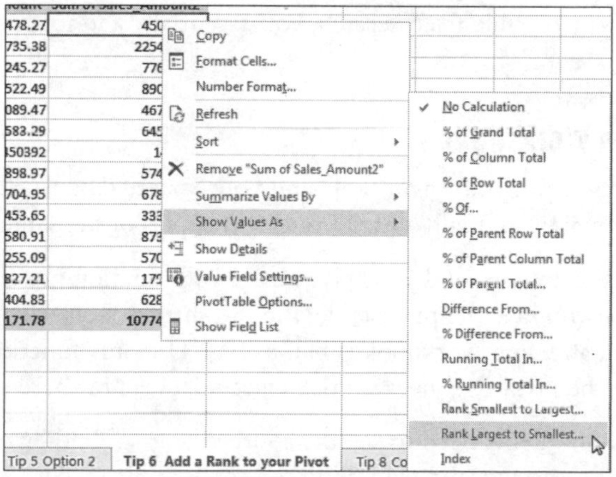

Figure 14.8
Adding a Rank field is simple with the Show Values As option.

14

When your ranking is applied, you can adjust the labels and formatting so it looks as shown in Figure 14.9. This gives you a clean-looking ranking report.

Figure 14.9
Your final pivot table, with ranking applied.

	A	B	C
1			
2			
3	Market ▼	Sum of Sales_Amount	Rank
4	BUFFALO	$450,478	12
5	CALIFORNIA	$2,254,735	1
6	CANADA	$776,245	5
7	CHARLOTTE	$890,522	3
8	DALLAS	$467,089	11
9	DENVER	$645,583	7
10	FLORIDA	$1,450,392	2
11	KANSASCITY	$574,899	9
12	MICHIGAN	$678,705	6
13	NEWORLEANS	$333,454	13
14	NEWYORK	$873,581	4
15	PHOENIX	$570,255	10
16	SEATTLE	$179,827	14
17	TULSA	$628,405	8
18	Grand Total	$10,774,172	

Tip 7: Reduce the Size of Pivot Table Reports

When you initiate the creation of a pivot table report, Excel takes a snapshot of your data set and stores it in a *pivot cache*, which is a special memory subsystem in which your data source is duplicated for quick access. That is to say, Excel literally makes a copy of your data and then stores it in a cache that is attached to your workbook.

Of course, the benefit you get from a pivot cache is optimization. Any changes you make to the pivot table report, such as rearranging fields, adding new fields, and hiding items, are made rapidly and with minimal overhead.

The downside of the pivot cache is that it basically doubles the size of a workbook. So every time you make a new pivot table from scratch, you essentially add to the file size of your workbook.

Delete the Source Data Worksheet

If your workbooks have both your pivot table and your source data worksheet, you are wasting space. That is, you are essentially distributing two copies of the same data.

You can delete your source data, and your pivot table will function just fine. After you delete the source data, when you save the pivot table, the file shrinks. Your clients can use the pivot table as normal, and your workbook is half as big. The only functionality you lose is the ability to refresh the pivot data because the source data is not there.

So what happens if your clients need to see the source data? Well, they can simply double-click the intersection of the row and column grand totals. This tells Excel to output the contents of the pivot table's cache into a new worksheet. So, with one double-click, your clients can re-create the source data that makes up the pivot table!

Tip 8: Create an Automatically Expanding Data Range

You will undoubtedly encounter situations in which you have pivot table reports that are updated daily (that is, records are constantly being added to the source data). When records are added to a pivot table's source data set, you must redefine the range that is captured before the new records are brought into the pivot table. Redefining the source range for a pivot table once in a while is no sweat, but when the source data is changed on a daily or weekly basis, it can start to get bothersome.

The solution is to turn your source data table into an Excel table before you create a pivot table. Again, Excel tables enable you to create a defined range that automatically shrinks or expands with the data. This means that any component, chart, pivot table, or formula tied to that range can keep up with changes in your data.

To implement this trick, simply highlight your source data and then click the Table icon on the Insert tab (see Figure 14.10). Confirm the range to be included in your table and then click OK.

After your source data has been converted to an Excel table, any pivot table you build on top of it automatically includes all records when your source data expands or shrinks.

Figure 14.10
Convert your source data into an Excel table.

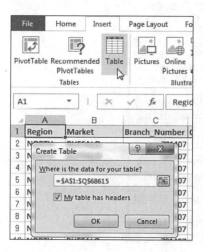

> **TIP**
> Keep in mind that although you won't have to redefine the source range anymore, you will still need to trigger a Refresh in order to have your pivot table show the current data.

Tip 9: Compare Tables Using a Pivot Table

If you've been an analyst for more than a week, you've been asked to compare two separate tables to come up with some brilliant analysis about the differences between them. This is a common scenario where leveraging a pivot table can save you some time.

Say that you have two tables that show customers in 2011 and in 2012. Figure 14.11 shows that these are two separate tables. For this example, the tables were made small for instructional purposes, but imagine that you're working with something bigger here.

Figure 14.11
You need to compare these two tables.

	A	B	C	D	E	F	G
1	2011 Customers				2012 Customers		
2	Customer_Name	Fiscal Year	Revenue		Customer_Name	Fiscal Year	Revenue
3	PHALCO Corp.	2011	$456.27		PHALSM Corp.	2012	$1,902.25
4	PHALLA Corp.	2011	$3,974.07		PHALTA Corp.	2012	$2,095.01
5	PHALSE Corp.	2011	$565.34		PHALWH Corp.	2012	$1,740.27
6	PHALSM Corp.	2011	$1,902.25		PHMAN Corp.	2012	$3,228.33
7	POMTRA Corp.	2011	$2,201.90		POPPIT Corp.	2012	$604.18
8	POPAUS Corp.	2011	$1,891.73		POPUSL Corp.	2012	$870.28
9	POPCOA Corp.	2011	$1,284.61		POPUSP Corp.	2012	$2,421.01
10	PORADA Corp.	2011	$10,131.22		PORADA Corp.	2012	$10,131.22
11	PORCFA Corp.	2011	$1,187.71		PORADY Corp.	2012	$1,012.94
12					PORCFA Corp.	2012	$1,187.71

The idea is to create one table you can use to pivot. Be sure you have a way to tag which data comes from which table. In Figure 14.12, a column called Fiscal Year serves this purpose.

Figure 14.12
Combine your tables into one table.

	Customer_Name	Fiscal Year	Revenue
2	Customer_Name	Fiscal Year	Revenue
3	PHALCO Corp.	2011	$456.27
4	PHALLA Corp.	2011	$3,974.07
5	PHALSE Corp.	2011	$565.34
6	PHALSM Corp.	2011	$1,902.25
7	POMTRA Corp.	2011	$2,201.90
8	POPAUS Corp.	2011	$1,891.73
9	POPCOA Corp.	2011	$1,284.61
10	PORADA Corp.	2011	$10,131.22
11	PORCFA Corp.	2011	$1,187.71
12	PHALSM Corp.	2012	$1,902.25
13	PHALTA Corp.	2012	$2,095.01
14	PHALWH Corp.	2012	$1,740.27
15	PHMAN Corp.	2012	$3,228.33
16	POPPIT Corp.	2012	$604.18
17	POPUSL Corp.	2012	$870.28
18	POPUSP Corp.	2012	$2,421.01
19	PORADA Corp.	2012	$10,131.22
20	PORADY Corp.	2012	$1,012.94
21	PORCFA Corp.	2012	$1,187.71

After you have combined the tables, use the combined data set to create a new pivot table. Format the pivot table so that the table tag (the identifier that tells which table the data came from) is in the column area of the pivot table. In Figure 14.13, years are in the column area and customers are in the row area. The data area contains the count records for each customer name.

As you can see in Figure 14.13, you instantly get a visual indication of which customers are only in the 2011 table, which are in the 2012 table, and which are in both tables.

Figure 14.13
Create a pivot table to get an easy-to-read visual comparison of the two data sets.

	A	B	C	D
1				
2	Count of Customer_Name	Fiscal Year ▼		
3	Customer_Name ▼	2011	2012	Grand Total
4	PHALCO Corp.	1		1
5	PHALLA Corp.	1		1
6	PHALSE Corp.	1		1
7	PHALSM Corp.	1	1	2
8	PHALTA Corp.		1	1
9	PHALWH Corp.		1	1
10	PHMAN Corp.		1	1
11	POMTRA Corp.	1		1
12	POPAUS Corp.	1		1
13	POPCOA Corp.	1		1
14	POPPIT Corp.		1	1
15	POPUSL Corp.		1	1
16	POPUSP Corp.		1	1
17	PORADA Corp.	1	1	2
18	PORADY Corp.		1	1
19	PORCFA Corp.	1	1	2
20	Grand Total	9	10	19

Tip 10: AutoFilter a Pivot Table

The conventional wisdom is that you can't apply an AutoFilter to a pivot table. Technically, that's true. But there is a way to trick Excel into making it happen.

The trick is to place your cursor directly adjacent to the last title in the pivot table, as shown in Figure 14.14. Once you have it there, you can go to the application menu, select Data, and then select AutoFilter.

Figure 14.14
Place your cursor just outside your pivot table.

	A	B	C	D
1	Market	(All) ▼		
2				
3	Customer_Name ▼	Revenue	Transaction Count	
4	ACASCO Corp.	$675	4	
5	ACECUL Corp.	$593	6	
6	ACEHUA Corp.	$580	4	
7	ACOPUL Corp.	$675	4	
8	ACORAR Corp.	$2,232	13	
9	ACSPUP Corp.	$730	4	

At this point, you have AutoFilter on your pivot table! You can now do cool things like apply a custom AutoFilter to find all customers with above-average transaction counts (see Figure 14.15).

This is a fantastic way to add an extra layer of analytical capabilities to pivot table reports.

14

Figure 14.15
With AutoFilter implemented, you can take advantage of custom filtering that's not normally available with pivot tables.

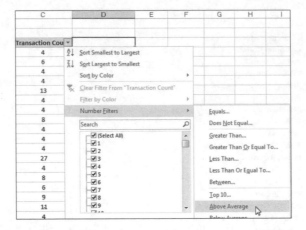

Tip 11: Force Two Number Formats in a Pivot Table

Every now and then, you have to deal with a situation where a normalized data set makes it difficult to build an appropriate pivot table. For example, the data set shown in Figure 14.16 contains metrics information for each market. Notice that there is a column that identifies the measure, and there is a column that specifies the corresponding value.

Figure 14.16
This metric table has many different data types in one Values field.

	A	B	C	D	E
1	Region	Market	Product_Description	Measure	Value
2	MIDWEST	DENVER	Cleaning & Housekeeping Services	Revenue	12563.91
3	MIDWEST	DENVER	Cleaning & Housekeeping Services	Conversion Rate	0.62
4	MIDWEST	DENVER	Facility Maintenance and Repair	Revenue	160324.22
5	MIDWEST	DENVER	Facility Maintenance and Repair	Conversion Rate	0.64
6	MIDWEST	DENVER	Fleet Maintenance	Revenue	170190.26
7	MIDWEST	DENVER	Fleet Maintenance	Conversion Rate	0.20
8	MIDWEST	DENVER	Green Plants and Foliage Care	Revenue	42408.61
9	MIDWEST	DENVER	Green Plants and Foliage Care	Conversion Rate	0.88
10	MIDWEST	DENVER	Landscaping/Grounds Care	Revenue	73621.62
11	MIDWEST	DENVER	Landscaping/Grounds Care	Conversion Rate	0.92
12	MIDWEST	DENVER	Predictive Maintenance/Preventative	Revenue	186474.67
13	MIDWEST	DENVER	Predictive Maintenance/Preventative	Conversion Rate	0.93
14	MIDWEST	KANSASCITY	Cleaning & Housekeeping Services	Revenue	65439.14
15	MIDWEST	KANSASCITY	Cleaning & Housekeeping Services	Conversion Rate	0.61

Although this is generally a nicely formatted table, notice that some of the measures are meant to be Number format, whereas others are meant to be Percentage. In the database where this data set originated, the Values field is a Double data type, so this works.

The problem is that when you create a pivot table out of this data set, you can't assign two different number formats for the Values field. After all, the rule is one field, one number format.

So as you can see in Figure 14.17, trying to set the number format for the percentage measures also changes the format for the measures that are supposed to be straight numbers.

Figure 14.17
You can have only one
number format assigned
to each data measure.

	A	B	C
1	Market	BUFFALO ▼	
2			
3	Sum of Value	Measure ▼	
4	Product_Description ▼	Conversion Rate	Revenue
5	Cleaning & Housekeeping Services	27.08%	6684485.00%
6	Facility Maintenance and Repair	99.53%	6956962.00%
7	Fleet Maintenance	75.26%	8646011.00%
8	Green Plants and Foliage Care	0.36%	3483113.00%
9	Landscaping/Grounds Care	5.38%	6546546.00%
10	Predictive Maintenance/Preventative Maintenanc	31.58%	12730710.00%

The solution is to apply a custom number format that formats any value greater than 1.5 as a number and any value less than 1.5 as a percentage. In the Format Cells dialog, click Custom and then enter the following syntax in the Type input box (see Figure 14.18):

```
[>=1.5]$#,##0;[<1.5]0.0%
```

Figure 14.18
Apply a custom number
format, telling Excel to
format any number less
than 1.5 as a percentage.

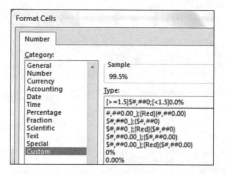

The result, shown in Figure 14.19, is that each measure is now formatted appropriately. Obviously, you have to get a little lucky with the parameters of the situation you're working in. Although this technique doesn't work in all scenarios, it does open up some interesting options.

Figure 14.19
Two formats in one Data
field. Amazing!

	A	B	C
1	Market	BUFFALO ▼	
2			
3	Sum of Value	Measure ▼	
4	Product_Description ▼	Conversion Rate	Revenue
5	Cleaning & Housekeeping Services	27.1%	$66,845
6	Facility Maintenance and Repair	99.5%	$69,570
7	Fleet Maintenance	75.3%	$86,460
8	Green Plants and Foliage Care	0.4%	$34,831
9	Landscaping/Grounds Care	5.4%	$65,465
10	Predictive Maintenance/Preventative Maintenance	31.6%	$127,307

14

Tip 12: Create a Frequency Distribution with a Pivot Table

If you've created a frequency distribution with the FREQUENCY function, you know it can quickly devolve into a confusing mess. The fact that it's an array formula doesn't help matters. Then there's the Histogram functionality you find in the Analysis ToolPak, which doesn't make life much better. Each time you have to change your bin ranges, you have to restart the entire process again.

In this tip, you'll learn how to use a pivot table to quickly implement a simple frequency distribution.

First, you need to create a pivot table where the data values are plotted in the Rows area (not the Values area). Notice that in Figure 14.20, the Sales_Amount field is placed in the Rows area.

Figure 14.20
Place your data measure in the Rows area.

Next, right-click any value in the Rows area and select Group. In the Grouping dialog (shown in Figure 14.21), set the start and end values and then set the intervals. This essentially creates the frequency distribution.

Figure 14.21
Use the Grouping dialog to create your frequency intervals.

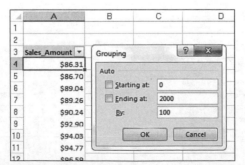

After you click the OK button, you can leverage the result to create a distribution view of your data.

In Figure 14.22, you can see that Customer_Name has been added to get a frequency distribution of the number of customer transactions by dollar amount.

The obvious benefit of this technique is you can use the pivot table's Report Filter to interactively filter the data based on other dimensions, such as Region and Market. Also, unlike with the Analysis ToolPak Histogram tool, you can quickly adjust your frequency intervals by simply right-clicking any number in the Rows area and selecting Group.

Figure 14.22
The frequency distribution of customer transactions by dollar amount.

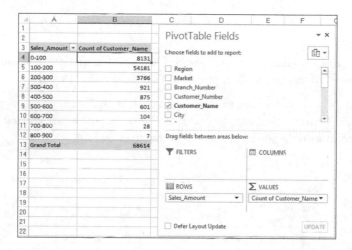

Tip 13: Use a Pivot Table to Explode a Data Set to Different Tabs

One of the most common requests an analyst gets is to create a separate pivot table report for each region, market, manager, or whatever. These types of requests usually lead to a painful manual process in which you copy a pivot table onto a new worksheet and then change the filter field to the appropriate region or manager. You then repeat this process as many times as you need to get through each selection.

Creating separate pivot table reports is one area where Excel really comes to the rescue. Excel has a function called Show Report Filter Pages that automatically creates a separate pivot table for each item in the filter fields. To use this function, simply create a pivot table with a filter field, as shown in Figure 14.23.

Figure 14.23
Start with a pivot table that contains a filter field.

	A	B	C	D
1	Market	(All) ▼		
2				
3	Sum of Sales_Amount	Sales_Period ▼		
4	Product_Description ▼	P01	P02	P03
5	Cleaning & Housekeeping Services	$80,083	$89,750	$78,182
6	Facility Maintenance and Repair	$121,304	$305,832	$115,232
7	Fleet Maintenance	$148,565	$297,315	$145,821
8	Green Plants and Foliage Care	$75,716	$135,529	$72,293
9	Landscaping/Grounds Care	$92,353	$99,173	$87,138
10	Predictive Maintenance/Preventative	$163,844	$189,317	$158,946
11	Grand Total	$681,865	$1,116,916	$657,611

14

Place your cursor anywhere on the pivot table and then go up to the ribbon to select the Analyze tab. On the Analyze tab, go to the PivotTable group and click the Options drop-down and then select Show Report Filter Pages, as shown in Figure 14.24.

Figure 14.24
Click the Show Report Filter Pages button.

A dialog opens, enabling you to choose the filter field for which you would like to create separate pivot tables. Select the appropriate filter field and click OK.

Your reward is a sheet for each item in the filter field, with each one containing its own pivot table. Figure 14.25 illustrates the result. Note that the newly created tabs are named to correspond with the filter item shown in the pivot table.

Figure 14.25
With just a few clicks, you can have a separate pivot table for each market!

NOTE

Be aware that you can use Show Report Filter Pages on only one filter field at a time.

Tip 14: Apply Restrictions on Pivot Tables and Pivot Fields

14

I often send pivot tables to clients, co-workers, managers, and other groups of people. In some cases, I'd like to restrict the types of actions users can take on the pivot table reports I send them. The macros outlined in this section demonstrate some of the protection settings available via VBA.

Pivot Table Restrictions

The PivotTable object exposes several properties that allow you as a developer to restrict different features and components of a pivot table:

- **EnableWizard**—Setting this property to False disables the PivotTable Tools context menu that normally activates when you click inside a pivot table.

- **EnableDrilldown**—Setting this property to False prevents users from getting to detailed data by double-clicking a data field.

- **EnableFieldList**—Setting this property to False prevents users from activating the field list or moving pivot fields around.

- **EnableFieldDialog**—Setting this property to False disables the users' ability to alter the pivot field via the Value Field Settings dialog box.

- **PivotCache.EnableRefresh**—Setting this property to False disables the ability to refresh the pivot table.

You can independently set any or all of these properties to either True or False. The following macro applies all the restrictions to the target pivot table:

```
Sub ApplyPivotTableRestrictions ()

'Step 1: Declare your Variables
    Dim pt As PivotTable

'Step 2: Point to the PivotTable in the activecell
    On Error Resume Next
    Set pt = ActiveSheet.PivotTables(ActiveCell.PivotTable.Name)

'Step 3:  Exit if active cell is not in a PivotTable
    If pt Is Nothing Then
    MsgBox "You must place your cursor inside of a PivotTable."
    Exit Sub
    End If

'Step 4:  Apply Pivot Table Restrictions
    With pt
        .EnableWizard = False
        .EnableDrilldown = False
        .EnableFieldList = False
        .EnableFieldDialog = False
        .PivotCache.EnableRefresh = False
    End With

End Sub
```

In this macro, step 1 declares the pt pivot table object variable that serves as the memory container for the pivot table.

Step 2 sets the pt variable to the name of the pivot table on which the active cell is found. It does this by using the ActiveCell.PivotTable.Name property to get the name of the target pivot table.

14

Step 3 checks to see whether the pt variable is filled with a pivot table object. If the pt variable is set to Nothing, the active cell was not on a pivot table, and thus no pivot table could be assigned to the variable. If this is the case, the macro says this to the user in a message box, and then it exits the procedure.

Step 4 applies the pivot table restrictions.

Once your chosen features have been restricted, Excel disables the menu commands for the features you turned off. You can see in Figure 14.26 that the Refresh, Pivot Table Options, and Show Field List commands are grayed out.

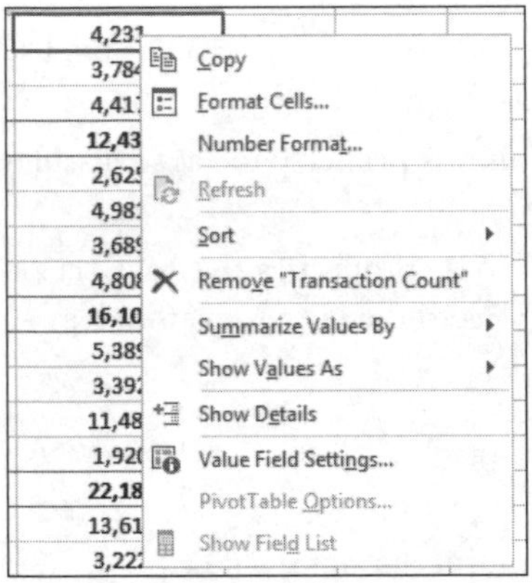

Figure 14.26
The commands for restricted features will be greyed out in all menus.

Pivot Field Restrictions

Like pivot table restrictions, pivot field restrictions enable you to restrict the types of actions users can take on the pivot fields in a pivot table. The macro shown in this section demonstrates some of the protection settings available via VBA.

The PivotField object exposes several properties that allow you as a developer to restrict different features and components of a pivot table:

- **DragToPage**—Setting this property to False prevents users from dragging any pivot field into the report filter area of the pivot table.

- **DragToRow**—Setting this property to False prevents users from dragging any pivot field into the row area of the pivot table.

- **DragToColumn**—Setting this property to False prevents users from dragging any pivot field into the column area of the pivot table.

- **DragToData**—Setting this property to False prevents users from dragging any pivot field into the data area of the pivot table.

- **DragToHide**—Setting this property to False prevents users from dragging pivot fields off the pivot table. It also prevents the use of the right-click menu to hide or remove pivot fields.

- **EnableItemSelection**—Setting this property to False disables the drop-down lists on each pivot field.

You can independently set any or all of these properties to either True or False. The following macro applies all the restrictions to the target pivot table:

```
Sub ApplyPivotFieldRestrictions()

'Step 1: Declare your Variables
    Dim pt As PivotTable
    Dim pf As PivotField

'Step 2: Point to the PivotTable in the activecell
    On Error Resume Next
    Set pt = ActiveSheet.PivotTables(ActiveCell.PivotTable.Name)

'Step 3:  Exit if active cell is not in a PivotTable
    If pt Is Nothing Then
    MsgBox "You must place your cursor inside of a PivotTable."
    Exit Sub
    End If

'Step 4:  Apply Pivot Field Restrictions
    For Each pf In pt.PivotFields
        pf.EnableItemSelection = False
        pf.DragToPage = False
        pf.DragToRow = False
        pf.DragToColumn = False
        pf.DragToData = False
        pf.DragToHide = False
    Next pf

End Sub
```

Step 1 declares two object variables, using pt as the memory container for the pivot table and pf as a memory container for the pivot fields. This allows looping through all the pivot fields in the pivot table.

Step 2 sets the pt variable to the name of the pivot table on which the active cell is found. It does this by using the ActiveCell.PivotTable.Name property to get the name of the target pivot.

Step 3 checks whether the pt variable is filled with a PivotTable object. If the pt variable is set to Nothing, the active cell was not on a pivot table, and thus no pivot table could be assigned to the variable. If this is the case, the macro notifies the user via a message box and then exits the procedure.

Step 4 of the macro uses a For Each statement to iterate through each pivot field and apply all the specified pivot field restrictions.

Once your chosen features have been restricted, Excel disables the menu commands for the features you set to FALSE.

Tip 15: Use a Pivot Table to Explode a Data Set to Different Workbooks

Imagine that you have a data set with 50,000+ rows of data. You have been asked to create a separate workbook for each market in this data set. In this tip, you'll discover how you can accomplish this task by using a pivot table and a little VBA.

Place the field you need to use as the group dimension (in this case, Market) into the filter field. Place the count of Market into the data field. Your pivot table should look like the one shown in Figure 14.27.

Figure 14.27
Create a simple pivot table with one data field and a filter.

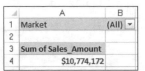

As you know, you can manually select a market in the page/filter field and then double-click Count of Market. This gives you a new tab containing all the records that make up the number you double-clicked. Imagine how you could do this for every market in the Market field and save the resulting tabs to their own workbook.

Using this same concept, you can implement the following VBA that goes through each item in the chosen page field and essentially calls the ShowDetail method for you, creating a raw data tab. The procedure then saves that raw data tab to a new workbook:

```
Sub ExplodeTable()
Dim PvtItem As PivotItem
Dim PvtTable As PivotTable

'Change variables to suit your scenario
        Const strFieldName = "Market"       '<-Change Field Name
        Const strTriggerRange = "B4"        '<-Change Trigger Range

'Set the pivot table name if needed
        Set PvtTable = ActiveSheet.PivotTables("PivotTable1") '<-Change Pivot-
Table Name if Needed

'Start looping through each item in the selected field
        For Each PvtItem In PvtTable.PivotFields(strFieldName).PivotItems
                PvtTable.PivotFields(strFieldName).CurrentPage = PvtItem.Name
                Range(strTriggerRange).ShowDetail = True

                'Name the temp sheet for easy cleanup later
                ActiveSheet.Name = "TempSheet"

                'copy data to new workbook and delete the temp sheet
                ActiveSheet.Cells.Copy
                Workbooks.Add
                ActiveSheet.Paste
                Cells.EntireColumn.AutoFit

                Application.DisplayAlerts = False
                ActiveWorkbook.SaveAs Filename:=ThisWorkbook.Path & "\" &
```

```
PvtItem.Name &".xls"
                ActiveWorkbook.Close
                Sheets("Tempsheet").Delete
                Application.DisplayAlerts = True

        Next PvtItem

    End Sub
```

To implement this technique, enter this code into a new VBA module. Be sure to change the following constants as appropriate for your scenario:

- `Const strFieldName`—This is the name of the field you want to separate the data by (that is, the field you put in the page/filter area of the pivot table).

- `Const strTriggerRange`—This is essentially the range that holds the one number in the pivot table's data area. For example, if you look at Figure 14.28, you see the trigger cell in A4.

As you can see in Figure 14.28, running this macro procedure outputs data for each market into its own separate workbook.

Figure 14.28
After running the macro, you will have a separate workbook for each filtered dimension.

Next Steps

In Chapter 15, "Dr. Jekyll and Mr. GetPivotData," you'll learn about one of the most hated pivot table features: the GetPivotData function. However, you'll also learn how to use this function to create refreshable reports month after month.

14

Dr. Jekyll
and Mr. GetPivotData

This chapter shows you a technique that solves many annoying pivot table problems. If you have been using pivot tables for a while, you might have run into the following problems:

- Formatting tends to be destroyed when you refresh a pivot table. Numeric formats are lost. Column widths go away.

- There is no easy way to build an asymmetric pivot table. Using named sets is one way, but they are available only in a pivot table model, not in a regular pivot cache pivot table.

- Excel cannot remember a template. If you frequently have to re-create a pivot table, you must redo the groupings, calculated fields, calculated items, and so on.

The technique shown in this chapter solves all these problems. It is not new. In fact, it has been around since Excel 2002. I have taught Power Excel seminars to thousands of accountants who use Excel 40–60 hours a week. Out of those thousands of people, I have had only three people say that they use this technique.

Ironically, far more than 0.3% of people know of this feature. One common question I get at seminars is "Why did this feature show up in Excel 2002, and how the heck can you turn it off?" This same feature, which is reviled by most Excellers, is the key to creating reusable pivot table templates.

The credit for this chapter must go to Rob Collie, who spent years on the Excel project management team. He spent the Excel 2010 development cycle working on the PowerPivot product. Rob happened to relocate to Cleveland, Ohio. Because Cleveland is not a hotbed of Microsoft developers, Dave Gainer gave me a heads-up that Rob was moving to my area, and we started having lunch.

Rob and I talked about Excel and had some great conversations. During our second lunch, Rob said something that threw me for a loop. He said, "We find that our internal customers use GetPivotData all the time to build their reports, and we are not sure they will like the way PowerPivot interacts with GetPivotData."

I stopped Rob to ask if he was crazy. I told him that in my experience with about 15,000 accountants, only 3 of them had ever admitted to liking GetPivotData. What did he mean that he finds customers actually using GetPivotData?

Rob explained the key word in his statement: He was talking about *internal* customers, which are the people inside Microsoft who use Excel to do their jobs. Those people had become incredibly reliant on GetPivotData. He agreed that outside Microsoft, hardly anyone ever uses GetPivotData. In fact, the only question he ever gets outside Microsoft is how to turn off the stupid feature.

I had to know more, so I asked Rob to explain how the evil GetPivotData could ever be used for good purposes. Rob explained it to me, and I use this chapter to explain it to you. However, I know that 99% of you are reading this chapter because of the following reasons:

■ You ran into the evil GetPivotData.

■ You turned to the index of this book to find information on GetPivotData.

■ You are expecting me to tell you how to turn off GetPivotData.

So, let's start there.

Avoiding the Evil GetPivotData Problem

GetPivotData has been the cause of many headaches since around the time of Excel 2002 when suddenly, without any fanfare, pivot table behavior changed slightly. Any time you build formulas outside a pivot table that point back inside the pivot table, you run into the evil GetPivotData problem.

For example, say you build the pivot table shown in Figure 15.1. Those years across the top are built by grouping daily dates into years. You would like to compare this year versus last year. Unfortunately, you are not allowed to add calculated items to a grouped field. So you follow these steps:

1. Add a **% Growth** heading in cell D4.
2. Copy the formatting from C4 over to D4.
3. In cell D5, type **=** (an equal sign).
4. Click cell C5.
5. Type **/** (a slash) for division.
6. Click B5.

Figure 15.1
You want to add a formula to show the percentage of growth year after year.

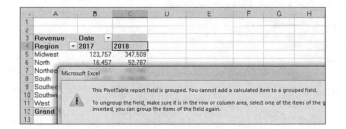

7. Type **-1** and press Ctrl+Enter to stay in the same cell. Format the result as a percentage. You see that the Midwest region grew by 180.8%. That is impressive growth (see Figure 15.2).

Figure 15.2
Build the formula in D5 using the mouse or the arrow keys.

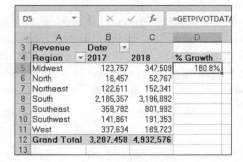

> **NOTE**
> If you started using spreadsheets back in the days of Lotus 1-2-3, you might like to use this alternative method to build the formula in D5: Type = (an equal sign) and press the left arrow once. Type / (for division). Press the left arrow twice. Press Enter. As you see, the evil GetPivotData problem strikes no matter which method you use.

8. After entering your first formula, select cell D5.

9. Double-click the tiny square dot in the lower-right corner of the cell. This is the fill handle, and it copies the formula down to the end of the report.

Immediately, you notice that something is wrong because every region managed to grow by exactly 180.8% (see Figure 15.3).

There is no way that this happens in real life. The data must be fabricated.

15

Figure 15.3
When the formula is copied down, somehow the growth is 180.8% for every region.

	A	B	C	D
3	Revenue	Date		
4	Region	2017	2018	% Growth
5	Midwest	123,757	347,509	180.8%
6	North	16,457	52,767	180.8%
7	Northeast	122,611	152,341	180.8%
8	South	2,185,357	3,196,892	180.8%
9	Southeast	359,782	801,992	180.8%
10	Southwest	141,861	191,353	180.8%
11	West	337,634	189,723	180.8%
12	Grand Total	3,287,458	4,932,576	180.8%
13				

Think about the formula you built: 2018 divided by 2017 minus 1. You probably could create that formula with your eyes closed (that is, if you use arrow keys to create formulas instead of your mouse).

This is what makes you not notice something completely evil when you built the formula. When you went through the steps to build the formula, as a rational person, you would expect Excel to create a formula such as =C5/B5-1. However, go back to cell D5 and press the F2 key to look at the formula (see Figure 15.4). Something evil has happened. The simple formula =C5/B5-1 is no longer there. Instead, Excel generated some GetPivotData nonsense. Although the formula works in D5, it does not work when you copy the formula down.

Figure 15.4
Where did GetPivotData come from?

	A	B	C	D	E	F	G	H	I
3	Revenue	Date							
4	Region	2017	2018	% Growth					
5	Midwest	123,757	347,509	=GETPIVOTDATA("Revenue",$A$3,"Region","Midwest","Date",2018)/					
6	North	16,457	52,767	GETPIVOTDATA("Revenue",$A$3,"Region","Midwest","Date",2017)-1					
7	Northeast	122,611	152,341	180.8%					
8	South	2,185,357	3,196,892	180.8%					
9	Southeast	359,782	801,992	180.8%					
10	Southwest	141,861	191,353	180.8%					
11	West	337,634	189,723	180.8%					
12	Grand Total	3,287,458	4,932,576	180.8%					
13									

When this occurs, your reaction is something like, "What is GetPivotData, and why is it messing up my report?" Your next reaction is, "How can I turn it off?" You might even wonder, "Why would Microsoft put this evil thing in there?"

Excel started inserting GetPivotData in Excel 2002. After being stung by GetPivotData repeatedly, I grew to hate it. I was thrown for a loop in one of the Power Analyst Boot Camps when someone asked me how it could possibly be used. I had never considered that question. In my mind, and in most other people's minds, GetPivotData was evil and no good.

If you are one of those users who would just like to avoid GetPivotData, I've got great news: There are two ways to do so, as presented in the following two sections.

Preventing GetPivotData by Typing the Formula

The simple method for avoiding GetPivotData is to create your formula without touching the mouse or the arrow keys. To do this, follow these steps:

1. Go to cell D5; type =.
2. Type **C5**.
3. Type /.
4. Type **B5**.
5. Type -**1**.
6. Press Enter.

You have now built a regular Excel formula that you can copy to produce real results, as shown in Figure 15.5.

Figure 15.5
Type =C5/B5-1, and the formula works as expected.

	A	B	C	D
3	Revenue	Date ▾		
4	Region ▾	2017	2018	% Growth
5	Midwest	123,757	347,509	180.8%
6	North	16,457	52,767	220.6%
7	Northeast	122,611	152,341	24.2%
8	South	2,185,357	3,196,892	46.3%
9	Southeast	359,782	801,992	122.9%
10	Southwest	141,861	191,353	34.9%
11	West	337,634	189,723	-43.8%
12	Grand Total	3,287,458	4,932,576	50.0%
13				

It is a relief to see that you can still build formulas outside pivot tables that point into a pivot table. I have run into people who simply thought this could not be done.

You might be a bit annoyed that you have to abandon your normal way of entering formulas. If so, the next section offers an alternative.

Simply Turning Off GetPivotData

If you do not plan to read the second half of this chapter, you can simply turn off GetPivotData forever. Who needs it? It is evil, so just turn it off.

In Excel 2016, follow these steps:

1. Move the cell pointer back inside a pivot table so that the PivotTable Tools tabs appear.
2. Click the Analyze tab.
3. Notice the Options icon on the left side of the ribbon (see Figure 15.6). Do not click the icon; rather, next to the options icon, click the drop-down arrow.

15

Figure 15.6
Don't click the large Options icon. Click the tiny drop-down arrow next to the icon.

4. Inside the Options drop-down is the choice Generate GetPivotData (see Figure 15.7). By default, this option is selected. Click that item to clear this check box.

Figure 15.7
Select Generate GetPivotData to turn off the feature.

The previous steps assume that you have a pivot table in the workbook that you can select in order to access the PivotTable Tool tabs. If you don't have a pivot table in the current workbook, you can use File, Options. In the Formulas category, uncheck Use GetPivotData Functions for PivotTable References.

Speculating on Why Microsoft Forced GetPivotData on Us

If GetPivotData is so evil, why did the fine people at Microsoft turn on the feature by default? Everyone simply wants to turn it off. Why would they bother to leave it on? Are they trying to make sure that there is a market for my Power Excel seminars?

I have a theory about this that I came up with during the Excel 2007 launch. I had written many books about Excel 2007—somewhere around 1,800 pages of content. When the Office 2007 launch events were happening around the country, I was given an opportunity to work at the event. I watched with interest when the presenter talked about the new features in Excel 2007.

There were at least 15 amazing features in Excel 2007. The presenter took three minutes and glossed over perhaps 2.5 of the features.

I was perplexed. How could Microsoft marketing do such a horrible job of showing what was new in Excel? Then I realized that this must always happen. Marketing asks the development team what is new. The project manager gives them a list of 15 items. The marketing guy says something like, "There is not room for 15 items in the presentation. Can you cut 80% of those items out of the list and give me just the ones with glitz and sizzle?"

The folks who worked on GetPivotData certainly knew that GetPivotData would never have enough sizzle to make it into the marketing news about Excel 2002. So, by making it the default, they hoped someone would notice GetPivotData and try to figure out how it could be used. Instead, most people, including me, just turned it off and thought it was another step in the Microsoft plot to make our lives miserable by making it harder to work in Excel.

Using GetPivotData to Solve Pivot Table Annoyances

You would not be reading this book if you hadn't realized that pivot tables are the greatest invention ever. Four clicks can create a pivot table that obsoletes the arcane process of using Advanced Filter, =DSUM, and data tables. Pivot tables enable you to produce one-page summaries of massive data sets. So what if the formatting is ugly? And so what if you usually end up converting most pivot tables to values so you can delete the columns you do not need but cannot turn off?

Figure 15.8 illustrates a typical pivot table experience: You start with raw data. You then produce a pivot table and use all sorts of advanced pivot table tricks to get it close. You conclude by converting the pivot table to values and performing the final formatting in regular Excel.

Figure 15.8
Typical pivot table process.

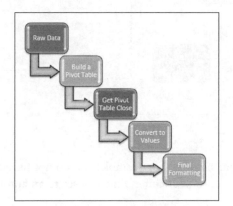

> **NOTE**
> I rarely get to refresh a pivot table because I never let pivot tables live long enough to have new data. The next time I get data, I start creating the pivot table all over again. If it is a long process, I write a macro that lets me fly through the five steps in Figure 15.8 in a couple of keystrokes.

The new method introduced by Rob Collie and described in the rest of this chapter puts a different spin on the pivot table experience. In this new method, which people inside Microsoft tend to use, you build an ugly pivot table. You do not care about the formatting of this pivot table. You then go through a one-time, relatively painful process of building a nicely formatted shell to hold your final report. Finally, you use GetPivotData to populate the shell report quickly.

From then on when you get new data, you simply put it on the data sheet, refresh the ugly pivot table, and print the shell report. Figure 15.9 illustrates this process.

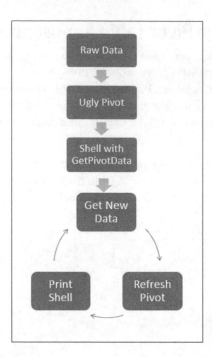

Figure 15.9
How people who work at Microsoft use pivot tables.

There are huge advantages to this method. For example, you do not have to worry about formatting the report after the first time. It comes much closer to an automated process.

The rest of this chapter walks you through the steps to build a dynamic report that shows actuals for months that have been completed and a forecast for future months.

Building an Ugly Pivot Table

Say that you have transactional data showing budget and actuals for each region of a company. The budget data is at a monthly level. The actuals data is at a daily level. Budget data exists for the entire year. Actuals exist only for the months that have been completed. Figure 15.10 shows the original data set.

Because you will be updating this report every month, it makes the process easier if you have a pivot table data source that grows as you add new data to the bottom. Whereas legacy versions of Excel would achieve this through a named dynamic range using the OFFSET function, you can do this in Excel 2016 by selecting one cell in your data and pressing Ctrl+T. Click OK to confirm that your data has headers.

You now have a formatted data set, as shown in Figure 15.10.

Figure 15.10
The original data includes budget and actuals.

	A	B	C	D
1	Region ▼	Date ▼	Measure ▼	Revenue ▼
2	Midwest	1/1/2018	Budget	248000
3	North	1/1/2018	Budget	90000
4	Northeast	1/1/2018	Budget	266000
5	South	1/1/2018	Budget	360000
6	Southeast	1/1/2018	Budget	675000
7	Southwest	1/1/2018	Budget	293000
8	West	1/1/2018	Budget	563000
9	Midwest	2/1/2018	Budget	248000
10	North	2/1/2018	Budget	90000
11	Northeast	2/1/2018	Budget	266000
12	South	2/1/2018	Budget	360000
13	Southeast	2/1/2018	Budget	675000

15

Your next step is to create a pivot table that has every possible value needed in your final report. You've learned that GetPivotData is powerful, but it can only return values that are visible in the actual pivot table. It cannot reach through to the pivot cache to calculate items that are not in the pivot table.

Create the pivot table by following these steps:

1. Select Insert, PivotTable, OK.

2. In the PivotTable Fields list, select the Date field. You will either see daily dates or years in the first column (see Figure 15.11). If you see years, it's due to the new Excel 2016 AutoGroup functionality, and you should skip Step 3.

Select Date cell   Group Field

Figure 15.11
Start with daily dates down the left.

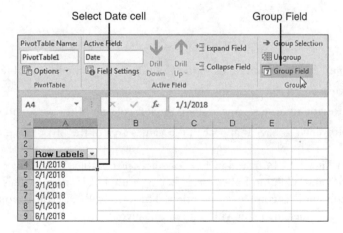

3. Select the first date cell in A4. From the PivotTable Options tab, select Group Field. Select Months and Years, as shown in Figure 15.12. Click OK. You now have actual month names down the left side, as shown in Figure 15.13.

Figure 15.12
Group the daily dates up to months and years.

Figure 15.13
You have month names instead of dates.

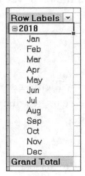

4. Drag the Years and Date fields to the Columns area in the Pivot Table Fields list.

5. Drag Measure to the Columns area.

6. Select Region to have it appear along the left column of the pivot table.

7. Select Revenue to have it appear in the Values area of the pivot table.

As shown in Figure 15.14, you now have one ugly pivot table. You might not like the words "Row Labels" and "Column Labels." And having a total of January Actuals plus January Budget in column D is completely pointless. This is ugly. But for once, you do not care because no one other than you will ever see this pivot table.

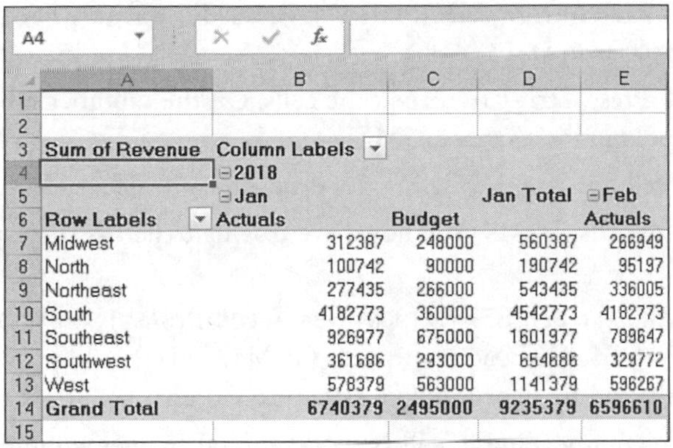

Figure 15.14
The world's ugliest pivot table. Summing Actuals and Budget in column D is completely meaningless.

	A	B	C	D	E
1					
2					
3	Sum of Revenue	Column Labels			
4		⊟2018			
5		⊟Jan		Jan Total	⊟Feb
6	Row Labels	Actuals	Budget		Actuals
7	Midwest	312387	248000	560387	266949
8	North	100742	90000	190742	95197
9	Northeast	277435	266000	543435	336005
10	South	4182773	360000	4542773	4182773
11	Southeast	926977	675000	1601977	789647
12	Southwest	361686	293000	654686	329772
13	West	578379	563000	1141379	596267
14	Grand Total	6740379	2495000	9235379	6596610
15					

At this point, the goal is to have a pivot table with every possible data point you could ever need in your final report. It is fine if the pivot table has extra data you will never need in the report.

Building the Shell Report

Now it's time to put away your pivot table hat and take out your straight Excel hat. You are going to use basic Excel formulas and formatting to create a nicely formatted report suitable for giving to your manager.

Insert a blank worksheet in your workbook and then follow these steps:

1. Put a report title in cell A1.

2. Use the Cell Styles drop-down on the Home tab to format cell A1 as a Title.

3. Put a date in cell A2 by using the formula =EOMONTH(TODAY(),0). This enters the serial number of the last day of the previous month in cell B1. If you want to see how the formula is working, you can format the cell as a Date. If you are reading this on July 14, 2018, the date that appears in cell B1 is June 30, 2018.

4. Select cell A2. Press Ctrl+1 to go to the Format Cells dialog. On the Number tab, click Custom. Type the custom number format **"Actuals Through" mmmm, yyyy**. This causes the calculated date to appear as text.

5. Because there is a chance that the text in cell A2 is going to be wider than you want column A to be, select both cells A2 and B2. Press Ctrl+1 to format the cells. On the Alignment tab, select Merge Cells. This allows the formula in cell A2 to spill over into B2 if necessary.

6. Type a Region heading in cell A5.

7. Down the rest of column A, type your region names. These names should match the names in the pivot table.

8. Where appropriate, add labels in column A for Division totals.

9. Add a line for Total Company at the bottom of the report.

10. Month names stretch from cells B4 to M4. Enter this formula in cell B4: `=DATE`
    `(YEAR ($A$2),COLUMN(A1),1)`.

11. Select cell B4. Press Ctrl+1 to format the cells. On the Number tab, select Custom and
    type the custom number format **MMM**.

12. Right-justify cell B4. Use the Cell Styles drop-down to select Heading 4.

13. Copy cell B4 to cells C4:M4. You now have true dates across the top that appear as
    month labels.

14. Enter this formula in cell B5: `=IF(MONTH(B4)<=MONTH($A$2),"Actuals","Budget")`.
    Right-justify cell B5. Copy across to cells C5:M5. This should provide the word *Actuals*
    for past months and the word *Budget* for future months.

15. Add a Total column heading in cell N5. Add a Total Budget column in cell O5. Enter
    Var % in cell P5.

16. Fill in the regular Excel formulas needed to provide division totals, the total company
    row, the grand total column, and the variance % column. For example:

    ■ Enter `=SUM(B6:B7)` in cell B8, and copy across.

    ■ Enter `=SUM(B6:M6)` in cell N6, and copy down.

    ■ Enter `=IFERROR((N6/O6)-1,0)` in cell P6, and copy down.

    ■ Enter `=SUM(B10:B12)` in cell B13, and copy across.

    ■ Enter `=SUM(B15:B16)` in cell B17, and copy across.

    ■ Enter `=SUM(B6:B18)/2` in cell B19, and copy across.

17. Apply the Heading 4 cell style to the labels in column A and to the headings
    in rows 4:5.

18. Apply the **#,##0** number format to cells B6:O19.

19. Apply the **0.0%** number format to column P.

> **NOTE**
>
> If the names in the pivot table are region codes, you can hide the codes in a new hidden column A and
> put friendly region names in column B.

You now have a completed shell report, as shown in Figure 15.15. This report has all the
necessary formatting your manager might desire. It has totals that add up the numbers that
eventually come from the pivot table.

In the next section, you'll use GetPivotData to complete the report.

Figure 15.15
The shell report before the GetPivotData formulas are added.

	Jan Actuals	Feb Actuals	Mar Actuals	Apr Actuals	May Actuals	Jun Actuals	Jul Actuals	Aug Budget	Sep Budget	Oct Budget	Nov Budget	Dec Budget	Total	Total Budget	Var. %
Actuals & Budget By Region															
Actuals Through July, 2018															
Region															
Northeast													0		0.0%
Southeast													0		0.0%
East Division Total	0	0	0	0	0	0	0	0	0	0	0	0	0		0.0%
Midwest													0		0.0%
North													0		0.0%
South													0		0.0%
Central Division Total	0	0	0	0	0	0	0	0	0	0	0	0	0	0	0.0%
West													0		0.0%
Southwest													0		0.0%
West Division Total	0	0	0	0	0	0	0	0	0	0	0	0	0		0.0%
Total Company	0	0	0	0	0	0	0	0	0	0	0	0	0	0	0.0%

15

Using GetPivotData to Populate the Shell Report

At this point, you are ready to take advantage of the thing that has been driving you crazy for years—that crazy Generate GetPivotData setting. If you cleared the setting back in Figure 15.7, go in and select it again. When it is selected, you see a check next to Generate GetPivotData.

Go to cell B6 on the shell report (this is the cell for Northeast region, January, Actuals), and then follow these steps:

1. Type = to start a formula (see Figure 15.16).

Figure 15.16
Start a formula on the shell report.

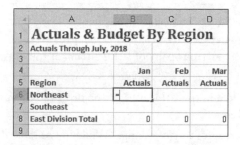

	A	B	C	D
1	**Actuals & Budget By Region**			
2	Actuals Through July, 2018			
3				
4		Jan	Feb	Mar
5	Region	Actuals	Actuals	Actuals
6	Northeast	=		
7	Southeast			
8	East Division Total	0	0	0
9				

2. Move to the pivot table worksheet and click the cell for Northeast, January, Actuals. In Figure 15.17, this is cell B9.

3. Press Enter to return to the shell report and complete the formula. Excel adds a GetPivotData function in cell B6.

The formula says that the Northeast region actuals are $277,435.

> **TIP**
>
> Jot down this number because you will want to compare it to the result of the formula that you later edit.

Figure 15.17
Using the mouse, click the correct cell in the pivot table.

| B9 | ▼ | : | ✕ | ✓ | *fx* | =GETPIVOTDATA("Revenue",UglyPi |

⊿	A	B	C	D	E
1					
2					
3	Sum of Revenue	Column Labels ▼			
4		⊟2018			
5		⊟Jan		Jan Total	⊟Feb
6	Row Labels ▼	Actuals	Budget		Actuals
7	Midwest	312387	248000	560387	266949
8	North	100742	90000	190742	95197
9	Northeast	277435	266000	543435	336005
10	South	4182773	360000	4542773	4182773
11	Southeast	926977	675000	1601977	789647
12	Southwest	361686	293000	654686	329772

The initial formula is as follows:

```
=GETPIVOTDATA("Revenue",UglyPivotTable!$A$3,"Region","Northeast",
"Date",1,"Measure","Actuals","Years",2018)
```

After years of ignoring the GetPivotData formula, you need to look at this monster formula closely to understand what it is doing. Figure 15.18 shows the formula in Edit mode, along with the formula tooltip.

Figure 15.18
The GetPivotData formula generated by Microsoft.

Jan	Feb	Mar	Apr	May	Jun	Jul	Aug	Sep	Oct	Nov
Actuals	Actuals	Actuals	Actuals	Actuals	Actuals	Actuals	Budget	Budget	Budget	Budget

```
=GETPIVOTDATA("Revenue",UglyPivotTable!$A$3,"Region","Northeast","Date",1,"Measure","Actuals","Years",2018)
```

The syntax for the function is =GetPivotData(data_field, pivot_table, [field1, item1], ...). In this case, there are four pairs of field*n*, item*n* arguments. Here are the arguments in the formula:

- **Data_field**—This is the field in the Value area of the pivot table. Note that you use Revenue, not Sum of Revenue.

- **Pivot_table**—This is Microsoft's way of asking, "Which pivot table do you mean?" All you have to do here is point to one single cell within the pivot table. The entry of UglyPivotTable!$A$3 is the first populated cell in the pivot table. You are free to choose any cell in the pivot table you want. However, because it does not matter which cell you choose, don't worry about getting clever here. Leave the formula pointing to $A$3, and you will be fine.

- **Field1, item1**—The formula generated by Microsoft shows Region as the field name and Northeast as the item value. Aha! So this is why the GetPivotData formulas that Microsoft generates cannot be copied. They are essentially hard-coded to point to one specific value. You want your formula to change as you copy it through your report. Edit the formula to change Northeast to $A6. By using only a single dollar sign before A, you are enabling the row portion of the reference to vary as you copy the formula down.

- **Field2, item2**—The next two pairs of arguments specify that the Date field should be 1. When the original pivot table was grouped by month and year, the month field retained the original field name Date. The value for the month is 1, which means January. You probably thought I was insane to build that outrageous formula and custom number format in cell B4. That formula becomes useful now. Instead of hard-coding a 1, use MONTH(B$4). The single dollar sign before row 4 indicates that the formula can get data from other months as it is copied across, but it should always reach back up to row 4 as it is copied down.

- **Field3, item3**—The field name is Measure, and the item is Actuals. This happens to be correct for January, but when you get to future months, you want the measure to switch to Budget. Change the hard-coded Actuals to point to B$5.

- **Field4, item4**—This is Years and 2018. I was almost ready to leave this one alone because it would be months before we have a new year. However, why not change 2018 to YEAR($A$2)?

The new formula is shown in Figure 15.19. Rather than a formula that is hard-coded to work with only one value, you have created a formula that can be copied throughout the data set.

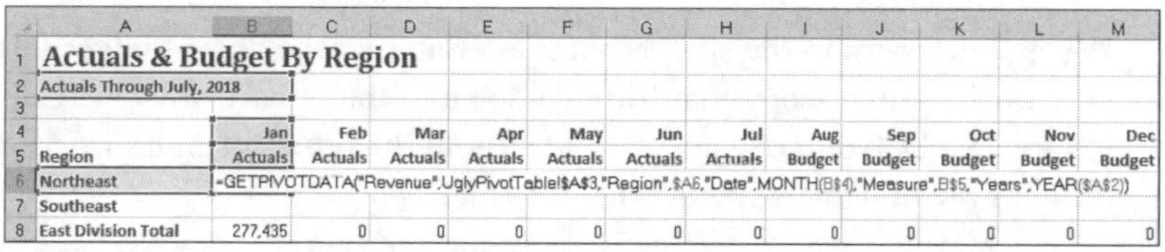

Figure 15.19
After being edited, the GetPivotData formula is ready for copying.

When you press Enter, you have exactly the same answer that you had before editing the formula. Compare this with the number you jotted down earlier to make sure.

The edited formula is as follows:

```
=GETPIVOTDATA("Revenue", UglyPivotTable!$A$3,"Region",$A6,
   "Date", MONTH(B$4),"Measure",B$5,"Years",YEAR($A$2))
```

Copy this formula to all the blank calculation cells in columns B:M. Do not copy the formula to column O yet. Now that you have real numbers in the report, you might have to adjust some column widths.

You can tweak the GetPivotData formula for the months to get the total budget. If you copy one formula to cell O6, you get a #REF! error because the word *Total* in cell O4 does not evaluate to a month. Edit the formula to the pairs of arguments for Month and Years. You still have an error.

> **CAUTION**
> For GetPivotData to work, the number you are looking for must be in the pivot table.

Because the original pivot table had Measure as the third column field, there is no actual column for Budget total. Move the Measure field to be the first Column field, as shown in Figure 15.20.

Figure 15.20
Tweak the layout of the Column Labels fields so you have a Budget Total column.

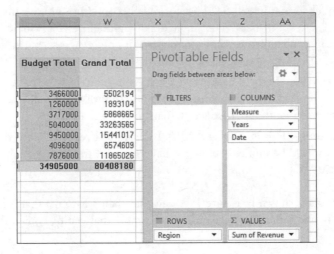

When you return to the shell report, you find that the Total Budget formula in cell O6 is now working fine. Copy that formula down to the other blank data cells in column O (see Figure 15.21). Note with amazement that all the other formulas work, even though everything in the underlying pivot table moved.

Figure 15.21
After rearranging the pivot table, you have a working formula for Total Budget.

	Total	
ɔtal	**Budget**	**Var. %**
665	3,717,000	3.1%
017	3,717,000	176.2%
682	7,434,000	89.7%

The formula in O6 is as follows:

```
=GETPIVOTDATA("Revenue",UglyPivotTable!$A$3,"Region",$A6,"Measure",O$5)
```

You now have a nicely formatted shell report that grabs values from a live pivot table. It certainly takes more time to set up this report for the first month that you have to produce it, but it will be a breeze to update the report in future months.

Updating the Report in Future Months

In future months, you can update your report by following these steps:

1. Paste actuals for the new month just below the original data set. Because the original data set is a table, the table formatting automatically extends to the new rows. The pivot table source definition also extends.

2. Go to the pivot table. Click the Refresh button on the Options tab. The shape of the pivot table changes, but you do not care.

3. Go to the shell report. In real life, you are done, but to test it, enter a date in cell B2 such as **8/30/2018**. You will initially see a #REF error, but it will disappear after you add August actuals to the real data and refresh the pivot table.

> **NOTE** Every month, these three steps are the payoff to this chapter. The first time you update, the data for July changes from Budget to Actuals. Formulas throughout recalculate. You do not have to worry about re-creating formats, formulas, and so on.

This process is so simple that you will probably forget about the pain that you used to endure to create these monthly reports. The one risk is that a company reorg will add new regions to the pivot table.

To be sure that your formulas are still working, add a small check section outside of the print range of the report. This formula in cell A22 checks to see if the budget total calculated in cell O19 matches the budget total back in the pivot table. Here is the formula:

```
=IF(GETPIVOTDATA("Revenue",UglyPivotTable!$A$3,"Measure","Budget")=$O$19,"", _
    "Caution!!! It appears that new regions have been added to the pivot
    table.
You might have to add new rows to this report for those regions."
```

In case the new region comes from a misspelling in the actuals, this formula checks the YTD actuals against the pivot table. Enter the following formula in cell A23:

```
=IF(SUMIF(B5:M5,"Actuals",B19:M19)=GETPIVOTDATA("Revenue",UglyPivotTable!$A$3, _
    "Measure","Actuals"),"","Caution!!! It appears that new regions have been _
    added to the pivot table. You might have to add new rows to this report for _
    those regions.")
```

Change the font color of both these cells to red. You do not even notice them down there until something goes wrong.

At one time I thought that I would never write these words: GetPivotData is the greatest thing ever. How could we ever live without it?

Conclusion

There you have it—everything that we know about pivot tables. You should have all of the tools you need to turn ugly detailed data into beautiful summary reports.

Index

G

T